TOEFL®
Strategies

A Complete Guide to the iBT

by

Bruce Stirling

Graphics and layout design by Bruce Stirling.
Audio written and produced by Bruce Stirling.
Sound engineer Jon Conine.

Editors

Marjan Sarraf Behbahani, Brenda Cariz, Kateryna Kucher, Shahla Morsali, Tamina Schaller, Hayedeh Sepehran, Patricia Stirling.

Audio Talent

Gretchen Anderson, Jon Conine, Jennie Farnell, Bill and Liz Foster, Ami Kothari, Bruce Stirling, Patricia Stirling.

ISBN-10: 1944595260

ISBN-13: 9781944595265

Published by Nova Press
P. O. Box 692023
West Hollywood, CA USA 90069
1-310-275-3513
info@novapress.net
www.novapress.net

Visit Bruce Stirling at www.LinkedIn.com

Contents

TOEFL Facts

TOEFL is one of the most popular English language tests in the world. TOEFL itself means *test of English as a foreign language*. The TOEFL PBT (paper-based test) was the original TOEFL test. It was replaced by the TOEFL CBT (computer-based test), which was replaced by the TOEFL iBT (internet-based test). The three test scores are compared below.

- **REMEMBER**: *On test day, you will take the TOEFL iBT. Since 2005, the year the TOEFL iBT was introduced, the average-yearly worldwide TOEFL iBT score for all test-takers has been 80/120.*

TOEFL iBT	TOEFL CBT	TOEFL PBT
120	300	677
110	270	637
100	250	600-603
90	233	577
80	213	550
70	193	523
60	170	497

The TOEFL iBT

The TOEFL iBT is four hours long and has four sections: reading, listening, speaking, and writing. Each section is worth 30 points for a total of 120 points (see *Task Order* next page).

TOEFL is designed and administered by New Jersey-based Educational Testing Service (ETS). You must take the test at an official ETS test center. Your responses will be sent by internet to ETS to be scored.

You can take the test as often as you wish. Your score is good for two years. You will receive your unofficial score by regular mail ten business days after the test. For security purposes, ETS will send your official TOEFL score directly to the school/agency of your choosing upon your request. You must pay ETS a fee for each official TOEFL score request.

- **REMEMBER**: *Visit www.ets.org/toefl for more information about the TOEFL iBT.*

Task Order

The TOEFL iBT has four test sections. You cannot change the task order. You must type your two written responses. You may take notes throughout the test.

Section	Task	Questions	Total Time	Score
Reading	3-4 passages	12-14 questions each	60-80 minutes	30/30
Listening	2-3 conversations	5 questions each		
	4-6 lectures	6 questions each	60-90 minutes	30/30
BREAK			**10 minutes**	
Speaking	independent	2 tasks	2 minutes	
	integrated	4 tasks	18 minutes	30/30
Writing	integrated	1 task	25 minutes	
	independent	1 task	30 minutes	30/30
TOTAL			**4 hours**	**120/120**

What does the TOEFL iBT measure?

The TOEFL iBT measures (tests) academic English language proficiency on a scale from 0 to 120. Specifically, TOEFL measures your ability to apply academic English across four skill sets: reading, listening, speaking, and writing. It also measures your ability to learn new topics, then answer questions about those topics.

Topics → *TOEFL is a Teaching Test*

The topics used for testing are found in first and second-year university life science and humanities courses, such as biology, art, geology, zoology, and literature. TOEFL does not test applied sciences, such as physics and mathematics, nor does it test current events.

- **REMEMBER:** *You do not need to study life sciences and/or the humanities before you take the test. TOEFL will teach you all you need to know to answer the questions. In this way, TOEFL is "a teaching test."*

Can I fail TOEFL?

No. You cannot pass or fail the TOEFL test. TOEFL simply measures your ability to understand and apply academic English on a scale from 0 to 120. The higher your score, the higher your English language proficiency.

What TOEFL iBT score do I need?

Undergraduate applicants to U.S. colleges should aim for at least 80/120. U.S. graduate school applicants should aim for at least 90/120.

- **REMEMBER:** *Each school has a different TOEFL requirement. Before you take the test, contact the schools of your choosing and ask for their TOEFL requirements. Professional-license applicants should consult their licensing agencies for their TOEFL requirements.*

How important is TOEFL?

Your TOEFL score is only one part of your college application. You will also be required to write a personal essay, submit your official grades, and provide letters of recommendation. Most U.S. and Canadian schools base admittance on your application as a whole.

What is the SAT?

If you are a non-native, English-speaking undergraduate college applicant, you will also have to submit an SAT score. SAT means *Scholastic Aptitude Test.* American high school students take the SAT upon graduation. The SAT tests high school reading, writing, and math.

- **REMEMBER:** *Visit www.collegeboard.org for more information about the SAT. Also, contact those schools to which you are applying and ask for their SAT requirements, and for any other test requirements.*

How do I register for TOEFL?

In the United States, the busiest testing times are at the end of each semester when TOEFL courses end and TOEFL students are ready to take the test. TOEFL is very popular. Seating is limited. Register early. For registration information, visit www.ets.org/toefl.

How should I prepare for TOEFL?

1. Take a TOEFL class. Chances are you will meet someone who has already taken the test. Learn from his/her experience.
2. Take academic English classes that focus on speaking and writing.
3. Read. Reading is the best way to acquire an academic English vocabulary.

- **WARNING:** *Do not take the TOEFL test without preparing. Many have taken the test without preparing only to realize that TOEFL was harder than they had expected. The result was a low score and a waste of money paying for the test.*

So, how can you maximize scoring on test day? For that, you need a new approach to the TOEFL iBT.

A New Approach to the TOEFL iBT

All TOEFL test-takers want to know how to get a high TOEFL score. Competing TOEFL guides say good grammar and a good vocabulary are the key. Yes, having a good vocabulary and knowing grammar are important; however, they will not get you the highest possible score on test day. To maximize scoring, you need a new TOEFL strategy. That strategy is a basic understanding of first year, college-level rhetoric. In other words, you need a crash course in American-style argument development and analysis. Why? Because the TOEFL iBT is all arguments.

The TOEFL iBT is all Arguments

Rhetoric is the Greek word for "the art of arguing." The Greeks believed that being able to argue was the foundation of a good education. The Greek tradition of rhetoric is carried on to this day in American universities. American college students read essays (written arguments), listen to lectures (verbal arguments), give presentations (verbal arguments), and write essays (written arguments). TOEFL, with its four test sections—reading, listening, speaking, writing—is designed to reflect the American college experience. That means that TOEFL, like U.S. colleges, is all arguments. It also means that to get a high TOEFL score, you must be able to apply basic argument strategies. This book will teach you those strategies, and more.

- **REMEMBER:** *The strategies in this guide have been designed for maximum scoring and have been tested on the TOEFL iBT by the author and his students.*

Argument Mapping with G+3TiC=C

The fastest way to learn essential argument strategies for the TOEFL iBT is to start with the last task on the test: the independent, or opinion-based, essay. I will teach you how to develop and deliver a proficient independent essay using the argument-map G+3TiC=C. G+3TiC=C is an algorithm that visually defines each step in the essay-writing process. All you have to do is memorize the map, then fill in the blanks on test day.

Once you learn how to map out an independent essay with G+3TiC=C, you will then recycle the map and apply it to all tasks on the TOEFL test. By recycling G+3TiC=C, you will reduce the time it takes to learn new strategies. More importantly, by recycling G+3TiC=C, you will realize that TOEFL predictably repeats the same questions and prompts. Because TOEFL is predictable, you will know which tasks to expect and how to analyze them with greater confidence and proficiency while managing your time. This will help you maximize scoring on test day.

TOEFL iBT Argument Chart

The chart below illustrates how the TOEFL iBT uses arguments for testing academic English language proficiency.

Section	Tasks	Arguments Used For Testing
Reading	3-4 passages	These tasks measure your ability to analyze written arguments.
Listening	2-3 conversations	These tasks measure your ability to analyze verbal arguments.
Listening	4-6 lectures	These tasks measure your ability to analyze verbal arguments.
Speaking	2 independent tasks	These tasks measure your ability to construct and deliver two verbal arguments.
Speaking	4 integrated tasks	These tasks measure your ability to summarize and integrate verbal and written arguments.
Writing	1 integrated summary	This task measures your ability to summarize and integrate a verbal and a written argument.
Writing	1 independent essay	This task measures your ability to construct and deliver a written argument.

As you can see, the TOEFL iBT is all arguments. That means to get a high score, you must know how to analyze, construct, and summarize written and verbal arguments on test day. This guide will teach you how.

We start with the writing section.

Writing Section → *Building a Foundation*

The writing section is the last section on the TOEFL test. There are two tasks: the integrated writing task followed by the independent writing task. Each task is scored out of 5 total points. Your scores will then be combined and converted to a section score out of 30 total points (see page 65, *Calculating Your Writing-Section Score*). You cannot change the task order. You must type your responses. You will have 55 minutes to complete this section.

TASK	TOTAL TIME
1. Integrated Writing Task	25 minutes
2. Independent Writing Task	30 minutes

Before you learn how to construct responses for both writing tasks using the argument map G+3TiC=C, you must first learn basic argument development and analysis strategies starting with the independent writing task. The strategies you will learn for this task you will recycle and apply to all TOEFL tasks. By doing so, you will maximize scoring on test day. So what is an argument?

What is an Argument?

An argument is the process of defending an opinion for the purpose of persuading an audience. This argument type is called *a subjective argument*. The TOEFL independent writing task (essay) is a subjective argument. On test day, you will construct a written subjective argument using your personal experience. When you write about yourself, and to maximize scoring, use your active-English vocabulary.

Your Passive and Active English Vocabularies

You have two English vocabularies: passive and active.

Your passive-English vocabulary consists of words and phrases you know but do not use regularly. Idioms are a good example. Like most non-native English speakers, you know more idioms than you use; thus, they are not part of your active (daily) vocabulary. Because you do not use some idioms regularly, you do not use them *proficiently* (see *Proficiency = Coherence* next page). This will result in more mistakes and a lower score on test day.

Your active-English vocabulary, in contrast, consists of English words you use every day. They describe you and your personal experience, for example:

"My name is Paula. I'm a graduate English student living in Sao Paulo, Brazil. In my free time, I love to travel and take photos. Last year I went to London and took lots of great pics. Next year, I will continue my education in the United States. I'm pursuing a PhD in sociolinguistics."

Note how Paula is writing subjectively about her experience using the first person *I am...I love...I went....*, etc. Because she is writing subjectively, she is confident about what she is writing thus makes no (or fewer) mistakes.

- **REMEMBER:** *When writing the independent essay, use your active-English vocabulary. Talk about your life experiences. By doing so, you will make fewer mistakes when writing and increase your score.*

- **REMEMBER:** *Your active-English vocabulary is an important writing strategy.*

Proficiency = Coherence

A subjective argument that successfully persuades demonstrates coherence. Coherence means your argument is clear and logical because it demonstrates *proficiency*. Proficiency means skill and knowledge of English. Skill means ability while knowledge means theory; thus, *skillfully applying your knowledge of English = proficiency* = coherence. Mistakes will indicate a lack of proficiency. For all TOEFL tasks, greater proficiency = greater coherence = a higher score.

Rhetorical Strategies

To construct a proficient independent essay, you need tools. Those tools are called rhetorical strategies. Speakers and writers use rhetorical strategies to construct and analyze arguments. For TOEFL, you need to know eight rhetorical strategies.

1. *Narration*

Narration describes the passing of time. When we arrange events according to time, we put them in chronological or time order, for example:

Yesterday, Jane got up at seven o'clock and took a shower. After that, she had breakfast, then rode the bus to work. When she got to work, she checked her email, then discussed the new business plan with her colleagues.

2. *Process*

Process means putting events in sequential or step-by-step order. In the following examples, notice how each step-by-step process also describes the passing of time.

When making tea, first boil water. Next, put a tea bag into a cup. When the water is boiling, pour the water into the cup. Finally, add milk.

3. *Description*

Description creates pictures of people, places, and things using adjectives and adverbs. Description appeals to the senses: smell, sight, taste, hearing, and touch.

Al, the bass player in the jazz band, is wearing a black-leather jacket and cologne that smells like a spice market.

4. _Illustration_

Illustration means you give supporting examples, for example:

When you visit Manhattan, I suggest you visit Times Square and Central Park.

5. _Compare-and-Contrast_

Compare-and-contrast describes the differences and similarities between two or more objects, people, or ideas. Compare-and-contrast also describes differences in opinion, for example:

Joan tried the apple pie and decided the cherry pie was sweeter.

6. _Definition_

A definition is a dictionary-like description of a person, place, object, or idea, for example:

TOEFL is an English language proficiency test developed and implemented by Educational Testing Service (ETS).

7. _Classification_

To classify means to put people, things, or ideas into subgroups under a main topic, for example:

There are three kinds of wine: red, white and rosé.

8. _Cause-and-Effect_

Cause-and-effect means action and result. We use cause-and-effect to describe an action and the results, or consequences, of that action, for example:

Cora studied hard and got a high TOEFL score.

- **REMEMBER:** _On test day, you will have to identify and develop reasons. Reasons are a fundamental part of argument development and analysis, and TOEFL. Reasons are created using cause-and-effect. The next section explains how._

What is a Reason?

A reason is the cause or the effect in a cause-and-effect relationship. Look at the following example. Note how the _cause_ is the reason in the first example.

Question: _Why did Cora get a high TOEFL score (effect)?_
            (Why means "What was the cause?"
Answer: _Because she studied hard (cause)._

Look at the next example. Note how the *effect* is the reason.

Man: *Why should I study (cause) for TOEFL?*
Woman: *Because you will get a higher score (effect).*
Man: *A higher score (effect)? That's a good reason to study for TOEFL.*

Starting an Argument → *Subjective Thesis*

One way to start a subjective argument is by first stating your opinion about the topic in question. Your opinion is what you believe. Your opinion is also called a *claim* or *position*, for example: *I believe in Santa Claus.* Some people, however, do not believe in Santa Claus. That is their opinion, their claim, their position.

When arguing subjectively in writing, or when speaking, your opinion is called a subjective thesis. A subjective thesis often starts with a <u>signal phrase</u>, for example:

> *Personally, I think that we need zoos.*

Below are common signal phrases that introduce a subjective thesis.

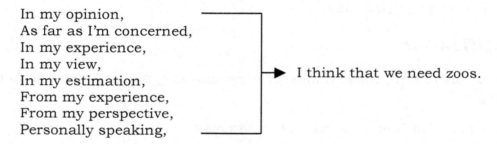

In my opinion,
As far as I'm concerned,
In my experience,
In my view,
In my estimation,
From my experience,
From my perspective,
Personally speaking,   → I think that we need zoos.

Subjective-Thesis Checklist

How do you know that what you are writing (or saying) is indeed a subjective thesis? Use this checklist. Let's work through the following example:

Statement: *Personally, I think that we need zoos.*

1) Is this statement arguable?
   ✓ Yes. Some believe that wild animals should be free, not caged.

2) Does it have one topic only?
   ✓ Yes: topic = "zoos".

3) Does it include an opinion, a topic, and a controlling idea?
   ✓ Yes: opinion = "I think"; topic = "zoos"; controlling idea = "we need".

4) Is it supportable? Can it be developed with body-paragraph examples?
   ✓ Yes. (See the zoo essay on page 21 for body-paragraph development, lines 3-20).

5) Is it a grammatically complete sentence?
   - ✓ Yes. It has a subject (I...) and a predicate (...think that we need zoos). A sentence fragment is not a thesis, for example: *Steve Jobs: genius.*

6) Is it a question?
   - ✓ No. A subjective thesis is never a question. A <u>rhetorical question</u>, however, often introduces the topic the subjective thesis will argue, for example: *"<u>Do we need zoos</u>? Yes. Personally, I think that we need zoos."*

7) Is it a fact?
   - ✓ No. A subjective thesis is arguable. Facts, in contrast, are not arguable, for example: *"A zoo is a place people can safely view protected wild animals."* This statement is a fact thus not arguable thus not an opinion.

8) Is it an announcement?
   - ✓ No. A thesis is not an announcement, for example: *"Today, I am going to talk about zoos."* An announcement is a fact thus not arguable.

9) Is the thesis an academic statement?
   - ✓ Yes. <u>Warning</u>: Stating a like/dislike is not a thesis, for example: *"I hate zoos."* This is an opinion; however, it is not an academic statement.

So what can we conclude? Is <u>*Personally, I think that we need zoos*</u> a subjective thesis? Yes. Why? Because it follows all the rules in the subjective-thesis checklist.

Subjective Thesis → *No Signal Phrase*

A subjective thesis will not always start with a signal phrase. However, if the statement follows the subjective thesis checklist, then we can infer that it is the writer's/speaker's claim, for example:

> <u>*In my opinion*</u>, *children under the age of ten should not drink soft drinks.*
>   *or...*
> *Children under the age of ten should not drink soft drinks.*

> <u>*As far as I am concerned*</u>, *we should ban plastic bottles and shopping bags.*
>   *or...*
> *Plastic bottles and shopping bags should be banned.*

Subjective Thesis → *Well-Developed*

A well-developed, subjective thesis will score higher, for example:

> *In my opinion, children under the age of ten should not drink soft drinks.*
>   *or....*
> *In my opinion, I think that children under the age of ten should not drink soft drinks because of the high risk of contracting diabetes.*

As far as I am concerned, we should ban plastic bottles and shopping bags.
or....
As far as I am concerned, we need to ban the use of plastic bottles and shop-ping bags to reduce pollution worldwide.

Independent Writing Task

The independent writing task, or opinion essay, is a subjective argument designed to persuade an audience. Your audience on test day is three TOEFL writing raters (see *Calculating Your Writing-Section Score*, page 65).

- **REMEMBER:** *The writing raters are trained to identify discrete elements in your essay that, when combined, create a coherent argument. In other words, the raters want to know only one thing: Can you construct a proficient, opinion-based essay in 30 minutes?*

The essay you write should have three parts.

1. introduction ⟶ introduces your subjective thesis
2. body ⟶ examples to support your thesis
3. conclusion ⟶ restates your thesis

When writing your independent essay, the first step is to read the prompt. The prompt describes the topic you will write about, for example:

Prompt: We need zoos. Do you agree or disagree? Why? Develop your posi-tion using examples and reasons.

In the prompt above, position means your opinion (subjective thesis), examples means illustrations, and reasons means use reasons based on cause-and-effect.

Next, state your position in the introduction. The raters are trained to look for your subjective thesis in the introduction, for example:

introduction → *Personally, I think that we need zoos.*

Next, add a rhetorical **Why**.

introduction → *Personally, I think that we need zoos.* **Why?**

Next, answer **Why** by providing an illustration in the body. The illustration is the answer to the rhetorical **Why**, for example:

introduction → *Personally, I think that we need zoos. Why?*

body → *For example, when I was twelve, my teacher took us to the zoo in Toronto. I had never seen wild animals before. I had just read about them in books and seen them on TV. But seeing them in real life was amazing, especially the lions. On TV, they looked so small, but seeing them live, I realized they were really big. By going to the zoo, I saw things in a whole new light.*

Note below how **Why** serves as a transitional word. A transitional word topically connects one idea to the next. In this example, **Why** connects the subjective thesis to the supporting example in the body. This creates a progression of ideas. The raters are trained to look for a progression of ideas through topical unity.

introduction → *Personally, I think that we need zoos.* **Why?**

body → *For example, when I was twelve, my teacher took us to the...*

Next, add a conclusion. The purpose of the conclusion is to connect topically the example in the body to your subjective thesis.

conclusion → *In conclusion, you can see why we need zoos. They are educational.*

→ **Finished! We now have a short written argument or essay.**

introduction → *Personally, I think that we need zoos. Why?*

body → *For example, when I was twelve, my teacher took us to the zoo in Toronto. I had never seen wild animals before. I had just read about them in books and seen them on TV. But seeing them in real life was amazing, especially the lions. On TV, they looked so small, but seeing them live, I realized they were really big. By going to the zoo, I saw things in a whole new light.*

conclusion → *In conclusion, you can see why we need zoos. They are educational.*

Next, let's map out this short argument.

Rhetorically, an introduction is called a general statement or <u>G</u>.

G → *Personally, I think that we need zoos. Why?*

Rhetorically, the body has three parts: **T** for transition or topic sentence, **i** for illustration or example, and **C** for conclusion.

T → *For example...*

i → *when I was twelve, my teacher took us to the zoo in Toronto. I had never seen wild animals before. I had just read about them in books and seen them on TV. But seeing them in real life was amazing, especially the lions. On TV, they looked so small, but seeing them live, I realized they were really big.*

C → *By going to the zoo, I saw things in a whole new light.*

Rhetorically, the <u>C</u>onclusion in the body should contain a reason stated using **cause**-and-*effect*.

    <u>C</u> → **By going to the zoo** *(cause), <u>I saw things in a whole new light</u> (effect)*.

Rhetorically, the end <u>C</u>onclusion is a general statement that restates the introduction-thesis (G).

    <u>C</u> → *In conclusion, you can see why we need zoos. They are educational.*

→ **Finished! We've just written a short independent essay using G+TiC=C.**

    <u>G</u> → *Personally, I think that we need zoos. Why?*

    <u>T</u> → *For example...*

    <u>i</u> → *when I was twelve, my teacher took us to the zoo in Toronto. I had never seen wild animals before. I had just read about them in books and seen them on TV. But seeing them in real life was amazing, especially the lions. On TV, they looked so small, but seeing them live, I realized they were really big.*

    <u>C</u> → *By going to the zoo, I saw things in a whole new light.*

    <u>C</u> → *In conclusion, you can see why we need zoos. They are educational.*

→ **The final argument maps out like this.**

    <u>G</u> → *Personally, I think that we need zoos. Why?*

    <u>TiC</u> → *For example, when I was twelve, my teacher took us to the zoo in Toronto. I had never seen wild animals before. I had just read about them in books and seen them on TV. But seeing them in real life was amazing, especially the lions. On TV, they looked so small, but seeing them live, I realized they were really big. By going to the zoo, I saw things in a whole new light.*

    <u>C</u> → *In conclusion, you can see why we need zoos. They are educational.*

Word Count → *Topic Development*

ETS says "an effective [independent essay] is typically about 300 words." Our short essay on page 20 is 96 words. Too short. We need more topic development. Do so by adding two more body paragraphs, or 2TiC (see below). We now have an independent essay written with the argument map G+3TiC=C.

1 2	<u>G</u> →	*Personally, I think that we need zoos. Why?*
3 4 5 6 7 8 9	<u>TiC</u> →	*For example, when I was twelve, my teacher took us to the zoo in Toronto. I had never seen wild animals before. I had just read about them in books and seen them on TV. But seeing them in real life was amazing, especially the lions. On TV, they looked so small, but seeing them live, I realized they were really big. By going to the zoo, I saw things in a whole new light.*
10 11 12 13 14 15	<u>TiC</u> →	*Now I have a family and we always go to the zoo every summer. My wife makes a picnic and we spend all day there. My kids love taking pictures and learning all about the animals, especially the gorillas. Being outside is good for my children. Best of all, they can leave the internet and the TV at home.*
16 17 18 19 20 21	<u>TiC</u> →	*Also, zoos look after endangered animals like pandas. I saw two in the Washington DC zoo last year and they had a baby. If there were no zoos, pandas would disappear because we are taking their habitat away. However, in zoos, pandas are safe. It is not perfect, but without zoos there might not be any pandas left.*
22 23	<u>C</u> →	*In conclusion, you can see why we need zoos. They are educational, fun for families, and protect animals.*

The word count is now <u>221</u> words. We still need more development. To determine where, we need to rate this essay using OPDUL=C.

OPDUL=C → *Rating this Task*

Three raters will rate your response out of five total points. Let's say rater one gives the response above a 4/5. Raters two and three also give it a 4/5. Your average rater score is 4/5. This score is then converted to a writing section score of 25/30. That is a good score. Okay, so why didn't you get 30/30? To figure out where you lost points, you must learn how to rate an independent essay like an official TOEFL writing rater. They are trained to rate responses against a rubric. A rubric is a checklist of argument writing rules. That rubric is defined by OPDUL=C.

OPDUL=C ("op-dull-see") is an argument analyzer that rates <u>C</u>oherence (intelligibility) using proficiency as a measure. Proficiency means your skill and knowledge of English. TOEFL will test your English proficiency in five discrete areas: <u>O</u>rganization, <u>P</u>rogression, <u>D</u>evelopment, <u>U</u>nity, and <u>L</u>anguage Use. For this task, if your argument (essay) demonstrates proficiency in all areas of OPDUL, then it will demonstrate <u>C</u>oherence. Next, we define each step of OPDUL=C.

O = <u>O</u>rganization

Under <u>O</u>rganization, there are two proficiency descriptors: deduction and induction. If your essay starts with a general statement, and is supported by examples and ends with a conclusion (G+3TiC=C), then you are demonstrating a method of organization called deduction. If your essay starts with examples, and ends with a conclusion-thesis (3TiC=C), then you are demonstrating a method of organization called induction (see graphic below).

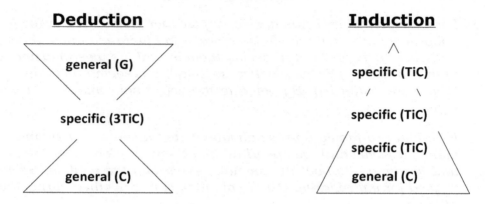

P = <u>P</u>rogression

Under <u>P</u>rogression, there are two proficiency descriptors. If your essay demonstrates deduction as the method of <u>O</u>rganization, the ideas will progress from general (intro) to specific (body) to general (conclusion; see graphic above). If your essay demonstrates induction, the examples will progress from specific (body) to general (conclusion-thesis).

D = <u>D</u>evelopment

Under <u>D</u>evelopment, there are three proficiency descriptors: introduction development (G), body development (3TiC), and conclusion development (C). Topic development in your introduction means your thesis is a true thesis (see checklist page 16). Topic development in the body means you have provided enough well-developed examples to support your thesis. Topic development in your conclusion means you restate your thesis.

- **REMEMBER**: *A big reason why test-takers score low on the independent essay is due to a lack of topic <u>D</u>evelopment in the body. The problem is not enough examples and/or the examples lack <u>D</u>evelopment.*

U = <u>U</u>nity

Under <u>U</u>nity, there are two proficiency descriptors: topical unity and grammatical unity. Topical unity means your essay focuses on the main topic in the prompt. You do not go off topic and write about unrelated topics. Grammatical unity means you are using transitional words proficiently to unite each part of your essay. Grammatical unity also means your grammar is proficient at the sentence level.

L = Language-Use

Under Language-Use, there are two proficiency descriptors: word choice and sentence variety. Word choice (including idioms) measures your ability to apply your English vocabulary proficiently. Sentence variety (including punctuation) measures your ability to write simple, compound, and complex sentences proficiently.

C = Coherence

If your independent essay proficiently demonstrates OPDUL, then it will demonstrate Coherence, and you will score a 5/5. Coherence means your essay is an intelligible whole. However, if your essay lacks proficiency in one or more areas of OPDUL, then Coherence (intelligibility) will be reduced, and your essay will score lower.

Holistic vs Analytical Rating Systems

The writing raters are trained to rate holistically. For example, if you make an error, such as "If I was a rich man..." instead of "If I were a rich man...", that is okay. The meaning is still clear despite the incorrect verb "was." In other words, "close enough is good enough." OPDUL=C, in contrast, is an analytical rating system. It is designed to help you identify the smallest errors in your writing so you can rewrite for greater proficiency and Coherence—and get a higher writing score on test day.

Rating an Independent Essay

Next, let's rate the zoo essay we wrote with G+3TiC=C (see page 21).

O = Does it (essay) demonstrate proficient Organization?

✓ Yes. The writer proficiently demonstrates deduction.

- **REMEMBER**: *G+3TiC=C is a deductive map. Just fill in the blanks and you will automatically write an independent essay that demonstrates deduction.*

P = Does it demonstrate proficient Progression?

✓ Yes. Because the essay is using deduction as the method of organization, the ideas progress from general (intro) to specific (body) to general (conclusion).

D = Does it demonstrate proficient Development?

✓ Yes. The introduction includes a subjective thesis that meets all the requirements of the subjective thesis checklist on page 16.

X **However, the intro needs a hook for greater topic development and to increase the final score.**

✓ Yes. The body proficiently develops three different examples that support the thesis.

✓ Yes. The conclusion restates the thesis and unites it topically with the topics in the body paragraphs and the thesis.

X However, the conclusion needs a conclusion strategy for greater topic development and to increase the final score.

U = Does it demonstrate proficient Unity?

✓ Yes. The essay focuses on the main topic of zoos and does not digress. The essay demonstrates proficient grammatical unity by the correct use of transitional words.

L = Does it demonstrate proficient Language-Use?

✓ Yes. The writer demonstrates proficient use of: 1) subjective grammar; 2) vocabulary specific to the task (lions, gorillas, pandas, endangered); 3) sentence variety, and; 4) the writer uses an idiom "...saw things in a whole new light."

C = Does it demonstrate Coherence?

✓ Yes. Because the writer proficiently demonstrates OPDUL, the writer demonstrates C. The result is a Coherent essay. However, to increase the score, the writer needs to develop the introduction (X) and the conclusion (X). Do so by rewriting.

Rewriting

The essay on page 21 scored a 4/5. According to OPDUL=C, we lost points due to a lack of Development in the introduction and the conclusion. That means we must develop the introduction and the conclusion. Let's start with the introduction. The thesis is fine. We just need to add a hook. A hook captures the reader's attention.

Developing the Introduction → *Hooks*

To maximize scoring, develop your introduction using one of the following hooks.

a. Or-Question Hook

Start with an *or question*. Next, write a **signal phrase**, then answer the question. The answer is your thesis, for example:

> *Do we need zoos or not?* ***From my point of view***, *I believe that we need zoos.*

b. Restate-the-Prompt Hook

Start by *paraphrasing the prompt*. Next, write a **signal phrase**, then state your thesis, for example:

> *The question is whether we need zoos or not.* ***As far as I am concerned***, *I assert that we need zoos.*

c. __Pro-Con Hook__

Start by *stating the pro (positive) side and the con (negative) side of the argument.* Next, write a **signal phrase**, then state your <u>thesis</u>, for example:

> *Some people think that we don't need zoos while others think that we do.* ***Personally speaking****,* <u>*I posit that we need zoos.*</u>

d. __General Fact + Or-Question Hook__

Start with a *general fact.* Next, ask an *or-question* about that fact including both the pro and the con sides of the argument. Next, write a **signal phrase**, then answer the question. The answer is your <u>thesis</u>, for example:

> *Zoos are popular all over the world. Yet do we need them or not?* ***In my estimation****,* <u>*I believe that we need zoos.*</u>

Developing the Conclusion → *Strategies*

To maximize scoring, develop the conclusion using one of these strategies.

a. __Suggestion__

Start with a **signal phrase**, restate your <u>opinion</u>, then end with a *suggestion.*

> ***As I have illustrated****,* <u>*I believe that we need zoos.*</u> *If you want to have fun and learn something new, you should go to a zoo.*

b. __Suggestion + Prediction__

Start with a **signal phrase**, restate your <u>opinion</u>, then end with a *suggestion and a prediction.*

> ***In the final analysis****,* <u>*I contend that we need zoos.*</u> *In fact, I think we should build more zoos. More zoos will make the world safer for endangered animals.*

c. __Warning + Prediction__

Start with a **signal phrase**, restate your <u>opinion</u>, then end with *a warning that contains a prediction of future events.*

> ***It goes without saying that*** <u>*we need zoos.*</u> *Without zoos, the endangered animals of this world will go extinct.*

d. __Call-To-Action + Rhetorical Question__

Start with a **signal phrase**, restate your <u>opinion</u>, *give a call-to-action,* then end with *a rhetorical question.*

> ***When all is said and done****,* <u>*I contend that we need zoos.*</u> *Support zoos! Don't you want to save the planet?*

e. Suggestion + Prediction + Rhetorical Question

Start with a **transition**, restate your <u>opinion</u>, make *a suggestion and a prediction,* then end with *a rhetorical question.*

> ***In the final analysis,*** *<u>I conclude that we need zoos</u>. If you are a parent, tell your kids to turn the internet off and go spend a day at the zoo. Doing so will definitely make your kids happier and healthier. They might even learn something too. <u>Isn't that how you want your kids to grow up?</u>*

Next, let's add an introduction hook and a conclusion strategy to the zoo essay. This essay is now <u>265</u> words. Because this essay demonstrates OPDUL=C for the independent essay, it is now a 5/5. <u>Note</u>: The thesis (G) and the conclusions (C) are <u>underlined</u>, the transitions (T) are in **bold**, and the supporting illustrations (i) are in *italics.*

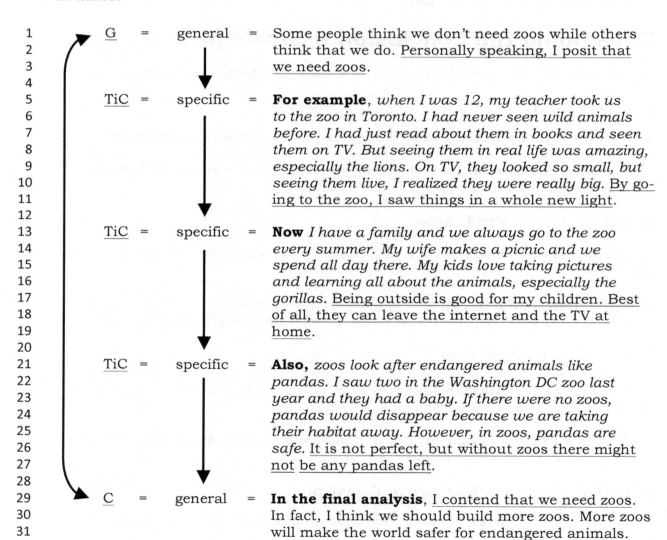

1 2 3 4	<u>G</u>	=	general	=	Some people think we don't need zoos while others think that we do. <u>Personally speaking, I posit that we need zoos.</u>
5 6 7 8 9 10 11 12	<u>TiC</u>	=	specific	=	**For example,** *when I was 12, my teacher took us to the zoo in Toronto. I had never seen wild animals before. I had just read about them in books and seen them on TV. But seeing them in real life was amazing, especially the lions. On TV, they looked so small, but seeing them live, I realized they were really big.* <u>By going to the zoo, I saw things in a whole new light.</u>
13 14 15 16 17 18 19 20	<u>TiC</u>	=	specific	=	**Now** *I have a family and we always go to the zoo every summer. My wife makes a picnic and we spend all day there. My kids love taking pictures and learning all about the animals, especially the gorillas.* <u>Being outside is good for my children. Best of all, they can leave the internet and the TV at home.</u>
21 22 23 24 25 26 27 28	<u>TiC</u>	=	specific	=	**Also,** *zoos look after endangered animals like pandas. I saw two in the Washington DC zoo last year and they had a baby. If there were no zoos, pandas would disappear because we are taking their habitat away. However, in zoos, pandas are safe.* <u>It is not perfect, but without zoos there might not be any pandas left.</u>
29 30 31	<u>C</u>	=	general	=	**In the final analysis,** <u>I contend that we need zoos. In fact, I think we should build more zoos. More zoos will make the world safer for endangered animals.</u>

▶ words: 265

G+3TiC=C + OPDUL=C → *Formula + Proof*

Mapped out, you can see how G+3TiC=C gives the writing raters exactly what they are trained to look for: an independent essay that proficiently demonstrates OPDUL=C. G+3TiC=C is the formula; OPDUL=C proves the formula is correct.

- **REMEMBER**: *There is no rule that says you must write three body paragraphs (3TiC). You can write an independent essay that demonstrates OPDUL=C using G+2TiC=C. If you do, remember to develop each body paragraph.*

Independent Essay → *Step-by-Step*

The independent writing task is the last task on the TOEFL test. This task measures your ability to write (construct) an opinion-based argument using your personal experience. You will have 30 minutes to complete this task. You will write your essay using a basic word processor that includes cut, copy and paste functions.

Paired-Choice Prompts

There are two prompt types: paired-choice and single-question. A paired-choice prompt gives you a choice between two opposing positions, for example:

- Prompt: We need zoos. <u>Do you agree or disagree</u>? Why? Give examples and reasons to develop your opinion.

> **When writing your independent essay, follow these steps.**

Step #1   Answer the prompt; write a hook; state your thesis (G).

Step #2   Develop body-paragraph examples (3TiC) and reasons.

Step #3   Restate your thesis; add a conclusion strategy (C).

Step #4   Check your first draft for <u>C</u>oherence using OPDUL=C.

Step #5   Revise your first draft; submit your essay.

Single-Question Prompts

A single-question prompt asks a question, for example:

- <u>Prompt</u>: Television is a good influence on children. What is your position? Use examples and reasons to support your argument.

In the essay below, the thesis (G) and the conclusions (C) are <u>underlined</u>, the transitions (T) are in **bold**, and the supporting illustrations (i) are in *italics*.

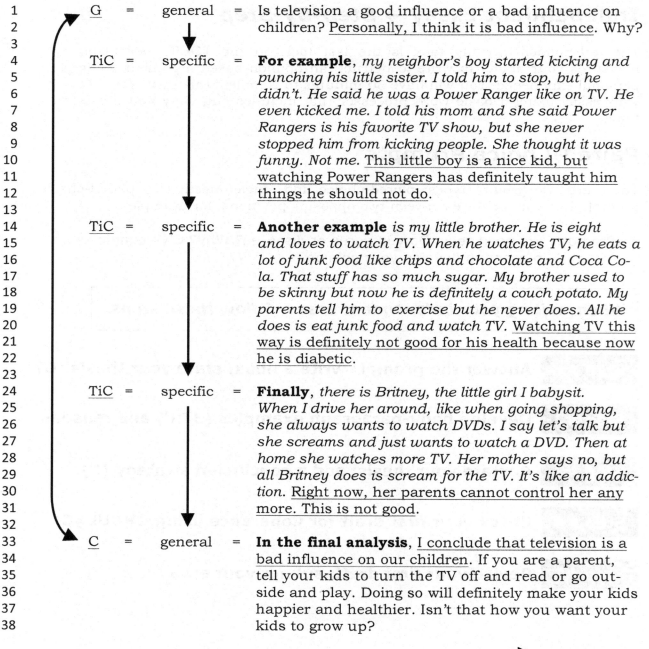

1	<u>G</u>	=	general	= Is television a good influence or a bad influence on
2				children? <u>Personally, I think it is bad influence.</u> Why?
3				
4	<u>TiC</u>	=	specific	= **For example**, *my neighbor's boy started kicking and*
5				*punching his little sister. I told him to stop, but he*
6				*didn't. He said he was a Power Ranger like on TV. He*
7				*even kicked me. I told his mom and she said Power*
8				*Rangers is his favorite TV show, but she never*
9				*stopped him from kicking people. She thought it was*
10				*funny. Not me.* <u>This little boy is a nice kid, but</u>
11				<u>watching Power Rangers has definitely taught him</u>
12				<u>things he should not do.</u>
13				
14	<u>TiC</u>	=	specific	= **Another example** *is my little brother. He is eight*
15				*and loves to watch TV. When he watches TV, he eats a*
16				*lot of junk food like chips and chocolate and Coca Co-*
17				*la. That stuff has so much sugar. My brother used to*
18				*be skinny but now he is definitely a couch potato. My*
19				*parents tell him to exercise but he never does. All he*
20				*does is eat junk food and watch TV.* <u>Watching TV this</u>
21				<u>way is definitely not good for his health because now</u>
22				<u>he is diabetic.</u>
23				
24	<u>TiC</u>	=	specific	= **Finally**, *there is Britney, the little girl I babysit.*
25				*When I drive her around, like when going shopping,*
26				*she always wants to watch DVDs. I say let's talk but*
27				*she screams and just wants to watch a DVD. Then at*
28				*home she watches more TV. Her mother says no, but*
29				*all Britney does is scream for the TV. It's like an addic-*
30				*tion.* <u>Right now, her parents cannot control her any</u>
31				<u>more. This is not good.</u>
32				
33	<u>C</u>	=	general	= **In the final analysis**, <u>I conclude that television is a</u>
34				<u>bad influence on our children.</u> If you are a parent,
35				tell your kids to turn the TV off and read or go out-
36				side and play. Doing so will definitely make your kids
37				happier and healthier. Isn't that how you want your
38				kids to grow up?

▶ words: 329

Common Problems for this Task

1. Serial-Topic Listing

Read the following body paragraph. Can you identify the problem?

1 *A new sports arena in my hometown will create new jobs for young people. A new*
2 *sports arena will also help increase taxes. In addition, a new sports arena will*
3 *bring more people to my hometown. Best of all, a new sports arena will help create*
4 *other businesses that will support the sports arena, such as hotels and restau-*
5 *rants. Finally, a new sports arena will reduce unemployment. As you can see, a*
6 *new sports arena is a good idea.*

This paragraph proficiently demonstrates Language-Use (OPDU**L**=C). However, note how each sentence introduces a new topic. Note below how we can put these same topics in a list. This style of writing is called serial-topic listing.

A new sports arena in my hometown will:

1. create new jobs for young people
2. increase taxes
3. bring more people ——— serial-topic listing
4. create support-businesses
5. reduce unemployment

Avoid serial-topic listing. Develop one topic per paragraph, for example:

1 *A new sports arena in my hometown will create new jobs for young people. For*
2 *example, in my hometown, when young people graduate from high school and*
3 *college, they leave right away and go to the big cities. In the cities, there are*
4 *more jobs and a better future. However, if we had a new sports arena, the*
5 *young people would stay because there would be new jobs. There would be*
6 *jobs like construction and catering, as well as other jobs like hotels and restau-*
7 *rants. This would be good because more new jobs would mean the young peo-*
8 *ple would have a reason to stay and develop the economy of my hometown.*

2. Topic Redundancy

Look at the following paragraph. Can you identify the problem?

1 *A new sports arena in my hometown will create new jobs for young people. In*
2 *my hometown, young people need jobs because jobs are good for young people.*
3 *Jobs are good because they give work to young people who need jobs. I am*
4 *young and I need a job, so new jobs are good for young people like me. New*
5 *jobs will help not only young people but also all people. So new jobs are good*
6 *for everyone, old and young. I support the new sports arena and new jobs.*

Note above how the test-taker is repeating the same topic (young people and jobs). This is an example of topic redundancy (repeating the same topic). Avoid topic redundancy by developing one topic per body paragraph.

3. Unable to Write → *Blanking Out*

To blank out means your mind is suddenly void (empty) of ideas or blank. In other words, you have stopped thinking. There are myriad reasons why you have blanked out: nerves, a dislike of writing, and/or pressure. Whatever the cause, the solution is to keep writing. Yes, it is painful. But writing is thinking. If you are not writing, you are not thinking. Do the following to keep writing.

Step #1   **Make sure you understand the prompt.**

- <u>Prompt</u>: What event changed your life? Why? Give examples and reasons to explain your position.

Step #2   **Write = 30 minutes.**

Do not state your opinion. Instead, tell a personal story using your active vocabulary. Do not worry about mistakes. Just write. This process is called brainstorming. Brainstorming stimulates ideas and will put you back on track.

- **WARNING:** *The worst thing you can do is stop writing. Even if you write garbage, do not stop. As you write, your ideas (your thoughts) will become clearer.*

Look at the following rough first-draft below. Note how the writer is using her active vocabulary and narration to develop a personal example.

1 *When I was in the university I always see this old woman. She was homeless she live*
2 *on the street she had a dog and some box she live on the corner. I saw her in good*
3 *weather and bad. When he see me she always wave and say hello. always she*
4 *smile. I thought was strange. But I talk to her and she was a nice. her name was Ana.*
5 *She never ask for money or nothin she just talk about life. Ana, she tell me something*
6 *I never forget. She say she wished she could go to school she never went she loved*
7 *history she want to be a teacher. She told me to always stay in school. Education*
8 *very important! I always remember her because I was thinking of leaving my universi-*
9 *ty but I did not. Ana was a big event in my life. change me life Her words give me*
10 *strength to study hard*

Step #3   **Revise your essay.**

When you revise your essay, make sure you establish <u>*the context*</u> (the time and the place). Correct the punctuation, the grammar, and add paragraph ***transitions***.

1 <u>*When I was a university student in Peru,*</u> *I always saw an old homeless woman. All*
2 *she had was a dog and some boxes. I saw her in good weather and bad. When she*
3 *saw me, she always waved and said hello. I thought she was strange, always so*
4 *happy, so I avoided her. But then one day I talked to her and she was really nice. Her*
5 *name was Ana. She never asked for money or anything. She just wanted to talk and*
6 *be friends.*

7   ***One day*** *Ana told me something I have never forgotten. She said she really wanted to*
8   *go to university when she was young. She said she always loved history. Unfortu-*
9   *nately, she came from a poor family and had no chance to go to school. She told me to*
10 *stay in school. Education, she said, is very important.*
11
12 ***In sum****, I will always remember what Ana said because I was thinking of leaving my*
13 *university. But I didn't. I graduated and got a good job.* ***As you can see, Ana really***
14 ***changed my life****. Her wisdom gave me strength to continue my studies and be who I*
15 *am today.*

words: 197

In the conclusion above, note how the test-taker answers the prompt by stating her **opinion**. Note also how the test-taker bases her opinion on the evidence (examples) she described. This indicates that the test-taker is using induction as the method of organization.

Notes

_____
_____
_____
_____
_____
_____
_____
_____
_____
_____
_____
_____
_____
_____
_____
_____
_____
_____
_____
_____

Predictor Thesis

Another way to develop your introduction (G) for maximum scoring is by creating a predictor thesis. Look at following theses.

Thesis #1 ▶ Personally, I think that we need zoos.

Thesis #2 ▶ Personally, I think that we need zoos because they are educational, they are fun for families, and they look after endangered animals.

Thesis #1 is a general thesis while #2 is *a predictor thesis*. To predict means *to identify in advance*. Note below how thesis #2 is predicting the three body paragraphs and the reasons in each.

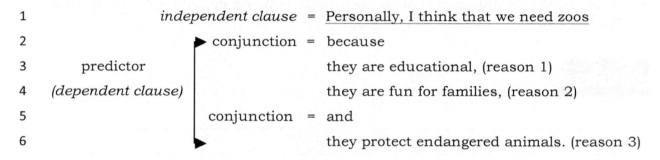

1		*independent clause*	=	Personally, I think that we need zoos
2		conjunction	=	because
3	predictor			they are educational, (reason 1)
4	*(dependent clause)*			they are fun for families, (reason 2)
5		conjunction	=	and
6				they protect endangered animals. (reason 3)

Note below how each predictor becomes a topic sentence in each body paragraph. Note also how **they** becomes the topic-identifier **Zoos** in each body paragraph topic sentence (**T**iC).

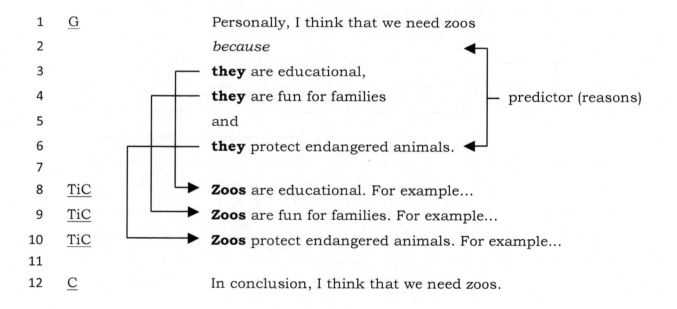

1	G	Personally, I think that we need zoos
2		*because*
3		**they** are educational,
4		**they** are fun for families
5		and
6		**they** protect endangered animals.
7		
8	TiC	**Zoos** are educational. For example...
9	TiC	**Zoos** are fun for families. For example...
10	TiC	**Zoos** protect endangered animals. For example...
11		
12	C	In conclusion, I think that we need zoos.

predictor (reasons)

To shorten the predictor, delete the subject and the verb in the *second* and *third* predictors.

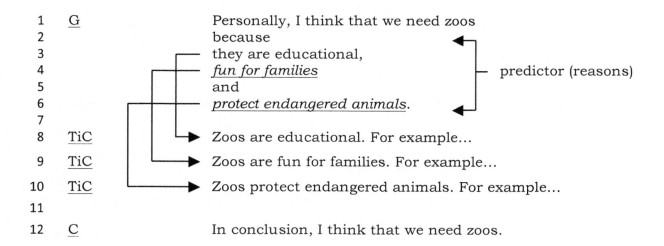

1	G	Personally, I think that we need zoos
2		because
3		they are educational,
4		*fun for families*
5		and
6		*protect endangered animals*.
7		
8	TiC	Zoos are educational. For example...
9	TiC	Zoos are fun for families. For example...
10	TiC	Zoos protect endangered animals. For example...
11		
12	C	In conclusion, I think that we need zoos.

Add transitions to signal the start of each body-paragraph topic sentence.

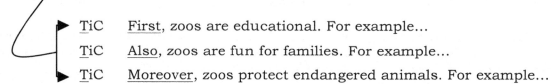

TiC   First, zoos are educational. For example...

TiC   Also, zoos are fun for families. For example...

TiC   Moreover, zoos protect endangered animals. For example...

Thesis Development → *Using Synonyms*

"Personally, I think..." is a common thesis signal phrase. To demonstrate Language Use (OPDU**L**=C) and thesis **D**evelopment (OPD**U**L=C), use synonymous phrases instead, for example:

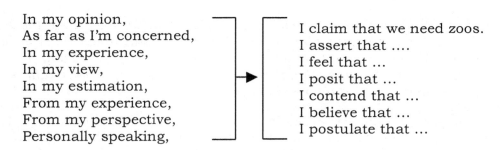

In my opinion,
As far as I'm concerned,
In my experience,
In my view,
In my estimation,
From my experience,
From my perspective,
Personally speaking,

I claim that we need zoos.
I assert that ....
I feel that ...
I posit that ...
I contend that ...
I believe that ...
I postulate that ...

1. In my opinion, I claim that there are advantages to working from home, such as privacy, cost and seeing my children more.

2. As far as I'm concerned, I assert that there are advantages to working from home, for example privacy, cost and seeing my children more.

3. In my experience, I <u>feel that</u> there are advantages to working from home, including privacy, convenience and less stress.

4. In my view, I <u>posit that</u> there are advantages to working from home, namely privacy, cost and spending more time with my children.

5. From my perspective, I <u>contend that</u> there are advantages to working from home, specifically privacy, cost and seeing my children more.

6. Personally speaking, I <u>believe that</u> there are advantages to working from home, including privacy, cost and seeing my children more.

7. In my estimation, I <u>conclude that</u> there are advantages to working from home, such as privacy, cost and seeing my children more.

8. In my opinion, I <u>postulate that</u> there are advantages to working from home, including privacy, convenience and seeing my children more.

Sample Independent Essays → *G+3TiC=C*

The following essays each score a 5/5 because each demonstrates OPDUL=C.

- **REMEMBER:** *ETS says your independent essay should be about 300 words. Don't worry if your word count is not exactly 300 words. <u>Remember</u>: You are demonstrating OPDUL=C, not counting words.*

Agree-Disagree Essay → Words 280

- <u>Prompt</u>: Do we need zoos? Give examples and reasons to develop your essay.

1 *Do we or don't we need zoos? Personally, I agree with the statement. I think that we*
2 *need zoos. We need zoos because they are educational, they are fun for families, and*
3 *they protect endangered animals.*
4
5 *Zoos are educational. For example, when I was 12, my teacher took us to the zoo in*
6 *Toronto. I had never seen wild animals before. I had just read about them in books*
7 *and seen them on TV. But seeing them in real life was amazing, especially the lions.*
8 *On TV, they looked so small, but seeing them live, I realized they were really big. By*
9 *going to the zoo, I saw things in a whole new light.*
10
11 *Zoos are also fun for families. For example, I have a family and we always go to the*
12 *zoo every summer. My wife makes a picnic and we spend all day there. My kids love*
13 *taking pictures and learning all about the animals, especially the gorillas. Being out-*
14 *side is good for my children. Best of all, they can leave the internet and the TV at*
15 *home.*
16
17 *Finally, zoos protect endangered animals. For example, I saw two pandas in the*
18 *Washington DC zoo last year and they had a baby. If there were no zoos, pandas*
19 *would disappear because we are taking their habitat away. However, in zoos, pan-*
20 *das are safe. It is not perfect, but without zoos there might not be any pandas left.*

21 *For those reasons, I believe that we need zoos because they are educational, they are*
22 *fun for families, and they protect endangered animals. If you want to have fun and*
23 *learn something new, you should go to a zoo.*

Preference Essay → Words 294

- Prompt: Do you prefer to use a laptop or a desktop computer? Explain.

1 *Today, people have a big choice between laptop computers and desktop computers.*
2 *So which do I prefer? Personally, I prefer a laptop because a laptop is great for taking*
3 *notes in class, portable, and affordable.*
4

5 *A laptop is great for taking notes in class. For example, I'm a university student and I*
6 *need a laptop for my classes. If I didn't have a laptop, I'd have to take notes by hand,*
7 *and that would be really slow. Also, my handwriting is really bad, but with my laptop*
8 *I can quickly take notes. This saves me a lot of time. I couldn't take notes with a desk-*
9 *top. It is too big and not made for carrying. As you can see, a laptop is definitely best*
10 *for taking notes in class.*
11

12 *Also, a laptop is portable. For example, I can take my laptop anywhere to study. This*
13 *is good because sometimes my roommate plays really loud music. This drives me*
14 *nuts. When he plays his music, I can't do any homework, so I go to the library or*
15 *Starbucks. There, I can use their wi-fi and do my homework. Because my laptop is*
16 *portable, I can do these things. Best of all, I don't have to listen to my roommate's mu-*
17 *sic.*
18

19 *In addition, a laptop is affordable. For example, a few years ago laptops, like my*
20 *Sony Vaio, were very expensive but now you can get a really fast laptop with lots of*
21 *memory for cheaper than a desktop. This is good because I can save money. With this*
22 *money, I can buy other school things like books.*
23

24 *In the final analysis, I definitely prefer a laptop because it is great for taking notes in*
25 *class, portable, and affordable. What more do I need?*

Compare-Contrast Essay → Words 300

➡ For this essay, note that the map is G+2TiC=C. Note also how the transitional "However" (line 11) topically connects contrasting body-paragraphs one and two.

- Prompt: What will your friend like and not like when visiting your hometown? Use examples and reasons to develop your argument.

1 *What will my friend like and not like when visiting the place I call home, New Delhi,*
2 *India? Personally speaking, I contend that my friend will like the food; however, he*
3 *will not be crazy about the summer temperatures or the crowds.*
4

5 *My friend will like the delicious food in New Delhi. When I am hungry, I go to*
6 *Sheshraj's, the best restaurant in New Delhi. The prices are very reasonable and you*
7 *get a lot of food. The lamb curry is excellent as is the aloo gobi. For a good meal, my*
8 *friend can spend maybe one American dollar. Eating at Sheshraj's will definitely give*
9 *my friend a real New Delhi experience that is both affordable and delicious.*
10

11 *However, my friend will not like summer in New Delhi. The temperature can reach*
12 *120F plus the humidity is high as well. This makes New Delhi uncomfortable in the*
13 *summer. Unlike America, air conditioning is not found everywhere in New Delhi. This*
14 *is most evident on the trains and buses. With the high temperatures and the high hu-*
15 *midity, this can make traveling difficult. Because of these factors, my friend may*
16 *want to avoid visiting New Delhi in the summer.*
17
18 *As mentioned, New Delhi is crowded. My friend might not like this because he comes*
19 *from a small town in Connecticut, so he does not feel the pressure of big city life. Also,*
20 *he does not see any poverty because Connecticut is wealthy unlike parts of New Del-*
21 *hi which are extremely poor. This might be a big shock for my friend since he is not*
22 *used to such cultural extremes.*
23
24 *As illustrated, there are many reasons why my friend will like and won't like New*
25 *Delhi. However, this should not stop him from visiting. I guarantee he will have a*
26 *wonderful time.*

Advantage-Disadvantage Essay → Words 269

- Prompt: What are the advantages and disadvantages of owning a car? Explain.

1   *The question is what are the advantages and disadvantages of owning a car. From*
2   *my experience, I can safely say that an advantage of owning a car is freedom and a*
3   *disadvantage is the cost.*
4
5   *A big advantage of owning a car is freedom. For example, I have a Honda. With my*
6   *car, I can go anywhere I want. Before I bought a car; however, I had to take the bus*
7   *everywhere. Sometimes the bus was late, so I got to work late. My boss didn't like*
8   *that. But since I bought a car, I've never been late for work. Also, I can go for a drive*
9   *in the country or go shopping and I don't have to worry about bus schedules or mon-*
10 *ey for tickets. This is a big advantage of owning a car.*
11
12 *In contrast, owning a car can be very expensive. For example, I drive to work every*
13 *day. The distance is fifty miles from my house to my office. That means I use a lot of*
14 *gasoline. In a week, I can spend more than $75.00 on gas. If the price of gas is high-*
15 *er, I spend more. Insurance and repairs can also be expensive. Tires and parking too.*
16 *As a result, I have to budget my money and spend less on clothes and video games,*
17 *and other things I like. This is definitely a disadvantage.*
18
19 *As I have illustrated, I think that there are advantages and disadvantages to owning a*
20 *car. Should you buy a car? Yes. It's a no-brainer. Go for it. Buy a car and be free!*
21 *Just watch your money!*

Advantage Essay → Words 296

- Prompt: What are the advantages of telecommuting? Explain.

1   *What is telecommuting? Telecommuting means you can work from home while being*
2   *connected to your office by the internet. Personally, I prefer to work from home. Work-*
3   *ing from home has many advantages, such as more privacy, less stress, and seeing*
4   *my children more.*
5

6   *First, telecommuting gives me more privacy. For example, at work I have a cubicle. It's*
7   *really noisy because people are always talking and using the copy machine. Also,*
8   *people are always stopping and saying hello to me. This is not good because it*
9   *wastes a lot of time. It also makes it hard for me to finish my work. But if I work from*
10 *home, nobody bothers me and I finish my work without interruption. This is an ad-*
11 *vantage of telecommuting.*
12
13 *Also, with telecommuting there is less stress. When I go to work, I must get up early*
14 *and drive. It takes an hour and the traffic is always bad. If there is an accident, I get*
15 *to work late. That means I have to stay late to finish my assignments. But if I work*
16 *from home, I don't have to worry about getting up early or stressing about traffic or*
17 *being late for work. This is another big advantage of telecommuting.*
18
19 *Finally, working from home lets me see my children more. My children are very*
20 *young, only seven and eight. I drop them off at day care when I go to work but when I*
21 *work from home, I can look after them. This really saves me money. Also, I can spend*
22 *more time with my children. This makes us all very happy. This is the best advantage*
23 *of telecommuting.*
24
25 *Suffice it to say, telecommuting has myriad advantages. Don't you wish you could*
26 *just fall out of bed and go to work?*

Disadvantage Essay → Words 276

- Prompt: What are the disadvantages of studying online? Explain.

1   *Last year, I wanted to get an MBA, so I took an online course. I thought I'd have time*
2   *to do all the work; however, I soon realized that I didn't have enough time. I couldn't*
3   *study during the week because I was too busy at work. On the weekends, I didn't*
4   *want to study either. I just wanted to be with my family and relax. As a result, I didn't*
5   *do any homework and I didn't finish the course. Obviously, if you have no time like*
6   *me, an online course is not a good way to get a university degree.*
7
8   *Also, if you are going to take an online course, you must be careful about the school's*
9   *reputation. For example, my friend Maria had a job interview at this company and*
10 *they asked about her diploma she got online. They thought it was fake because*
11 *they'd never heard of her school before. This made Maria feel two-inches small be-*
12 *cause she'd worked so hard to get her degree. Unfortunately, she didn't get the job.*
13
14 *Something like this also happened to my friend Hiroshi. He's really good with com-*
15 *puters, so he took an IT course because he wanted a computer job. The course cost*
16 *him a lot of money, but he took it anyway because he could finish in six months and*
17 *get a job. However, the day after he started studying, the school suddenly closed and*
18 *Hiroshi lost all his money. Now, he has no school, no money and no job.*
19
20 *As you can see, studying online is like gambling. Does this mean you should not take*
21 *an internet course? No. Just look before you leap!*

Reason Essay → Words 347

- <u>Prompt</u>: Which technology has changed your life? Explain.

1 *Because I'm a scientist, I use many technologies. However, I can honestly say that the*
2 *technology that has changed my life the most is the internet. Using the internet makes*
3 *communication fast and easy, is good for research, and saves me money.*
4
5 *First, the internet makes communication fast and easy. For example, I'm from China*
6 *and I'm now working in the United States. That means my family and friends back in*
7 *Beijing are very far away. Yet, by using the internet, I can talk to them as much as I*
8 *want. The best way is Skype. Using Skype, I can see their faces and they can see*
9 *mine. Before the internet, people like my parents had to send letters. That took so*
10 *long. But the internet has changed all that. The internet makes communication fast*
11 *and easy for me and my family. It's like magic. Best of all, I don't get homesick.*
12
13 *Next, the internet is good for research. I'm a research physicist developing lasers for*
14 *weather testing. To research my ideas, I always use the internet. It's good for finding*
15 *articles and the latest research papers that can help me with my research. If I didn't*
16 *have the internet, I'd have to go to libraries. But with the internet, all I have to do is*
17 *search with Google and I have the information right at my fingertips.*
18
19 *Finally, the internet saves me money. When I have questions about my work, I can*
20 *email scientists all over the world for answers. This saves money because I don't*
21 *have to travel. Also, scientists can contact me and ask questions. For example, last*
22 *week a scientist from Norway emailed me and asked about my work. Before the in-*
23 *ternet, he would have had to have flown or called long distance. This is very expen-*
24 *sive. But now scientists can save time and money using the internet.*
25
26 *In sum, the internet has changed my life the most. Using the internet is fast and easy,*
27 *is great for research, and it saves me money. Can you imagine a world without the*
28 *internet?*

Quality Essay → Words 283

- <u>Prompt</u>: What are the qualities of a good university? Explain.

1 *What are the qualities of a good university? Personally, I posit that a good university*
2 *should have many qualities, such as excellent teachers, lots of good courses, and a*
3 *convenient location.*
4
5 *A good university should have excellent teachers. For example, I study ESL at Shelton*
6 *University. The teachers there have lots of teaching experience. Also, many of them*
7 *have taught English in foreign countries. This is good because the teachers at Shelton*
8 *University can understand my situation in America. In other words, the teachers can*
9 *see life through my eyes and know that learning a new language is not easy, espe-*
10 *cially when living in a new culture.*
11
12 *Moreover, a good university should have a variety of courses. For example, at Shelton*
13 *University there are lots of great ESL courses. I can take grammar, idioms and com-*
14 *position. I can even take TOEFL! For me, the best course was English for Business. In*

15 *that class, Professor Morrison showed me how to write a resume and a cover letter.*
16 *Because of this, I now have a part time job as a Spanish-English translator.*
17

18 *Furthermore, a good university should have a convenient location. Shelton University*
19 *has a great location. It's right downtown and very close to the subway station. It takes*
20 *me just five minutes from the station to school. This is so convenient. Best of all, I*
21 *don't have to drive my car and find a parking place, which is always a hassle.*
22

23 *As the aforementioned examples have illustrated, a good university should have*
24 *many qualities, such as excellent teachers, lots of great courses, and a convenient lo-*
25 *cation. If you want to study ESL in America, you should check out Shelton University.*
26 *You won't be disappointed.*

Contrarian Essay

What if you think the prompt is not asking the right question? What should you do?
<u>Answer</u>: Write a contrarian essay. Read the following prompt, then read the contrarian response that follows.

- <u>Prompt</u>: Television is a good influence on children. What is your position?

Contrarian Response → Words 247

1 *The prompt claims that television is good for children. Personally, I don't agree or dis-*
2 *agree. The fact is television is neither good nor bad for children. Television is just an*
3 *electronic device that delivers information. The real problem is those parents who do*
4 *not control what their children watch.*
5

6 *For example, my friend Pierre lets his kids watch TV all the time. Whenever I go over*
7 *to his house, his kids are always watching violent movies like Terminator and Die*
8 *Hard. When Pierre tells them to do their homework or go outside and play, his kids*
9 *just yell and fight, and Pierre does nothing to stop them. His kids want to watch gar-*
10 *bage all day, so he lets them watch garbage all day. Pierre is a great guy but as you*
11 *can see, the TV is controlling him. As a result, his kids are out of control.*
12

13 *In contrast, my friend Carla lets her kids watch only two hours of TV every night. Be-*
14 *fore her kids can watch TV; however, they must do their homework. Then, when they*
15 *watch TV, Carla tells her kids which shows they can watch, like National Geographic,*
16 *and which shows they can't watch, like violent movies. This way, Carla controls the*
17 *TV. By doing so, she makes sure that television is a good influence on her kids.*
18

19 *As illustrated, television is neither good nor bad for children. The question should be*
20 *about parents, and how well they control what their kids watch.*

➔ In a contrarian essay, such as the one above, the test-taker is arguing that the prompt is asking the wrong question. The test-taker then constructs a contrarian response with a new thesis using compare-and-contrast and G+2TiC=C, then concludes by suggesting what the prompt should be.

- **REMEMBER:** *A well-developed contrarian response is acceptable on test day.*

Writing Practice

Using the strategies discussed, write an independent essay that demonstrates OPDUL=C. You have 30 minutes. Check your responses for coherence using the *Independent Writing → Proficiency Checklist* on page 329, then rate each response using the *Independent Writing → Rating Guide* on page 330.

Note: Google "TOEFL writing prompts" for more samples.

1. Before an important exam, do you think it is better to prepare for a long time or only for a few days? Give examples and reasons to support your argument.

2. Students are less political than before. What is your opinion? Use examples and reasons to support your claim.

3. Which teacher has had the greatest influence on your life? Why? Give examples and reasons to support and develop your opinion.

4. Some prefer to stay home while on vacation while others prefer to travel. Which do you prefer? Why? Give examples and reasons to support your position.

5. Honesty is the best policy. What is your belief? Give illustrations and reasons to support your argument.

6. How do you measure success? Support your position with examples and reasons.

7. Advertising has a positive influence. What is your position? Use examples and reasons to defend your position.

8. Is it better to buy a product when you want it at the regular price or wait for the product when it is on sale? Use examples and reasons to argue your position.

9. In America, customers can return a purchased item for a full refund within thirty days. Do you agree or disagree with this policy? Develop your position with illustrations and reasons.

10. University education should be free. Do you agree or disagree? Why? Use examples and reasons to develop your argument.

11. Compare and contrast the advantages and disadvantages of using a smartphone. Give illustrations and reasons to support your opinion.

12. Do you agree or disagree? Every student should travel or work for a year before going to university or college. Support your argument using examples and reasons.

13. It is easy to waste time these days. Give illustrations and reasons to support your opinion

14. Progress is good. Give illustrations and reasons to support your opinion.

Integrated Writing Task

The integrated writing task is the first task in the writing section. For this task, you will summarize two arguments. One is a short reading. The other is a short lecture. They are on the same topic, yet argue opposing positions. In your summary, you will integrate the two arguments and show how *the lecture argues against the reading*. Your summary should be about <u>225</u> words The task order follows.

Reading = 3 minutes
Lecture = 2 minutes
Writing = 20 minutes

● **REMEMBER**: *You hear the lecture only once. You cannot replay it. When you write your summary, the reading will return to your computer screen.*

Reading and Lecture → *Analysis*

Read the passage and lecture tapescript below. You can listen to the lecture on audio track #1. Note how each argument maps out using G+3TiC=C. Note as well how *the lecture argues against the reading.*

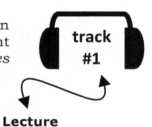

track #1

	Reading	**Lecture**
G →	Personally, I believe that oil companies are a vital part of the American economy.	On the contrary, oil companies do more harm than good.
TiC →	First, oil companies create thousands of jobs. They need geologists to find new oil reserves and engineers to bring them to market. Economists predict this segment of the job market will continue to grow.	For starters, big oil eliminates jobs to increase profits. Last year, oil companies reduced their work force by 25% while profits were up 50% percent. This trend does not appear to be changing.
TiC →	In addition, oil companies pay taxes that build roads and bridges. Last year, big oil paid over $100 billion dollars in tax revenue. America needs this money to maintain its infrastructure.	Also, oil companies avoid paying taxes by moving overseas. One company, Hamilton, moved to Dubai to reduce its U.S. corporate tax rate. How does this help our roads and bridges?
TiC →	Finally, the products oil companies make are the life-blood of many industries. Oil is vital for the transportation and plastics industries. These segments of the economy would disappear without oil.	Worse, petroleum products are the number one cause of global warming. Every day, cars pour billions of tons of CO_2 into the atmosphere. CO_2 has been directly linked to the greenhouse effect.
C →	In sum, oil companies are critical to America's health and well-being.	The evidence is clear. Oil companies do more harm than good.

Pro-Con Format

As you can see on the previous page, the reading passage is pro (supports) oil while the lecture is con (against) oil. You will see this format and structure on test day. It is predictable: two independent essays arguing opposite positions.

- **REMEMBER**: *If the reading says "pro," the lecture will say "con." If the reading says "No," the lecture will say "Yes," etc. Being able to predict the opposing arguments this way will help you anticipate the main points to summarize in both arguments and to take notes more proficiently.*

Integrated Summary → *Step-by-Step*

Follow these steps when writing your integrated summary on test day.

Step #1   **Make a G+3TiC-C note map.**

Write READING and LECTURE at the top of a piece of paper. Next, map out G+3TiC=C twice. Because time is short, simply write O for opinion (G), 1, 2, 3 for each body paragraph (3TiC), and C for conclusion.

READING	LECTURE
O	O
1	1
2	2
3	3
C	C

Step #2   **Read the passage; you have 3 minutes.**

When the task directions end, the reading passage will appear on your screen. You will have 3 minutes to read it. Read the following passage. As you do, identify the G+3TiC=C structure. Note each section on your note map.

1 *Music. We all love it. In fact, I'm listening to my favorite band right now, music I*
2 *downloaded off the internet. I had to pay for it, but I didn't. For that, many*
3 *would call me a criminal. Well, go right ahead. As far as I'm concerned, down-*
4 *loading music off the internet without paying is not a crime. Why not?*
5

6 *Let's start with a little history. The internet was originally invented to be a*
7 *source of free information benefiting all. Downloading music off the internet*
8 *without paying for it is a perfect example of this democratic ideal in action. In*
9 *this light, I am not criminal. I am simply exercising my democratic right to move*
10 *freely in the vast new democracy called cyberspace.*
11
12 *Now if you're like me, you love to share music with your friends by download-*
13 *ing it from their computers. This is not stealing music. Hardly. My friends and I*
14 *are simply sharing songs. In fact, I share music with people all over the world,*
15 *people I don't know and will never meet. This process is called P2P or peer-to-*
16 *peer file sharing. Now think: Is sharing something you love a crime? I don't*
17 *think so.*
18
19 *Finally, and this point I really want to stress: What I do in the privacy of my*
20 *home is nobody's business but my own. Period. I don't need the government*
21 *telling me what I can or can't do with my computer. The United States is a de-*
22 *mocracy not a dictatorship.*
23
24 *To sum up, just because I refuse to pay for internet music does not make me a*
25 *felon. The real criminals are those in government and business determined to*
26 *deny music-loving individuals their right to freedom and privacy.*

Step #3   Identify and note the reading thesis and examples.

To locate the reading thesis, check the introduction. Look for signal words, such as those below. They will identify the start of the author's opinion.

Personally, I believe...I feel that...I think that...In my experience...From my per-
spective...In my estimation...It goes without saying that...I argue that...etc.

If the thesis is not in the introduction, check the conclusion. As you read, look for signal words, such as the following.

In sum...In conclusion...To sum up...As you have seen...In the end...All in all...To
restate...As illustrated...In closing...In the final analysis...Indeed...etc.

In the reading, the thesis is in the introduction. The author says: *"As far as I'm concerned, downloading music off the internet without paying is not a crime."* This is the author's thesis-opinion. Why? Because it is arguable and supportable (see the thesis checklist on page 16).

Next, note the thesis on your note map beside O under READING. Write objectively using third-person singular and the present tense. Say, *"The reading argues...It says..."* or *"The author argues...He argues...She argues,"* etc.

READING

O   the reading says downloading music off web without pay-
     ing is not a crime

Next, note the reasoning in the thesis. It will be stated using **cause**-and-*effect*.

READING

O   the reading says **downloading music off web without paying (cause)** *is not a crime* (effect)

Next, note the start of each body paragraph. Look for **signal words** such as:

First...Let's start with...Let me begin by saying... Also...Moreover...In addition...Next...Furthermore...Not only that but...On top of that...Finally...etc.

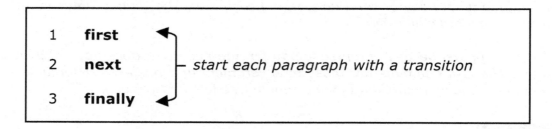

1   **first**

2   **next**   — *start each paragraph with a transition*

3   **finally**

Next, note the **topic** of each body paragraph.

---

1   first reading says **internet is a democracy**; downloading music example of internet democracy

2   next friends just **sharing music** example P2P

3   finally author argues **right to privacy** in home

Next, note the reason in each body paragraph stated using **cause**-and-*effect*.

---

1   first reading says internet is a democracy; downloading music example of internet democracy
     because internet is democracy, *music is free*

2   next friends just sharing music example P2P
     sharing love for music *not stealing, not a crime*

3   finally author argues right to privacy in home
     what he does in home *no business of government or music companies*

Next, note the restated thesis in the conclusion and the **cause**-and-*effect* reason.

> C   in sum reading says not a felon...
> **government + music companies deny freedom and privacy,** *they are the criminals*
> US democracy not dictatorship

 Your reading note map is now complete!

> Reading
>
> O   reading says downloading music off web without paying is not a crime
>
> 1   first reading says internet is a democracy; downloading music is example of internet democracy
> because internet is democracy, music is free
>
> 2   next friends just sharing music, example P2P
> sharing love for music is not stealing, not a crime
>
> 3   finally author argues right to privacy in home
> what he does at home is no business of government or music companies
>
> C   in sum reading says not a felon...
> government + music companies deny freedom and privacy, they are the criminals
> US democracy not a dictatorship

- **REMEMBER**: *This task measures your ability to identify quickly the reading argument's structure (G+3TiC+C) and the cause-and-effect reasoning in each body paragraph.*

Step #4   Listen to the lecture; take notes while listening.

When the reading time is up, the passage will leave your screen.

- **REMEMBER**: *The reading will return when you write your summary.*

The lecture will replace the reading. The lecture will last 2-3 minutes. To take proficient lecture notes, you must anticipate each counter-argument in the lecture as you listen.

Listening Strategies → *How to Listen*

For many test-takers, taking notes while listening to the lecture is a challenge. To take more proficient notes, do the following while listening.

1. **Predict:** The lecture is mapped out the same as the reading. That structure is G+3TiC=C. It is predictable.

2. **Visualize**: As you listen, visualize G+3TiC=C. Follow the map in your mind.

3. **Anticipate:** Because the lecture structure is predictable, you know the thesis (G) will come first followed by three body paragraphs (3TiC) and the conclusion (C). As you visualize G+3TiC=C, anticipate each step as the lecture progresses.

4. **Signal Words:** As the lecture progresses, listen for signal words. They will tell you when the thesis is transitioning into the body, when the body paragraphs are changing, and when the lecture is concluding.

5. **Reasons:** Each point in the lecture will argue against each point in the reading using a cause-and-effect reasoning. As you listen, look at each reason in your reading note map. The lecture will argue the opposite. Note it.

Sample Lecture: Internet Music → *Tapescript*

track #2

Below is the tapescript for the lecture. Read as you listen.

1 *It happens every second of every day all over the world. One click and that new*
2 *song—the one you didn't pay for—is on your iPod. You may think it's legal. After all,*
3 *downloading music is fast and easy, right? Think again. It goes without saying that*
4 *downloading music off the web without paying for it is a crime.*
5
6 *I know. I know. Some will argue that "It's my democratic right to download music*
7 *without paying for it." Nonsense. The internet might have started out with the inten-*
8 *tion of being a democracy, but believe me, those days are long gone. The internet the-*
9 *se days is about two things: information and money. Big money. One of the biggest*
10 *money makers on the web is music, and music is protected by law. If you download*
11 *U2's latest album, let's say, and you don't pay for it, then you are breaking the copy-*
12 *right law that says U2 owns that music. It is their property and you just stole it. If you*
13 *want to listen to U2, you've got to buy it, no ifs, ands or buts.*
14
15 *Also, the artist has a legal right to get paid for his or her work no matter how or where*
16 *it is downloaded. How would you like it if somebody were stealing your music? This*
17 *is exactly what Napster was doing. Napster was the first peer-to-peer music sharing*
18 *site. Musicians, however, took Napster to court for not paying royalties, money owed*
19 *each time a song was downloaded via Napster. Napster argued that it was just help-*
20 *ing friends share music. The courts disagreed. Napster paid a big fine and is now a*
21 *pay site.*

22 *Moreover, illegally downloading music off the web is not a privacy issue. If you break*
23 *the law by illegally downloading music, you are a criminal. I'm sorry, but you can't*
24 *have it both ways. You can't break the law and hide behind the privacy issue. The*
25 *law is clear. Criminals have no right to privacy. Period.*
26
27 *It bears repeating that downloading music without paying for it is a crime no matter*
28 *what anyone says about "the freedom of cyberspace." Just because downloading*
29 *music is fast and easy doesn't mean you have the right to steal it.*

- -

Next, look at the finished note map for the lecture. Note the **cause**-and-*effect* reasoning. Note also the third-person singular grammar in the present tense.

Lecture

O   lecture says **downloading music without paying** *is a crime!*

1   lecture says web is not democracy, all info and money, example U2
    not pay for U2? *break copyright law*
    want new U2? you must pay

2   lecture says musicians have right to get paid
    example Napster
    Napster said P2P sharing *okay, no crime*
    court disagreed, if artist makes music *court says musicians should get paid*
    napster now pay site

3   lecture says it is not a privacy issue
    download without paying *means you are a criminal*
    criminals have *no right to privacy*
    you can't have your cake *and eat it too*

C   lecture says that **downloading music and not paying is easy** *but still a crime*

Next, look at the two note maps side-by-side mapped out with G+3TiC=C. Note **however** on the lecture side. Note also how the lecture counter-argues the reading *point-by-point* even in rough form.

	Reading		**Lecture**
1			
2			
3			
4	G reading says downloading	⬅	G **however** lecture says
5	music off web without paying		downloading music without
6	is not a crime		paying is a crime
7			
8	Ti **first** reading says internet	⬅	Ti **however** lecture says web
9	is a democracy; down-		is not democracy,
10	loading music is example		all info and money
11	of internet democracy		example U2
12	C because internet is		C not pay for U2? break
13	democracy music is free		copyright law
14			want new U2? you must pay
15			
16			
17	Ti **next** friends just sharing	⬅	Ti **however** lecture says
18	music, example P2P		musicians have right to get
19	C sharing love for music is		paid, example Napster
20	not stealing, not a crime		C Napster said P2P sharing
21			okay, no crime
22			court disagreed,
23			if artist makes music court
24			says musicians should get
25			paid, napster now pay
26			site
27			
28	Ti **finally** author argues right	⬅	Ti **however** lecture says not
29	to privacy in home		a privacy issue
30	C what he does at home is		C download without paying
31	no business of gov't or music		means you are a criminal,
32	companies		criminals have no right to
33			privacy, you can't have
34			your cake and eat it too
35			
36	C **in sum** author says he is not	⬅	C **however** lecture says that
37	a felon if he doesn't pay,		downloading music and not
38	government + record		paying is easy but still a
39	companies deny freedom and		crime
40	privacy, they are criminals,		
41	US democracy not dictatorship		

Step #5   **Prompt analysis.**

When the lecture ends, the reading passage will return to your screen. The prompt will also appear on your screen. Below is the prompt for this task.

Prompt   Summarize the points made in the lecture and show how they cast doubt on the points made in the reading.

The prompt, translated using G+3TiC=C, reads like this.

Prompt   Identify and describe the opinion (G) and the supporting illustrations (3TiC) in the lecture and show how they counter-argue the opinion (G) and the supporting illustrations (3TiC) in the reading.

Writing → *Point-by-Point Style*

One way to write your summary is by using point-by-point style. Start by summarizing the reading thesis, then summarize the lecture thesis counterpoint. Do the same with the body paragraphs. <u>Note</u>: "pt." means point.

Line		Text
1 2 3	pt.	The reading says that downloading music off the internet without paying for it is not a crime. ***However***, *the lecture believes it's a crime.*
4 5 6 7 8	pt.	First, the reading states that the internet was invented to be a source of free information. Downloading music without paying for it is an example of this democratic ideal. ***In contrast***, *the lecture states that copyright laws protect music. If you don't pay for U2's latest album, you're breaking the law.*
9 10 11 12 13 14	pt.	Next, the reading says that downloading music from a friend's computer is not stealing but file sharing, which is not a crime. ***However***, *the lecture says that musicians should get paid. For example, Napster, a P2P site, didn't pay musicians. Napster said file sharing wasn't a crime. The court disagreed and fined Napster for not paying.*
15 16 17 18 19	pt.	Finally, the author says that what he does in the privacy of his home is no business of the government. ***In contrast***, *the lecture believes that if you steal music, you're a thief and have no right to privacy. The law is black and white. You can't have your cake and eat it too.*
20 21 22 23	pt.	In sum, the reading states that downloading music off the internet without paying for it isn't a crime. The criminals are the government and record companies trying to take away people's freedom. ***However***, *the lecture asserts that ripping music off the web is a crime.*

words: 221

Word Count: *According to ETS's Official Guide to the TOEFL Test, 4th Edition, page 199, your summary should be "between 150 and 225 words. You will not be penalized if you write more, so long as what you write answers the question."*

Writing → *Block Style*

Block style is another way to organize your summary. Note below how the reading is summarized first followed by the lecture. Note the transition-of-contrast **however**. This transition connects the reading (R) and the lecture (L) below.

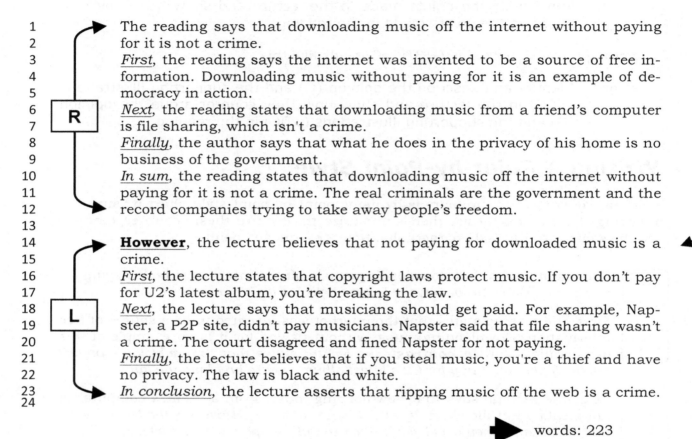

1	The reading says that downloading music off the internet without paying
2	for it is not a crime.
3	*First*, the reading says the internet was invented to be a source of free in-
4	formation. Downloading music without paying for it is an example of de-
5	mocracy in action.
6 **R**	*Next*, the reading states that downloading music from a friend's computer
7	is file sharing, which isn't a crime.
8	*Finally*, the author says that what he does in the privacy of his home is no
9	business of the government.
10	*In sum*, the reading states that downloading music off the internet without
11	paying for it is not a crime. The real criminals are the government and the
12	record companies trying to take away people's freedom.
13	
14	**However**, the lecture believes that not paying for downloaded music is a
15	crime.
16	*First*, the lecture states that copyright laws protect music. If you don't pay
17	for U2's latest album, you're breaking the law.
18 **L**	*Next*, the lecture says that musicians should get paid. For example, Nap-
19	ster, a P2P site, didn't pay musicians. Napster said that file sharing wasn't
20	a crime. The court disagreed and fined Napster for not paying.
21	*Finally*, the lecture believes that if you steal music, you're a thief and have
22	no privacy. The law is black and white.
23 24	*In conclusion*, the lecture asserts that ripping music off the web is a crime.

words: 223

- **REMEMBER:** *You can write your summary using either point-by-point or block style. One style is not better than the other. Both are acceptable. Some, however, prefer point-by-point while others prefer block style. Determine which style you prefer by practicing, then use it on test day.*

Step #6   **Check your summary for Coherence using OPDUL=C.**

OPDUL=C → *Rating this Task*

Three raters will rate your summary out of five total points. Let's say, for example, rater one and two give the point-by-point summary on page 49 a 5/5. Rater three also gives it a 5/5. The average rater score is 5/5. The average rater score is then converted to a writing section score of 30/30. That is a perfect score. Okay, so why did you get 30/30? Because, according to the integrated writing task rubric on the next page (and on pages 331-332), you demonstrated proficiency in all areas of OPDUL=C for integrated writing.

O = Organization

Under Organization, there are two proficiency descriptors: deduction and induction. If your summary starts with a general statement (G), and is supported by examples (3TiC) and ends with a conclusion (C), then you are demonstrating a method of organization called deduction. If your summary starts with examples (3TiC), and ends with conclusion-thesis (C), then you are demonstrating a method of organization called induction.

P = Progression

Under Progression, there are two proficiency descriptors. If your summary demonstrates deduction as the method of Organization, the ideas will progress from *general* (intro) to *specific* (body) to *general* (conclusion). If your essay demonstrates induction, the examples will progress from *specific* (body) to *general* (conclusion-thesis).

D = Development-Summarization

Under Development-Summarization, there are three proficiency descriptors: introduction development (G), body development (3TiC), and conclusion development (C). Topic development in your introduction means you have proficiently summarized the two opposing theses and the opposing reasons therein. Topic development in the body means you have proficiently summarized each example and the opposing reasons therein. Topic development in your conclusion means you have proficiently summarized the restated theses and the opposing reasons therein.

- **REMEMBER**: *A big reason why test-takers score low on the integrated writing task is because the reasons in each body paragraph have not been summarized using cause-and-effect and/or have been left out.*

U = Unity-Synthesis

Under Unity-Synthesis, there are two proficiency descriptors: topical unity and grammatical unity. Topical unity means your summary has proficiently integrated (united) the topics and the reasons in the reading and lecture using either point-by-point style or block style. Grammatical unity means you are using words of contrast (*however, in contrast*) to unite proficiently the reading and the lecture, topically and grammatically. Grammatical unity also means your grammar is proficient at the sentence level.

- **WARNING**: *Do not include your opinion in your summary. Your opinion is off topic and will demonstrate a lack of topical unity. This will result in a lower score.*

- **REMEMBER**: *Your opinion is subjective; whereas, the integrated writing task measures your ability to think and write objectively.*

L = Language-Use-Paraphrasing

Under Language-Use-Paraphrasing, there are two proficiency descriptors: word choice and sentence variety. Word choice measures your ability to paraphrase the reading and lecture using synonyms (see page 53). Sentence variety (including punctuation) measures your ability to summarize using simple, compound, and complex sentences proficiently.

C = Coherence

If your integrated summary demonstrates OPDUL, you will score a 5/5. However, if your summary lacks proficiency in one or more areas of OPDUL, then Coherence will be reduced, and your summary will score lower.

Rating an Integrated Summary

Next, let's rate the point-by-point summary we wrote on internet music on page 49.

O = Does it (summary) demonstrate proficient Organization?

✓ Yes. The writer proficiently demonstrates deduction as the method of organization.

P = Does it demonstrate proficient Progression?

✓ Yes. Because the summary is using deduction as the method of organization, the ideas progress from *general* (G) to *specific* (3TiC) to *general* (C)

D = Does it demonstrate proficient Development?

✓ Yes. The introduction proficiently summarizes the opposing subjective theses and the reasons therein. The body proficiently summarizes the opposing examples and the reasons therein. The conclusion proficiently summarizes the restated-opposing theses and the reasons therein.

U = Does it demonstrate proficient Unity?

✓ Yes. The summary focuses on the main topic of internet music and does not digress. The summary demonstrates proficient topical and grammatical unity by the correct use of transitional words.

L = Does it demonstrate proficient Language-Use-Paraphrasing?

✓ Yes. The writer proficiently demonstrates paraphrasing (see page 53).

C = Does the summary demonstrate Coherence?

✓ Yes. Because the writer proficiently demonstrates OPDUL, the writer demonstrates C. The result is a Coherent summary rating a 5/5.

Paraphrasing

To paraphrase means to summarize using synonyms. When you paraphrase, you demonstrate <u>L</u>anguage-Use-Paraphrasing (OPDU**L**=C), for example:

1. <u>original</u> The author of the reading states that downloading music off the internet without paying for it is not a crime.

   paraphrase The reading says that it is not a crime to download music off the web and not pay for it.

2. <u>original</u> First, the reading says that the internet was originally invented to be a source of free information. Downloading music without paying for it is an example of this democratic ideal in action.

   paraphrase First, the reading states that the internet is a democracy. Therefore, everything on the internet is free, including music.

3. <u>original</u> Next, the reading states that downloading music from a friend's computer is not stealing. It is peer-to-peer file sharing. File sharing, he says, is not a crime.

   paraphrase Next, the reading claims that P2P file sharing isn't a crime. You're simply sharing what you love: music.

4. <u>original</u> Finally, the author says that what he does in the privacy of his own home is no business of the government or the record companies. The U.S. is a democracy not a dictatorship.

   paraphrase Finally, the author of the reading believes that this is a privacy issue. Record companies and the government can't tell him what he can or can't do.

- **REMEMBER**: *On the official ETS integrated writing task rubric, paraphrasing is not included as a proficiency descriptor. However, you should paraphrase as much as possible. By doing so, you will demonstrate language use and maximize scoring.*

| Step #7 | **Submit your integrated summary.** |

After you check your summary using OPDUL=C, rewrite areas that lack proficiency, then submit your summary.

Mapped out, you can see on the next page how G+3TiC=C gives the writing raters what they are trained to look for: an integrated written summary that meets all the requirements of OPDUL=C for integrated writing. The summarized opinions (G) and conclusions (C) are <u>underlined</u>, the transitions (T) are in **bold**, and the summarized supporting illustrations (i) are in *italics*.

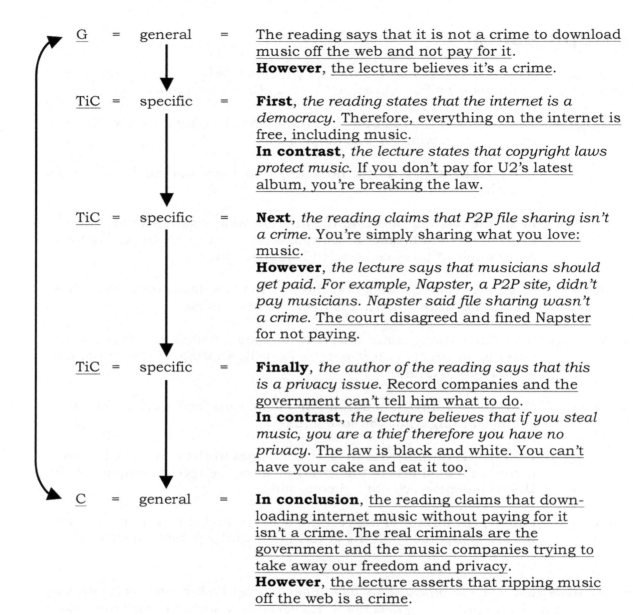

G	=	general	=	The reading says that it is not a crime to download music off the web and not pay for it. **However**, the lecture believes it's a crime.
TiC	=	specific	=	**First**, *the reading states that the internet is a democracy.* Therefore, everything on the internet is free, including music. **In contrast**, *the lecture states that copyright laws protect music.* If you don't pay for U2's latest album, you're breaking the law.
TiC	=	specific	=	**Next**, *the reading claims that P2P file sharing isn't a crime.* You're simply sharing what you love: music. **However**, *the lecture says that musicians should get paid. For example, Napster, a P2P site, didn't pay musicians. Napster said file sharing wasn't a crime.* The court disagreed and fined Napster for not paying.
TiC	=	specific	=	**Finally**, *the author of the reading says that this is a privacy issue.* Record companies and the government can't tell him what to do. **In contrast**, *the lecture believes that if you steal music, you are a thief therefore you have no privacy.* The law is black and white. You can't have your cake and eat it too.
C	=	general	=	**In conclusion**, the reading claims that downloading internet music without paying for it isn't a crime. The real criminals are the government and the music companies trying to take away our freedom and privacy. **However**, the lecture asserts that ripping music off the web is a crime.

words: 235

Common Problems for this Task

1. Reversed Argument --

For this task, you must demonstrate how the lecture argues against the reading. Do so by summarizing *the reading* first, then summarizing how *the lecture* counter-argues the reading. Do not do this.

Wrong *The lecture believes that global warming is just a natural warming cycle that poses no threat to mankind;* ***however***, *the reading argues that global warming is destroying the planet.*

Right   *The reading argues that global warming is destroying the planet;* **however,** *the lecture believes that global warming is just a natural warming cycle that poses no threat to mankind.*

2. Lack of Topic Identification -------------------------------

Many test-takers do not identify **the source** of each argument, for example:

Weak   *Downloading music off the internet without paying for it is not a crime; however, if you steal music off the web, you are a criminal.*

Good   **The reading argues** *that downloading music off the internet without paying for it is not a crime; however,* **the lecture asserts** *that if you steal music off the web, you are a criminal.*

3. Lack of Unity-Synthesis ----------------------------------

Make sure you use the correct connecting word/phrase of contrast when uniting opposing reasons. This will demonstrate proficient topical and grammatical Unity and Language-Use (OPD**UL**=C), for example:

Wrong   *The reading argues that zoos benefit all mankind* **and** *the lecture asserts that zoos are inhumane and should be abolished.*

Right   *The reading argues that zoos benefit all mankind;* **however,** *the lecture asserts that zoos are inhumane and should be abolished.*

4. Lack of Reason Identification --------------------------

When summarizing the reading and the lecture, make sure you identify and describe the reasons using **cause**-and-*effect*.

Weak   The reading argues for zoos while the lecture doesn't.

Better   The reading argues that **zoos** *benefit all mankind* while the lecture asserts that **zoos** *are inhumane* and **should be abolished**.

Good   First, the reading argues against organic food. In contrast, the lecture supports this idea.

Better   First, the reading argues that **organic food** *is too expensive,* **especially when trying to feed a large family**; however, the lecture counters by arguing that **organic food** *is an investment in your family's health* **and is worth the extra cost**.

5. Can't Write → *Blanked Out Listening to the Lecture* ----

As you write your integrated summary, you can refer to the reading passage. However, you hear the lecture only once. Therein lies the challenge: listening to an academic lecture full of new words and information while trying to take notes. In other words, you have to multi-task in English. For some, the result is panic. They blank out and fail to understand the lecture. If this happens, you can still write a response. Do the following.

Using block-style (see page 50), summarize the reading. As you summarize, you will familiarize yourself with the points in the reading argument.

1 2	The reading argues that milk is a health risk and we should not drink it.
3 4 5 6 7	First, the reading says that cows are injected with a hormone called rBGH. rBGH forces cows to produce far more milk than is naturally possible. RBGH stays in the milk and enters your body. The author says rBGH causes cancer.
8 **R** 9 10 11	Next, the reading states that a study in England says that children with attention-deficit-hyperactivity disorder (ADHD) are allergic to milk. This allergy increases hyper activity and attention problems in children with ADHD.
12 13 14	Finally, the reading claims that drinking milk reduces calcium absorption, making bones more fragile in older women.
15	For those reasons, the reading argues that milk is a health risk.

➡ Next, when summarizing the lecture, state the opposite of what each reading point is arguing.

1 2	**However,** the lecturer claims that milk **is not a health risk.**
3 4	First, the lectures argues that rBGH **does not cause cancer**.
5 **L** 6 7	Next, the lecture asserts that kids with ADHD are **not more allergic to milk**.
8 9 10	Finally, the lecture says that **older women who drink milk do not have more bone loss and fractures**.
11	In sum, the lecturer believes that **milk is not a health risk**.

1

➡ words: 180

When writing a point-by-point summary, state the opposite of the reading when summarizing the lecture (see below).

1 The reading argues that milk is a health risk and we should not drink it. ***However,***
2 *the lecture claims that milk is not a health risk.*
3
4 First, the reading says that cows are injected with a hormone called rBGH. RBGH
5 forces cows to produce far more milk than is naturally possible. rBGH stays in the
6 milk and enters your body. The author says rBGH causes cancer. ***However,*** *the lec-*
7 *ture argues that rBGH does not cause cancer.*
8
9 Next, the reading states that a study in England says that children with attention-
10 deficit-hyperactivity disorder (ADHD) are allergic to milk. This allergy increases hy-
11 per activity and attention problems in children with ADHD. ***However,*** *the lecture*
12 *asserts that children with ADHD are not more allergic to milk.*
13
14 Finally, the reading claims that drinking milk reduces calcium absorption, making
15 bones more fragile in older women. ***However,*** *the lecture posits that older women*
16 *who drink milk do not have more bone loss and fractures.*
17
18 For those reasons, the reading argues that milk is a health risk. ***However,*** *the lec-*
19 *ture argues that milk is not a health risk.*

 words: 180

Show-Support Writing Task

According to ETS, there are two integrated writing tasks for the TOEFL test: the pro-con integrated writing task you have just learned about and the show-support integrated writing task.

For the show-support integrated writing task, you must show how information in the lecture (specific supporting material) supports the topic in the reading (general introduction to the topic).

The strategies for the show-support writing task are the same as those for speaking task #4 (see page 97). The only difference is for the show-support writing task, you must write your response while for speaking task #4, you must deliver your response verbally. Other than that, the strategies for both tasks are the same.

Author's Note: As of this writing, the official TOEFL test uses only the pro-con integrated writing task for testing purposes. If you want to prepare for the show-support integrated writing task as well, use the test samples at the end of speaking task #4; however, instead of delivering verbal responses, write your responses, then rate them using the integrated writing guides on pages 331 and 332.

- **REMEMBER:** *On test day, expect the pro-con integrated writing task.*

Integrated Writing Practice

For each of the following tasks, read the passage, listen to the lecture, then write an integrated summary using the strategies discussed. Check each response for proficiency using the *Integrated Writing → Proficiency Checklist* on page 331. Rate each using the *Integrated Writing → Rating Guide* on page 332.

Task #1

Reading → *Teleconferencing* → 3:00 minutes

1   In this article, I will take a closer look at teleconferencing. For starters, perhaps the
2   greatest benefit of teleconferencing is convenience. No longer do business people
3   have to fly around the world to meet face-to-face with customers or colleagues. Now
4   they can simply dial into a conference line or click open a webcam and they're
5   ready to do business. Not only that, but with teleconferencing you can schedule
6   meetings all day long from the comfort of your office or home. Never has there been
7   a more convenient way to do business.
8
9   Another big advantage is the savings. These days, with the average business class
10 airline ticket costing well over four thousand dollars—not to mention the cost of
11 hotels, meals and transportation—the cost saving advantages of teleconferencing
12 are enormous. According to *Economy Magazine,* the average blue-chip company
13 saved over $40 million last year by cutting back on travel costs. Now ask yourself:
14 What's better, wasting time and money getting from point A to point B—and feeling
15 exhausted in the process—or simply using same-time messaging? The choice is ob-
16 vious.
17
18 Teleconferencing also allows business people from a wide variety of cultures to
19 come together to solve time-sensitive problems. For example, if you're working to-
20 wards a deadline, and you don't have a solution to your problem, one of your col-
21 leagues in Brazil or Spain might have the solution you are looking for. By sharing
22 experiences, business people can, via teleconferencing, offer insights and solutions
23 to problems by simply turning on a webcam or picking up a phone.

After you read, listen to the lecture   **track #3**

Prompt: Summarize the points made in the lecture and show how they cast doubt on the points made in the reading.

Writing Time = 20 minutes

audio script page 337

Task #2

Reading → *Global Warming* → *3:00 minutes*

1 Are humans responsible for global warming? This is a contentious issue. But let's
2 be clear: The increase in CO_2 in the atmosphere is not a result of man's burning of
3 fossil fuels. To the contrary, the increase in CO_2 specifically, and greenhouse gases
4 generally, is a direct result of the Earth naturally warming itself. Where then, you
5 might ask, is all that CO_2 coming from if not from man? It is coming from carbon
6 sinks. Simply put, a carbon sink is a place where carbon dioxide is naturally
7 stored. The largest carbon sinks are the Arctic tundra and the oceans. As the Earth
8 warms, carbon sinks release CO_2. To state otherwise is to ignore the fact that over
9 the past 250,000 years, periods of global warming were a direct result of large
10 amounts of CO_2 being naturally released from carbon sinks.
11
12 In this debate, computer modeling is held up as evidence that global warming is a
13 man-made phenomenon. Let's put this issue to rest as well. Yes, computers are
14 capable of immense calculations. However, when it comes to predicting future cli-
15 mate patterns, computers fail repeatedly. Case in point: computers cannot accu-
16 rately measure the global mean ocean surface temperature, or GMST. If scientists
17 agree that measuring the GMST is the best indicator of climate change, and since
18 we can't measure it, how can anyone state with any degree of certainty that man is
19 responsible for global warming? Simple. They can't.
20
21 The last point I want to make concerns water vapor. Water vapor is a naturally oc-
22 curring greenhouse gas. Not only that but it is also the most abundant greenhouse
23 gas. Concentrations of water vapor are natural events caused by storms and are
24 driven globally by the movement of ocean currents. According to one study, water
25 vapor in the stratosphere increased the global warming rate in the 1990's by 30%.
26 The conclusion? Why blame man when it is obvious that global warming is a natu-
27 ral phenomenon we are just beginning to understand.

After you read, listen to the lecture  track #4

Prompt: Summarize the points made in the lecture and show how they cast
doubt on the points made in the reading.

Writing Time = 20 minutes

audio script page 338

Task #3

Reading → *America and Oil* → 3:00 minutes

1 Whenever an oil spill occurs, environmentalists are quick to remind us that we
2 need to move away from a petroleum-based economy. Yet what environmentalists
3 fail to realize is that the petroleum industry is an integral part of the American way
4 of life.
5
6 Let's start with a few statistics. According to the *American Petroleum Institute*, in the
7 year ending 2010, over 9.2 million people worked in the American oil industry, do-
8 ing everything from designing software to finding new oil reserves to transporting
9 food to offshore oil rigs. Those 9.2 million jobs added over one-trillion dollars to the
10 U.S. economy in the form of taxes, taxes that helped build and maintain America's
11 infrastructure. It doesn't take a rocket scientist to realize that a move away from oil
12 would spell the end of the American way of life as we now know it.
13
14 If you are still not convinced that oil is the life-blood of the American economy, take
15 a look around you. Those plastic bottles used for water? The natural gas we use for
16 cooking and heating? That wrapper or box your Big Mac comes in? Let's face it. We
17 are surrounded by oil-based products. Without them, our lives would be less con-
18 venient. And if there is one thing Americans love, it is convenience.
19
20 Finally, there is the political imperative. There is no denying that the majority of
21 the world's oil is controlled by foreign governments not always friendly to the Unit-
22 ed States. As a result, we need to secure a safe and reliable source of petroleum.
23 That source is in our own backyard. Less than twenty miles off our coasts is the oil
24 that will free us from unreliable foreign governments. By exploiting that oil reserve,
25 we will be investing in America's security and economic future.
26
27 In closing, consider this: By the time you are finished reading this paragraph, the
28 U.S. will have used over 8,000 barrels of oil. That's about 340,000 gallons. Contra-
29 ry to what environmentalists might argue, turning off the oil tap is easier said than
30 done.

After you read, listen to the lecture  **track #5**

Prompt: Summarize the points made in the lecture and show how they cast doubt on the points made in the reading.

Writing Time = 20 minutes

audio script page 339

Task #4

Reading → *Computer Games* → *3:00 minutes*

1 In 2016, seven of the top-ten selling computer games were rated mature due to vio-
2 lent content. Is it any wonder then that computer games are having a detrimental
3 effect on our children's behavior?
4
5 For starters, computer games teach children that violence is the way to solve prob-
6 lems. This idea is reinforced by the design of violent computer games. To survive,
7 the hero must kill to advance (read: win). Such a scenario teaches adolescents and
8 teens that violence is an acceptable part of reaching a goal. The more a child kills,
9 the more this notion is reinforced. Reaching the end of the game confirms the idea
10 that violence is the solution to all problems, be they emotional or physical. School
11 shootings prove this beyond a doubt.
12
13 Even more alarming is the fact that video games teach a false sense of reality. Wit-
14 ness military recruiting centers in shopping malls. These high-tech centers give
15 boys a taste of war using computer games. The boys spend hours freely killing en-
16 emies with virtual weapons. The boys are so captivated, so thrilled by the virtual
17 experience, that they feel immortal and want to join the military. Now I ask you: Is
18 that any way to recruit soldiers? By fooling them into believing that war is just a
19 computer game in which only the bad guys die?
20
21 Finally, the women in such games are ugly stereotypes. They are there to support
22 the hero in his violent quest and to act as eye-candy. Sadly, their violent behavior
23 runs contrary to the idea of woman being the symbol of life, not the taker of it. If
24 anyone tries to tell you that these women are role models, then they need to take a
25 good hard look in the mirror.

After you read, listen to the lecture  track #6

Prompt: Summarize the points made in the lecture and show how they cast doubt on the points made in the reading.

Writing Time = 20 minutes

audio script page 339

Task #5

Reading → *Standardized Testing* → *3:00 minutes*

1 A standardized test measures the general knowledge of a particular student group.
2 The SAT (Scholastic Aptitude Test), taken nation-wide by graduating high-school
3 seniors, is perhaps the most well-known standardized test in the U.S. Standardized
4 tests, such as the SAT, do indeed have their detractors; however, as an experienced
5 educator, I support standardized testing for both high-school and middle-school
6 students.
7
8 One of the benefits of standardized testing is the statistics gathered. Statistics pro-
9 vide valuable insight into a school's academic performance. Administrators can
10 then compare their school's performance to other schools. The result is administra-
11 tors can accurately assess the efficacy of the educational system at the local, state,
12 and national level. By doing so, administrators know which schools are performing
13 below average and can take the appropriate action to improve those scores.
14
15 Teachers also benefit from standardized testing. For example, if students in a par-
16 ticular middle school are scoring consistently low in math, their teachers can
17 spend more class time on math. By targeting low-scoring subjects, teachers can
18 make better use of class time. In short, standardized testing helps teachers plan
19 their curriculum with a particular focus on maximizing standardized test scores.
20
21 Finally, standardized testing measures teacher performance as well. High-school
22 students who score consistently high on the SAT, for example, obviously have re-
23 sults-driven teachers. Conversely, if high-school students score consistently low on
24 the SAT, a teacher review is warranted. More often than not, low standardized test
25 scores are directly traceable to a lack of teacher performance. Armed with the in-
26 formation, administrators can replace teachers as needed.

After you read, listen to the lecture

track #7

Prompt: Summarize the points made in the lecture and show how they cast
doubt on the points made in the reading.

Writing Time = 20 minutes

audio script page 340

Task #6

Reading → *Organic Food* → *3:00 minutes*

1 Organic food is very trendy these days. I used to be organic. Believe me, I'd bought
2 all the arguments, like the one that says that organic food is priced the same as
3 non organic. Right. Let me give you an example of just how wrong that argument
4 is. At my local grocery store, a small box of organic strawberries costs four dollars.
5 Four dollars for maybe twelve strawberries! I can buy twice that many non-organic
6 strawberries for half that price. The fact is organic fruits and vegetables are a good
7 forty to fifty percent more expensive than non-organic. Imagine trying to feed a
8 family of four at those prices. You'd have to take out a bank loan every time you
9 went shopping.
10
11 Another thing about organic is that it's not always easy to get. At my local grocery
12 store, I can buy organic fruit and vegetables no problem, but not organic rice or
13 grains like barley and wheat. If I want organic rice, I have to drive ten miles across
14 town through heavy traffic to a health food store that doesn't take credit cards.
15 Then I have to drive all the way back home. All that for five pounds of rice. Believe
16 me, it's easier just to grab a bag of good old non-organic rice at my local grocery
17 store.
18
19 And what about taste? Does my family even know the difference between organic
20 and non-organic? No. A good example is organic milk. I used to buy it all the time,
21 but I stopped because it was more expensive than non-organic. Did my husband
22 and kids miss the organic milk? Did they suddenly notice a taste change from or-
23 ganic to non-organic milk? Not at all. Think about that the next time you go shop-
24 ping.

After you read, listen to the lecture

track
#8

Prompt: Summarize the points made in the lecture and show how they cast
doubt on the points made in the reading.

Writing Time = 20 minutes

audio script page 341

Task #7

Reading → *Cell Phones* → 3:00 minutes

1 Cell phones. It's hard to imagine life without one. But are they safe? A growing
2 body of research says no. Case in point: beneath a cell phone's innocuous exterior
3 are dangerous electronics, which produce radio-frequency radiation (RF). Re-
4 search shows that RF can damage genetic material in the blood and cause cancer.
5 In fact, Swedish researchers have evidence indicating that acoustic neuroma, an
6 ear nerve cancer, is more prevalent on the side of the head on which a cell phone
7 is regularly placed.
8
9 Distraction is another way that cell phones pose a threat to human safety. How
10 often do you see someone chatting or texting while driving even though most
11 states prohibit it? Yet people still do it despite the danger and the law. The result
12 is that in the year ending 2016, the National Safety Council (NSC) states that 28%
13 of all traffic crashes (1.6 million) were caused by drivers using cell phones while
14 driving. To underscore the danger, a University of Utah report says that a person
15 driving while texting is as impaired as a drunk driver with a .08 blood alcohol lev-
16 el, (.08 g alcohol per 100 ml blood), .08 being the legal limit in all 50 states.
17
18 Cell phones are a danger to the environment as well, particularly to honey bees.
19 To prove it, researchers at India's Panjab University put a cell phone on top of a
20 healthy honey-bee hive. The cell phone was powered twice each day for fifteen
21 minutes. The results are shocking. After only three months, the bees stopped
22 producing honey while the queen's egg production was cut by half. This sudden
23 and drastic destruction of a bee hive is called colony collapse disorder (CCD). CCD
24 is happening in the wild as well. If action is not taken soon, the British Bee Keep-
25 ers Association (BBKA) predicts that the honey bee will disappear from Britain by
26 2018.

After you read, listen to the lecture  track #9

<u>Prompt</u>: Summarize the points made in the lecture and show how they cast doubt on the points made in the reading.

Writing Time = 20 minutes

audio script page 341

Calculating Your Writing-Section Score

ETS says that each written response will be rated by 3 raters on a scale from 0 to 5. For example, the three raters below have rated your independent essay. Their three raw scores are averaged to determine your raw independent-essay score.

$$Rater\ 1\ =\ 4/5$$
$$Rater\ 2\ =\ 4/5$$
$$Rater\ 3\ =\ 4/5$$

$$average\ =\ 12/15$$

$$12\ /\ 3\ raters\ =\ 4/5\ =\ your\ raw\ independent\text{-}essay\ score$$

Your integrated summary will be scored the same way. Your two writing-task scores will then be averaged.

$$Integrated\ Writing\ Task\ =\ 4/5$$
$$Independent\ Writing\ Task\ =\ 4/5$$

$$total\ =\ 8/10$$

$$8\ /\ 2\ tasks\ =\ 4/5\ =\ your\ raw\text{-}averaged\ writing\ score$$

Your raw-averaged writing score (4/5) will be converted to a final writing-section score out of 30 total points.

$$4/5 = 25/30$$

Notes

Speaking Section

The speaking section is the third section on the TOEFL test. The task order follows.

TASK DESCRIPTION	PREPARATION TIME	SPEAKING TIME
1. Independent Speaking - *speak only*	15 seconds	45 seconds
2. Independent Speaking - *speak only*	15 seconds	45 seconds
3. Integrated Speaking - *read, listen, speak*	30 seconds	60 seconds
4. Integrated Speaking - *read, listen, speak*	30 seconds	60 seconds
5. Integrated Speaking - *listen, speak*	20 seconds	60 seconds
6. Integrated Speaking - *listen, speak*	20 seconds	60 seconds

Tasks #1 and #2 → *Independent Speaking*

These subjective tasks measure your ability to use your experience to develop and deliver an opinion-based argument in response to a prompt. The task order follows.

read the prompt +
prepare your response   = 15 seconds
deliver your response   = 45 seconds

For speaking task #1, you will answer <u>a single-question</u> prompt, for example:

- <u>Prompt</u>:   We need zoos. <u>What is your position</u>? Use examples and reasons to support your argument.

For speaking task #2, you will answer <u>a paired-choice</u> prompt, for example:

- <u>Prompt</u>:   Exercising reduces stress. <u>Do you agree or disagree</u>? Use examples and reasons to support your argument.

G+3TiC=C → *G+TiC=C*

You can construct and deliver responses for speaking tasks #1 and #2 by changing G+3TiC=C to G+TiC=C. Note below how you can recycle and convert an independent essay into a response for speaking tasks #1 and #2.

independent essay ⟶ speaking tasks #1 + #2

G → *Personally, I think that we need zoos. Why?*

TiC → *For example, when I was twelve, my teacher took us to the zoo in Toronto. I had never seen wild animals before. I had just read about them in books and seen them on TV. But seeing them in real life was amazing, especially the lions. On TV, they looked so small, but seeing them live, I realized they were really big. By going to the zoo, I saw things in a whole new light.*

TiC → *Now I have a family and we always go to the zoo every summer. My wife makes picnic and we spend all day there. My kids love taking pictures and learning all about the animals, especially the gorillas. Being outside is good for my children. Best of all, they can leave the internet and the TV at home.*

TiC → *Also, zoos look after endangered animals like pandas. I saw two in the Washington DC zoo last year and they had a baby...*

C → *In conclusion, you can see why we need zoos. They are educational.*

G → *Personally, I think that we need zoos. Why?*

TiC → *For example, when I was twelve, my teacher took us to the zoo in Toronto. I had never seen wild animals before. I had just read about them in books and seen them on TV. But seeing them in real life was amazing, especially the lions. On TV, they looked so small, but seeing them live, I realized they were really big. By going to the zoo, I saw things in a whole new light.*

C → *In conclusion, you can see why we need zoos. They are educational.*

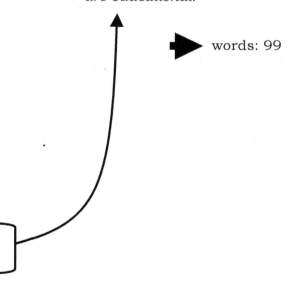

words: 99

- **REMEMBER:** *Speaking tasks #1 and #2 are the same task. You answer them the same way. The only difference is the prompt type.*

Speaking Tasks #1 and #2 → *Step-by-Step*

Follow these steps when developing and delivering a response for both tasks.

Step #1   **Make a note map; visualize the map.**

As you listen to the task instructions, make a note map, as illustrated below.

G	=	opinion
TiC	=	example
C	=	in sum

- **REMEMBER**: *Visualize the map. It will guide you through this task. If you get lost, just remember each part of G+TiC=C, and get back on track.*

When the task instructions end, the prompt will appear on your screen.

- Prompt: People like to travel. Why? Use examples and reasons to support your argument.

Step #2   **Preparing to speak = 15 seconds.**

You will have 15 seconds to prepare your response. The clock will count down (15, 14, 13...). On your note map, rough out your opinion (subjective thesis, see page 16) and one example.

Step #3   **Speak = 45 seconds.**

When the preparation clock reaches zero, you will hear a "Beep!" At this point, the response clock will start counting down (45, 44, 43...). Look at your note map. Follow it as you speak.

- **REMEMBER**: *Speak subjectively. Talk about your personal experience. Use your active-English vocabulary.*

- **WARNING**: *Do not talk about DNA or Steve Jobs or global warming. These topics are unnecessarily difficult. Plus, the raters do not care about your opinion. They just want to know if you can develop and deliver a short, verbal argument that demonstrates OPDUL=C for independent speaking (see pages 333-334).*

Mapped out, you can see how G+TiC=C gives the speaking raters what they are trained to listen for: a short, verbal argument that meets all the requirements of OPDUL=C for independent speaking. The opinion (G) and the conclusions (C) are underlined, the transitions (T) are in **bold**, and the supporting illustration (i) is in *italics*.

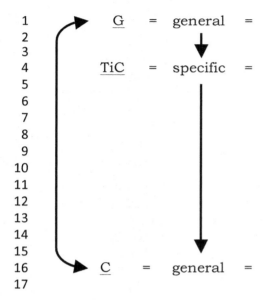

1	<u>G</u>	= general =	<u>Personally, I like traveling because it's a learning experience.</u> Why?
2			
3			
4	<u>TiC</u>	= specific =	**For example**, *last year I went to Manhattan. I visited many famous places like The Met and Radio City Music Hall. The most interesting place was Ground Zero. Ground Zero is where the World Trade Center once stood. Now it is nothing but a big hole. On TV, it doesn't look so big. But seeing it in person, I had no idea it was so huge. It's like a big hole in the heart of the city.* <u>Looking at it made me realize that sometimes you just have to see things with your own eyes. That way you can understand what really happened.</u>

16	<u>C</u>	= general =	**For those reasons**, <u>traveling to Manhattan was definitely a great learning experience.</u>
17			

 words: 126

Note below how the concluding sentence in the paragraph (Ti**C**) states a reason using **cause**-and-*effect*. This reason supports the opinion (G). This is what the raters look for.

> **Looking at it** *made me realize that sometimes you just have to see things with your own eyes.* **That way** *you can understand what really happened.*

For the conclusion (C), simply repeat your opinion (G). By doing so, you will know exactly what to say at the end—and you will save time.

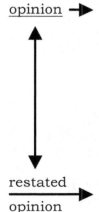

opinion ➤ Personally, *I like traveling because it's a learning experience*. Why?

For example, last year I went to Manhattan. I visited many famous places like The Met and Radio City Music Hall. The most interesting place was Ground Zero. Ground Zero is where the World Trade Center once stood. Now, it's nothing but a big hole. On TV, it doesn't look so big. But seeing it in person, I had no idea it was so huge. It's like a big hole in the heart of the city. Looking at it made me realize that sometimes you just have to see things with your own eyes. That way you can understand what really happened.

restated opinion ➤ For those reasons, *traveling to Manhattan was definitely a great learning experience*.

Step #4 **Task end.**

Your recorded responses will be sent to ETS for rating (see page 130, *Calculating Your Speaking-Section Score*). The raters will rate your responses with a rubric. OPDUL=C for independent speaking defines that rubric.

OPDUL=C → *Rating this Task*

Each verbal response is rated out of 4 total points. By delivering responses for speaking tasks #1 and #2 with G+TiC=C, you will demonstrate what the raters are trained to listen for: a verbal, mini-independent argument that demonstrates OPDUL=C for independent speaking. A description of the rubric follows.

O = Organization

Under Organization, there are two proficiency descriptors: deduction and induction. If your response starts with a general statement (G), and is supported by an example (TiC) and ends with a conclusion (C), then you are demonstrating a method of organization called deduction. If your response starts with an example (TiC), and ends with a conclusion-thesis (C), then you are demonstrating induction.

P = Progression

Under Progression, there are two proficiency descriptors. If your response demonstrates deduction as the method of Organization, the ideas will progress from *general* (intro) to *specific* (body) to *general* (conclusion). If your response demonstrates induction, the example(s) will progress from *specific* (body) to *general* (conclusion-thesis).

D = Development

Under Development, there are three proficiency descriptors: introduction development (G), body development (TiC), and conclusion development (C). Topic development in your intro means your thesis is a true thesis (see checklist page 16). Topic development in the body means you provide a well-developed example(s) to support your thesis. Topic development in your conclusion means you restate your thesis.

- **REMEMBER**: *One reason why test-takers score low on speaking tasks #1 and #2 is due to a lack of topic development in the body (TiC). Specifically, the illustration lacks development.*

U = Unity

Under Unity, there are two proficiency descriptors: topical unity and grammatical unity. Topical unity means your response focuses on the main topic in the prompt. You do not go off topic and talk about unrelated topics. Grammatical unity means you are using transitional words proficiently to unite each part of your response. Grammatical unity also means your grammar is proficient at the sentence level.

L = Language-Use

Under Language-Use, there are three proficiency descriptors: word choice, sentence variety, and delivery. Word choice (including idioms) measures your ability to apply your English vocabulary proficiently. Sentence variety measures your ability to apply simple, compound, and complex sentences proficiently. Delivery describes how you speak. Under delivery there are four proficiency descriptors: fluency, automaticity, pronunciation, and ease-of-understanding.

1. **Fluency** describes how easily (naturally) you speak. Do you speak smoothly and confidently, or do you hesitate and speak in fragments?

2. **Automaticity** describes how fast you think and speak. Do you pause to translate, or do you think and speak automatically without pausing to translate?

3. **Pronunciation** describes how you produce the sound of English words. Do you stress the right syllables with accurate intonation and volume, or not?

4. **Ease-of-understanding** describes how easy or difficult it is to hear and understand you. Do you speak in a loud or a soft voice? Must the rater listen harder to rate you?

C = Coherence

If your response proficiently demonstrates OPDUL, then it will demonstrate Coherence, and you will score a 4/4. However, if your response lacks proficiency in one or more areas of OPDUL, then Coherence will be reduced, and your response will score lower.

NOTE: *The sample responses for speaking tasks #1 (pg. 67) and #2 (pg. 69) both score a 4/4 based on OPDU only. We can't rate Language-Use (OPDUL=C). To rate it, we need to hear a recorded/live response. However, if you did demonstrate all aspects of OPDUL=C when speaking, then the scores would remain at 4/4.*

Introduction and Conclusion Strategies

You can develop your introduction and conclusion using the same strategies used to develop the introduction and conclusion of your independent essay. The introduction strategies are on page 24. The conclusion strategies are on page 25.

- **REMEMBER:** *Memorize one introduction strategy and one conclusion strategy and use them when delivering responses for speaking tasks #1 and #2. By memorizing strategies, they will come to you automatically, you will deliver them more proficiently, and you will save time when speaking. This, in turn, will help you maximize scoring on test day.*

On the next page, note the *introduction strategy* and the *conclusion strategy* in the sample response.

1 *People travel for many reasons. Some travel for fun. Others travel to learn about new*
2 *cultures.* From my experience, I like traveling because it's a learning experience.
3
4 For example, last year I went to Manhattan. I visited many famous places like The
5 Met and Radio City Music Hall. The most interesting place was Ground Zero.
6 Ground Zero is where the World Trade Center once stood. Now, it's nothing but a
7 big hole. On TV, it doesn't look so big. But seeing it in person, I had no idea it was
8 so huge. It's like a big hole in the heart of the city. Looking at it made me realize
9 that sometimes you just have to see things with your own eyes. That way you can
10 understand what really happened.
11
12 It goes without saying that traveling to Manhattan was a great learning experience
13 *If you want to learn about a new culture, you should travel. Go for it! You'll have a*
14 *great time.*

▶ words: 164

G+2TiC=C

Develop your responses by adding a second body paragraph using G+2TiC=C.

- <u>Prompt</u>: Exercising reduces stress. Do you agree or disagree? Use examples and reasons to support your argument.

Mapped out, you can see how G+2TiC=C gives the speaking raters what they are trained to look for: a short, well-developed, verbal argument that demonstrates OPDUL=C. The opinion (G) and the conclusions (C) are <u>underlined</u>, the transitions (T) are in **bold**, and the supporting illustrations (i) are in *italics*.

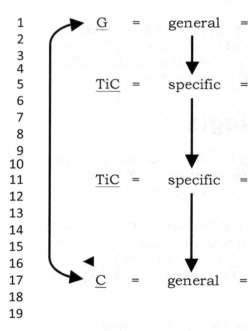

1   <u>G</u> = general = The prompt asks whether exercising reduces stress
2   or not. <u>Personally, I believe that exercising does re-</u>
3   <u>duce stress.</u> Why?
4
5   <u>TiC</u> = specific = **First**, *after class, I run up and down a big hill near my*
6   *university. The distance is ten miles. It is definitely*
7   *hard work, but I love it. If I don't run every day, I have*
8   *a hard time sleeping. After I run, I feel stress free.* <u>Best</u>
9   <u>of all, I sleep like a log.</u>
10
11   <u>TiC</u> = specific = **Next** *is my girlfriend. She loves to exercise too. After a*
12   *hard day of work, she hits the gym near our house*
13   *and does yoga and Pilates.* <u>She says it is a great way</u>
14   <u>to relieve the pressures of being a new lawyer in a big</u>
15   <u>law firm.</u>
16
17   <u>C</u> = general = **In sum**, <u>exercising definitely reduces stress.</u> If you
18   want to stay happy and healthy, you should exercise
19   every day.

▶ words: 143

Develop Transitions (T)

You can demonstrate Language-Use using these **transitions**. You can use these same transitions when writing your independent essay as well.

1 *Personally, I contend that people are living longer because they are taking better*
2 *care of themselves.*
3
4 **A good example** is my grandfather.

5 **A salient example** is my grandfather (salient means important/noticeable).

6 **A perfect illustration** is my grandfather.

7 **An excellent example** is my grandfather.

8 **An excellent illustration** is my eighty-year-old grandfather.

9 **An apt illustration** to support my opinion is my grandfather.

10 **A salient illustration** to support my argument is my grandfather.

How Long Should My Response Be?

The map below illustrates how to manage your time for speaking tasks #1 and #2.

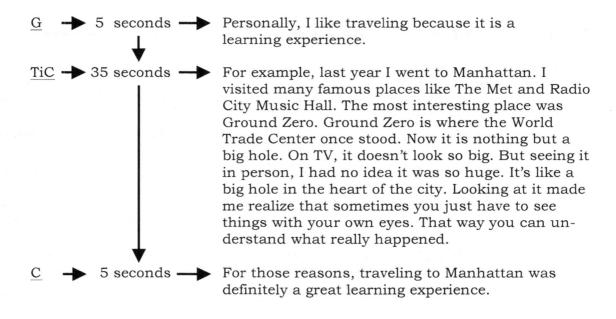

G → 5 seconds → Personally, I like traveling because it is a learning experience.

TiC → 35 seconds → For example, last year I went to Manhattan. I visited many famous places like The Met and Radio City Music Hall. The most interesting place was Ground Zero. Ground Zero is where the World Trade Center once stood. Now it is nothing but a big hole. On TV, it doesn't look so big. But seeing it in person, I had no idea it was so huge. It's like a big hole in the heart of the city. Looking at it made me realize that sometimes you just have to see things with your own eyes. That way you can understand what really happened.

C → 5 seconds → For those reasons, traveling to Manhattan was definitely a great learning experience.

- **REMEMBER:** *The speaking section will test your time-management skills.*

Common Problems for this Task

The response below demonstrates four common speaking problems.

- <u>Prompt</u>: In your view, what was the greatest invention of the twentieth century? Give examples and reasons to support your argument.

1 *Personally, I believe that the greatest invention of the twentieth century was women*
2 *developing and winning many special rights they never had before from countries*
3 *that didn't care about them, and I believe this is a good thing for all women.*
4
5 *For example, women were very successful. They did a lot of very important things*
6 *that changed their lives. They won many rights they never had before.*
7
8 *Women winning rights was the greatest invention of the twentieth century because it*
9 *helped them so much.*

1. Opinion is Too Long ---

In the response above, the test-taker's opinion (G) is too long. Avoid overstating your opinion by delivering it in one concise sentence, for example:

> *Personally, I believe that the greatest invention of the twentieth century was women winning many rights.*

2. Lack of Topic Development -----------------------------

In the response above, the test-taker's body paragraph example lacks development. Specifically, there is no personal example to support the test-taker's opinion (G). This demonstrates a lack of topic <u>D</u>evelopment (OP**D**UL=C).

- **REMEMBER:** *Developing an example to support your thesis (G) is the hardest part of speaking tasks #1 and #2. Why? Because example development will test your automaticity. Automaticity means your ability to develop examples quickly and proficiently without translating.*

- **REMEMBER:** *If you can't think of a real-life example, make one up. Tell a story.*

3. Off-Topic Response ---

Read the prompt once again.

- <u>Prompt</u>: In your view, what was the greatest invention of the twentieth century? Give examples and reasons to support your argument.

The topic of the prompt is <u>the greatest invention of the twentieth century</u>. The test-taker, however, talks about "women's rights." Women's rights is not an invention. It is a political idea. The speaker is therefore off topic (talking about the wrong subject). An invention, in this context, means an original material idea, i.e., Edison inventing the phonograph, Steve Jobs and the iPhone, etc.

- **REMEMBER:** *Read the prompt carefully. Make sure you understand it before you respond. Make sure you are "on topic" (talking about the topic in the prompt).*

4. Lack of Active Vocabulary ----------------------------------

Note how this test-taker was trying to develop an academic topic in 45 seconds. To do so, the test-taker had to use her passive-English vocabulary. The result is she knew what she wanted to say, but she had trouble applying her passive-English vocabulary proficiently. This resulted in a lack of topic development.

- **REMEMBER:** *For speaking tasks #1 and #2, avoid academic topics. Maximize scoring by talking subjectively about yourself using your active-English vocabulary.*

The following example corrects the four problems illustrated above.

1   *What was the greatest invention of the twentieth century? Good question. From my*
2   *experience, it was definitely the electric hair dryer. Why?*
3
4   *For example, I have really long curly hair, and I hate when it is wet. It makes me cra-*
5   *zy. After I shower, it takes forever to dry if I use a towel. I waste time and I am late for*
6   *work. However, if I use my electric hair dryer, I can quickly dry my hair and be ready*
7   *for work on time. As you can see, my hair dryer is a real time saver.*
8
9   *Also, when traveling, some hotels do not have hair dryers. That's why I always take*
10 *my hair dryer when traveling. After taking a shower, I don't have to worry about us-*
11 *ing a towel and getting a cold from wet hair. As you can see, my hair dryer is also*
12 *good for my health.*
13
14 *For the aforementioned reasons, my hair dryer was the greatest invention of the twen-*
15 *tieth century. You should buy one. It will save you time and prevent colds.*

▶ words: 174

5. Blanking Out --

For speaking tasks one and two, blanking out is a common problem, especially at the start and/or after stating your opinion. When you blank out, you might think there is no time left, so you do not restart. Yes, this task is short, only 45 seconds to speak; however, if you know G+TiC=C, you can deliver a proficient response in 30 seconds and still score high. Do the following if you blank out at the start or have to restart. First, read the prompt below.

- Prompt: What event changed your life? Why? Give examples and reasons to explain your position.

Do not state your opinion at the start. Instead, tell a personal story using your active-English vocabulary. Do not worry about mistakes. Just speak. This process is called brainstorming. Brainstorming stimulates ideas and will put you back on track. Look at the following response. Note how the speaker is using her active-English vocabulary and narration to develop a personal story using induction.

1   *My younger brother has autism and for a long time he never talked to anybody. Also,*
2   *he would get angry really easily for reasons nobody could understand. Then one day*
3   *the doctor told my parents they should get a dog. We never had a dog or any pets be-*
4   *fore, but my parents wanted to make my brother happy, so we got a dog and called*
5   *him Happy. Well, I'm telling you, it was amazing. Before my brother was always quiet*
6   *and angry, but with Happy, he is always smiling. The change was amazing. As you*
7   *can see, a pet can really change someone's life. If you have a brother or sister with*
8   *autism, I recommend that you get a dog. It will change his or her lives.*

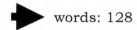 words: 128

- **REMEMBER**: *We all love to tell stories. Use this innate human ability to develop a response for speaking tasks #1 and #2, and for the independent essay.*

Help! → *My Response is Too Long!*

The following are reasons why your response is longer than 45 seconds.

Reason #1   Your opinion is too long.

Solution
1. Make your opinion shorter.
2. State your opinion in one concise sentence.
3. State your opinion in 5 seconds or less.
4. Speak faster; try not to hesitate.

Reason #2   When the clock starts, you are not speaking right away. As a result, you are losing valuable seconds at the start.

Solution   Start speaking right after the beep. Remember: *The speaking tasks come up fast. Be ready for them.*

Reason #3   You are being too careful. When you are too careful, you slow down to pronounce correctly. When you slow down, you waste time. You also decrease fluency and automaticity.

Solution
1. Speak at a natural pace.
2. Record your voice, then play it back. You will know if you are speaking too slowly. If so, speak faster.

Reason #4   You are pausing or hesitating too much. Record your voice and play it back. You will soon know if you are pausing or hesitating too much. Pausing and hesitating waste time. Pausing and hesitating will also decrease fluency and automaticity.

Solution
1. Practice reading sample responses for correct speed and accuracy.
2. Go to youtube.com. Google "How to speak like a native-English speaker." There are lots of great videos to help you speak more proficiently.

Reason #5   You are pausing and/or hesitating too much because you have not memorized G+TiC=C.

Solution
1. Memorize G+TiC=C.
2. Practice reading sample responses using G+TiC=C.

Reason #6   Your supporting illustration (T**i**C) contains too much information.

Solution
1. Do not include information that is not important or off topic.
2. Develop one example only (G+TiC=C). Remember: *One well-developed example is better than two examples that lack development.*

Reason #7   Your conclusion is too long.

Solution
1. State your conclusion in five seconds or less.
2. Simply repeat your opinion.

Reason #8   The clock makes you so nervous, you can't speak.

Solution
1. Do not time yourself when you practice. Just speak. When you are more confident, time yourself.

Help! → *My Response is Too Short!*

The following are reasons why your response is too short.

Reason #1   You are nervous. When you are nervous, you speak too fast and finish too soon.

Solution
1. Record your voice and play it back. You will soon know if you are speaking too fast. If so, slow down.

Reason #2   Your supporting illustration is too short. If your example is too short, it will lack development.

Solution
1. Include more details when you develop your supporting example. Identify all place names and people names. Remember: *Be specific. If you studied mechanical engineering at Tsinghua University in China from 2016 to 2019, say, "I studied mechanical engineering at Tsinghua University in China from 2016 to 2019."*

Reason #3   You speak, then suddenly stop because you are shy, afraid, or feel stupid.

Solution
1. Practice reading into a recording device. Read an English magazine article or a book while recording. This will help you develop confidence speaking into a microphone.
2. Take an ESL class to develop your speaking skills and your confidence.
3. Practice. Practice. Practice.

Reason #4   You are not confident using G+TiC=C.

Solution   1. Practice developing and delivering responses until you have memorized G+TiC=C and you can remember it automatically without notes.

Reason #5   You blank out.

Solution   1. You are trying too hard and/or are too nervous. Try to relax. When you practice speaking, don't time yourself. Just speak until you are confident. When you are more confident, then time yourself.
2. Forget about trying to demonstrate OPDUL=C. Just speak. The more you speak, the more confident you will become.

Sample Responses

- **Prompt:** Should students work during high school? Give illustrations and reasons to develop your argument.

1 *The question is should students work during high school. As far as I'm concerned, I*
2 *think that students should work while going to high school. Why?*
3
4 *A salient example is myself. Back in Hungary, I worked every Saturday and Sunday,*
5 *and sometimes at night during the week at a bookstore. I loved it because I was al-*
6 *ways meeting foreigners who spoke English. By helping them find books, I was able*
7 *to practice my English. It was great because at school, I only learned grammar from*
8 *books, but at the bookstore I was learning conversational English. Not only that but I*
9 *made money for myself. This helped me because I didn't always have to ask my par-*
10 *ents for money for books and other things. As you can see, by working at the*
11 *bookstore I killed two birds with one stone.*
12
13 *To sum up, I believe that all high school students should work part-time during high*
14 *school. It's a great experience that will open many new doors. Isn't that what life's all*
15 *about?*

 words: 170

- -

- **Prompt:** People are living longer. Why? Develop your argument using examples and reasons.

1 *Why are people living longer? Personally, I contend that people are living longer be-*
2 *cause they are taking better care of themselves.*
3
4 *An excellent illustration is my grandfather. He is eighty. When he was younger, he*
5 *used to smoke and drink a lot. Also, he never ate very well. Then, when he was fifty,*
6 *he had heart attack. He was in the hospital for a long time. The doctor told him he*
7 *should stop smoking and drinking, and start eating better. That's what my grandfa-*
8 *ther did. Now, he doesn't drink or smoke anymore. Also, he eats lots of healthy food*
9 *like salads and fish, and he exercises every day. As a result, he feels much better*
10 *than before and has lots more energy.*

11 *As you can see, by changing his lifestyle, my grandfather is definitely going to live*
12 *longer because he is taking better care of himself. If you want to live longer, you*
13 *should take care of yourself too.*

➤ words: 159

- **Prompt:** Which person has been the greatest influence in your life? Why? Give examples and reasons to support and develop your opinion.

1   *A lot of people have influenced my life. However, it goes without saying that my*
2   *mother has been the biggest influence in my life because she encourages and inspires*
3   *me.*
4
5   *My mother encourages me. For example, I'm now in America working as an au pair.*
6   *An au pair is like a babysitter who lives with an American family. I'm doing this for a*
7   *year in Westport, Connecticut. At first I didn't want to come to America and leave all*
8   *my friends in Brazil, but my mother said it would be a great experience and a great*
9   *way to develop my English. She was right. Living with an American family has been a*
10 *wonderful experience and my English is so much better.*
11
12 *Also, my mother inspires me. When I was growing up, my mother was a high-school*
13 *teacher. This was strange because all my friends' mothers were housewives. But my*
14 *mother wanted to work. She always told me to just follow your heart. I remember the-*
15 *se words whenever I have problems in America, and they give me strength.*
16
17 *It goes without saying that my mother has been the biggest influence in my life. She*
18 *has encouraged and inspired me. I hope that when I have a daughter, I can encour-*
19 *age and inspire her too.*

➤ words: 212

Argument Counter-Argument

- **Prompt:** Some prefer to shop online while others prefer to shop at stores. Discuss both options, then state your preference. Use illustrations and reasons to develop your position.

In the response below, note the transition **However**. This transition-of-contrast connects the two arguments: the *pro argument* supporting online shopping vs. the speaker's *con argument* (the preference for shopping at stores/a mall).

1   *Some people prefer to shop at stores while others prefer to shop online. Personally, I*
2   *prefer to shop at a mall.*
3
4   *These days the internet makes everything so easy, especially shopping. You can find*
5   *a big selection and lots of really good prices online, and you don't even have to leave*
6   *your home.*
7

8   ***However***, *I prefer to go to a mall, especially for shoes. When I buy shoes, I need to try*
9   *them on. If I buy them online, I never know how they will fit. This is a hassle because*
10 *if they don't fit, it takes a lot of time to return them and get my money back. But if I*
11 *buy shoes at a mall, and they don't fit, I can exchange them or get the right size right*
12 *away. This is much more convenient.*
13
14 *For those reasons, I definitely prefer to shop at a mall.*

▶ words: 149

Advantage-Disadvantage

When answering this prompt type, use G+2TiC=C. Develop an advantage in body paragraph one and a disadvantage in body paragraph two, or vice versa.

Note below how body paragraph one develops a *disadvantage* of homeschooling while body paragraph two develops an *advantage*. Note as well how **However** connects the two opposing arguments.

- **Prompt:** What are the advantages and disadvantages to homeschooling? Use examples and reasons to support your position.

1   *Personally, I think there are advantages and disadvantages to homeschooling.*
2
3   *For example, my friend Sarah studied at home with her mom. Sarah was really*
4   *smart, but she never knew how to talk to people. She never went to parties or had a*
5   *boyfriend. All she did was study with her mom. That is one big disadvantage of home*
6   *schooling. You don't have many friends.*
7
8   ***However***, *by studying all the time, Sarah got really good grades. She is now going to*
9   *Harvard. She wants to be a doctor. To be a doctor, you must study very hard. That is*
10 *one big advantage of studying at home. You can study with no distractions like sports*
11 *or band practice.*
12
13 *For those reasons, there are advantages and disadvantages to homeschooling. Per-*
14 *sonally, I think you need a balance between making friends and studying.*

▶ words: 139

Notes

_____
_____
_____
_____
_____

Speaking Practice

Using the strategies discussed, construct responses for each of the following prompts. Check each response for Coherence using the *Independent Speaking → Proficiency Checklist* on page 333. Rate each response using the *Independent Speaking → Rating Guide* on page 334.

1. Which technology in the past ten years has changed your life? Why? Develop your position using examples and reasons.

2. Can a pet change a person's behavior? Explain your position using supporting illustrations and reasons.

3. Many people leave their home country. Why? Give examples and reasons to support your argument.

4. Do you prefer reading paper-based books or off a computer screen? Why? Support your position with illustrations and reasons.

5. Why is a car important in daily life? Develop your response using examples and reasons.

6. Why do people take photographs? Support your argument using examples and reasons.

7. What is a problem facing your country? Why? Support your position with illustrations and reasons.

8. How do you measure success? Why? Use examples and reasons to develop your
    position.

9. How can recycling make a difference? Support your argument with examples and reasons.

10. Which area of English do you need to improve? Why? Develop your response using examples and reasons.

11. Are you the type of person who leads or follows? Give examples and reasons to support your opinion.

12. Education should be free. Do you agree or disagree? Give illustrations and reasons to support your answer.

13. What are the advantages and disadvantages of text messaging? Support your argument with examples and reasons.

14. Historic buildings should be saved. What is your position? Use examples and reasons to support your argument.

Task #3 → *Integrated Speaking*

This task measures your ability to integrate three skills: reading, listening, and speaking. You will integrate these skills while summarizing an announcement and a student's opinion of the announcement. You can construct a response for this task using G+3TiC=C. The task order follows.

1. Read a short university announcement = 45 seconds
2. Listen as two students discuss the announcement = 60-90 seconds
3. Read the prompt; prepare your response = 30 seconds
4. Deliver your response = 60 seconds

Speaking Task #3 → *Step-by-Step*

Follow these steps when constructing a response for this task.

Step #1   Make a note map; visualize the map.

As you listen to the task instructions, make a note map (see below). Under MAN and WOMAN, write G+3TiC=C. To save time, write O for opinion, number each body paragraph, then write C for conclusion.

```
READING


MAN                          WOMAN


O                            O


1                            1


2                            2


3                            3


C                            C
```

Step #2   Read the announcement + take notes = 45 seconds.

When the instructions end, the announcement will appear on your screen. You will have 45 seconds to read it.

New Organic-Food Policy

1   *Starting next semester, all food sold at Shelton University will be organic. This will*
2   *include all food prepared and served in the main cafeteria, as well as snacks bought*
3   *in vending machines throughout campus. This policy also includes beverages as well,*
4   *both hot and cold. When possible, the university will contract local growers to provide*
5   *fresh organic produce. Student meal tickets will continue to be honored. The universi-*
6   *ty is implementing this policy in order to regulate the sugar and fat content in student*
7   *diets. This change in policy reflects health awareness programs being implemented at*
8   *other colleges and universities across the nation.*

Under READING on your note map below, identify the topic of the announcement and the reason(s) for it.

- **REMEMBER:** *The reason is the purpose for the announcement. Later, in the listening, the two students will argue (debate) the reason for the announcement.*

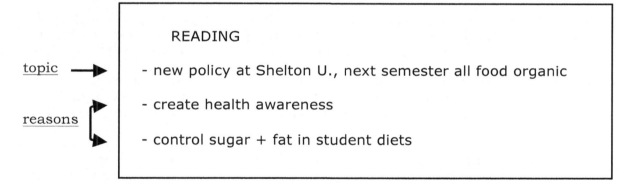

- **WARNING:** *When the 45-second reading time ends, the announcement will leave your screen. It will not return, so take notes.*

Step #3   Listen to the conversation + take notes = 60-90 secs.

After the reading, you will listen as two students discuss the announcement. One student will support the new policy (pro), one student will be against it (con).

- **REMEMBER:** *The student conversation is a pro-con argument.*

- **REMEMBER:** *The integrated writing task is also a pro-con argument (see pg. 42).*

Sample → *Student Conversation* ⟶ track #10

1	Man:	Hi, Wendy.
3	Woman:	Hey, Tom. Have you heard about the new organic food policy?
5	Man:	Yeah. What a great idea. It's about time the school did something to improve the food around here.
8	Woman:	If you ask me, I think the new policy is all wrong.
10	Man:	Why?
12	Woman:	Because organic food is way more expensive. In some cases, at least fifty-percent more. Add that to labor costs, you know, money to pay the cafeteria staff, and I'm going to be paying a lot more for my coffee and the milk I put in it. I hate to think what a salad will cost. Organic may be cheaper in the future, but right now it's for people with money not poor students like me.
19	Man:	But think of all the health benefits. You'll be eating food that doesn't have any chemicals or antibiotics in it. Not only that but all that good organic food will be lower in fat and calories. I mean, that's got to be good, right?
24	Woman:	Don't be fooled. A hamburger is a hamburger whether the meat is organic or not. Both will have the same amount of fat and calories. The only difference is the organic hamburger has no pesticides or antibiotics in it.
28	Man:	Well, I still think it's a good idea. By offering organic food, we'll be eating a lot better. Even the snacks in the vending machines will be organic. It's definitely the wave of the future. Best of all, we'll be helping local farmers.
33	Woman:	What I don't like is the university telling us what we can and can't eat. Not everybody wants to eat organic, you know. If I want to eat non-organic, that's my choice. Sorry, but the school should not be in the healthcare business.

In the conversation above, note how the man is for (pro) the new policy while the woman is against it (con). Note also how their opposing arguments develop using point-by-point style. In the integrated writing task, the reading and the lecture also argue using point-by-point style (see page 49). As you can see, TOEFL is repeating the same testing method.

- **REMEMBER:** *Because the conversation is short, the two students will immediately state their opposing opinions. If you are not listening at the start, if you are distracted, you will miss the two opinions; therefore, focus from start to finish.*

- **WARNING:** *You hear the conversation once. You cannot replay it, so take notes.*

Below is a summary of both arguments in note form.

	MAN		WOMAN
O	supports policy	O	against policy
1	first thinks it is a good idea improve university food	1	first organic 50% more expensive she is poor and will pay more
2	next organic means less fat + fewer calories good for students' health	2	next organic does not mean fat + calorie-free can get fat eating organic
3	finally students will eat better wave of the future help farmers	3	finally school should not tell students what to eat no choice = no freedom
C	for those reasons supports policy	C	for those reasons against policy

Step #4 Prompt + prepare your response = 30 seconds.

When the listening ends, it will leave your screen. You cannot replay it. The listening will be replaced by the prompt.

- Prompt: The woman expresses her opinion about the announcement. State her opinion and explain the reasons she gives for holding that opinion.

You will have 30 seconds to prepare your response (30, 29, 28...)

- **WARNING:** *On test day, you might summarize either the man's or the woman's argument. While listening, there is no way to determine which argument you will summarize. Do not try and guess; instead, note each argument and be ready to summarize either. For this task, you will summarize the woman's argument.*

- **REMEMBER:** *For this task, to maximize scoring, you must take proficient notes. Do so using the note map above. On test-day, each argument will develop point-by-point. Anticipate each point and counterpoint by following your note map.*

Step #5   Speak = 60 seconds.

When you speak, follow your note map. Start by giving the context. Use the present tense and speak objectively using third-person (*He says...She says...*).

Context: *Two students are discussing the new organic food policy at Shelton University.*

Next, summarize the announcement. Identify the <u>new policy</u> (topic) and the reason for the new policy. State the reason using **cause**-and-*effect*.

Policy: *Starting next semester, <u>all the food at Shelton University will be organic</u>.*
*The university says that **organic food** will be healthier for the students and that **other schools are making the same changes**.*

Next, summarize the woman's argument using block style (see block style summarizing, page 50). Note the **transitions** (T) below.

Student: *The woman believes that the new policy is a bad idea.*

__First__, she says that organic food is fifty-percent more expensive than regular food. That means she will have to pay more for her coffee and salads. She says organic food is for rich people, not poor students like her.

__Next__, she says that organic food does not mean healthy food. For example, she says a regular hamburger and an organic hamburger have the same calories and fat. Organic food, she says, is not healthier.

__Finally__, she doesn't want the university telling her what she should eat. The university is taking away her freedom to choose. If she wants to eat regular food, that is her choice.

__For those reasons__, the woman is against the new food policy.

- **REMEMBER:** *On test day, each student might give two illustrations and reasons (G+2TiC=C). Be prepared for three (G+3TiC=C).*

- **REMEMBER:** *There is no official rule that says you must speak continuously for 60 seconds. If you finish early, just sit there and wait for the next task.*

- **WARNING:** *Do not summarize both arguments. Summarize the argument indicated in the prompt, in this case the woman's. Summarizing both arguments will demonstrate a lack of Topical <u>U</u>nity (OPD<u>UL</u>=C), and will result in a lower score.*

- **WARNING:** *This is an objective-speaking task. Do not state your opinion. Your opinion is subjective. Stating your opinion demonstrates a lack of Topical <u>U</u>nity (OPD<u>UL</u>=C), and will result in a lower score.*

Mapped out, you can see how G+3TiC=C gives the raters what they are trained to listen for: an integrated verbal summary that meets all the requirements of OPDUL=C for integrated speaking (see pages 335-336). The context and the woman's opinion (G) and conclusions (C) are <u>underlined</u>, the transitions (T) are in **bold**, and the supporting illustrations (i) are in *italics*.

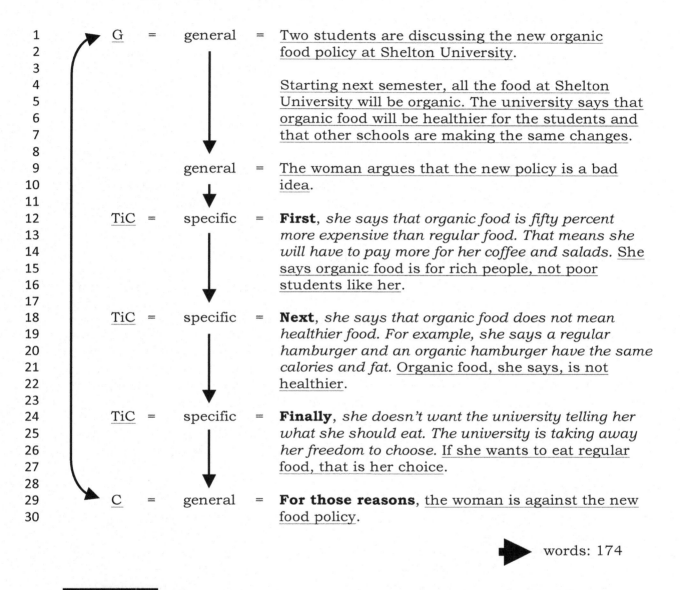

1 2	G	=	general	=	<u>Two students are discussing the new organic food policy at Shelton University.</u>

1   **G** = general = <u>Two students are discussing the new organic</u>
2   <u>food policy at Shelton University.</u>
3
4   <u>Starting next semester, all the food at Shelton</u>
5   <u>University will be organic. The university says that</u>
6   <u>organic food will be healthier for the students and</u>
7   <u>that other schools are making the same changes.</u>
8
9   general = <u>The woman argues that the new policy is a bad</u>
10   <u>idea.</u>
11
12   **TiC** = specific = **First**, *she says that organic food is fifty percent*
13   *more expensive than regular food. That means she*
14   *will have to pay more for her coffee and salads.* <u>She</u>
15   <u>says organic food is for rich people, not poor</u>
16   <u>students like her.</u>
17
18   **TiC** = specific = **Next**, *she says that organic food does not mean*
19   *healthier food. For example, she says a regular*
20   *hamburger and an organic hamburger have the same*
21   *calories and fat.* <u>Organic food, she says, is not</u>
22   <u>healthier.</u>
23
24   **TiC** = specific = **Finally**, *she doesn't want the university telling her*
25   *what she should eat. The university is taking away*
26   *her freedom to choose.* <u>If she wants to eat regular</u>
27   <u>food, that is her choice.</u>
28
29   **C** = general = **For those reasons**, <u>the woman is against the new</u>
30   <u>food policy</u>.

words: 174

Step #6   **Task end.**

Your recorded response will be sent via internet to ETS for rating. Raters will rate your response with a rubric. OPDUL=C for integrated speaking (see next page) defines that rubric.

OPDUL=C → *Rating this Task*

O = Organization

Under Organization, there are two proficiency descriptors: deduction and induction. If your summary starts with a general statement (G), and is supported by examples (3TiC) and ends with a conclusion (C), then you are demonstrating a method of organization called deduction. If your summary starts with examples (3TiC), and ends with conclusion-thesis (C), then you are demonstrating a method of organization called induction.

P = Progression

Under Progression, there are two proficiency descriptors. If your summary demonstrates deduction as the method of Organization, the ideas will progress from *general* (intro) to *specific* (body) to *general* (conclusion). If your essay demonstrates induction, the examples will progress from *specific* (body) to *general* (conclusion-thesis).

D = Development-Summarization

Under Development-Summarization, there are three proficiency descriptors: introduction development (G), body development (3TiC), and conclusion development (C). Topic development in your introduction means you have proficiently summarized the topic of the announcement and the reason(s) for it, and you have proficiently summarized the student's opinion. Topic development in the body means you have proficiently summarized each reason in the body of the student's argument (TiC). Topic development in your conclusion (C) means you have proficiently restated-summarized the student's opinion about the announcement.

- **REMEMBER**: *Test-takers score low on this task because they did not proficiently summarize the student's reasoning and/or one or more reasons were left out.*

U = Unity-Synthesis

Under Unity-Synthesis, there are two proficiency descriptors: topical unity and grammatical unity. Topical unity means your summary has proficiently integrated (united) the announcement and the student's argument. Grammatical unity means you proficiently unite the announcement and the student's opinion grammatically. Grammatical unity also means your grammar is proficient at the sentence level.

L = Language-Use-Paraphrasing

Under Language-Use-Paraphrasing, there are two proficiency descriptors: word choice and sentence variety. Word choice measures your ability to paraphrase the reading and lecture using synonyms. Sentence variety measures your ability to summarize using simple, compound, and complex sentences proficiently.

Also, see page 71 for these proficiency descriptors: fluency, automaticity, pronunciation, and ease-of-understanding.

C = Coherence

If your integrated summary demonstrates OPDUL, you will score a 4/4. However, if your summary lacks proficiency in one or more areas of OPDUL, then Coherence will be reduced, and your summary will score lower.

NOTE: *The sample response below scores a 4/4 based on OPDU only. We cannot rate Language-Use (OPDUL=C). To rate it, we need to hear a recorded/live response. However, if you did demonstrate all aspects of OPDUL=C when speaking, including Language-Use, then your score would be 4/4.*

How Long Should My Response Be?

The following map illustrates how to manage your time for this response.

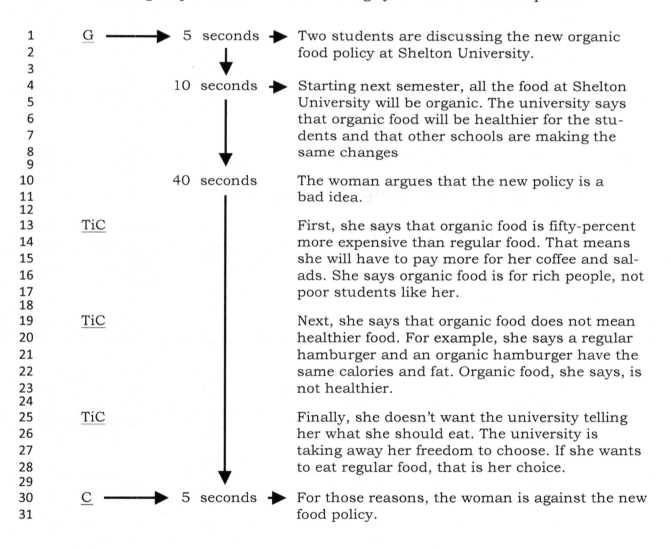

1	G ⟶ 5 seconds ▸	Two students are discussing the new organic
2		food policy at Shelton University.
3		
4	10 seconds ▸	Starting next semester, all the food at Shelton
5		University will be organic. The university says
6		that organic food will be healthier for the stu-
7		dents and that other schools are making the
8		same changes
9		
10	40 seconds	The woman argues that the new policy is a
11		bad idea.
12		
13	TiC	First, she says that organic food is fifty-percent
14		more expensive than regular food. That means
15		she will have to pay more for her coffee and sal-
16		ads. She says organic food is for rich people, not
17		poor students like her.
18		
19	TiC	Next, she says that organic food does not mean
20		healthier food. For example, she says a regular
21		hamburger and an organic hamburger have the
22		same calories and fat. Organic food, she says, is
23		not healthier.
24		
25	TiC	Finally, she doesn't want the university telling
26		her what she should eat. The university is
27		taking away her freedom to choose. If she wants
28		to eat regular food, that is her choice.
29		
30	C ⟶ 5 seconds ▸	For those reasons, the woman is against the new
31		food policy.

Common Problems for this Task

1. Lack of Development-Summarization --------------------

Test-takers tend to focus on the student's argument more than the announcement. As a result, they summarize the announcement in one sentence, then summarize the student's position. Make sure you summarize both the topic of the announcement and the reason for it. Also, when summarizing the student's argument, make sure you summarize each supporting illustration and the reasoning therein using cause-and-effect.

- **WARNING:** *A lack of Development-Summarization (OPDUL=C) of the announcement will result in a lack of Topical-Unity-Synthesis (OPDUL=C) between the announcement and the student's argument. This will result in a lack of Coherence (OPDUL=**C**) and a lower score.*

2. Summarizing Both Students -----------------------------

This task measures your ability to summarize one student argument only. That argument will be indicated in the prompt. If you are asked to summarize the man's argument, for example, do not summarize the woman's position. It is off topic.

- **WARNING:** *Summarizing both arguments will not result in a higher score.*

3. Reading the Announcement → *Blanking Out* ------------

If you blank out reading the announcement, refocus and analyze the first three sentences. They are the most important sentences in the announcement. Sentence one is typically a general introduction to the policy while sentence two states the policy and sentence three develops the policy in detail. Summarize accordingly. Also, the reason is often stated/restated in the last sentence

4. Listening to the Dialogue → *Blanking Out* --------------

If you blank out listening to the dialogue, try to refocus and identify each student's position using tone. A positive-student tone will infer support for the policy while a negative tone will infer opposition. Identify which student is tonally positive and which is negative. Next, identify the policy they are debating by listening for policy restatements made by the students. For example, when a student says, "If you ask me, I think the new parking policy is all wrong," you know that the topic of the announcement they are debating is a new parking policy. When you speak, summarize what you have heard after the point at which you refocused.

- **REMEMBER:** *The dialogue has a specific purpose: to present two opposing arguments. Practice listening for those arguments by anticipating each step of G+3TiC=C as each student speaks.*

Help! → *My Response is Too Long!*

The following are reasons why your response is longer than 60 seconds.

Reason #1   Your summary of the reading is too long.

Solution   1. Make your summary shorter. Do not include details (dates, etc.).
2. Summarize the reading in 10 seconds or less.
3. Speak faster; try not to hesitate.

Reason #2   When the clock starts, you are not speaking right away. That means you are losing valuable seconds at the start.

Solution   1. Start speaking right after the beep. <u>Remember</u>: *The speaking tasks come up fast. Be ready for them.*

Reason #3   You are being too careful. When you are too careful, you slow down to pronounce correctly. When you slow down, you waste time. You also decrease fluency and automaticity.

Solution   1. Speak at a normal pace.
2. Record your voice, then play it back. You will know if you are speaking too slowly. If so, speak faster.

Reason #4   You are pausing or hesitating too much. Record your voice and play it back. You will soon know if you are pausing or hesitating too much. Pausing and hesitating waste time. Pausing and hesitating will also decrease fluency and automaticity.

Solution   1. Practice reading sample responses for correct speed and accuracy.
2. Go to youtube.com. Google "How to speak like a native-English speaker." There are lots of great videos to help you speak more proficiently.

Reason #5   You are pausing or hesitating too much because you did not summarize the student's argument using G+3TiC=C.

Solution   1. Memorize G+3TiC=C.
2. Practice summarizing student arguments using sample responses.

Reason #6   Your summary of the student's supporting illustrations (3TiC) contains too much information.

Solution   1. Identify the topic in each body paragraph and the reason stated by the cause-and-effect relationship.
2. Do not include details (dates, scores, costs, etc.).

Reason #7   Your conclusion is too long.

Solution   1. State the conclusion in one sentence.
2. State the conclusion in 5 seconds or less.
3. Simply repeat the student's opinion.

Reason #8   The clock makes you so nervous you blank out.

Solution   1. Do not time yourself when you practice. Just speak. When you are more confident, time yourself.

Help! → *My Response is Too Short!*

The following are reasons why your response is too short.

Reason #1   You are nervous. When you are nervous, you speak too fast and finish too soon.

Solution   1. Record your voice and play it back. You will soon know if you are speaking too fast. If so, slow down.
2. Do not time yourself. Just speak at a regular speed.

Reason #2   Your summary of the student's supporting illustrations (3TiC) is too short.

Solution   1. Make sure you have identified the topic in each supporting example.
2. Make sure you have identified the cause-and-effect relationship in each example.
3. Make sure you have summarized all supporting examples.

Reason #3   You speak, then suddenly stop because you are shy, afraid, or feel stupid.

Solution   1. Practice reading into a recording device. Read an English magazine article or a book while recording. This will help you develop confidence speaking into a microphone.
2. Take an ESL class to develop your speaking skills and confidence.
3. Practice. Practice. Practice.

Reason #4   You are not confident using G+3TiC=C.

Solution   1. Practice developing and delivering responses until you have memorized G+3TiC=C, and you remember it automatically without notes.
2. Practice. Practice. Practice.

Reason #5   You blank out.

Solution   1. You are trying too hard or are too nervous. Try to relax. When you practice speaking, don't time yourself. Just speak until you are confident. When you are more confident, then time yourself.
2. Forget about trying to demonstrate OPDUL=C. Just speak. The more you speak, the more confident you will become.

Speaking Practice

Using the strategies discussed, complete the following tasks. Check each for Coherence using the *Integrated Speaking → Proficiency Checklist* on page 335. Rate them using the *Integrated Speaking → Rating Guide* on page 336.

Task #1 → *New Bookstore Policy*

<u>Directions</u>: Darien College is changing its textbook policy. Read about the policy change in the following announcement. You have 45 seconds.

1 *In order to reduce the school's carbon footprint, and to reduce the rising cost of paper-*
2 *based textbooks, the campus bookstore will go digital starting next semester. Stu-*
3 *dents will have two e-text buying options. Using a computer terminal at the bookstore,*
4 *students can purchase e-texts with a credit card, then download their purchase to a*
5 *storage device. Students will also be able to download e-texts via the school website.*
6 *The move to digital texts will result in greater savings for students when purchasing*
7 *required texts. Please note: Due to the policy change, campus bookstores will no long-*
8 *er buy back student books purchased at campus bookstores. If you have any ques-*
9 *tions, please contact the Dean's office.*

<u>Directions</u>: Now listen as two students discuss the announcement.

track #11

- <u>Prompt</u>: The man gives his opinion about the new policy. State his position and explain the reasons he gives for holding that opinion.

Preparation Time = 30 seconds	Speaking Time = 60 seconds

audio script page 343

- -

Task #2 → *New Dress-Code Policy*

<u>Directions</u>: Wilton University is introducing a new policy. Read about the new policy in the following announcement. You have 45 seconds.

1 *Starting next semester, Wilton University will introduce a new dress-code policy. This*
2 *policy pertains to students, faculty and support staff. Starting next semester, the*
3 *wearing of shorts will no longer be permitted inside campus buildings. Also, tank*
4 *tops, and any other top that does not completely cover the mid-section down to the*
5 *belt, will be prohibited. Sandals and other open-toed shoes will also be prohibited, as*
6 *will the wearing of hats and caps. This policy is to ensure and maintain a consistent*
7 *dress code that reflects the high academic standards of Wilton University.*

Directions: Now listen as two students discuss the announcement.

track #12

- Prompt: The woman gives her opinion about the new policy. State her position and explain the reasons she gives for holding that opinion.

Preparation Time = 30 seconds   Speaking Time = 60 seconds

audio script page 343

- -

Task #3 → *New School Mascot*

Directions: Read the following announcement from the student government at Greenwich College. You have 45 seconds.

1 *With the opening of the new football stadium, the student body was invited to submit*
2 *ideas for a new mascot to replace Old Sparky the dog. The final two choices are a*
3 *bear and a chicken. When voting, please keep in mind that the new mascot should,*
4 *like Old Sparky, symbolize the strengths and traditions of our three-hundred-year-old*
5 *institution. Please remember as well that the mascot's image will appear on a variety*
6 *of media, including school uniforms, the school website, and clothing. Voting will oc-*
7 *cur next Monday in room 310. Each student will get one vote. If you have any ques-*
8 *tions, please contact the Mascot Committee, room SC-229. Don't forget to vote!*

Directions: Now listen as two students discuss the announcement.

track #13

- Prompt: The woman gives her opinion about the new policy. State her position and explain the reasons she gives for holding that opinion.

Preparation Time = 30 seconds   Speaking Time = 60 seconds

audio script page 344

Task #4 → *No-Pets Policy*

<u>Directions</u>: Stamford College is introducing a new policy. Read about the new policy in the following announcement. You have 45 seconds.

1   *Starting immediately, students will no longer be able to bring pets to campus and/or*
2   *keep pets in the dormitories. This policy includes all cats, dogs, fish, birds, monkeys,*
3   *and snakes. Exclusions to this policy are seeing-eye dogs and those animals brought*
4   *on to campus for safety/security reasons, or for teaching purposes. Those wishing to*
5   *bring an animal on campus must fill out a permission form. If a student is found keep-*
6   *ing a pet, the student will be asked to relinquish the animal. If the student does not*
7   *comply, the animal in question will be taken away by the proper authority. This policy*
8   *will ensure a healthier and safer campus for all.*

<u>Directions</u>: Now listen as two students discuss the announcement.

track #14

- <u>Prompt</u>: The man gives his opinion about the new policy. State his position and explain the reasons he gives for holding that opinion.

Preparation Time = 30 seconds   **Speaking Time = 60 seconds**

audio script page 344

Task #5 → *No-Laptops Policy*

<u>Directions</u>: Shelton University is introducing a new computer policy. Read about the new policy. You have 45 seconds.

1   *Starting next semester, students at Shelton University will not be allowed to use lap-*
2   *top computers during class time. Any student using a laptop computer during class*
3   *time will be asked to turn it off or leave the room. This policy is in response to com-*
4   *plaints saying that increased laptop usage during class time is noisy and distracting.*
5   *Laptop usage will be permitted in all main campus areas, including libraries and food*
6   *service areas. If you have any questions regarding this policy, please contact the*
7   *Dean. Office hours are Monday-Friday 9 to 5pm.*

<u>Directions</u>: Now listen as two students discuss the announcement.

track #15

- <u>Prompt</u>: The woman gives her opinion about the new policy. State her position and explain the reasons she gives for holding that opinion.

Preparation Time = 30 seconds   **Speaking Time = 60 seconds**

audio script page 345

Task #6 → *New School President*

<u>Directions:</u> Old Lovell College has a new president. Read the announcement
about the new president. You have 45 seconds.

1 *It is with great honor and pleasure that Old Lovell College announces the appointment*
2 *of its new president, William Liddell. Mr. Liddell brings to his new position a wealth of*
3 *academic and private-sector experience. Prior to joining Old Lovell, Mr. Liddell was*
4 *Dean of Saint Lionel's, one of New England's most prestigious preparatory schools.*
5 *Prior to Saint Lionel's, Mr. Liddell was CEO of Golf, Inc., a developer of golf courses.*
6 *Mr. Liddell's experience as a business leader will help prepare Old Lovell for the chal-*
7 *lenges of the future. Please join me in welcoming Mr. Liddell. For more information,*
8 *please contact the President's office.*

track #16

<u>Directions:</u> Now listen as two students discuss the announcement.

- <u>Prompt:</u> The woman gives her opinion about the new policy. State her
position and explain the reasons she gives for holding that opinion.

Preparation Time = 30 seconds	Speaking Time = 60 seconds

audio script page 345

Notes

_____
_____
_____
_____
_____
_____
_____
_____
_____
_____
_____
_____

Task #4 → *Integrated Speaking*

This task measures your ability to integrate three skills: reading, listening, and speaking. You will integrate these skills while summarizing a short academic reading and a short lecture on the same topic. You can construct a response for this task using G+3TiC=C. The task order follows.

1. Read a short academic passage = 45 seconds
2. Listen to a short academic lecture = 60-90 seconds
3. Read the prompt; prepare your response = 30 seconds
4. Deliver your response = 60 seconds

Speaking Task #4 → *Step-by-Step*

Follow these steps when constructing a response for this task.

Step #1   Make a note map; visualize the map.

As you listen to the task instructions, make a note map, as illustrated below.

```
                          READING

   G



                          LECTURE

   1


   2


   3


   C
```

Step #2   **Read the passage + take notes = 45 seconds.**

When the task instructions end, the passage will appear on your screen. You will have 45 seconds to read it.

Animal Behavior

1 *Animal behavior can be classified according to the time of day an animal is active.*
2 *Animals, such as horses, elephants and most birds, are said to be diurnal because*
3 *they are active during the day and rest at night. Those animals active at dawn and*
4 *dusk are said to be crepuscular. Beetles, skunks and rabbits fall into this category.*
5 *The third group are those animals that sleep during the day and are active at night.*
6 *They are called nocturnal. A good example is the bat. Bats have highly developed*
7 *eyesight, hearing and smell. This helps them avoid predators and locate food. Being*
8 *nocturnal also helps them avoid high temperatures during the day, especially in de-*
9 *serts where temperatures can reach well over one hundred degrees Fahrenheit.*

- **WARNING:** *When the 45-second reading time ends, the passage will leave your screen. It will not return, so take notes.*

- **REMEMBER:** *Don't worry if you don't understand the topic in the reading. TOEFL will teach it to you. By doing so, TOEFL is measuring your ability to learn and apply new ideas. In this way, TOEFL is a teaching test. Learning about the topic starts with note-taking.*

Note-Taking

The purpose of the reading is to teach you about the topic using a general intro-duction. The topic itself will be predictably stated in the first (topic) sentence using a rhetorical strategy. For example, a date in the topic sentence will signal the rhetorical strategy of narration, for example:

> *In America, the 1920's was a period of great innovation.*

The topic might also be introduced using the rhetorical strategy of process.

> *Making microprocessors starts at a high-tech factory.*

→ **Or description...**

> *J. D. Salinger, an eccentric recluse, penned The Catcher in the Rye, a seminal, coming-of-age novel which introduced a new literary character: the rebellious teenager.*

→ **Or cause-and-effect...**

> *Nicotine in cigarettes is more addictive than heroin.*

→ **Or definition...**

> *Estrogen is a hormone that regulates sexual characteristics in women.*

➔ **Or illustration...**

> *Louis Comfort Tiffany, an American artist and designer, is best known for his stained glass.*

➔ **Or compare-and-contrast...**

> *Scientists have recently discovered that the Aspen finch and the Pine finch are in fact the same species of bird.*

Note below how the topic sentence in the reading uses <u>definition</u> and **cause**-and-*effect* to teach and introduce the topic of animal behavior.

1	*Animal behavior can be classified **according to the time of day an animal is***
2	***active**.*

Note below how the topic of animal behavior is then classified into *three groups* with a definition of each group and examples.

1	Animal behavior can be classified according to the time of day an animal is
2	active.
3	
4	*Animals, such as horses, elephants and most birds, are said to be **diurnal** be-*
5	*cause they are active during the day and rest at night.*
6	
7	*Those animals active at dawn and dusk are said to be **crepuscular**. Beetles,*
8	*skunks and rabbits fall into this category.*
9	
10	*The third group are those animals that sleep during the day and are active at*
11	*night. They are called **nocturnal**. A good example is the bat.*

Note this general information on your note map.

READING

<u>G</u>   animal behavior classified according to time of day

    day = diurnal, active day, sleep night ie humans, horses
    crepuscular = active dawn + dusk ie beetles, rabbits
    night = nocturnal, sleep day, active night ie bats

● **WARNING:** *Do not note every point. <u>Remember</u>: You only have 45 seconds. Simply identify the topic and how it is developed, as illustrated above.*

Step #3   Listen to the lecture + take notes = 60-90 secs.

When the reading ends, it will leave your screen.

- **WARNING:** *The reading will not return, so take notes.*

The purpose of the lecture is to develop the topic in the reading by developing it with specific examples. This testing method is predictable.

Next, as you listen to the lecture and read along with the tapescript below, identify the illustrations (TiC) that develop and support the topic of animal behavior in the reading.

Sample Lecture → *Animal Behavior* ⟶ track #17

1   1 ➔ *Good afternoon. In this lecture, we'll focus on a common nocturnal animal: the*
2   *bat. There are two types of bat: micro-bats, or true bats, and mega-bats, also called*
3   *fruit bats.*
4
5   2 ➔ *Let's start with mega-bats. Size-wise, mega-bats are from two to sixteen inches in*
6   *length. Mega-bats have extremely sensitive sight and smell. This helps them locate*
7   *the flowers and fruit upon which they feed. It is while eating that mega-bats play an*
8   *important role in the distribution of plants. Like bees, mega-bats serve as pollinators.*
9   *When they lick nectar or eat flowers, their bodies become covered in pollen which*
10   *they, in turn, carry to other trees and plants, thereby acting as pollinators. In fact,*
11   *many of the fruits and vegetables on our tables, such as bananas and peaches,*
12   *would not be there if mega-bats did not pollinate plants and trees.*
13
14   3 ➔ *Next are micro-bats. As the name implies, micro-bats are quite small, about the*
15   *size of a mouse. To find food, micro-bats use echolocation, high-frequency sounds*
16   *they bounce off insects. The most common micro-bat is the vesper or evening bat. Like*
17   *mega-bats, micro-bats play an important role in the environment. The average vesper*
18   *bat, for example, can eat one thousand mosquitoes in one night. By doing so, they*
19   *control the mosquito population.*

As you can see, the lecture above develops two examples (2TiC) of a nocturnal animal: the mega-bat and the micro-bat. These examples develop and support the reading (G).

Next, look at the lecture notes. Note the description and the **cause**-and-*effect* reasoning in the conclusion of each body paragraph (Ti**C**).

LECTURE

1.   first mega bat, 2 - 16 inches
good eyesight and smell helps bat find food = flowers and fruit
mega bats pollinate plants + trees *good for environment, we get peaches, bananas*

2.   next micro bat, size of mouse
uses echolocation to find food = insects
micro bats eat 1,000 mosquitoes a night *good for controlling mosquitoes*

Step #4   **Prompt + prepare your response = 30 seconds.**

When the listening ends, it will leave your screen. You cannot replay it. The listening will be replaced by the prompt (see below). You will have 30 seconds to prepare your response.

- Prompt: Summarize how the reading and the lecture define and develop the idea of animal behavior.

The prompt can be phrased various ways, for example:

1. Prompt: According to the reading, animals are classified by their behavior. How does the lecture develop and illustrate this point?

2. Prompt: How does the lecture support the classification of bats?

3. Prompt: How do bats benefit the environment? Include in your response points made in the reading and in the lecture.

- **REMEMBER:** *The prompts for this task—no matter how they are written—all mean the following.*

   Prompt: Summarize the specific points (TiC) made in the lecture and show how they add to and support the general information in the reading (G).

Step #5   Speak = 60 seconds.

When speaking, follow your note map. Summarize the reading, then the lecture.

READING (G)

G   animal behavior classified according to time of day

       day = diurnal, active day, sleep night ie humans, horses
       crepuscular = active dawn + dusk ie beetles, rabbits
       night = nocturnal, sleep day, active night ie bats

LECTURE (2TiC)

1   first mega bat, 2 - 16 inches
      good eyesight and smell helps bat find food = flowers
      and fruit
      mega bats pollinate plants + trees, good for environment, we
      get peaches, bananas

2   next micro bat, size of mouse
      uses echolocation to find food = insects
      micro bats eat 1,000 mosquitoes a night good for controlling
      mosquitoes

C

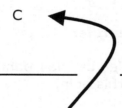

Note that the conclusion (C) is still blank. When stating the conclusion (see below), answer by answering the prompt, for example:

Prompt: Summarize how the reading and the lecture define and develop the idea of animal behavior.

    C: *That's how the reading and the lecture define and develop the idea of animal behavior.*

Prompt: How do the reading and lecture support the classification of bats?

    C: *That's how the reading and lecture support the classification of bats.*

- **REMEMBER:** *Stating the conclusion is the least important part of your response. The most important part is connecting the lecture to the reading.*

Mapped out, you can see how G+2TiC=C gives the speaking raters what they are trained to listen for: a summary that demonstrates OPDUL=C for integrated speaking. The summary of the reading (G) and the conclusions (C) are underlined, the transitions (T) are in **bold**, and the summarized supporting illustrations (i) are in *italics*.

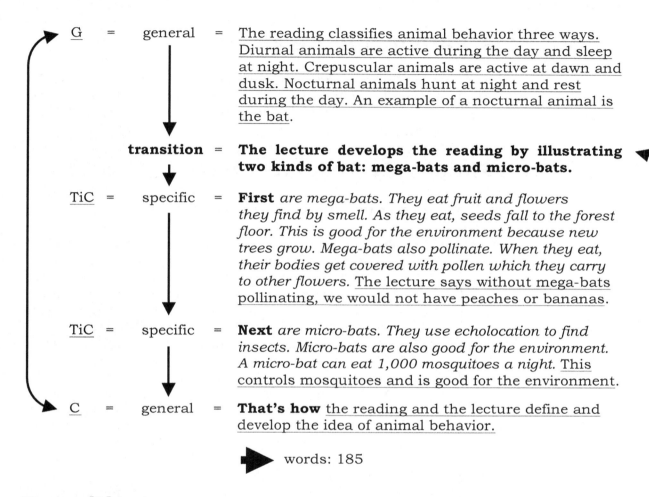

<u>G</u>	=	general	=	<u>The reading classifies animal behavior three ways. Diurnal animals are active during the day and sleep at night. Crepuscular animals are active at dawn and dusk. Nocturnal animals hunt at night and rest during the day. An example of a nocturnal animal is the bat.</u>
		transition	=	**The lecture develops the reading by illustrating two kinds of bat: mega-bats and micro-bats.**
<u>TiC</u>	=	specific	=	**First** *are mega-bats. They eat fruit and flowers they find by smell. As they eat, seeds fall to the forest floor. This is good for the environment because new trees grow. Mega-bats also pollinate. When they eat, their bodies get covered with pollen which they carry to other flowers.* <u>The lecture says without mega-bats pollinating, we would not have peaches or bananas.</u>
<u>TiC</u>	=	specific	=	**Next** *are micro-bats. They use echolocation to find insects. Micro-bats are also good for the environment. A micro-bat can eat 1,000 mosquitoes a night.* <u>This controls mosquitoes and is good for the environment.</u>
<u>C</u>	=	general	=	**That's how** <u>the reading and the lecture define and develop the idea of animal behavior.</u>

words: 185

Transition

Note the transition ➜

> The lecture develops the reading by illustrating two kinds of bat: mega-bats and micro-bats.

This transition is critical. It connects the reading and the lecture, topically, grammatically, and rhetorically. The raters listen for this transition. It demonstrates <u>U</u>nity-Synthesis (OPD**UL**=C) between the reading (general) and the lecture (specific).

- **REMEMBER:** *The lecture sample above gives two supporting examples (2TiC). On the test day, there might be three lecture examples (3TiC) or one extended example (TiC). Be prepared for three.*

Step #6   **Task end.**

Your recorded response will be sent via internet to ETS for rating. Raters will rate your response with a rubric. OPDUL=C for integrated speaking (see pages 335-336) defines that rubric.

OPDUL=C → *Rating This Task*

The sample response for speaking task #4 (page 103) scores a 4/4 based on OPDU only. We cannot rate <u>L</u>anguage-Use (OPDU<u>L</u>=C). To rate it, we need to hear a recorded/live response. However, if you did demonstrate all aspects of OPDUL=C when speaking, including <u>L</u>anguage-Use, then your score would be 4/4.

How Long Should My Response Be?

The following map illustrates how to manage your time for this task.

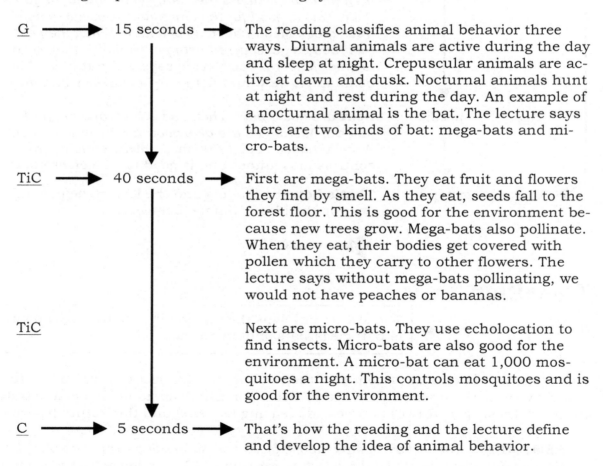

<u>G</u> ⟶ 15 seconds ⟶ The reading classifies animal behavior three ways. Diurnal animals are active during the day and sleep at night. Crepuscular animals are active at dawn and dusk. Nocturnal animals hunt at night and rest during the day. An example of a nocturnal animal is the bat. The lecture says there are two kinds of bat: mega-bats and micro-bats.

TiC ⟶ 40 seconds ⟶ First are mega-bats. They eat fruit and flowers they find by smell. As they eat, seeds fall to the forest floor. This is good for the environment because new trees grow. Mega-bats also pollinate. When they eat, their bodies get covered with pollen which they carry to other flowers. The lecture says without mega-bats pollinating, we would not have peaches or bananas.

<u>TiC</u> — Next are micro-bats. They use echolocation to find insects. Micro-bats are also good for the environment. A micro-bat can eat 1,000 mosquitoes a night. This controls mosquitoes and is good for the environment.

<u>C</u> ⟶ 5 seconds ⟶ That's how the reading and the lecture define and develop the idea of animal behavior.

Common Problems for this Task

1. Lack of Development-Summarization --------------------

Test-takers tend to focus on the lecture more than the reading. As a result, they summarize the reading in one sentence, then summarize the lecture. When summarizing the reading, make sure you identify the topic _and_ supporting details/reasoning therein. When summarizing the lecture, make sure you summarize each supporting illustration and the reason(s) therein using cause-and-effect.

- **WARNING:** _A lack of Development-Summarization (OPDUL=C) of the reading will result in a lack of Topical-Unity-Synthesis (OPDUL=C) between the reading passage and the lecture. This will result in a lack of Coherence (OPDUL=**C**) and a lower score._

2. No Transition Between the Reading and Lecture -------

Test-takers tend to forget the transition that connects the reading and the lecture (see page 103).

- **WARNING:** _If you do not connect the reading and the lecture, the result will be a lack of Topical-Unity-Synthesis. This will result in a lack of Coherence (OPDUL=**C**) and a lower score._

3. Reading the Passage → _Blanking Out_ --------------------

If you blank out reading the passage, try to refocus and concentrate on the first three sentences. They are the most important sentences in the passage. Sentence one is typically a general introduction to the topic while sentences two and three will develop it. Summarize accordingly.

4. Listening to the Lecture → _Blanking Out_ ----------------

If this happens, try to refocus. Listen for how the professor is connecting the topic in the reading to the details he/she is developing, and summarize accordingly. Remember that the lecture has a specific purpose: to support the reading with examples. Before taking the test, practice listening for supporting examples in lectures. Knowing how to anticipate what you will hear will create greater confidence. Confidence, in turn, will help you concentrate and not blank out.

Help! → _My Response is Too Long!_ → _see page 91._

Help! → _My Response is Too Short!_ → _see page 92._

Speaking Practice

Using the strategies discussed, construct a response for the following tasks. Check each response for Coherence using the *Integrated Speaking → Proficiency Checklist* on page 335. Rate them using the *Integrated Speaking → Rating Guide* on pg. 336.

Task #1 → *Bestsellers*

Read the passage about bestsellers. You have 45 seconds.

1   *The term bestseller describes a book that is popular because it sells well hence the*
2   *term bestseller. Bestsellers can be both fiction and non-fiction. The most famous best-*
3   *seller list in America is the New-York-Times bestseller list. A book that makes it onto*
4   *this list will substantially increase its sales. Yet just because a book makes the New-*
5   *York-Times bestseller list does not mean that the book is of the highest literary quali-*
6   *ty. On the contrary, many of the books on the New-York-Times bestseller list are*
7   *aimed at a general audience more interested in being entertained than educated.*

Directions: Now listen to a lecture on the same topic.

track #18

Prompt: How do the reading and the lecture add to our understanding of the term bestseller in a contemporary and in an historical sense?

Preparation Time = 30 seconds   **Speaking Time = 60 seconds**

audio script page 346

Task #2 → *The Green Revolution*

Read the following passage about the Green Revolution. You have 45 seconds.

1   *The Green Revolution of the 1960's had one goal: to eliminate hunger worldwide. It*
2   *did so by introducing the concept of industrialized agriculture. Prior to the Green Revo-*
3   *lution, farming in less-developed nations had changed little since man first planted*
4   *seeds. Crop yields were unpredictable, insects uncontrollable, and disease impossi-*
5   *ble to fight. At the same time, the world's population was skyrocketing. To feed the*
6   *world, scientists developed high-yielding cereal grains that were disease resistant.*
7   *They also developed synthetic fertilizers and pesticides. The result was the Green*
8   *Revolution, a global revolution in which technology took control of the agricultural pro-*
9   *cess. The results were immediate. Countries like Mexico were soon net exporters of*
10 *wheat while in Pakistan and India, wheat yields doubled between 1965 and 1970.*

Directions: Now listen to a lecture on the same topic.

track
#19

Prompt: What is the Green Revolution and what are its short and long-term effects?

Preparation Time = 30 seconds   Speaking Time = 60 seconds

audio script page 347

Task #3 → *Seamounts*

Read the passage about seamounts. You have 45 seconds.

1   *Seamounts are undersea mountains rising off the ocean floor. Approximately half of*
2   *the world's seamounts are found in the Pacific Ocean. Currents flowing up the sea-*
3   *mounts from the ocean floor bring life-sustaining nutrients into the photosynthetic*
4   *zone, a place where sunlight and carbon dioxide are converted into food energy for*
5   *plants and other organisms. As a result, a great variety of plants and fish make sea-*
6   *mounts their home. Some of these fish are native species, fish that are found only*
7   *around seamounts. Such biodiversity, in turn, attracts larger fish, such as sharks and*
8   *tuna, as well as marine mammals, such as seals. It also attracts commercial fishing.*

Now listen to a lecture on the same topic.

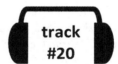

track
#20

Prompt: Seamounts are under threat. Why? Using information from the reading and the lecture, illustrate the threat and the reason for it.

Preparation Time = 30 seconds   Speaking Time = 60 seconds

audio script page 347

Task #4 → *Brown-Headed Cowbird*

Read the passage about the brown-headed cowbird. You have 45 seconds.

1   *Brown-headed cowbirds are native to North America. They are about eight inches*
2   *long. Before European settlers arrived in North America, the cowbird followed the*
3   *buffalo across the Great Plains, eating the insects stirred up by the passing herds.*
4   *In this way, cowbirds were nomadic, always on the move in search of food, much*
5   *like the buffalo. However, with settlers clearing the land and the introduction of*

6   *grazing animals, such as cows and sheep, cowbirds found a new food source: in-*
7   *sects stirred up by domesticated animals. As a result, the cowbird became a per-*
8   *manent resident in agricultural areas. Today, cowbirds are a common sight at*
9   *backyard birdfeeders, arriving in early spring and staying till late September when*
10   *they head south for winter.*

Directions: Now listen to a lecture on the same topic.

Prompt: The brown-headed cowbird is a brood-parasite. How do the reading
          and lecture define and develop this classification?

Preparation Time = 30 seconds   Speaking Time = 60 seconds

audio script page 348

Task #5 → *A Census of Population*

Read the passage about a census of population. You have 45 seconds.

1   *Before demographers can study a population, they have to know how many people*
2   *comprise that population. To determine the size of a population, the population must*
3   *be counted. The process of counting people is called a census of population, or simply*
4   *a census. The United Nations broadens the definition of a census by stating that a*
5   *census of population is "the total process of collecting, compiling and publishing de-*
6   *mographic, economic and social data pertaining, at a specified time or times, to all*
7   *persons in a country or...territory."*

Directions: Now listen to a lecture on the same topic.

Narrator: Summarize the points made in the lecture and show how they add to
           and support the information in the reading.

Preparation Time = 30 seconds   Speaking Time = 60 seconds

audio script page 348

Task #5 → *Integrated Speaking*

This task measures your ability to integrate two skills: listening and speaking. You will integrate these skills while summarizing a student conversation in which solutions for a problem are offered. You will then state your opinion about which solution you prefer and why. You can construct a response for this task using G+3TiC=C. The task order follows.

1. Listen to a student conversation = 60-90 seconds
2. Read the prompt; prepare your response = 20 seconds
3. Deliver your response = 60 seconds

Speaking Task #5 → *Step-by-Step*

Follow these steps when constructing a response for this task.

Step #1 **Make a note map; visualize the map.**

As you listen to the task instructions, make a note map as illustrated below.

PROBLEM	SOLUTIONS		MY OPINION
	G		G
	1 *first*		TIC
	2 *second*		C
	C		

Step #2 **Listen to the conversation + take notes = 60-90 secs.**

The student conversation is a problem-solution scenario. One student describes a personal problem and does not know how to solve it. The other student will offer two solutions and the reasons for those solutions. The problem is a general statement (G) while the solutions are specific advice (2TiC).

As you listen to the student conversation, follow the tapescript below. Listen for the problem followed by the two solutions. Take notes.

Sample → *Student Dialogue* ➡️ track #23

1	Man:	Hi, Betty. What's wrong?
3	Woman:	Well, there's good news and bad.
5	Man:	Okay, so what's the good news?
7	Woman:	I got accepted into Harvard law.
9	Man:	Congratulations! That's fantastic.
11	Woman:	Thanks. Now for the bad news. Harvard is not cheap. I nearly died when I saw the tuition.
14	Man:	Yeah, but it's Harvard. Ivy League.
16	Woman:	I know. I want to go, but I can't afford it. I already have four years' worth of undergrad loans at this school. If I do three years of Harvard law, I'll be even more in debt. I'm not sure what to do.
20	Man:	What about applying for a scholarship? How are your grades?
22	Woman:	I'm at the top of my class.
24	Man:	There you go. You'd have a really good chance of getting a scholarship. Some scholarships pay all your tuition. If you don't get a full scholarship, you should at least get something for books. I got a scholarship here, and boy did I save a bundle.
29	Woman:	Applying for a scholarship is definitely an option. I'll have to check it out.
32	Man:	You could also take time off and work for a year or two, you know, postpone admittance. That way you could save money for tuition. You might not be able to pay off the full cost, but you could at least pay off some of it. That way you'd owe less in the long run.
37	Woman:	Yeah. Obviously, I have a decision to make.

- **REMEMBER:** *Because the conversation is short, the problem will be stated at the very start. Make sure you are focused. If not, you will miss the problem.*

- **REMEMBER:** *On test day, the problem-student will describe his/her problem and then the solution-student will do all the talking, or you might get a more natural conversation like the sample above. Answer both using these strategies.*

● **REMEMBER:** *There will be two solutions. Not three. Not one. Two.*

As you listen to the conversation, note the problem and the solutions. Note how they are reasons expressed using **cause**-and-*effect*.

PROBLEM		SOLUTIONS
student got into Harvard *but can't go; can't afford it*	G	
	1	first = apply for scholarship; she has good grades **scholarship** *pay tuition and/or books*
	2	second = take time off and work **work** *save money for tuition or pay for some + pay less*

Step #3 **Prompt + prepare your response = 20 seconds.**

When the conversation ends, it will leave your screen. You cannot replay it. The conversation will be replaced by the prompt. You will have 20 seconds to prepare your response.

● Prompt: The students discuss two solutions to the woman's problem. Describe the problem, then state which solution you prefer and why.

Step #4 **Speak = 60 seconds.**

Mapped out on the next page, you can see how G+2TiC=C combined with G+TiC=C gives the raters what they are trained to listen for: an integrated summary that demonstrates OPDUL=C for integrated speaking. The student's problem (G) and the conclusions (C) are underlined, the solutions are *italicized*, and the transitions (T) are in **bold**.

As you read the response on the next page, note how the speaker's opinion is an independent-speaking-task response, mapped out like speaking tasks #1 and #2 (see page 66).

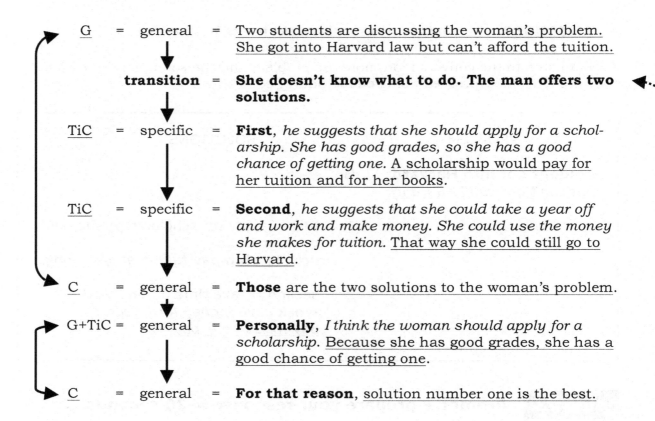

G	= general	=	Two students are discussing the woman's problem. She got into Harvard law but can't afford the tuition.
transition		=	**She doesn't know what to do. The man offers two solutions.**
TiC	= specific	=	**First**, *he suggests that she should apply for a scholarship. She has good grades, so she has a good chance of getting one.* A scholarship would pay for her tuition and for her books.
TiC	= specific	=	**Second**, *he suggests that she could take a year off and work and make money. She could use the money she makes for tuition.* That way she could still go to Harvard.
C	= general	=	**Those** are the two solutions to the woman's problem.
G+TiC	= general	=	**Personally**, *I think the woman should apply for a scholarship.* Because she has good grades, she has a good chance of getting one.
C	= general	=	**For that reason**, solution number one is the best.

Transition

Note the transition ➤

> She doesn't know what to do. The man offers two solutions.

This transition is critical. It connects the problem and the solutions, topically, grammatically, and rhetorically. The raters listen for this transition. It demonstrates Unity-Synthesis (OPD**U**L=C) between the problem (general) and the solutions (specific).

Step #5 **Task end.**

Your recorded response will be sent via internet to ETS for rating. Raters will rate your response with a rubric. OPDUL=C for integrated speaking (see pages 335-336) defines that rubric.

OPDUL=C → *Rating This Task*

The sample-response above for speaking task #4 scores a 4/4 based on OPDU only. We cannot rate Language-Use (OPDU**L**=C). To rate Language-Use, we need to hear a recorded/live response. However, if you did demonstrate all aspects of OPDUL=C when speaking, including Language-Use, then your score would be 4/4.

How Long Should My Response Be?

The following map illustrates how to manage your time for this task.

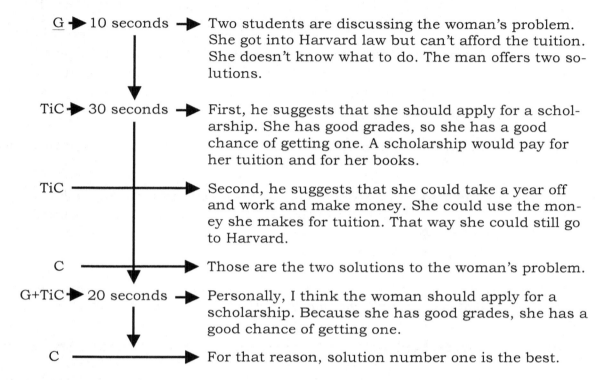

G ▶ 10 seconds ▶ Two students are discussing the woman's problem. She got into Harvard law but can't afford the tuition. She doesn't know what to do. The man offers two solutions.

TiC ▶ 30 seconds ▶ First, he suggests that she should apply for a scholarship. She has good grades, so she has a good chance of getting one. A scholarship would pay for her tuition and for her books.

TiC ▶ Second, he suggests that she could take a year off and work and make money. She could use the money she makes for tuition. That way she could still go to Harvard.

C ▶ Those are the two solutions to the woman's problem.

G+TiC ▶ 20 seconds ▶ Personally, I think the woman should apply for a scholarship. Because she has good grades, she has a good chance of getting one.

C ▶ For that reason, solution number one is the best.

Common Problems for this Task

1. Lack of Problem Development-Summarization ----------

When summarizing the problem, make sure you state the cause-and-effect reason. This will demonstrate greater Development-Summarization (OP**D**UL=C), for example:

Good   The woman can't go to Harvard.
Better The woman can't go to Harvard because she can't afford it.

2. Lack of Solution Development-Summarization ----------

When summarizing the solutions, make sure you summarize the cause-and-effect reasons. This will demonstrate greater Development-Summarization (OP**D**UL=C), for example:

Good   The man thinks the woman should apply for a scholarship.
Better The man thinks the woman should apply for a scholarship in order to pay for her tuition.

Good   The man thinks the woman should take a year off.
Better The man thinks the woman should take a year off and work to make money for tuition so she can still go to Harvard.

3. Lack of Topical-Unity Synthesis --------------------------

When summarizing the problem, remember to conclude by saying, "The student doesn't know what to do." This transition is critically important. It connects the problem with the solutions, for example:

> problem ➡ Two students are discussing the woman's problem. She got into Harvard law but can't afford the tuition.
> transition ➡ She doesn't know what to do. The man offers two solutions.
> solutions ➡ First, he suggests...

If you forget "The student doesn't know what to do," your summary will lack Topical-Unity-Synthesis between the problem and the solutions.

> problem ➡ Two students are discussing the woman's problem. She got into Harvard law but can't afford the tuition.
> transition ➡ _____ . The man offers two solutions.
> solutions ➡ First, he suggests...

- **WARNING:** *A lack of Topical-Unity-Synthesis between the problem and the solutions will result in a lack of Coherence (OPDUL=C) and a lower score.*

4. Mixing Verb Tenses ---------------------------------------

This task measures your ability to summarize using objective third-person grammar (*He said...She said...The problem is...It is...*), then switching to subjective first-person grammar (*I think...I believe...*). Make sure your tenses are consistent from start to finish. Do not mix tenses, for example:

> context ➡ Two students **are** discussing the woman's problem.
> problem ➡ She **got** into Harvard law but **couldn't** afford the tuition.
> transition ➡ She **didn't** know what to do. The man **will offer** two solutions. First, he **suggested**...

- **WARNING:** *Mixing verb tenses demonstrates a lack of Unity-Synthesis, specifically a lack of grammatical unity (OPDUL=C). This will result in a lack of Coherence (OPDUL=C) and a lower score.*

5. Blanking Out ---

If you blank out listening to the student dialogue, try to refocus. Remember that the student dialogue is a problem-solution scenario. One student will be offering solutions to a problem. The solutioning-student will typically restate his/her fellow student's problem, for example, "That [solution] is how I think you can pay for your trip to Los Angeles." From this statement, we can infer the topic and the problem: the student's inability to travel to Los Angeles. Listen for topic-problem restatements and solutions, and summarize accordingly.

Help! → *My Response is Too Long!*

The following are reasons why your response is longer than 60 seconds.

Reason #1   Your summary of the context-problem is too long.

Solution
1. Make your summary shorter.
2. Avoid details like dates, places, costs, etc.
3. Summarize the context-problem in 15 seconds or less.
4. Speak faster; try not to hesitate.

Reason #2   When the clock starts, you are not speaking right away. That means you are losing valuable seconds at the start.

Solution
1. Start speaking right after the beep. Remember: *The speaking tasks come up fast. Be ready for them*

Reason #3   You are being too careful. When you are too careful, you slow down to pronounce correctly. When you slow down, you waste time. You also decrease fluency and automaticity.

Solution
1. Speak at a normal pace.
2. Record your voice, then play it back. You will know if you are speaking too slowly. If so, speak faster.

Reason #4   You are pausing or hesitating too much. Record your voice and play it back. You will soon know if you are pausing or hesitating too much. Pausing and hesitating waste time. Pausing and hesitating will also decrease fluency and automaticity.

Solution
1. Practice reading sample responses for correct speed and accuracy.
2. Go to youtube.com. Google "How to speak like a native-English speaker." There are lots of great videos to help you speak more proficiently.

Reason #5   You are pausing or hesitating too much because you did not summarize the problem and the solutions using G+2TiC=C.

Solution
1. Practice summarizing sample dialogues using G+2TiC=C.
2. Practice one response over and over until you are confident summarizing the problem and the solutions using G+2TiC=C.

Reason #6   Your summary of the two solutions contains too much information.

Solution
1. Summarize only the topic in each solution and the cause-and-effect relationship.
2. Reduce the number of specific details (dates, costs, ages, etc.).

Reason #7   You are summarizing each solution, then explaining why it is not a good idea.

Solution   1. Do not analyze each solution in detail. This will waste time. Also, it is not part of the task.
2. Summarize each solution only.
3. State your argument (solution preference) at the end.

Reason #8   Your summary of the dialogue conclusion is too long.

Solution   1. State the conclusion in one sentence.
2. State the conclusion in 5 seconds or less.

Reason #9   Your solution preference (G+TiC=C) is too long.

Solution   1. Reduce the number of details in your argument.
2. Develop only one solution preference.
3. State your argument in 20 seconds or less.

Reason #10   The clock makes you so nervous you blank out.

Solution   1. Do not time yourself when you practice. Just speak. When you are more confident, time yourself.

Help! → *My Response is Too Short!*

Listed below are reasons why your response is too short.

Reason #1   You are nervous. When you are nervous, you speak too fast and finish too soon.

Solution   1. Record your voice and play it back. You will soon know if you are speaking too fast. If so, slow down.
2. Do not time yourself. Just speak at a regular speed.

Reason #2   You speak, then suddenly stop because you are shy, afraid, or feel stupid.

Solution   1. Practice reading into a recording device. Read an English magazine article or a book while recording. This will help you develop confidence speaking into a microphone.
2. Take an ESL class to develop your speaking skills and confidence.
3. Practice. Practice. Practice.

Reason #3   You are not confident using G+2TiC=C.

Solution   1. Practice developing and delivering one response until you have memorized G+2TiC=C and can remember it automatically without notes.
2. Practice. Practice. Practice.

Reason #4   You blank out.

Solution   1. You are trying too hard or are too nervous. Try to relax. When you practice speaking, don't time yourself. Just speak until you are confident. When you are more confident, then time yourself.
2. Don't worry about fluency, automaticity and pronunciation. Just speak. The more you speak, the more confident you will become.

Reason #5   Your summary of the context-problem is too short.

Solution   1. Make sure you have accurately identified the context and the problem.

Reason #6   Your summary of the two solutions is too short.

Solution   1. Make sure you have accurately summarized each solution.
2. Make sure you have accurately summarized the cause-and-effect relationship in each solution.

Reason #7   Your solution-preference argument (G+TiC=C) is too short.

Solution   1. Identify which solution you think is best.
2. Develop your argument with a cause-and-effect reason.
3. Use a personal example to support your position.

Notes

_____

_____

_____

_____

_____

_____

_____

_____

_____

_____

_____

_____

_____

_____

_____

Speaking Practice

Using the strategies discussed, construct a response for the following tasks. Check each for Coherence using the *Integrated Speaking → Proficiency Checklist* on page 335. Rate each using the *Integrated Speaking → Rating Guide* on page 336.

Task #1 → *Pet Policy*

Directions: Listen to a conversation between two students.

Prompt   The students discuss two solutions to the woman's problem. Identify the problem and the solutions, then state which solution you think is best and why.

| Preparation Time = 20 seconds | Speaking Time = 60 seconds |

audio script page 349

- -

Task #2 → *Euthanasia Debate*

Directions: Listen to a conversation between two students.

Prompt: The students discuss two solutions to the man's problem. Identify the problem and the solutions, then state which solution you think is best and why.

| Preparation Time = 20 seconds | Speaking Time = 60 seconds |

audio script page 350

- -

Task #3 → *Job Offer*

Directions: Listen to a conversation between two students.

Prompt: The students discuss two solutions to the woman's problem. Identify the problem and the solutions, then state which solution you think is best and why.

| Preparation Time = 20 seconds | Speaking Time = 60 seconds |

audio script page 350

Task #4 → *Roommate Problem*

Directions: Listen to a conversation between two students.

Prompt: The students discuss two solutions to the man's problem. Identify the problem and the solutions, then state which solution you think is best and why.

Preparation Time = 20 seconds	Speaking Time = 60 seconds

audio script page 351

Task #5 → *Professor Plagiarizes*

Directions: Listen to a conversation between two students.

Prompt: The students discuss two solutions to the woman's problem. Identify the problem and the solutions, then state which solution you think is best and why.

Preparation Time = 20 seconds	Speaking Time = 60 seconds

audio script page 352

Notes

Task #6 → *Integrated Speaking*

This task measures your ability to integrate two skills: listening and speaking. You will integrate these skills while summarizing a short academic lecture. You can construct a response for this task using G+3TiC=C. The task order follows.

1. Listen to a short lecture = 60-90 seconds
2. Read the prompt; prepare your response = 20 seconds
3. Deliver your response = 60 seconds

This task is similar to speaking task #4 (see pg. 97). The difference is task #4 starts with a reading passage. For task #6, the reading (the teaching segment) is integrated into the lecture, as illustrated below.

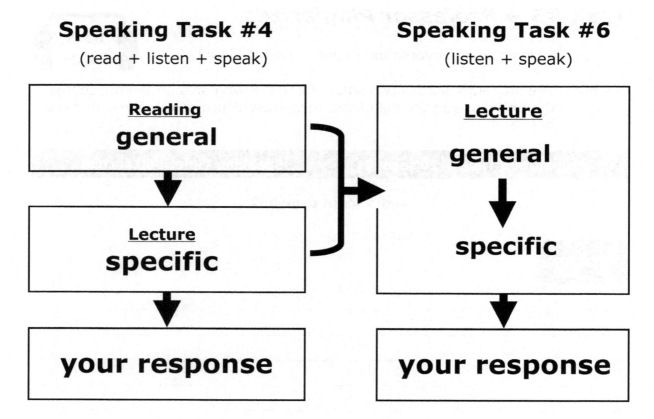

Speaking Task #6 → *Step-by-Step*

Follow these steps when constructing a response for this task.

Step #1　**Make a note map; visualize the map.**

As you listen to the task instructions, make a note map, as illustrated on the next page. To save time, write G, then 1, 2, 3 for body paragraphs.

```
G


1


2


3


C
```

Step #2 Listen to the lecture + take notes = 60-90 secs.

As you listen to the lecture, follow the tapescript below.

- **REMEMBER:** *The lecture will start by teaching you about the topic. This information is general (G). As the lecture progresses, the professor will give illustrations to develop the topic (TiCs). The number of examples depends on the task.*

Sample Lecture → *Zoology Class* → track #29

1　1 → *Animal behavior can be classified according to the time of day an animal is ac-*
2　*tive. Animals, such as horses, elephants, and most birds, are said to be diurnal be-*
3　*cause they are active during the day and rest at night. Those animals active at dawn*
4　*and dusk are said to be crepuscular. Beetles, skunks, and rabbits fall into this cate-*
5　*gory. The third group are those animals that sleep during the day and are active at*
6　*night. They are called nocturnal. A good example is the bat. Bats have highly-*
7　*developed eyesight, hearing and smell. This helps them avoid predators and locate*
8　*food. Being nocturnal also helps them avoid high temperatures during the day, espe-*
9　*cially in deserts where temperatures can reach well over one-hundred degrees Fahr-*
10　*enheit. There are two types of bat: micro-bats, or true bats, and mega-bats, also called*
11　*fruit bats.*
12
13　2 → *Let's start with mega-bats. Size wise, mega-bats range from two to sixteen inches*
14　*in length. Mega-bats have extremely sensitive sight and smell. This helps them locate*
15　*the flowers and fruit upon which they feed. It is while eating that mega-bats play an*
16　*important role in the distribution of plants. Like bees, mega-bats serve as pollinators.*
17　*When they lick nectar or eat flowers, their bodies become covered in pollen which*
18　*they, in turn, carry to other trees and plants, thereby acting as pollinators. In fact,*

19 *many of the fruits and vegetables on our tables, such as bananas and peaches,*
20 *would not be there if mega-bats did not pollinate plants and trees.*
21
22 3 → *Next are micro-bats. As the name implies, micro-bats are quite small, about the*
23 *size of a mouse. To find food, micro bats use echolocation, high-frequency sounds*
24 *they bounce off insects. The most common micro-bat is the vesper or evening bat. Like*
25 *mega-bats, micro-bats play an important role in the environment. The average vesper*
26 *bat, for example, can eat one-thousand mosquitoes in one night. By doing so, they*
27 *control the mosquito population.*

Note-Taking

The professor will introduce the topic in the first two-or-three sentences. A date in the topic sentence will signal the rhetorical strategy of narration, for example:

> *In 1793, Eli Whitney invented the cotton gin and revolutionized the cotton industry in the American south.*

The professor might use the rhetorical strategy of process to introduce the topic.

> *Extracting DNA from old bones is a complicated and time-consuming process. First, you must...*

→ **Or description...**

> *Pangea was a supercontinent that existed during the Mesozoic and the Paleozoic eras approximately 250 million years ago.*

→ **Or cause-and-effect...**

> *A snake sheds its skin in order to keep growing and to get rid of parasites.*

→ **Or compare-and-contrast...**

> *In the mid-nineteenth century, two distinct art movements emerged: Impressionism in France and the Pre-Raphaelite Brotherhood in England.*

→ **Or definition...**

> *Revolution 1.0 and 2.0 refer to the Tunisian and Egyptian revolutions of 2011, popular uprisings that used social media to spread their messages.*

Note below how the topic sentence uses definition and **cause**-and-*effect* to introduce the topic of animal behavior.

1 *Animal behavior can be classified **according to the time of day an animal is***
2 ***active.***

Note below how the topic of animal behavior is classified into ***three groups*** with a definition of each group and examples. Note this general information on your note map (see below).

1　　Animal behavior can be classified according to the time of day an animal is
2　　active.
3
4　　*Animals, such as horses, elephants, and most birds, are said to be **diurnal** be-*
5　　*cause they are active during the day and rest at night.*
6
7　　*Those animals active at dawn and dusk are said to be **crepuscular**. Beetles,*
8　　*skunks, and rabbits fall into this category.*
9
10　　*The third group are those animals that sleep during the day and are active at*
11　　*night. They are called **nocturnal**. A good example is the bat.*

Next, the professor's general introduction will progress to the supporting examples (points 1 and 2 below). Note the **cause**-and-*effect* reasons in the conclusions of each body paragraph (Ti**C**).

LECTURE

G　animal behavior classified according to time of day

　　day = diurnal, active day, sleep night ie humans, horses
　　crepuscular = active dawn + dusk ie beetles, rabbits
　　night = nocturnal, sleep day, active night ie bats

1　first mega bat, 2 - 16 inches
　good eyesight and smell, helps bat find food = flowers
　and fruit
　mega bats pollinate plants + trees *good for environ-*
　ment, we get peaches, bananas

2　next micro bat, size of mouse
　uses echolocation to find food = insects
　micro bats eat 1,000 mosquitoes a night *good for*
　controlling mosquitoes

- **REMEMBER:** *As you can see, note-taking for this task is the same as note-taking for speaking task #4 (see page 102).*

Step #3   **Prompt + prepare your response = 20 seconds.**

When the lecture ends, it will leave your screen. You cannot replay it. It will be re-placed by the prompt. You will have 20 seconds to prepare your response.

• <u>Prompt</u>: How does the lecture develop the topic of animal behavior?

Step #4   **Speak = 60 seconds.**

Mapped out, you can see how G+2TiC=C gives the raters what they are trained to listen for: a lecture summary that demonstrates OPDUL=C for integrated speaking (see page 335-36). The topic (G) and the conclusions (C) are <u>underlined</u>, the transitions (T) are in **bold**, and the supporting illustrations (i) are in *italics*.

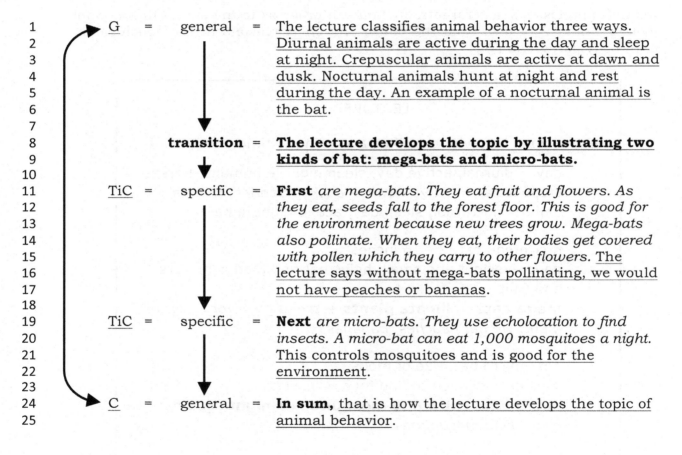

1	G	=	general	=	The lecture classifies animal behavior three ways. Diurnal animals are active during the day and sleep at night. Crepuscular animals are active at dawn and dusk. Nocturnal animals hunt at night and rest during the day. An example of a nocturnal animal is the bat.

1 — G = general = <u>The lecture classifies animal behavior three ways.</u>
2 — <u>Diurnal animals are active during the day and sleep</u>
3 — <u>at night. Crepuscular animals are active at dawn and</u>
4 — <u>dusk. Nocturnal animals hunt at night and rest</u>
5 — <u>during the day. An example of a nocturnal animal is</u>
6 — <u>the bat.</u>
7
8 — **transition** = **The lecture develops the topic by illustrating two**
9 — **kinds of bat: mega-bats and micro-bats.**
10
11 — TiC = specific = **First** *are mega-bats. They eat fruit and flowers. As*
12 — *they eat, seeds fall to the forest floor. This is good for*
13 — *the environment because new trees grow. Mega-bats*
14 — *also pollinate. When they eat, their bodies get covered*
15 — *with pollen which they carry to other flowers.* <u>The</u>
16 — <u>lecture says without mega-bats pollinating, we would</u>
17 — <u>not have peaches or bananas.</u>
18
19 — TiC = specific = **Next** *are micro-bats. They use echolocation to find*
20 — *insects. A micro-bat can eat 1,000 mosquitoes a night.*
21 — <u>This controls mosquitoes and is good for the</u>
22 — <u>environment.</u>
23
24 — C = general = **In sum,** <u>that is how the lecture develops the topic of</u>
25 — <u>animal behavior.</u>

Step #5   **Task end.**

Your recorded response will be sent via internet to ETS for rating. Raters will rate your response with a rubric. OPDUL=C for integrated speaking (see pages 335-36) defines that rubric.

OPDUL=C → *Rating This Task*

The sample response on the previous page would score a 4/4 based on OPDU only. We cannot rate Language-Use (OPDU**L**=C). To rate Language-Use, we need to hear a recorded/live response. However, if you did demonstrate all aspects of OPDUL=C when speaking, including Language-Use, then your score would be 4/4.

How Long Should My Response Be?

The following map illustrates how to manage your time for this task.

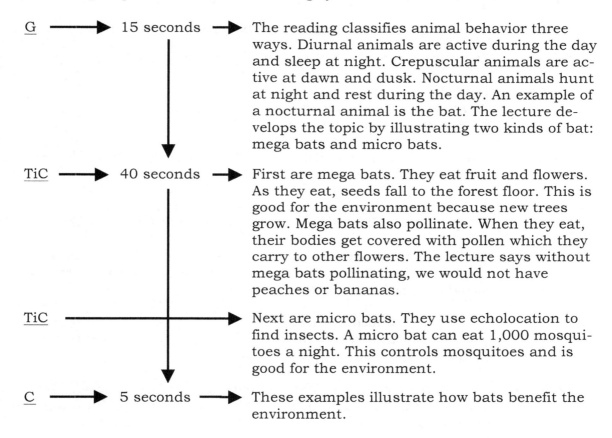

G → 15 seconds → The reading classifies animal behavior three ways. Diurnal animals are active during the day and sleep at night. Crepuscular animals are active at dawn and dusk. Nocturnal animals hunt at night and rest during the day. An example of a nocturnal animal is the bat. The lecture develops the topic by illustrating two kinds of bat: mega bats and micro bats.

TiC → 40 seconds → First are mega bats. They eat fruit and flowers. As they eat, seeds fall to the forest floor. This is good for the environment because new trees grow. Mega bats also pollinate. When they eat, their bodies get covered with pollen which they carry to other flowers. The lecture says without mega bats pollinating, we would not have peaches or bananas.

TiC → Next are micro bats. They use echolocation to find insects. A micro bat can eat 1,000 mosquitoes a night. This controls mosquitoes and is good for the environment.

C → 5 seconds → These examples illustrate how bats benefit the environment.

Common Problems for this Task

1. Lack of Development-Summarization --------------------

Test-takers tend to summarize the topic in one sentence, then start summarizing the supporting examples. When summarizing the topic, make sure you identify it and describe it in detail.

- **WARNING:** *A lack of Development-Summarization (OP**D**UL=C) of the topic and of the supporting illustrations will result in lack of Coherence (OPDUL=**C**) and a lower score.*

2. Blanking Out --

If you blank out, try and refocus. Listen for how the professor is connecting the topic to the details. Remember also that the professor will restate the topic and connect it to each detail, for example: "And that's why honey is so healthy. It is full of antioxidants." From this statement, we can infer that the lecture topic is honey and a supporting detail is its nutritional value (antioxidants). Note these and summarize accordingly.

Help! → *My Response is Too Long!*

The following are reasons why your response is longer than 60 seconds.

Reason #1   Your summary of the general topic is too long.

Solution
1. Make your summary shorter.
2. Avoid details like dates, places, costs, etc.
3. Speak faster; try not to hesitate.

Reason #2   When the clock starts, you are not speaking right away. That means you are losing valuable seconds at the start.

Solution
1. Start speaking right after the beep. <u>Remember</u>: *The speaking tasks come up fast. Be ready for them.*

Reason #3   You are being too careful. When you are too careful, you slow down to pronounce correctly. When you slow down, you waste time. You also decrease fluency and automaticity.

Solution
1. Speak at a normal pace.
2. Record your voice, then play it back. You will know if you are speaking too slowly. If so, speak faster.

Reason #4   You are pausing or hesitating too much. Record your voice and play it back. You will soon know if you are pausing or hesitating too much. Pausing and hesitating waste time. Pausing and hesitating will also decrease fluency and automaticity.

Solution
1. Practice reading sample responses for correct speed and accuracy.
2. Go to youtube.com. Google "How to speak like a native-English speaker." There are lots of great videos to help you speak more proficiently.

Reason #5   You are pausing or hesitating too much because you did not summarize the lecture using G+3TiC=C.

Solution
1. Memorize G+3TiC=C.
2. Practice one response over and over until you are confident summarizing the lecture using G+3TiC=C.

Reason #6   Your summary of the lecture contains too much information.

Solution   1. Summarize only the main topic in each supporting illustration.
2. Reduce the number of details (dates, costs, ages, etc.).

Reason #7   The conclusion is too long.

Solution   1. State the conclusion in one sentence.
2. State the conclusion in 5 seconds or less.

Reason #8   The clock makes you nervous so you blank out.

Solution   1. Do not time yourself when you practice. Just speak. When you are more confident, time yourself.

Help! → *My Response is Too Short!*

The following are reasons why your response is too short.

Reason #1   You are nervous. When you are nervous, you speak too fast and finish too soon.

Solution   1. Record your voice and play it back. You will soon know if you are speaking too fast. If so, slow down.
2. Do not time yourself. Just speak at a regular speed.

Reason #2   Your summary of the lecture is too short.

Solution   1. Make sure you have identified the main topic in the general introduction.
2. Make sure you have identified each supporting illustration in the body.

Reason #3   You speak, then suddenly stop because you are shy, afraid, or feel stupid.

Solution   1. Practice reading into a recording device. Read an English magazine article or a book while recording. This will help you develop confidence speaking into a microphone.
2. Take an ESL class to develop your speaking skills and confidence.
3. Practice. Practice. Practice.

Reason #4   You are not confident using G+3TiC=C.

Solution   1. Practice developing and delivering one response until you have memorized G+3TiC=C and can remember it automatically without notes.
2. Practice. Practice. Practice.

Reason #5   You blank out.

Solution   1. You are trying too hard or are too nervous. Try to relax. When
                 you practice speaking, don't time yourself. Just speak until you
                 are confident. When you are more confident, then time yourself.
              2. Don't worry about fluency, automaticity and pronunciation. Just
                 speak. The more you speak, the more confident you will become.

Speaking Practice

Using the strategies discussed, construct a response for the following tasks. Check
each response for <u>C</u>oherence using the *Integrated Speaking → Proficiency Checklist*
on page 335. Rate them using the *Integrated Speaking → Rating Guide* on page 336.

Task #1 → *Charles Darwin*

<u>Directions</u>: Listen to a lecture in a biology class.

<u>Prompt</u>: According to the lecture, how did Charles Darwin revolutionize agricul-
tural science?

Preparation Time = 20 seconds	Speaking Time = 60 seconds

audio script page 353

- -

Task #2 → *Estrogen and HRT*

<u>Directions</u>: Listen to a lecture in a women's studies class.

<u>Prompt</u>: The lecture talks about hormone replacement therapy (HRT).
Summarize the recent history of HRT usage in the United States and
its impact on women's health.

Preparation Time = 20 seconds	Speaking Time = 60 seconds

audio script page 353

Task #3 → *White-Collar Crime*

Directions: Listen to a lecture in a sociology class.

Prompt: How does the lecture define and develop the concept of white-collar crime?

Preparation Time = 20 seconds   Speaking Time = 60 seconds

audio script page 354

Task #4 → *Space Junk*

Directions: Listen to a lecture in an astronomy class.

Prompt: According to the lecture, what are the origins of space junk and why is it a problem?

Preparation Time = 20 seconds   Speaking Time = 60 seconds

audio script page 354

Task #5 → *Sharks*

Directions: Listen to a lecture in a marine biology class.

Prompt: What does the lecture teach us about sharks?

Preparation Time = 20 seconds   Speaking Time = 60 seconds

audio script page 355

Task #6 → *Aristotle's Three Appeals*

track #35

Directions: Listen to a lecture in a composition class.

Prompt: According to the lecture, what are Aristotle's three appeals? Use examples to support your summary.

Preparation Time = 20 seconds	Speaking Time = 60 seconds

audio script page 355

Calculating Your Speaking-Section Score

According to ETS, each spoken response will be scored by three raters from 0 to 4. The average of their raw scores will then be converted to a speaking section score from 0 to 30. For example, three raters scored your independent speaking task #1. The average of their raw scores is your raw score for speaking task #1.

$$\text{Rater 1} = 4.0/4$$
$$\text{Rater 2} = 4.0/4$$
$$\text{Rater 3} = 4.0/4$$

$$\text{average} = 12/12$$

12 / 3 raters = 4/4 = your averaged raw score for task #1

ETS will do the same for all six speaking tasks.

$$\text{Speaking Task 1} = 4.0/4$$
$$\text{Speaking Task 2} = 3.0/4$$
$$\text{Speaking Task 3} = 4.0/4$$
$$\text{Speaking Task 4} = 3.0/4$$
$$\text{Speaking Task 5} = 4.0/4$$
$$\text{Speaking Task 6} = 3.0/4$$

$$\text{total} = 21/24$$

21 / 6 tasks = 3.5/4 = your averaged raw speaking score

Your averaged raw speaking score (3.5) will then be converted to a speaking-section score out of 30 total points.

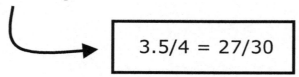

$$3.5/4 = 27/30$$

Listening Section

The listening section is the second section on the TOEFL test. It will last about 60 minutes. It measures your ability to understand "authentic" speech patterns used in academic (formal) and non-academic (informal) situations. Authentic-speech patterns include hesitations, self-corrections, repetitions, tone, and false starts. The task description follows.

PROMPT	NUMBER	LENGTH	QUESTIONS
Conversations	2-3	2-3 minutes each	5 per
Lectures	4-6	4-6 minutes each	6 per

- **REMEMBER:** *The questions are all multiple-choice. You will select answers with a mouse. You must answer the questions in order. You can take notes.*

- **REMEMBER:** *Before you begin, you will do a sound check. Follow the on-screen directions. Adjust the settings as needed. Alert the site manager to problems.*

Listening Section → *All Arguments*

The listening section consists of conversations, lectures, and discussions. They are all three-part arguments that can be mapped out using G+3TiC=C. Topically, the conversations are problem-solution scenarios while the lectures and discussions are academic arguments that teach, then test, you about the topic.

- **WARNING:** *You cannot replay the tasks or the questions, so take notes.*

- **REMEMBER:** *The clock will not run when you listen to a conversation or lecture. The clock will run only when you answer questions. You control how much time you need to answer each question.*

- **REMEMBER:** *When you listen, you will not see the questions on your screen. The questions will appear after the conversations and lectures end.*

- **REMEMBER:** *If you do not know an answer, guess. You will not lose points for a wrong answer, so answer everything. Never leave a question unanswered.*

Conversation Prompts

There are two types of conversation prompt: office-hours and service-encounters. You will hear one of each on test day. We start with office-hours.

Office-Hours Conversation

On test day, expect one office-hours prompt followed by five questions. For this prompt type, a student has an academic problem, such as late homework or a missed assignment. The student will ask his/her professor for advice. The professor will help the student solve his/her problem. This scenario is mapped out in the sample tapescript below.

Introduction Analysis → *Noting General Ideas*

The introduction serves three purposes: 1) to introduce the context; in this example, the context is a student asking a professor for help, 2) to introduce the topic; in this example, the topic is the student's last essay, and; 3) the problem: the student wants to know "why I didn't get an A?" Note each as you listen. These points are predictable, occur at the start, and are designed to teach you about the topic.

Introduction = General Information = <u>G</u>

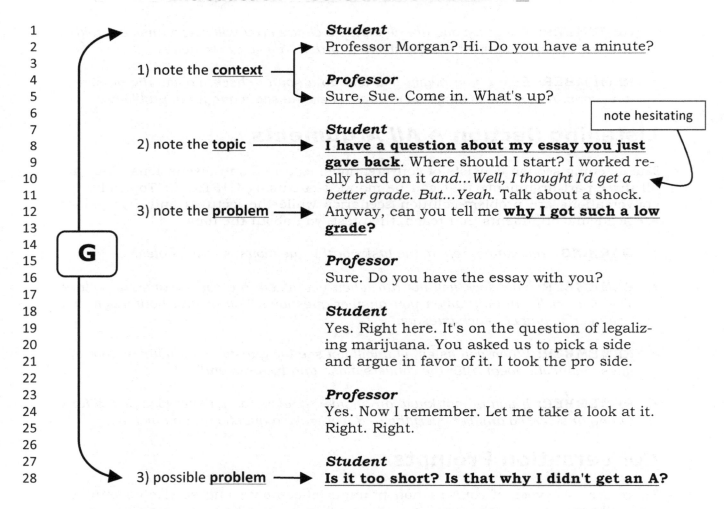

1
2
3   **Student**
4   1) note the **context** ──   Professor Morgan? Hi. Do you have a minute?
5   **Professor**
                                     Sure, Sue. Come in. What's up?
6   ┌─────────────────┐
7   **Student**   │ note hesitating │
8   2) note the **topic** ──→   **I have a question about my essay you just**
9   **gave back**. Where should I start? I worked re-
10   ally hard on it *and...Well, I thought I'd get a*
11   *better grade. But...Yeah.* Talk about a shock.
12   3) note the **problem** ──→   Anyway, can you tell me **why I got such a low**
13   **grade?**
14
     G
15   **Professor**
16   Sure. Do you have the essay with you?
17
18   **Student**
19   Yes. Right here. It's on the question of legaliz-
20   ing marijuana. You asked us to pick a side
21   and argue in favor of it. I took the pro side.
22
23   **Professor**
24   Yes. Now I remember. Let me take a look at it.
25   Right. Right.
26
27   **Student**
28   3) possible **problem** ──→   **Is it too short? Is that why I didn't get an A?**

- **REMEMBER:** *You will answer a general question about the introduction. It could be about the 1) context, 2) the topic, or 3) the student's problem. Note each.*

Body Analysis → *Noting Specific Ideas*

In the body, the professor will give advice. He/she will identify the student's problem areas and suggest solutions using cause-and-effect reasoning. Note below the three pieces of advice (3TiC) the professor gives the student about her essay.

Body = Specific Information = TiC

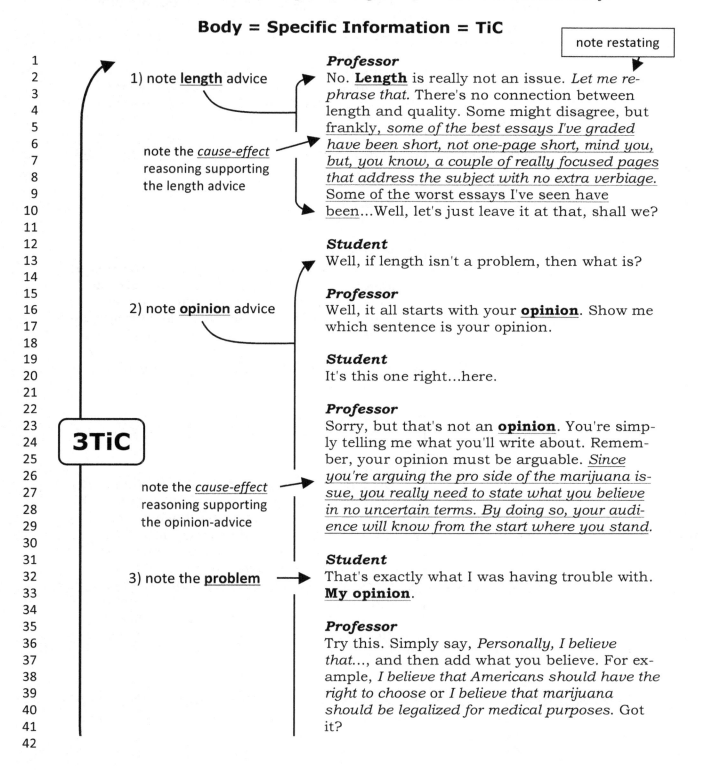

note restating

Professor

1) note **length** advice

No. **Length** is really not an issue. *Let me re-phrase that.* There's no connection between length and quality. Some might disagree, but frankly, *some of the best essays I've graded have been short, not one-page short, mind you, but, you know, a couple of really focused pages that address the subject with no extra verbiage.* Some of the worst essays I've seen have been...Well, let's just leave it at that, shall we?

note the *cause-effect* reasoning supporting the length advice

Student

Well, if length isn't a problem, then what is?

Professor

2) note **opinion** advice

Well, it all starts with your **opinion**. Show me which sentence is your opinion.

Student

It's this one right...here.

3TiC

Professor

Sorry, but that's not an **opinion**. You're simply telling me what you'll write about. Remember, your opinion must be arguable. *Since you're arguing the pro side of the marijuana issue, you really need to state what you believe in no uncertain terms. By doing so, your audience will know from the start where you stand.*

note the *cause-effect* reasoning supporting the opinion-advice

Student

3) note the **problem**

That's exactly what I was having trouble with. **My opinion**.

Professor

Try this. Simply say, *Personally, I believe that...*, and then add what you believe. For example, *I believe that Americans should have the right to choose* or *I believe that marijuana should be legalized for medical purposes.* Got it?

43
44
45
46
47
48   4) note **support** advice
49
50
51
52
53
54
55   note the *cause-effect*
56   reasoning supporting
57   the support advice
58
59
60
61
62   **3TiC**
63
64
65
66
67
68
69
70
71
72
73
74
75
76
77
78
79
80   note **advice**
81
82
83   note the *cause-effect*
84   reasoning supporting
85   the support advice
86
87

Student
Yeah. Okay. I see.

note restating

Professor
Also, your opinion must be supportable. When I say supportable, I mean each sentence—*sorry, I meant each body paragraph*—must have one specific topic, then you must develop that topic in detail. Look at body paragraph one. *You start off by saying "legalizing marijuana would be good for the economy" in the first sentence, then you suddenly switch to "it has many medical benefits" in the next sentence. This signals a clear lack of development of both topics.*

Student
But that's what I believe.

Professor
Yes. But now we're talking **the mechanics of developing and supporting your opinion**. Do so by giving each supporting topic its own body paragraph. In this case, *"legalizing marijuana would be good for the economy"* is the topic of your first body paragraph, and *"the medical benefits"* is the topic of your second body paragraph.

Student
You mean, do what I did in paragraph three?

Professor
Exactly. In body paragraph three, you focus on how legalizing marijuana will decrease the crime rate. However, you still need to develop this topic in detail. **Give an example**. One with statistics. You know what I mean. Do the same for body paragraphs one and two. *Remember: The more you develop your supporting examples, the more persuasive your argument will be. Right now, you're just scratching the surface. To be honest, this reads more like a first draft.*

- **REMEMBER:** *You will answer questions about specific information in the body. The most important specific information is the advice the professor gives the student, advice designed to help the student solve his/her problem. Note it.*

Conclusion Analysis → *Noting General Ideas*

By the conclusion, the professor will have solved the student's problem (Student: "I see what you mean."). The conclusion will typically suggest a future-action, such as the student below rewriting and handing in her essay for a higher grade.

Conclusion = General Information = C

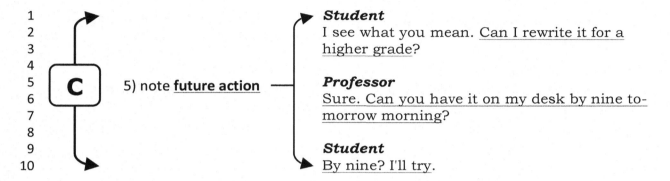

Student
I see what you mean. <u>Can I rewrite it for a higher grade?</u>

Professor
<u>Sure. Can you have it on my desk by nine tomorrow morning?</u>

Student
<u>By nine? I'll try.</u>

Rejoinders → *Identifying Topic Transitions*

In the conversation, topic transitions are signaled by rejoinders. A rejoinder is a short reply of affirmation. Rejoinders are transitional signal words telling you that *this is the conclusion of this topic and the start of the next*, for example:

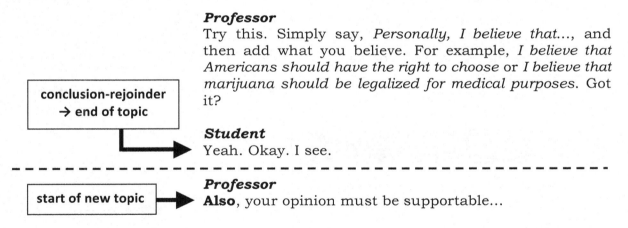

Professor
Try this. Simply say, *Personally, I believe that...*, and then add what you believe. For example, *I believe that Americans should have the right to choose* or *I believe that marijuana should be legalized for medical purposes*. Got it?

Student
Yeah. Okay. I see.

Professor
Also, your opinion must be supportable...

- **REMEMBER:** *Rejoinders are like road signs telling you a change is about to occur. The change, in this case, is a topic change. Note it as you listen.*

How to Listen → *Visualize the Argument* → 🎧 track #36

Next, listen to the same conversation, then answer the questions on the next page. As you listen, visualize how the ideas illustrated above progress from general to specific to general. By doing so, you will be able to anticipate and note the important ideas in the conversation, and answer questions more proficiently.

Sample Office-Hours Conversation → *Questions*

<u>Directions</u>: Now get ready to answer the questions. Answer each question based on what is stated or implied in the conversation.

#1

What are the student and the professor mainly discussing?

A) the student's opinion
B) the student's essay about illegal drugs
C) the student's attendance record
D) the student's most recent grade

#4

What does the professor think about short essays?

A) One focused page is best.
B) Short essays always get high grades.
C) A focused, short essay is best.
D) A short essay never has an opinion.

#2

Why does the student visit the professor?

A) to learn how to write better essays
B) to find out why she got a low grade on her essay
C) to discuss the pros and cons of the marijuana debate
D) to ask for an extension

#3

In which areas does the student's essay need revising? **Select two. This is a 1-point question.**

A) the developer
B) the body
C) the thesis
D) the sentence variety

#5

Listen again to part of the conversation, then answer the question.

What does the professor imply when she says this? 🎧

A) She thinks the student hates essay writing.
B) She thinks parts of the student's essay are scratched.
C) She thinks the student's essay lacks depth.
D) She thinks the student is on the wrong track.

This is an authentic speech-pattern question. It tests <u>Language</u>-Use. You cannot replay it.

This is a 2-point question. You must answer both right to get 1 point. One wrong = 0.

→ Answers page 318.
→ Scoring multi-answer questions page 328.

Expect the following questions on test day.

1. Content Questions

Content questions measure your ability to synthesize and paraphrase the main information in an office-hours prompt. Content questions can be paraphrased a variety of ways, for example:

- What is the student's problem?
- What topic are the student and the professor talking about?
- What is the focus of the conversation?

- **REMEMBER:** *Do not look for perfect answers. There are no perfect answers. Instead, look for the closest possible answer. If you do not know the answer, guess and move on. You will not be penalized for a wrong answer.*

- **WARNING:** *Do not change your answers. Classroom experience proves that test-takers who change their answers get them wrong. Trust your intuition.*

Look at a sample content question.

1. What are the student and the professor mainly discussing?

A) the student's opinion
B) the student's essay about illegal drugs
C) the student's attendance record
D) the student's most recent grade

Question Analysis: *Signal Words*

As you read the question, look for signal words. Signal words are clues that help you identify the topic of the question. Look at the following question. The signal words are the phrase <u>mainly discussing</u>. <u>Mainly discussing</u> means *generally talking about.*

1. What are the student and the professor <u>mainly discussing</u>?

- **WARNING:** *Test-takers often choose the wrong answer because they did not carefully read the question and identify the signal words. Read the question carefully. Make sure you understand it before you answer.*

- **WARNING:** *You can't change your answer after you have clicked "Ok" and "Next."*

Choice Analysis: *Process of Elimination*

After you have identified signal words in the question, analyze the answer choices using the strategy called *process of elimination.* Look for choices that are:

1) off topic	3) too general	5) not known
2) too specific	4) not true	6) not accurate

Next, read each answer choice carefully. As you read, analyze the language used. In the following example, choice C is off topic. The student and the professor do not discuss this topic. Because C is off topic, eliminate it as a choice.

1.   What are the student and the professor discussing?

         A)   the student's opinion
         B)   the student's essay about illegal drugs
off topic   C)   the student's attendance record
         D)   the student's most recent grade

Next, look at A. The student's opinion is a detail the student and the professor develop in the body of the conversation. A detail does not "mainly" (generally) describe the focus of the discussion. Because A is too specific, eliminate it as a choice.

1.   What are the student and the professor mainly discussing?

too specific A)   the student's opinion
            B)   the student's essay about illegal drugs
off topic   C)   the student's attendance record
            D)   the student's most recent grade

You now have two choices left: B and D. This is the position TOEFL wants you to be in. You now have a 50-50 chance of choosing the correct answer. But which one is correct? Both sound good. Yet one is correct and the other is *the distractor.*

Identifying the Distractor

One of the four answer choices will be a distractor. Distractors are designed to look and sound like the correct answer (see page 154, *Homophone Distractors*). Distractors test your listening and Language-Use proficiency, specifically your vocabulary. In the following example, B is the distractor.

1. What are the student and the professor mainly discussing?

too specific   A)   the student's opinion
distractor   **B)   the student's essay about illegal drugs**
off topic   C)   the student's attendance record
            D)   the student's most recent grade

Why is B the distractor? Look at it closely. Yes, the student and the professor are talking about "the student's essay." But did the student write an essay about one illegal drug or about many "illegal drugs"? She wrote about one drug: marijuana.

As you can see, B uses the plural "illegal drugs" to distract you into believing that illegal drugs means marijuana, the topic of the student's essay and the topic the student and the professor are "mainly discussing". This is how a distractor will test your Language-Use proficiency (OPDU**L**=C). That leaves D. D is correct because in the introduction, the student says, "I have a question about my essay you just gave back." In this context, "just gave back" means *most recent grade*, wherein *grade* is a synonym for essay. This, in turn, introduces the main topic, which the student and the professor discuss.

1. What are the student and the professor mainly discussing?

too specific	A) the student's opinion
distractor	B) the student's essay about illegal drugs
off topic	C) the student's attendance record
correct	**D) the student's most recent grade**

- **WARNING:** *Analyze each answer choice carefully. Classroom experience proves that test-takers often select the distractor because they did not carefully analyze the language used in each answer choice.*

Notes

_____

_____

_____

_____

_____

_____

_____

_____

_____

_____

_____

_____

_____

Practice: *Content Questions*

<u>Directions</u>: Listen to each prompt, then answer the question.

Audio Track #37

#1

Listen as a student talks to a professor.

What is the topic of discussion?

A) changing professors
B) changing classes
C) transferring majors
D) changing registrars

#2

Listen as a student talks to a professor.

What are the speakers mainly talking about?

A) The student's earthquake experience.
B) The student's academic record.
C) The student's new job.
D) The student's attendance record.

#3

Listen as a student talks to a professor.

What is the student's problem?

A) She always fails her presentations.
B) She always gets nervous in class.
C) She is nervous about her presentation.
D) She is too nervous to practice.

#4

Listen as a student talks to a professor.

What is the focus of the conversation?

A) the student's problem
B) illegal downloads
C) the student's need to save money
D) the course text

→ Answers page 318.
→ Audio script page 358.

2. Purpose Questions

Purpose questions measure your ability to identify reasons. A purpose question can be paraphrased a variety of ways, for example:

- Why is the student seeking the professor's help?
- Why does the student visit her professor?
- Why does the professor want to talk to the student?

Look at a sample purpose question.

1. Why does the student visit the professor?

A) to learn how to write better essays
B) to find out why she got a low grade on her essay
C) to discuss the pros and cons of the marijuana debate
D) to ask for an extension

Question Analysis: *Signal Words*

As you read the question, look for signal words. Look at the following question.

1. Why does the student visit the professor?

The signal words above are Why and visit. Why and visit point to a reason based on cause-and-effect.

Choice Analysis: *Process of Elimination*

After you have identified signal words in the question, analyze the answer choices using the process of elimination. Look for choices that are:

1) off topic	3) too general	5) not known
2) too specific	4) not true	6) not accurate

As you read each choice, analyze the language used. Eliminate choices you think fall into one of the above-six categories.

1. Why does the student visit the professor?

A) to learn how to write better essays
B) to find out why she got a low grade on her essay
not true C) to discuss the pros and cons of the marijuana debate
not true D) to ask for an extension

Identifying the Distractor

Next, identify the distractor. In this example, A is the distractor.

1. Why does the student visit the professor?

distractor	A)	to learn how to write better essays
correct	**B)**	**to find out why she got a low essay grade**
not true	C)	to discuss the pros and cons of the marijuana debate
not true	D)	to ask for an extension

From the conversation, we know that the student was unhappy about her low essay grade, so she went to her professor to discuss it. The professor told the student why she got a low grade, then advised her how to improve her essay; thus, A is a result of B. Also, did visiting the professor help the student write "better essays"? We do not know. Therefore, B is correct.

Notes

_____

_____

_____

_____

_____

_____

_____

_____

_____

_____

_____

_____

_____

_____

_____

_____

_____

Practice: *Purpose Questions*

<u>Directions</u>: Listen to each prompt, then answer the question.

Audio Track #38

#1

Listen as a student talks to a professor.

Why does the student visit the professor?

A) to get permission to use the lab
B) to get a tech job in security
C) to get his signature to use the lab
D) to approve his lab work

#2

Listen as a student talks to a professor.

What is the student's purpose for talking to her professor?

A) to see if her friend is attending a lecture
B) to see if her friend likes the professor
C) to see if her friend can attend a lecture
D) to get permission for her friend

#3

Listen as a student talks to a professor.

What does the student need clarified?

A) the cause of the American Revolution
B) the causes of the Canadian compact
C) the difference between Canadians
D) how Canadians and Americans view government

#4

Listen as a student talks to a professor.

Why did the professor ask to see the student?

A) to argue a woman's right to choose
B) to encourage her to publish her argument
C) to encourage her to rewrite her essay
D) to talk about agents and publishing

➔ Answers page 318.
➔ Audio script page 360.

3. Detail Questions: *Single-Answer*

Single-answer detail questions measure your ability to identify facts that support and develop the student's problem and the professor's advice-giving process. A single-answer detail question can be paraphrased a variety of ways, for example:

- What does the student say about her opinion?
- Why does the professor mention statistics?
- Why does the professor like the student's topic?

Look at a sample detail question.

1. What does the student say about her opinion?

A) She worked on it a long time.
B) It gave her ideas for another essay.
C) She thinks she did a good job.
D) It gave her a lot of trouble.

Question Analysis: *Signal Words*

As you read the question, look for signal words. The signal words in this question are student say about her opinion.

1. What does the student say about her opinion?

Choice Analysis: *Process of Elimination*

After you have identified signal words in the question, analyze the answer choices. Eliminate choices that are: 1) off topic; 2) too general; 3) not true; 4) not known; 5) not accurate; 6) too specific.

1. What does the student say about her opinion?

not known	A)	She worked on it a long time.
not known	B)	It gave her ideas for another essay.
distractor	C)	She thinks she did a good job.
correct	**D)**	**It gave her a lot of trouble.**

Identifying the Distractor

Next, identify the distractor. In the example above, C is the distractor. It is too general. "A good job" doing what? It is not clear. Therefore, D is correct. The student tells the professor on page 133, line 32 that she was "having trouble with [her opinion]."

Practice: *Single-Answer Detail Questions*

<u>Directions</u>: Listen as a student talks to a professor, then answer the questions.

#1 →

What can't the student do?

A) the presentation
B) biology
C) vivisection
D) the test

#2

What are the "objects of investigation"?

A) rats
B) mice
C) snakes
D) apes

#3 →

What can't be done virtually?

A) vivisection
B) the procedure
C) predicting the future
D) the course

#4

What percentage of the final grade is the assignment?

A) 4%
B) 14%
C) 30%
D) 40%

#5 →

What is the student dropping out of?

A) the program
B) school
C) the course
D) the experiment

#6

The professor says, "Life is full of..."

A) challenges
B) crossroads
C) assignments
D) choices

→ Answers page 318.
→ Audio script page 362.

4. <u>Detail Questions</u>: *Multi-Answer*

Multi-answer detail questions measure your ability to identify facts that support and develop the student's problem and/or the professor's advice-giving process. A multi-answer detail question can be paraphrased a variety of ways, for example:

- What does the professor say about the length of an essay?
- The professor says that each body paragraph must have...
- In which areas does the student's essay need revising?

Look at a sample question below. <u>Note</u>: Some questions have <u>3</u> answer choices.

1.   In which areas does the student's essay need revising?

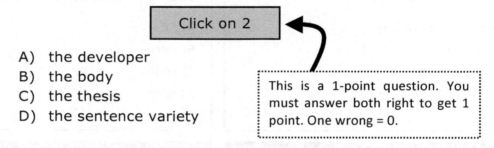

Click on 2

A) the developer
B) the body
C) the thesis
D) the sentence variety

This is a 1-point question. You must answer both right to get 1 point. One wrong = 0.

Question Analysis: *Signal Words*

As you read the question, look for signal words. The signal words in this question are <u>which areas</u>, <u>essay</u>, and <u>need revising</u>.

1.   In <u>which areas</u> does the student's <u>essay</u> <u>need revising</u>?

Choice Analysis: *Process of Elimination*

After you have identified signal words in the question, analyze the answer choices. Eliminate choices that are: 1) off topic; 2) too general; 3) not true; 4) not known; 5) not accurate; 6) too specific. As you read each choice, analyze the language used. Eliminate choices that fall into one of the above categories.

1.   In which areas does the student's essay need revising?

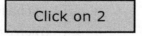

Click on 2

A) the developer
B) the body
C) the thesis
not known D) the sentence variety

Identifying the Distractor

Next, identify the distractor. In this example, A is the distractor. A is a noun for a person, i.e., a software developer. If it were *development*—a noun describing the condition of being developed, as in *essay development*—it would be correct. If you choose A, you would be confusing developer (person) with development (process). This is an example of how a noun with a similar spelling and sound, but with a different meaning, is a distractor. Your ability to distinguish between similarly spelled words and their meanings will test your Language-Use proficiency (OPDU**L**=C). A is also a homophone distractor (see page 154, *Homophone Distractors*).

1. In which areas does the student's essay need revising?

> Click on 2

distractor	A)	the developer
correct	**B)**	**the body**
correct	**C)**	**the thesis**
not known	D)	the sentence variety

This is a 1-point question. You must answer both right to get 1 point. One wrong = 0.

Notes

Practice: *Multi-Answer Detail Questions*

<u>Directions</u>: Listen to each prompt, then answer the question.

Audio Track #40

#1

Listen as a student talks to a professor.
This is a 2-point question.

What must the student do to complete the assignment? Select three.

A) give a presentation
B) hand in a list of interviewers
C) write a summary
D) hand in a bibliography
E) hand in a list of interviewees

#2

Listen as a student talks to a professor.
This is a 1-point question.

What does the student need from her professor? Select two.

A) an interview for a new job
B) letters recommending the position
C) signed letters of recommendation
D) to be interviewed by phone

#3

Listen as a student talks to a professor.
This is a 2-point question.

What will the student take to the Amazon? Select three.

A) malaria pills
B) malaria spray
C) bug pills
D) bug spray
E) a charger

#4

Listen as a student talks to a professor.
This is a 1-point question.

Which two graduate English degrees does the professor describe? Select two.

A) MBA
B) MFA
C) MA
D) PhD

➔ Answers page 318.
➔ Scoring multi-answer questions page 328.
➔ Audio script page 363.

5. Function Questions: *Authentic-Speech Patterns*

Function questions measure your ability to judge how a speaker uses authentic (natural) speech patterns, such as tone, hesitations, self-corrections, repetitions, restatements, idioms, and homophone distractors. There are two types of function question: question-first and segment-first.

- **REMEMBER:** *The headset symbol* *indicates a function question.*

Question-First

For this question type, you will hear the instructions followed by a question. You will then hear a dialogue segment and answer the question. You will not see the replayed dialogue text on your screen. It is here for demonstration purposes only.

Narrator: 6. Listen to part of a conversation, then answer the question.

              What does the student imply when she says this?

Student: "But...Yeah."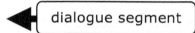

              A) She forgot what she wanted to say.

correct   **B) She is surprised by her low grade.**
              C) She is disappointed by her poor performance.
              D) She is not surprised she got a low grade.

Sometimes the segment comes before the question.

Narrator: 6. Listen to part of a conversation, then answer the question.

Student: "But...Yeah."

Narrator: What does the student imply when she says this?

              A) She forgot what she wanted to say.
              B) She is surprised by her low grade.
              C) She is disappointed by her poor performance.
              D) She is not surprised she got a grade.

Segment-First

For this question type, you will hear the instructions and an extended dialogue segment first. You will then hear the question. The question will be based on a replayed segment of the conversation, for example:

Narrator: 5. Listen to part of a conversation, then answer the question.

Professor: "Remember: the more you develop your supporting examples, the more persuasive your argument will be. Right now, you're just scratching the surface. To be honest, this reads more like a first draft."

Narrator: What does the professor imply when she says this?

Professor: "Right now, you're just scratching the surface. To be honest, this reads more like a first draft."

        A) She thinks the student hates essay writing.
        B) She thinks parts of the student's essay are scratched.
correct   **C) She thinks the student's essay lacks depth.**
        D) She thinks the student is on the wrong track.

TOEFL tests the following authentic-speech patterns.

a. Tone

Tone describes the emotion in a speaker's voice. Tone includes doubt, surprise, disbelief, excitement, anger, and relief. From a speaker's tone, we can infer meaning. Look at the dialogue segment below. The student thought she would get a high grade on her essay. We know because the student says, *"Talk about a shock."* On the audio track, the tone of surprise and disbelief in the student's voice matches her words. This is an example of inferring meaning from a speaker's tone.

Student

*I have a question about my essay you just gave back. Where should I start? I worked really hard on it and...Well, I thought I'd get a better grade. But...Yeah. **Talk about a shock**. Anyway, can you tell me why I got such a low grade?*

Look at a sample question.

Narrator: 9. Listen to part of a conversation, then answer the question.

        Why does the student say this?

Student: "Talk about a shock."

        A) because she thinks the professor made a mistake
        B) because she believes she deserves a better grade

correct **C) because her poor essay grade <u>surprised her</u>**
D) because the topic in her essay is quite shocking

The phrase <u>surprised her</u> in choice C means her low essay grade shocked and surprised her; therefore, C is correct. B is the distractor. Better grade in what subject area? We do not know. B is too general thus not correct.

- **REMEMBER:** *Note tone. It is a predictable testing point.*

b. Hesitation

In the dialogue segment below, the student says, *"But...Yeah."* This is a hesitation. Hesitating is an example of authentic-language use that includes tone as well.

Student
*I have a question about my essay you just gave back. Where should I start? I worked really hard on it and...Well, I thought I'd get a better grade. **But...Yeah.** Talk about a shock. Anyway, can you tell me why I got such a low grade?*

Look at a sample question.

Narrator: 5. Listen to part of a conversation, then answer the question.

What does the student imply when she says this?

Student: "But...Yeah."

A) She forgot what she wanted to say.
correct **B) She is surprised by her low grade.**
C) She is disappointed by her poor performance.
D) She is not surprised she got a low grade.

To answer this question correctly, we must infer that the student thought she was going to get a higher grade. She was going to say, *"But...[I really thought I was going to get a higher grade],"* then hesitated and stopped. "Yeah" infers *"Wow, was I wrong and surprised—and now I'm speechless."* Therefore, B is correct. Her tone of surprise supports B. C is the distractor. Poor performance in what area? We do not know. As a result, C is too general thus not correct.

- **REMEMBER:** *Note hesitations. They are predictable testing points.*

c. Self-Correction

In the dialogue segment on the next page, the professor says, *"—sorry, I meant each body paragraph."* This is an example of a self-correction. Self-correcting is an example of authentic-language use.

Professor
*Also, your opinion must be supportable. When I say supportable, I mean each sentence—**sorry, I meant each body paragraph**—must have one specific topic, then you must develop that topic in detail.*

Look at a sample question.

Narrator: 4. Listen to part of a conversation, then answer the question.

Why does the professor say this?

Professor: "Sorry, I meant each body paragraph."

correct   **A) She made a mistake and is correcting it.**
B) She wants to change the topic.
C) She feels the student doesn't know what she means.
D) She thinks the student should rethink her topic.

In English, "Sorry, I meant" signals a self-correction. In this case, the professor did not mean "each sentence." Instead, the professor meant "each body paragraph." The professor recognized her mistake and self-corrected. Therefore, A is correct. Her apologetic tone ("sorry") supports A. The distractor is B. Change the topic to what? We do not know. As a result, B is too general thus not correct.

- **REMEMBER:** *Note self-corrections. They are predictable testing points.*

d. Repetition

In the dialogue segment below, the professor says, *"Right. Right."* This is an example of repetition. Repetition is an example of authentic-language use.

Professor
*Yes. Now I remember. Let me take a look at it. **Right. Right.***

Look at a function question based on this repetition.

Narrator: 5. Listen to part of a conversation, then answer the question.

Why does the professor say this?

Professor: "Right. Right."

A) because by looking at the student, the professor remembers the student
B) because the professor believes the student did the right thing coming to see her
correct   **C) because the professor is <u>confirming</u> that she remembers the student's essay**
D) because the professor is approving the student's revisions

By repeating "Right. Right," the professor signals that she is reading the student's essay. As she reads, she remembers and <u>confirms</u> the fact by repeating, "Right. Right." In this context, "Right. Right" means, "Yes, yes. Now I remember this essay." The tone in the professor's voice confirms C thus C is correct. D is the distractor. The positive tone in the professor's voice could infer approval. However, we know that the student is there to discuss a problem not get approval; thus, D is the distractor.

- **REMEMBER:** *Note repetitions. They are predictable testing points.*

e. Restatement

In the dialogue segment below, the professor says ***In other words***. This is a restatement. Restating is a process of redefining for greater understanding or coherence. It is an example of authentic-language use.

Professor
Carcharodon carcharias is a rapacious killing machine. **In other words**, *the great white shark will eat anything that enters the water.*

Look at a sample question.

Narrator: 5. Listen to part of a conversation, then answer the question.

Why does the professor say this?

Professor: "**In other words**, the great white shark will eat anything that enters the water.

A) to give examples of sharks
B) to signal that the lecture is on great white sharks

correct   **C) to redefine his main point in simpler terms**
D) to warn about the dangers of entering the water

In the dialogue segment, the phrase ***In other words*** signals that the professor is restating (redefining) a prior point for greater coherence. That point is the Latin name for the great white shark ("*Carcharodon carcharias*") and its eating habits ("rapacious killing machine"). Since we probably do not understand Latin (and may not know the meaning of rapacious), the professor translates the Latin name of the great white shark into English and "rapacious killing machine" into "[it] will eat anything." As you can see, this restatement simplifies and clarifies the Latin definition of the great white shark for greater coherence; therefore, C is correct.

B is the distractor. Yes, the lecture is on great white sharks; however, the prepositional phrase "in other words" infers the process of restating-redefining to simplify for greater understanding. B does not indicate this process. It is, instead, off topic. As a result, it is not correct.

- **REMEMBER:** *Note restatements. They are predictable testing points.*

f. <u>Idioms</u>

To understand an idiom's function, you must infer its meaning specific to the context in which the idiom is used. This process is called contextualizing. Look at the dialogue segment below. The professor says, *"Right now, you're just scratching the surface."* This idiom is an example of authentic-language use.

> **Professor**
> *Right now, you're just scratching the surface.*

Look at a question based on this idiom.

Narrator: 4. Listen to part of a conversation, then answer the question. What does the professor imply when she says this?

Professor: "Right now, you're just scratching the **surface**."

A) She thinks the student hates essay writing.
B) She thinks parts of the student's essay are scratched.
correct   **C) She thinks the student's essay lacks <u>depth</u>.**
D) She thinks the student is on the wrong track.

In the dialogue segment, note the word **surface**. Surface means shallow or not deep. Note the noun **depth** in choice C. In this context, depth means very deep or a lot of hard work. "Lacks depth" in choice C, however, means a lack of work. A lack of work = a lack of development. Instead of being deep into the topic (well-developed because of hard work), the student's essay is still on the **surface** (not well-developed because of a lack of work). As you can see, the idiom the professor uses functions both as a statement of fact and as an indirect warning ("You need to work harder if you want a higher grade"). Therefore, C is correct. B is a homophone distractor (see *Homophone Distractors* below) thus not correct.

• **REMEMBER:** *Note idioms. They are predictable testing points.*

g. <u>Homophone Distractors</u>

Homophone is a Greek word that means *having the same sound*. In choice B below, the homophone distractor is <u>scratched</u>. It sounds like—and has the same root as—<u>scratching</u> in the replayed segment. Therefore B is a homophone distractor and C is correct.

Professor: "Right now, you're just **scratching** the surface. To be honest, this reads more like a first draft."

A) She thinks the student hates essay writing.
B) She thinks parts of the student's essay are **scratched**.
C) She thinks the student's essay lacks depth.
D) She thinks the student is on the wrong track.

If you thought B was the answer because <u>scratched</u> and <u>scratching</u> share the same sound and root (same sound + same root = answer!), then you will have done what TOEFL expected you would do: fallen into the homophone-distractor trap.

- **WARNING:** *If an answer choice shares the same root and sound, and/or is spelled the same as a signal word in the question, it is a homophone distractor. Do not select it. Do not fall into the homophone-distractor trap.*

- **REMEMBER:** *Note homophones. Do not choose them.*

Notes

_____

_____

_____

_____

_____

_____

_____

_____

_____

_____

_____

_____

_____

_____

_____

_____

_____

_____

_____

_____

_____

_____

_____

Practice: *Question-First Function Questions*

Directions: Answer each question based on what is stated or implied.

Audio Track #41

#1

Why does the professor say this?

A) to help the student with late homework assignments
B) to warn the student that he is always late with work
C) to encourage the student to complete all the homework assignments
D) to warn the student that he is not following the homework policy

---

#2

Why does the professor say this?

A) to bring the student up to date
B) to remind the student that he must research the topic of Rome and taxes
C) to summarize a point made in the lecture
D) to help the student make the connection between armies and populations

---

#3

Why does the professor say this?

A) to avoid talking to the student
B) to suggest another time to meet
C) to invite the student to lunch
D) to remind the student that he can't meet because it is raining

---

#4

Why does the student say this?

A) to explain the results of her research
B) to signal her excitement over the find
C) to explain the importance of research
D) to signal that she needs only a minute to explain her research topic

---

→ Answers page 318.
→ Audio script page 365.

Practice: *Segment-First Function Questions*

<u>Directions</u>: Answer each question based on what is stated or implied.

#1 →

Listen to part of a conversation, then answer the question.

Why does the professor say this?

A) to repeat her point for accuracy
B) to signal that she will try to make her point clearer
C) to point out her mistake by rephrasing it
D) to teach the student about rephrasing

#2

Listen to part of a conversation, then answer the question.

Why does the professor say this?

A) to explain how easy it is to steal music
B) to stress her point through repetition
C) to summarize an important point
D) to support her point with historical facts

#3 →

Listen to part of a conversation, then answer the question.

What does the professor mean when he says this?

A) Computer modeling is important.
B) Computer modeling is out of date.
C) Computer modeling is dangerous.
D) Computer modeling is popular.

#4

Listen to part of a conversation, then answer the question.

What does the professor mean when she says this?

A) to acknowledge her mistake
B) to make the comparison clearer
C) to express her anger
D) to indicate a change in topic

→ Answers page 318.
→ Audio script page 365.

6. Direct-Attitude Questions

Attitude questions measure your ability to identify a speaker's opinion (also called position or stance), degree of certainty, and/or feelings. Direct attitude means the speaker's opinion is stated as a fact. Direct-attitude questions can be paraphrased a variety of ways, for example:

- What does the professor think about short essays?
- What is the professor's opinion of the student's essay?
- How does the student feel about her last essay grade?

Look at a sample question.

1. What does the professor think about short essays?

A) One focused page is best.
B) Short essays always get high grades.
C) A short, focused essay is best.
D) A short essay never has an opinion.

Question Analysis: *Signal Words*

As you analyze the question, identify <u>signal words</u>.

1. What does the <u>professor think about short essays?</u>

Choice Analysis: *Process of Elimination*

After you have identified signal words in the question, use the process of elimination to eliminate choices that are: 1) off topic; 2) too general; 3) not true; 4) not known; 5) not accurate; 6) too specific.

1. What does the professor think about short essays?

	A)	One <u>focused</u> page is best.
not known	B)	Short essays always get high grades.
	C)	A short, <u>focused</u> essay is best.
not true	D)	A short essay never has an opinion.

Identifying the Distractor

Note above how, by the process of elimination, A and C are the best choices. Note also that both contain the adjective "<u>focused</u>." Which answer is right and which is the distractor, "focused page" or "focused essay"? The answer will depend on the accuracy of your notes.

Choice A below is the distractor. The professor does not directly (factually) state that *"one focused page is best."* Instead, she directly states that some of the *"best essays"* she has read were only *"a couple of really focused pages...not one-page short, mind you..."* Therefore, C is correct. The professor is directly addressing the topic of essay length (C), and not the quality of one page of writing (A).

1. What does the professor think about short essays?

distractor	A)	One focused page is best.
not true	B)	Short essays always get high grades.
correct	**C)**	**A short, focused essay is best.**
not true	D)	A short essay never has an opinion.

Notes

_____

_____

_____

_____

_____

_____

_____

_____

_____

_____

_____

_____

_____

_____

_____

_____

_____

_____

_____

Practice: *Direct-Attitude Questions*

Directions: Listen to each prompt, then answer the questions.

Audio Track #43

#1

Listen as a student talks to a professor.

What does the professor believe?

A) The debating team will lose terribly.
B) The debating team will run out of time.
C) The debating team will win decisively.
D) The debating team will enjoy the challenge.

#2

Listen as a student talks to a professor.

What does the student believe?

A) Her presentation was great.
B) Her presentation was awful.
C) Her presentation needs more work.
D) Her presentation was a failure.

#3

Listen as a student talks to a professor.

What is the student's opinion of grades?

A) They are not part of the rewriting process.
B) They are necessary.
C) They are superfluous.
D) They really mean a lot.

#4

Listen as a student talks to a professor.

What is the professor's opinion of the student's thesis?

A) It is arguable therefore a thesis.
B) It needs more facts.
C) It is perfect for the topic.
D) It is not an opinion but a fact.

➜ Answers page 319.
➜ Audio script page 366.

7. Inferred-Attitude Questions

Inferred attitude means the speaker's opinion or position is not stated as a fact in the conversation. Instead, it is suggested or implied. From the suggestion or implication, you must infer a conclusion based on the facts presented. Inferred-attitude questions can be paraphrased a variety of ways, for example:

- What does the professor imply about long essays?
- What can we infer about the student's essay?
- What can we infer about the professor's submission policy?

Look at a sample question.

1. What can we infer about the professor's submission policy?

A) Her assignments are based on controversial topics.
B) She permits a rewrite for an improved grade.
C) Her submission policy changes regularly.
D) She gives her students all the time they need to rewrite.

Question Analysis: *Signal Words*

As you analyze the question, identify signal words.

1. What can we infer about the professor's submission policy?

Choice Analysis: *Process of Elimination*

Listen to the conclusion ending the sample conversation, track #36, then analyze the question below. Use process of elimination to eliminate choices that are: 1) off topic; 2) too general; 3) not true; 4) not known; 5) not accurate; 6) too specific.

1. What can we infer about the professor's submission policy?

not known A) Her assignments are based on controversial topics.
B) She permits a rewrite for an improved grade.
not known C) Her submission policy changes regularly.
D) She gives her students all the time they need to rewrite.

Identifying the Distractor

In the question on the next page, D is the distractor. From the sample conclusion, it is clear that the student can rewrite her essay for a better grade. Yes, the professor gives her more time, but not *"all the time [the student needs] to rewrite."* The student must hand in the rewrite the next morning. Therefore, B is correct.

1.   What can we infer about the professor's submission policy?

not known A) Her assignments are based on controversial topics.

correct B) She permits a rewrite for an improved grade.

not known C) Her submission policy changes regularly.

distractor D) She gives her students all the time they need to rewrite.

Notes

_____

_____

_____

_____

_____

_____

_____

_____

_____

_____

_____

_____

_____

_____

_____

_____

_____

_____

_____

_____

Practice: *Inferred-Attitude Questions*

Directions: Listen to each prompt, then answer the question.

Audio Track #44

#1

Listen as a student talks to a professor.

What can we infer about having the debate outside?

A) The professor approves of the idea.
B) The professor is against the idea.
C) The professor needs a change of pace.
D) The professor needs time to think it over.

#2

Listen as a student talks to a professor.

What can we infer from the conversation?

A) The student will rewrite her essay.
B) The student will ask for more time.
C) The student will change her opinion.
D) The student will avoid using clichés.

#3

Listen as a student talks to a professor.

What is the professor suggesting?

A) The student must not attend class with his cell phone.
B) The student must look for a new job.
C) The student must change phones.
D) The student is not following school policy regarding cell phones.

#4

Listen as a student talks to another student.

How does the man feel about having a chicken for a mascot?

A) He thinks it is a novel idea.
B) He would prefer the Earth instead.
C) He is far from persuaded.
D) He thinks it will be good for school spirit.

→ Answers page 319.
→ Audio script page 367.

8. Inferred-Action Questions

Inferred-action questions measure your ability to identify what action a speaker will do next or in the future. To answer this question type, you must make an inference based on the facts presented in the conversation. Inferred-action questions can be paraphrased a variety of ways, for example:

- What will the student do next?
- What will the student probably do tonight?
- What will the professor look for in the rewritten essay?

Look at a sample question.

1. What will the student probably do tonight?

A) She will do homework.
B) She will think about her professor's advice.
C) She will rewrite her opinion.
D) She will rewrite her essay.

Question Analysis: *Signal Words*

As you analyze the question, identify signal words.

1. What will the student probably do tonight?

Choice Analysis: *Process of Elimination*

Listen to the conclusion of the sample conversation, track #36 (page 135), then analyze the question below. Eliminate choices that are: 1) off topic; 2) too general; 3) not true; 4) not known; 5) not accurate; 6) too specific.

1. What will the student probably do tonight?

not known A) She will do homework.
not known B) She will think about her professor's advice.
distractor C) She will rewrite her opinion.
correct D) She will rewrite her essay.

Identifying the Distractor

Choice C is the distractor. Yes, the student will rewrite her opinion. We can infer this from the conclusion. However, her opinion is part of her essay. Therefore, D is correct. In the end, the student says, *"I'll try."* Try what? Try to rewrite her essay that night so she can hand it in *"By nine tomorrow morning"*, as the professor says.

Practice: *Inferred-Action Questions*

<u>Directions</u>: Listen to each prompt, then answer the question.

Audio Track #45

#1

Listen as a student talks to a professor.

What will the professor probably do?

A) give the student an A+
B) tell the student to rewrite his essay
C) suggest that the student try and publish his work
D) give the student an average grade

#2

Listen as a student talks to a professor.

We can infer from the conversation that the professor has not...

A) been to a mall
B) visited a high-tech recruitment center
C) listened to the student's comments
D) been in the military

#3

Listen as a student talks to a professor.

From the conversation, we can infer that the student will probably continue to...

A) disagree with her professor
B) support the right to privacy
C) disagree with the government
D) drop out of the class

#4

Listen as a student talks to a professor.

What will student probably do?

A) look for a job on Wall Street
B) look for a job in qualitative finance
C) ask the professor for a recommendation
D) expand her job search

→ Answers page 319.
→ Audio script page 368.

Service-Encounter Conversation

On test day, expect one service-encounter conversation followed by five questions. For this prompt, a campus employee will help a student solve a campus-related issue, such as a parking ticket, a bad roommate, or applying for a scholarship. This prompt, like an office-hours conversation, is a problem-solution task.

- **REMEMBER:** *Structurally, a service-encounter conversation is the same as an office-hours conversation. Both are problem-solution tasks with three parts: intro, body, conclusion. The difference is the characters and the context. An office-hours conversation is academic (student-professor); whereas, a service-encounter is non-academic (student-employee).*

- **REMEMBER:** *Service-encounter questions are the same as office-hours questions.*

How to Listen → *Visualize the Argument* → track #46

Next, listen to a service-encounter conversation, then answer the questions on the next page. As you listen, visualize how the ideas progress from general to specific to general. By doing so, you will be able to anticipate and note the student's problems and the solutions, and answer questions more proficiently.

Notes

_____

_____

_____

_____

_____

_____

_____

_____

_____

_____

_____

_____

_____

_____

Sample Service-Encounter Conversation → *Questions*

<u>Directions</u>: Now get ready to answer the questions. Answer each question based on what is stated or implied in the conversation.

#1

What are the student and the IT staffer mainly discussing?

A) the student's new iPhone
B) the student's wi-fi issue
C) the school's security system
D) the latest virus going around

#2

What is the student's problem?

A) Her new iPod has a virus.
B) She needs a new wi-fi connection.
C) She can't connect to the school's wireless network.
D) She is having problems with the net-work.

#3

What are the wireless security settings? Select three. This is a 2-point question.

A) WPA
B) WEP2
C) WEP
D) WPA2
E) WPA-A

#4

Why does the student say this?

A) because IT-support fixed her iPod
B) because IT-support was helpful
C) because IT-support disconnected her
D) because IT-support solved her issue

#5

Listen again to part of the conversation, then answer the question.

What does the student mean by this?

A) She needs more information.
B) She is missing the point.
C) She understands completely.
D) She is apologizing for her mistake.

→ Answers page 319.
→ Scoring multi-answer questions page 328.
→ Audio script page 370.

Expect the following questions on test day.

1. Practice: *Content Questions*

<u>Directions</u>: Listen to each prompt, then answer the question.

Audio Track #47

#1

Listen as a student talks to a security guard.

What is the main topic of discussion?

A) the student's parking ticket
B) the color of the parking lines
C) the lack of parking space
D) when the garage will close

#2

Listen as a student talks to an admin.

What is the focus of the conversation?

A) the student's ID card
B) the recent policy memo about tuition
C) the school's new policy
D) the government cutting back

#3

Listen as a student talks to a security guard.

What is the subject of discussion?

A) opening the lab
B) calling security
C) accessing the bio lab
D) completing an assignment

#4

Listen as a student talks to a librarian.

What is the subject of discussion?

A) a book the library has
B) a book the student has requested
C) a book the student wants to borrow
D) a book the library does not have

→ Answers page 319.
→ Audio script page 371.

2. **Practice:** *Purpose Questions*

Directions: Listen to each prompt, then answer the question.

#1

Listen as a student talks to an admin.

Why does the student visit financial aid?

A) to get course information
B) to learn about borrowing money
C) to pay back money borrowed
D) to find out about scholarships

#2

Listen as a student talks to maintenance.

Why does the student call maintenance?

A) to report a problem with her laptop
B) to report a wild animal problem
C) to report a problem with her room
D) to report a problem with her dorm

#3

Listen as a student talks to a security guard.

Why does the student visit security?

A) to get her stolen laptop back
B) to fill out a report
C) to request an investigation
D) to try and find her missing laptop

#4

Listen as a student talks to an admin.

Why does the student talk to the admin?

A) to buy tickets for her boyfriend and his family
B) to buy and sell game tickets on eBay
C) to purchase tickets for the big game
D) to purchase tickets for her boyfriend's family

➔ Answers page 319.
➔ Audio script page 373.

3. **Practice:** *Single-Answer Detail Questions*

<u>Directions</u>: Listen as a student talks to a campus employee, then answer the questions.

#1

To whom does the student speak?

A) the manager of an art gallery
B) the manager of the school's gallery
C) the editor of Art House Magazine
D) her art professor

#2

What can't the student remember?

A) the last time she bought computer parts
B) the last time she talked to her professor
C) the last time she bought art material
D) the last time she went to class

#3

What is the student pushing with her art?

A) the envelope
B) her portfolio
C) her prices
D) her schedule

#4

How long will the student's exhibition last?

A) a month
B) two weeks
C) one week
D) a day

#5

How many days does the student have to prepare her exhibition?

A) three
B) two
C) seven
D) one

#6

Who is Karen Goldblatt?

A) a magazine publisher
B) the student's art professor
C) an art expert
D) a famous artist

➔ Answers page 319.
➔ Audio script page 375.

4. Practice: *Multi-Answer Detail Questions*

<u>Directions</u>: Listen to each prompt, then answer the question.

#1

Listen as a student talks to an admin. This is a 1-point question.

What information is required for the scholarship application? Select two.

A) a driver's license
B) high grades
C) letters of recommendation
D) volunteer experience

#2

Listen as a student talks to a librarian. This is a 1-point question.

Which books does the student put on reserve? Select two.

A) Howard's Human Prehistory
B) Mitchell's Methods of Archeology
C) Swift-Lee's Guide to Ancient Tools
D) Swift-Scott's Guide to Ancient Tools

#3

Listen as a student talks to an admin. This is a 1-point question.

How will the student pay for the tickets? Select two.

A) half Visa
B) half debit card
C) half cash
D) half MasterCard

#4

Listen as a student talks to a campus employee. This is a 1-point question.

What did the student order? Select two.

A) Pepsi
B) chicken wrap with onions, cheese, and jalapenos
C) turkey wrap with avocado and sprouts
D) Coke

➔ Answers page 319.
➔ Scoring multi-answer questions page 328.
➔ Audio script page 376.

5. <u>Practice</u>: *Question-First Function Questions*

<u>Directions</u>: Answer each question based on what is stated or implied.

Audio Track #51

#1 →

Why does the student say this?

A) to indicate that his Visa card is lost; therefore, he can't pay for the tickets
B) to explain that he has a lot of Visa cards
C) to indicate that he needs to use up the maximum amount available on his card
D) to indicate that he can't use his Visa because he has reached his limit

---

#2

Why does the admin say this?

A) to stress that the student needs as many high grades as possible
B) to emphasize the fact that high grades are given to good students only
C) to remind the student that he must give his grades to the financial office
D) to stress that high grades are important when applying for a scholarship

---

#3 →

Why does the student say this?

A) to suggest a growing interest
B) to suggest that she has no money
C) to suggest that it is time to leave
D) to suggest a lack of interest

#4

Why does the student say this?

A) to express her joy and excitement
B) to express her shock and surprise
C) to express her doubt and confusion
D) to express her love and affection

→ Answers page 320.
→ Audio script page 377.

6. Practice: *Segment-First Function Questions*

<u>Directions:</u> Listen to each prompt, then answer the question.

Audio Track #52

#1

Listen to part of a conversation, then answer the question.

Why does the student say this?

A) because she wants to reserve the book
B) because she does not want to reserve *Methods of Archeology*
C) because *Guide to Tools* is a better book
D) because she wants to reserve all three books

#2

Listen to part of a conversation, then answer the question.

What does security mean by this?

A) the student must pay the fine
B) the student does not have to pay the fine
C) the student needs to move her car
D) security will report the student

#3

Listen to part of a conversation, then answer the question.

What does the student mean by this?

A) You can say that again.
B) Tell me once more, please.
C) Of course.
D) Fantastic, isn't it?

#4

Listen to part of a conversation, then answer the question.

What does the student mean by this?

A) I prefer Coke.
B) Pepsi is fine.
C) I want neither Coke nor Pepsi.
D) I want to cancel my order.

➜ Answers page 320.
➜ Audio script page 378.

7. Practice: *Direct-Attitude Questions*

<u>Directions</u>: Listen to each prompt, then answer the question.

Audio Track #53

#1

Listen then answer the question.

How does the student feel about getting a scholarship?

A) amused
B) indifferent
C) relieved
D) worried

#2

Listen then answer the question.

What is the student's opinion of *Dummies* books?

A) You get a lot for a great price.
B) They are overpriced and lacking detail.
C) You never know what you will get.
D) They cover every subject.

#3

Listen then answer the question.

How does the student feel about putting titles on her work?

A) She loves to think up new titles.
B) She thinks it is a good idea for her show.
C) She thinks her titles are original.
D) She is against the idea.

#4

Listen then answer the question.

What does the admin think about buying so many tickets?

A) It is definitely not a wise idea.
B) It is definitely a risky decision.
C) It is definitely a great idea.
D) It is definitely worth considering.

→ Answers page 320.
→ Audio script page 379.

8. Practice: *Inferred-Attitude Questions*

<u>Directions</u>: Listen to each prompt, then answer the question.

#1

Listen then answer the question.

How does the student feel about the new policy?

A) She can't support it.
B) She can't afford it.
C) She can't allow it.
D) She can't believe it.

#2

Listen then answer the question.

What does the student think about selling his used texts on eBay?

A) It's a great idea.
B) It's too complicated.
C) It's not an option.
D) It's fast and convenient.

#3

Listen then answer the question.

How does the admin react to the student's request?

A) mysteriously
B) sympathetically
C) skeptically
D) suspiciously

#4

Listen then answer the question.

How does the student feel about the staffer's help?

A) wonderful
B) excited
C) grateful
D) fruitful

➔ Answers page 320.
➔ Audio script page 380.

9. Practice: *Inferred-Action Questions*

<u>Directions</u>: Listen to each prompt, then answer the question.

Audio Track #55

#1 →

Listen then answer the question.

Where will the student probably go?

A) to pick up her reward
B) to financial aid
C) to the scholarship office
D) to the bank

#2

Listen then answer the question.

What will the student probably do?

A) go to the campus security office
B) buy a new cell phone
C) call campus security later
D) buy a silicone sleeve with red hearts

#3 →

Listen then answer the question.

What will the student probably do?

A) buy the book
B) reserve the book
C) pay the fine
D) contest the fine

#4

Listen then answer the question.

What will the student probably do?

A) reconsider taking the class
B) come back next week
C) make an appointment
D) get a medical release form

 Answers page 320.
→ Audio script page 381.

Lecture → *Professor Only*

On test day, expect 3-4 professor-only lectures followed by six questions. The professor will give a short lecture on an academic topic. You cannot replay the lecture.

Lecture Analysis → *Noting General and Specific Ideas*

The lecture will develop predictably. The ideas will progress from general to specific to general. Note those points below. Expect questions on those points.

- **REMEMBER:** *The introduction (G) will be short. If you are not paying attention, you will miss the topic. If you miss the topic, you will miss the most important part of the lecture—and the question on it.*

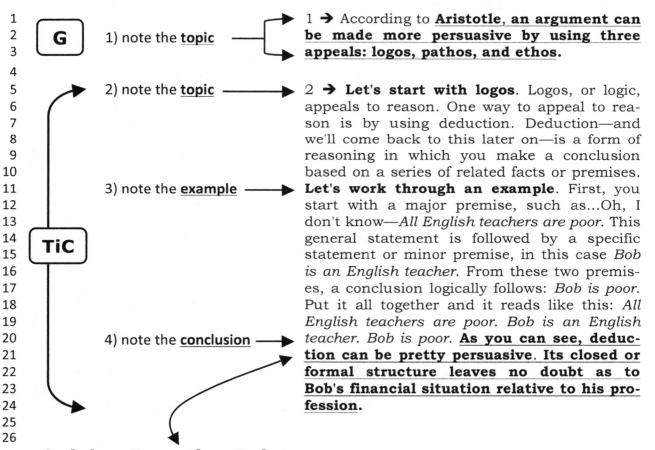

1
2   **G**   1) note the **topic** ——→ 1 → According to **Aristotle, an argument can be made more persuasive by using three appeals: logos, pathos, and ethos.**
3
4
5   2) note the **topic** ——→ 2 → **Let's start with logos**. Logos, or logic, appeals to reason. One way to appeal to reason is by using deduction. Deduction—and we'll come back to this later on—is a form of reasoning in which you make a conclusion based on a series of related facts or premises.
6
7
8
9
10
11   3) note the **example** ——→ **Let's work through an example**. First, you start with a major premise, such as...Oh, I don't know—*All English teachers are poor*. This general statement is followed by a specific statement or minor premise, in this case *Bob is an English teacher*. From these two premises, a conclusion logically follows: *Bob is poor*. Put it all together and it reads like this: *All English teachers are poor. Bob is an English teacher. Bob is poor.* **As you can see, deduction can be pretty persuasive. Its closed or formal structure leaves no doubt as to Bob's financial situation relative to his profession.**
12
13
14   **TiC**
15
16
17
18
19
20   4) note the **conclusion** ——→
21
22
23
24
25
26

Opinion-Insertion Points

The professor will insert his/her opinion throughout. Opinion-insertion points are often in the Conclusions, ("As you can see, deduction can be pretty persuasive.")

- **REMEMBER:** *Note professor and student opinion-insertion points. They are predictable testing points.*

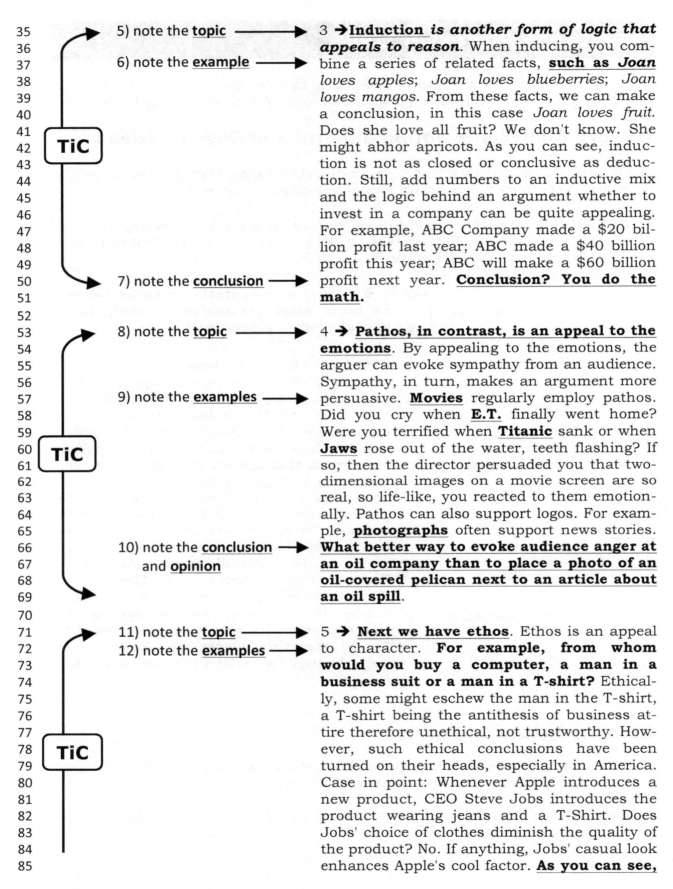

TiC

5) note the **topic** →
6) note the **example** →
7) note the **conclusion** →

3 → ***Induction is another form of logic that appeals to reason***. When inducing, you combine a series of related facts, ***such as Joan*** *loves apples; Joan loves blueberries; Joan loves mangos*. From these facts, we can make a conclusion, in this case *Joan loves fruit*. Does she love all fruit? We don't know. She might abhor apricots. As you can see, induction is not as closed or conclusive as deduction. Still, add numbers to an inductive mix and the logic behind an argument whether to invest in a company can be quite appealing. For example, ABC Company made a $20 billion profit last year; ABC made a $40 billion profit this year; ABC will make a $60 billion profit next year. **Conclusion? You do the math.**

TiC

8) note the **topic** →
9) note the **examples** →
10) note the **conclusion** and **opinion** →

4 → **Pathos, in contrast, is an appeal to the emotions**. By appealing to the emotions, the arguer can evoke sympathy from an audience. Sympathy, in turn, makes an argument more persuasive. **Movies** regularly employ pathos. Did you cry when **E.T.** finally went home? Were you terrified when **Titanic** sank or when **Jaws** rose out of the water, teeth flashing? If so, then the director persuaded you that two-dimensional images on a movie screen are so real, so life-like, you reacted to them emotionally. Pathos can also support logos. For example, **photographs** often support news stories. **What better way to evoke audience anger at an oil company than to place a photo of an oil-covered pelican next to an article about an oil spill**.

TiC

11) note the **topic** →
12) note the **examples** →

5 → **Next we have ethos**. Ethos is an appeal to character. **For example, from whom would you buy a computer, a man in a business suit or a man in a T-shirt?** Ethically, some might eschew the man in the T-shirt, a T-shirt being the antithesis of business attire therefore unethical, not trustworthy. However, such ethical conclusions have been turned on their heads, especially in America. Case in point: Whenever Apple introduces a new product, CEO Steve Jobs introduces the product wearing jeans and a T-Shirt. Does Jobs' choice of clothes diminish the quality of the product? No. If anything, Jobs' casual look enhances Apple's cool factor. **As you can see,**

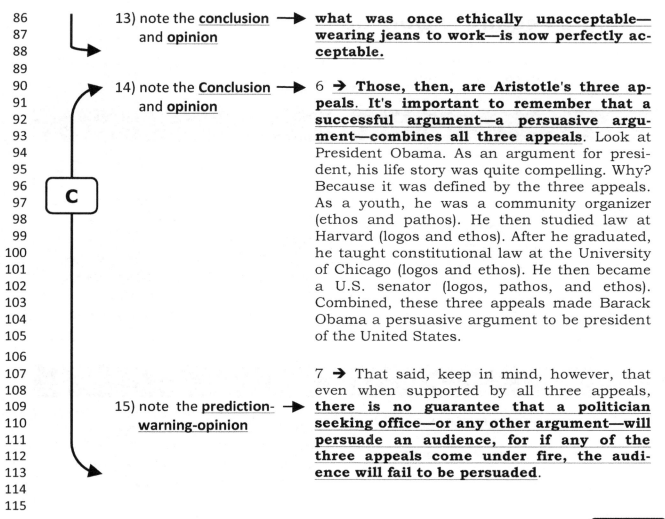

86	13) note the **conclusion** ➔	what was once ethically unacceptable—wearing jeans to work—is now perfectly acceptable.
87	and **opinion**	
88		
89		
90	14) note the **Conclusion** ➔	6 ➔ **Those, then, are Aristotle's three appeals**. **It's important to remember that a successful argument—a persuasive argument—combines all three appeals**. Look at President Obama. As an argument for president, his life story was quite compelling. Why? Because it was defined by the three appeals. As a youth, he was a community organizer (ethos and pathos). He then studied law at Harvard (logos and ethos). After he graduated, he taught constitutional law at the University of Chicago (logos and ethos). He then became a U.S. senator (logos, pathos, and ethos). Combined, these three appeals made Barack Obama a persuasive argument to be president of the United States.
91	and **opinion**	
92		
93		
94		
95		
96		
97	**C**	
98		
99		
100		
101		
102		
103		
104		
105		
106		
107		7 ➔ That said, keep in mind, however, that even when supported by all three appeals, **there is no guarantee that a politician seeking office—or any other argument—will persuade an audience, for if any of the three appeals come under fire, the audience will fail to be persuaded**.
108		
109	15) note the **prediction-** ➔	
110	**warning-opinion**	
111		
112		
113		
114		
115		

How to Listen → *Visualize the Argument* ➔

Next, listen to the same lecture, then answer the questions on the next page. As you listen, visualize how the ideas illustrated above progress from general to specific to general. By doing so, you will be able to anticipate and note the important ideas in the lecture, and answer questions more proficiently.

Notes

_____

_____

_____

_____

Sample Lecture → *Questions*

<u>Directions</u>: Now get ready to answer the six questions. Answer each based on what is stated or implied in the lecture.

#1

What is the topic of the lecture?

A) Aristotle's philosophy
B) Aristotle's writing style
C) Aristotle's ancient lesson
D) Aristotle's modes of appeal

#2

What is the purpose of the lecture?

A) to demonstrate three different types of persuasive argument
B) to illustrate how an argument can be made more persuasive
C) to highlight Aristotle's influence
D) to highlight how audiences have been persuaded

#3

According to Aristotle, which appeals make a lecture more persuasive? Select three. This is a 2-point answer.

A) ethos
B) bathos
C) pathos
D) chaos
E) logos

#4

Why does the professor say this ?

A) to warn that even the best arguments can fail to persuade an audience
B) to warn that persuaded people often change their minds during elections
C) to reinforce the idea that persuasive arguments guarantee results
D) to highlight the need for arguments

#5

The professor describes President Obama's personal history. Put President Obama's personal history in the proper order. This is a 2-point question.

a. graduated from Harvard Law
b. became a U.S. Senator
c. was a community organizer
d. taught constitutional law

1. _____

2. _____

3. _____

4. _____

#6

In the lecture, the professor describes Aristotle's three appeals and their functions in an argument. Indicate whether each of the following is a function of Aristotle's three appeals. This is a 3-point question.

	YES	NO
Logos appeals to reason using deduction or induction		
Ethos appeals to logos.		
Pathos appeals to the emotions using both words and images.		
Logos combines both ethos and pathos.		
Ethos appeals to character.		

→ Answers page 320.
→ Scoring multi-answer questions page 328.
→ Audio script page 382.

Notes

_____

_____

_____

_____

_____

_____

_____

_____

_____

_____

_____

_____

Expect the following questions on test day.

1. <u>Practice</u>: *Content Questions*

<u>Directions</u>: Listen to each prompt, then answer the question.

Audio Track #57

#1

Listen to a professor, then answer the question.

What is the main topic of the lecture?

A) photoautotrophs
B) essential chemical processes
C) photosynthesis
D) classifying photosynthetic plants, algae, and bacteria

#2

Listen to a professor, then answer the question.

What is the focus of the lecture?

A) computers
B) algorithms
C) brownies
D) software

#3

Listen to a professor, then answer the question.

What is the main topic of the lecture?

A) the evolution of early civilizations
B) the word civilization
C) the world's first spreadsheets
D) the importance of writing

#4

Listen to a professor, then answer the question.

What is the focus of the lecture?

A) translating Egyptian hieroglyphs
B) an important discovery
C) the Rosetta Stone
D) France's and Britain's historical claims

→ Answers page 320.
→ Audio script page 383.

2. __Practice__: *Purpose Questions*

Directions: Listen to each prompt, then answer the question.

Audio Track #58

#1 →

Listen to a professor, then answer the question.

Why does the professor introduce four more thinking tools?

A) to introduce more material
B) to indicate which tools are important
C) to develop and expand thinking styles
D) to expand and develop the topic

#2

Listen to a professor, then answer the question.

Why does the professor describe Frank Sinatra's breathing style?

A) to illustrate why Sinatra was talented
B) to illustrate how Sinatra could sing
C) to illustrate why Sinatra was original
D) to illustrate Sinatra's passion for words

#3 →

Listen to a professor, then answer the question.

Why does the professor stress fossil fuels?

A) to compare old and new societies
B) to contrast kings and despots
C) to contrast industrial and preindustrial societies
D) to illustrate one type of energy source

#4

Listen to a professor, then answer the question.

Why does the professor mention Europe in 2003?

A) as evidence of serious weather patterns
B) as evidence of how summer can kill
C) as evidence to support NOAA's claim
D) as evidence we need to drink more water

→ Answers 320 page.
→ Audio script page 385.

3. **Practice**: *Single-Answer Detail Questions*

<u>Directions</u>: Listen to a lecture about education, then answer the questions.

Audio Track #59

#1

The first public schools in America were...

A) focused on teaching Protestant beliefs
B) free to all students, rich and poor
C) an alternative to Catholic schools
D) created for new immigrants

#2

In which year was the Boston Latin School founded?

A) 1735
B) 1837
C) 1600
D) 1635

#3

According to the lecture, the literacy rate for women in colonial America was...

A) very high
B) the same as for men
C) extremely low
D) improving

#4

What was the condition of the public school system in 1837?

A) growing rapidly as planned
B) a model of excellence around the world
C) in desperate need of reform
D) divided between Puritans and Catholics

#5

How did Horace Mann change the school year?

A) He added a six-week summer vacation.
B) He limited it to six years.
C) He added six days.
D) He increased it to six months.

#6

According to the lecture, what did Horace Mann believe?

A) Education decreased taxes.
B) Education was moral training.
C) Education was only for the rich.
D) Education was a religious duty.

→ Answers page 321.
→ Audio script page 386.

4. <u>Practice</u>: *Multi-Answer Detail Questions*

<u>Directions</u>: Listen to each prompt, then answer the question.

Audio Track #60

#1

Listen then answer the question. This is a 2-point question.

What three weapons did a Roman legionnaire carry? Select three.

A) gladius
B) gladiator
C) pugio
D) polio
E) pilum

#2

Listen then answer the question. This is a 2-point question.

What are the essential parts of a business plan? Select three.

A) a description of the profits
B) a statement describing the goals
C) the reason why the goals are attainable
D) a plan of action
E) how to maintain a competitive edge

#3

Listen then answer the question. This is a 2-point question.

According to the professor, the best ways to study marine life are... Select three.

A) in a laboratory
B) by submersibles
C) with specially designed cameras
D) by scuba diving
E) by computer simulation

#4

Listen then answer the question. This is a 1-point question.

What were the first major battles of the American Revolutionary War? Select two.

A) the Battle of White Plains
B) the Battle of Brooklyn
C) the Battle of the Heights
D) the Battle of Harlem Heights

➔ Answers page 321.
➔ Scoring multi-answer questions page 328.
➔ Audio script page 387.

5. <u>Practice</u>: *Question-First Function Questions*

<u>Directions</u>: Answer each question based on what is stated or implied.

Audio Track #61

#1

Why does the professor say this?

A) to mention Sinatra's love of sports
B) to point out Sinatra's place in history
C) to detail Sinatra's many talents
D) to stress how original Sinatra was

#2

Why does the professor say this?

A) to highlight the job of a marine biologist
B) to stress the need to respect nature
C) to reinforce the need for more research
D) to warn that the water should not be disturbed

#3

Why does the professor say this?

A) to illustrate how different societies define civilization
B) to illustrate how taboos play a part in most societies
C) to warn against defining all societies the same way
D) to redefine the nature of society

#4

Why does the professor say this?

A) to compare New York City today with New York City during the Revolutionary War
B) to contrast buildings now and buildings during the Revolutionary War
C) to illustrate two battles that took place on Manhattan island
D) to suggest that the students should go for an historical walk around New York City

Practice: (cont'd)

#5

Why does the professor say this?

A) to highlight a commonly known fact about weather-related deaths
B) to illustrate weather-related deaths in the United States
C) to classify hurricanes and tornadoes by how deadly they are
D) to state a little-known fact about hurricanes and tornadoes

#6

Why does the professor say this?

A) to highlight Rome's need for an army
B) to illustrate how a census gave the Roman government accurate statistics
C) to define how ancient empires raised tax money by employing a census
D) to illustrate how a census was taken two-thousand years ago

#7

Why does the professor say this?

A) to warn against global warming
B) to illustrate how an insect is destroying a local species in Asia
C) to show how global warming is affecting both bees and hornets in Europe
D) to illustrate the destructive power of the Asian hornet, an invasive species

#8

Why does the professor say this?

A) to stress how astonished everyone was, then and now
B) to highlight how bad news affects people
C) to remind people what happened on December 11
D) to explain where she was on December 11, 2008

➔ Answers page 321.
➔ Audio script page 388.

6. <u>Practice</u>: *Segment-First Function Questions*

<u>Directions</u>: Answer each question based on what is stated or implied.

Audio Track #62

#1 ➡️

Listen to part of a lecture, then answer the question.

Why does the professor say this?

A) to stress that the battle is still going on
B) to suggest that France is the rightful owner of the Rosetta Stone
C) to suggest that the rightful owner of the Rosetta Stone is still in question
D) to suggest that Britain and France debate

#2

Listen to part of a lecture, then answer the question.

Why does the professor say this?

A) to invite an argument
B) to invite a debate
C) to invite a review
D) to invite questions

#3 ➡️

Listen to part of a lecture, then answer the question.

Why does the professor say this?

A) to introduce the next debate
B) to introduce the next question
C) to introduce the next topic
D) to introduce the next reason

#4

Listen to part of a lecture, then answer the question.

Why does the professor say this?

A) to illustrate using a simple example
B) to classify using a simple recipe
C) to compare food to algorithms
D) to illustrate a simple exercise

➔ Answers page 321.
➔ Audio script page 389.

7. **Practice:** *Direct-Attitude Questions*

<u>Directions</u>: Listen to each prompt, then answer the question.

Audio Track #63

#1

Listen then answer the question.

The professor thinks corporate rehiring is...

A) a reliable economic indicator
B) one type of economic indicator
C) an unreliable economic indicator
D) a good indicator of sales

#2

Listen then answer the question.

What is the professor's position on drilling for oil offshore?

A) She is convinced it is a good idea.
B) She believes it needs more research.
C) She is not convinced it is a good idea.
D) She thinks a jury should decide the issue.

#3

Listen then answer the question.

What is the professor's view of Thomas Edison?

A) He thinks Edison had scruples.
B) He believes Edison was a divided man.
C) He thinks Edison coined great ideas.
D) He thinks Edison's quotes are memorable.

#4

Listen then answer the question.

The professor thinks that genetically modified food is...

A) affordable
B) dangerous
C) delicious
D) innocuous

→ Answers page 321.
→ Audio script page 390.

8. <u>Practice</u>: *Inferred-Attitude Questions*

<u>Directions</u>: Listen to each prompt, then answer the question.

#1 →

Listen then answer the question.

How does the professor feel about what happened off the Farallon Islands?

A) curious
B) confused
C) cautious
D) amazed

#2

Listen then answer the question.

What is the professor's view of Microsoft?

A) It is no longer the industry leader.
B) It was founded by Bill Gates.
C) It competes directly with Apple.
D) It still controls the computer market.

#3 →

Listen then answer the question.

What is the professor's opinion of Cro-Magnon cave art?

A) Its purpose remains a mystery.
B) It needs to be preserved.
C) It is equal to the art of today.
D) It is best viewed on slides.

#4

Listen then answer the question.

The professor believes that...

A) It's possible that Cuban nationalists assassinated Kennedy.
B) The military complex probably killed Kennedy.
C) Kennedy was killed in Viet Nam.
D) Neither Cuban nationalists nor the military complex killed Kennedy.

→ Answers page 321.
→ Audio script page 391.

9. <u>Practice</u>: *Inferred-Action Questions*

<u>Directions</u>: Listen to each prompt, then answer the question.

#1 →

Listen then answer the question.

What will the professor probably do next?

A) teach jargon using student examples
B) teach skateboarding jargon and slang
C) teach examples of skateboarding slang using student examples
D) teach the code of skateboarding

#2

Listen then answer the question.

What will the professor talk about next?

A) Sinatra's early career
B) Sinatra's ethics
C) Sinatra's work habits
D) Sinatra's breathing techniques

#3 →

Listen then answer the question.

What will the professor probably do next?

A) give another lecture
B) take a break
C) take a nap
D) take a vacation

#4

Listen then answer the question.

What will the professor demonstrate?

A) how to make an axe
B) how to make a primitive tool
C) how to make a hand axe
D) how to complete the assignment

→ Answers page 321.
→ Audio script page 392.

Ordering Questions

For this task, you will also answer ordering questions. They are detail questions. They measure your ability to identify the steps in a process or event, such as a moment in history, or the stages in a person's and/or animal's life.

Practice: *Ordering Questions*

Directions: Listen to each prompt, then answer the question.

Audio Track #66

#1 →

Listen then answer the question.

The professor talks about the sockeye salmon. Put the life cycle of the sockeye in the correct order. This is a 2-point question.

a. return to the home river
b. alevin grow into fry
c. smolt head for the ocean
d. spawn in shallow water

1. _____
2. _____
3. _____
4. _____

#2

Listen then answer the question.

The professor talks about Jonathan James. Put James' computer hacking career in the proper order. This is a 2-point question.

a. accused of hacking major retailers
b. hacked the Defense Reduction Agency
c. hacked Bell-South
d. hacked the Miami-Dade school system

1. _____
2. _____
3. _____
4. _____

#3 →

Listen then answer the question.

The professor describes the life of F. Scott Fitzgerald. Put Fitzgerald's writing career in the proper order. This is a 2-point question.

a. screenplay contract with MGM
b. sold short stories to magazines
c. published *The Great Gatsby*
d. published *This Side of Paradise*

1. _____
2. _____
3. _____
4. _____

#4

Listen then answer the question.

The professor talks about the persistence hunt. Put the steps of the persistence hunt in order. This is a 2-point question.

a. move the herd
b. isolate and chase one kudu
c. find kudu
d. make a kill

1. _____
2. _____
3. _____
4. _____

→ Answers page 322.
→ Scoring multi-answer questions page 328.
→ Audio script page 393.

Yes-No Questions

For this task, you will also answer yes-no questions. They are detail questions. They measure your ability to identify correct and incorrect information.

Practice: *Yes-No Questions*

<u>Directions</u>: Listen to each prompt, then answer the question.

Audio
Track
#67

#1

The professor describes Black Friday. Indicate whether each of the following is true of Black Friday in the United States. This is a 3-point question.

	YES	NO
Black Friday is an official holiday.		
Black Friday is a bellwether for retailers and manufacturers.		
Black Friday prices are generally better than Cyber Monday prices.		
Black Friday marks the start of the Christmas shopping season.		
Black Friday is popular only on the east coast.		

#2

The professor talks about microcredit. Indicate whether each of the following is true of microcredit. This is a 3-point question.

	YES	NO
It is based on group financing called solidarity lending.		
It is a system of finance that extends credit to the very poor.		
The average size of the borrowing group is fifteen.		
It encourages relatives to borrow credit to start small businesses.		
It is popular around the world.		

#3

The professor talks about the Situationist International. Indicate whether each of the following is true of the Situationist International. This is a 3-point question.

	YES	NO
It combined Marxism and Surrealism to fight consumerism.		
It was founded in 1957.		
They believed that the individual was a slave to advertising.		
Guy Debord believed in capitalism.		
The Situationist International is no longer active.		

#4

The professor talks about hybrid cars. According to the professor, which of the following are true of hybrid cars? This is a 3-point question.

	YES	NO
They are very popular.		
They are more expensive than conventional gas-powered cars.		
Their only source of energy is a large nickel battery.		
They average 50 miles per liter.		
They are environmentally friendly.		

→ Answers page 322.
→ Scoring multi-answer questions page 328.
→ Audio script page 395.

Connecting Questions

For this task, you will also answer connecting questions. They are detail questions. They measure your ability to identify specific topics and identify connections between those topics. Look at the following example.

The professor describes the three parts of an independent essay. Match each part of an independent essay in the top row with its corresponding part in the bottom row. This is a 2-point question.

a. thesis	b. body	c. conclusion

details	introduction	restated thesis

Using the mouse, click-and-drag each top-row example under the corresponding space in the bottom row to make a topic match or connection.

The professor describes the three parts of an independent essay. Match each part of an independent essay in the top row with its corresponding part in the bottom row. This is a 2-point question.

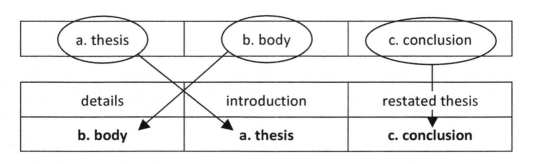

Practice: *Connecting Questions*

<u>Directions</u>: Listen to each prompt, then answer the question.

Audio
Track
#68

#1

The professor describes three military battles that changed history. Match each battle with each defeated military leader. This is a 2-point question.

a. Waterloo	b. Marathon	c. Teutoburg Forest

Varus	Darius	Napoleon

#2

The professor identifies three herbs used for plant-based medicine. Match each herb with its corresponding application. This is a 2-point question.

a. aloe vera	b. willow bark	c. milk thistle

aches and pains	liver health	burns and wounds

#3

The professor describes the parts of a prokaryote cell. Connect each part of a prokaryote cell with its corresponding function. This is a 2-point question.

a. cytoplasmic region	b. envelope	c. exterior

contains the genome	flagella for motion	protective filter

#4

The professor illustrates the life cycle of the sockeye salmon. Match each stage of the sockeye salmon's life cycle with a corresponding description of that stage. This is a 2-point question.

a. alevin	b. fry	c. smolt

a sockeye salmon approximately six months old	lives off the nutrient-rich yolk of the egg sack	will mature in the Pacific Ocean and return to the home river as an adult

→ Answers page 322.
→ Scoring multi-answer questions page 328.
→ Audio script page 397.

Discussion → *Professor-Students*

On test day, expect 1-2 discussion prompts followed by six questions. The professor and the students will discuss an academic topic. Typically, the professor will introduce the topic and the students will develop the supporting details.

Discussion Analysis → *Noting General and Specific Ideas*

The discussion will develop predictably with the ideas progressing from general to specific to general. Listen for this topic progression. Note it.

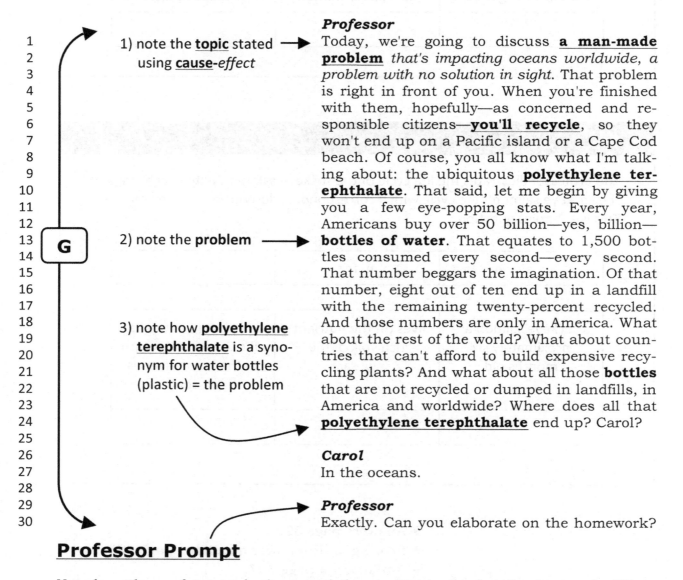

1) note the **topic** stated using **cause**-*effect*

2) note the **problem**

3) note how **polyethylene terephthalate** is a synonym for water bottles (plastic) = the problem

Professor
Today, we're going to discuss **a man-made problem** *that's impacting oceans worldwide, a problem with no solution in sight.* That problem is right in front of you. When you're finished with them, hopefully—as concerned and responsible citizens—**you'll recycle**, so they won't end up on a Pacific island or a Cape Cod beach. Of course, you all know what I'm talking about: the ubiquitous **polyethylene terephthalate**. That said, let me begin by giving you a few eye-popping stats. Every year, Americans buy over 50 billion—yes, billion— **bottles of water**. That equates to 1,500 bottles consumed every second—every second. That number beggars the imagination. Of that number, eight out of ten end up in a landfill with the remaining twenty-percent recycled. And those numbers are only in America. What about the rest of the world? What about countries that can't afford to build expensive recycling plants? And what about all those **bottles** that are not recycled or dumped in landfills, in America and worldwide? Where does all that **polyethylene terephthalate** end up? Carol?

Carol
In the oceans.

Professor
Exactly. Can you elaborate on the homework?

Professor Prompt

Note how the professor asks (prompts) the student to develop the next topic. When a student speaks, it often signals the start of a new body paragraph-topic-idea.

- **REMEMBER:** *Note professor and student prompts. They are predictable testing points.*

1
2
3
4
5
6
7
8
9
10
11
12
13
14
15
16
17
18
19
20
21
22
23
24
25
26
27
28
29
30
31
32
33
34
35
36
37
38
39
40
41
42
43
44
45
46
47
48
49

TiC

4) note the **topic**

5) note the **interjection**
followed by a *definition*

TOEFL is teaching you new words.

6) note the **interjection**
followed by a *definition*

7) note the **topic**
and *example*

Carol
Sure. According to the reading, **there's this huge floating patch of garbage in the North Pacific**. It's made up mostly of plastic bottles, but you can also find fish nets and micro pellets used for abrasive cleaning, plus all the stuff tossed off freighters and cruise ships. All this garbage is being swept along on what's **called the North Pacific gyre**.

Professor
Sorry, what exactly is that? **A gyre?**

Carol
It's the prevailing ocean current. In the North Pacific, the gyre moves west along the equator, then up past Japan to Alaska, then down the west coast of North America to the equator again. It's kind of like water spinning in a toilet bowl.

Professor
Good. So what's the connection between the North Pacific gyre and pelagic plastic?

Ann
Sorry, professor, what does pelagic mean again?

Professor
It means living or occurring at sea. The albatross, for example, is a pelagic bird. Carol?

Carol
Right, so where was I? Okay, so the stuff, I mean, you know, **all that pelagic plastic, is swept along clockwise by the gyre**. Eventually, all that plastic junk finds its way into the center of the gyre and becomes stationary, you know, just sits there in an area called the Horse Latitudes, this area of calm in the center of the gyre. *Years ago, sailors would get trapped there due to a lack of wind and current.* Today, it's basically one big, continuously-fed garbage dump in which pelagic plastic is the prevailing contaminant.

50
51
52
53
54
55
56
57
58
59
60
61
62
63
64
65
66
67
68
69
70
71
72
73
74
75
76
77
78
79
80
81
82
83
84
85
86
87
88
89
90
91
92
93
94
95
96
97
98
99
100

TiC

8) note the **topic** and *example*

note processes

note comparisons

9) note the **topic** and *examples*

TiC

10) note the **topic**

TiC

Professor
And it isn't going anywhere. In fact, it's spreading due to the decomposing nature of the contaminants themselves. **Ann, can you jump in here and talk about the photodegradation process?**

Ann
So when all this floating plastic is exposed to the sun, it begins to photodegrade until it reaches the molecular level. *For example, take this book*. Let's say it's floating in the center of the gyre, okay? The first thing to go are the covers, then the pages decompose freeing all the words. Next, the words break apart into letters. Finally, the ink in the letters photodecomposes into molecules. All that ends up in the gyre forming this thick, soupy liquid full of floating plastic particles that look like confetti.

Professor
A sea of confetti. That's a good way to put it. Beautiful, I'm sure, what with all that colored plastic floating around, but deadly. Very. **All that particulate matter?** It doesn't sink. Instead, it stays in the upper water column where it poses a significant threat to endemic wildlife. *Pelagic birds, for example, consume the particulate matter mistaking it for food*. They, in turn, feed it to their young who die of starvation or are poisoned by the toxic nature of polyethylene terephthalate. Other contaminants identified in the patch are PCB, DDT and PAH. When ingested, some of these toxins imitate estradiol which, as you know, is a naturally occurring estrogenic hormone secreted mainly by the ovaries. You can imagine the effect these toxins have on the reproduction systems of endemic species, *such as whales. Fish* too ingest the decomposed plastic and become contaminated.

Carol
Professor, is it **possible to clean it up?**

Professor
So far? No. The particulate matter is so small, you need extremely fine nets—micronets basically—to scoop it up. But even if we had such nets, remember, the North Pacific is vast. **It**

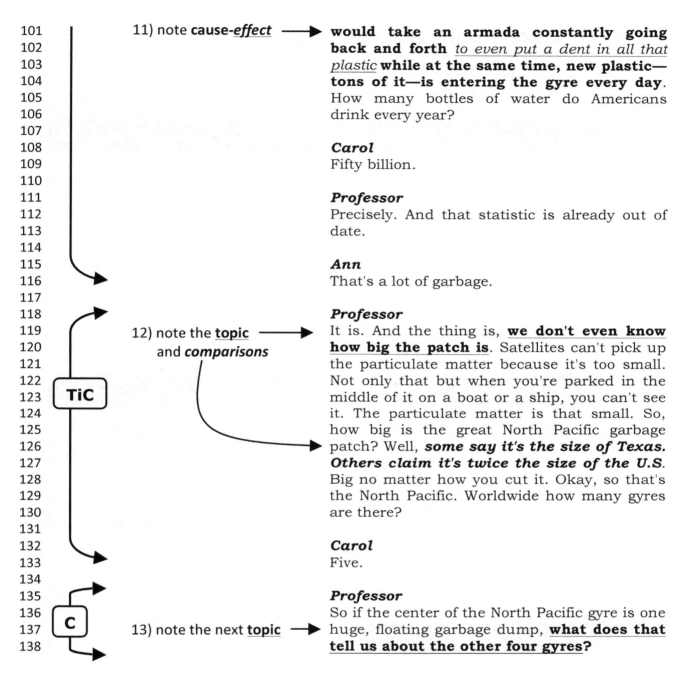

101	11) note **cause-*effect*** →	**would take an armada constantly going back and forth** *to even put a dent in all that plastic* **while at the same time, new plastic—tons of it—is entering the gyre every day.** How many bottles of water do Americans drink every year?
102		
103		
104		
105		
106		
107		
108		*Carol*
109		Fifty billion.
110		
111		*Professor*
112		Precisely. And that statistic is already out of date.
113		
114		
115		*Ann*
116		That's a lot of garbage.
117		

101–116

TiC **118–133**

12) note the **topic** and *comparisons* →

Professor
It is. And the thing is, **we don't even know how big the patch is**. Satellites can't pick up the particulate matter because it's too small. Not only that but when you're parked in the middle of it on a boat or a ship, you can't see it. The particulate matter is that small. So, how big is the great North Pacific garbage patch? Well, ***some say it's the size of Texas. Others claim it's twice the size of the U.S.*** Big no matter how you cut it. Okay, so that's the North Pacific. Worldwide how many gyres are there?

Carol
Five.

C **135–138**

13) note the next **topic** →

Professor
So if the center of the North Pacific gyre is one huge, floating garbage dump, **what does that tell us about the other four gyres?**

How to Listen → *Visualize the Argument* →

track #69

Next, listen to the same discussion, then answer the questions on the next page. As you listen, visualize how the ideas illustrated above progress from general to specific to general. By doing so, you will be able to anticipate and note the important ideas in the discussion, and answer questions more proficiently.

Sample Discussion → *Questions*

<u>Directions</u>: Now get ready to answer the questions. Answer each question based on what is stated or implied in the discussion.

#1

What is the discussion mainly about?

A) the North Pacific gyre
B) how plastic is polluting the Pacific
C) the North Pacific garbage patch
D) plastic and pelagic species

#2

What is the purpose of the discussion?

A) to highlight how pollution affects ocean currents
B) to illustrate how plastic garbage is polluting the North Pacific
C) to define an environmental disaster
D) to show the relationship between a gyre and plastic water bottles

---

#3

Why does the professor say this?

A) to warn that plastic bottles are a growing problem
B) to stress his disbelief at the amount of plastic in daily use
C) to illustrate how much plastic he uses on a daily basis
D) to introduce the next topic

#4

Which pelagic species does the professor mention? Select three. This is a 2-point question.

A) whales
B) crabs
C) birds
D) sea turtles
E) fish

#5

The professor describes how plastic becomes part of the eco-system. Put those steps in order. This is a 2-point question.

a. Plastic photodegrades into particles.
b. Plastic ends up in the Horse Latitudes.
c. Plastic enters the North Pacific.
d. Plastic is swept along by the gyre.

1. _____
2. _____
3. _____
4. _____

#6

In the lecture, the professor describes the Horse Latitudes. Indicate whether each of the following is a characteristic of the Horse Latitudes. This is a 3-point question.

	YES	NO
They flow clockwise.		
Worldwide there are five.		
The center is a calm area that once trapped sailing ships.		
They are home to a variety of pelagic species.		
Plastic photodecomposes on the surface into toxic particulates.		

→ Answers page 322.
→ Scoring multi-answer questions page 328.
→ Audio script page 398.

Notes

_____
_____
_____
_____
_____
_____
_____
_____
_____
_____
_____
_____

Practice: *Discussion #1*

track
#70

Directions: Now get ready to answer the questions. Answer each question based on what is stated or implied in the discussion.

#1

What is the discussion mainly about?

A) malicious computers
B) Trojan horses
C) viruses
D) malware

#2

What is the purpose of the discussion?

A) to highlight various internet dangers
B) to identify types of malicious software and their effects
C) to describe the history of the internet in America
D) to classify methods of virus protection

#3

Why does the student say this?

A) to compare the fate of the Trojans to users infected with Trojan horses
B) to illustrate where the name Trojan comes from
C) to develop the history of malware
D) to stress that Trojan horses are the most dangerous malware

---

#4

The student describes the history of computer viruses. Put that history in order. This is a 2-point question.

a. The Elk Clone virus attacks Apple computers.
b. The Brain appears to defend against software pirating.
c. The Creeper virus appears on AR-PANET.
d. Computer scientists started writing about computer viruses.

1. _____
2. _____
3. _____
4. _____

#5

In the discussion, the student describes Trojan horses and computer viruses. Identify the characteristics of each. This is a 3-point question.

	Trojan horse	virus
Designed to disrupt or crash a host computer.		
Designed to secretly download a host computer's files.		
Spreads via portable media, such as flash drives.		
Often shows up as a legitimate link in an email message.		
First appeared on ARPANET as an innocuous experiment.		

#6

Listen to part of the discussion, then answer the question.

Why does the student say this?

A) to express empathy
B) to express shock
C) to express disgust
D) to express anger

➜ Answers page 322.
➜ Scoring multi-answer questions page 328.
➜ Audio script page 400.

Practice: *Discussion #2*

Audio
Track
#71

Directions: Now get ready to answer the questions. Answer each question based on
what is stated or implied in the discussion.

#1

What is the topic of the discussion?

A) comparing systems
B) borders
C) the Earth's atmosphere
D) homeostasis

#2

What is the purpose of the discussion?

A) to introduce a new lecture topic
B) to review material from the last lecture
C) to prepare for an upcoming exam
D) to give the students a chance to ask questions

#3

According to the discussion, all systems have what?

A) interdependence
B) permeability
C) balance
D) originality

#4

Why does the professor say this?

A) because the student was not clear
B) because the student changed topics
C) because the student was precise
D) because the student was energetic

#5

In the discussion, the following topics are mentioned. Identify which are open systems and which are closed systems. This is a 3-point question.

	closed	open
the Earth		
the U.S. economy		
the human circulatory system		
the human body		
a computer network		

#6

Listen to part of the discussion, then answer the question.

Why does the student say this?

A) to add to the definition of systems
B) to illustrate how open systems are like closed systems
C) to rephrase the definition of an open system
D) to describe how mass and energy cannot cross borders

→ Answers page 323.
→ Scoring multi-answer questions page 328.
→ Audio script page 402.

Reading Section

The reading section is the first section on the TOEFL test. It is one hour. This section measures your ability to read academic passages and answer questions on them.

- **REMEMBER:** *You manage the clock. You decide how much time to spend on each passage and question. One passage takes about 20 minutes to complete.*

TASK	WORDS	TIME	QUESTIONS
passage 1	650-750	20 minutes	12-14
passage 2	650-750	20 minutes	12-14
passage 3	650-750	20 minutes	12-14

TOEFL Recycles

By working through this text, you have seen how TOEFL recycles the same prompts and questions. In other words, TOEFL is predictable. That means you can apply the strategies discussed to the short reading test below. Remember to note the three-part argument structure (G+3TiC=C) as you read.

- **REMEMBER:** *On test day, you can answer the questions in any order. For example, you can answer question nine first, then scroll back to question one, etc.*

- **REMEMBER:** *If you don't know the answer, guess. You will not lose points for wrong answers.*

Short Reading Test

Task: You have 20 minutes to read the passage and answer the questions.

1 1 ➔ Adam Smith was born in Scotland in 1723. As a young man, he studied moral
2 philosophy at the University of Glasgow and at Oxford. He eventually went on to
3 tutor a nobleman's son. The position freed Smith from his daily work while afford-
4 ing him the opportunity to tutor while traveling throughout Europe. In France,
5 Smith met Rousseau and Voltaire, leading proponents of the European Enlighten-
6 ment. At its core, the European Enlightenment, guided by reason and science,
7 questioned customs, morals, and traditional institutions, namely monarchies. Re-
8 turning to Scotland, Smith set about writing his seminal *An Inquiry into the Nature*
9 *and Causes of the Wealth of Nations.*
10
11 2 ➔ In *The Wealth of Nations*, Smith argues that building national economic wealth
12 begins with a division of labor. Smith supports his argument by using a pin facto-

13   ry. In a typical pin factory of the day, each worker was responsible for making pins
14   from start to finish. A worker would start by cutting the pin to size from a piece of
15   wire, then straighten it, then sharpen the end, affix a head, polish it, then package
16   it. In short, one man was responsible for each step of the pin-making process.
17   Smith argued that such an approach was not only counter-productive but also
18   time consuming inasmuch as once a worker finished one part of the task—say pol-
19   ishing a pin—he would pause before moving onto the next task. Such an approach,
20   Smith argued, was inefficient, for workers were likely to "saunter" or pause be-
21   tween steps, which wasted time and substantially reduced productivity. Smith ar-
22   gued that the most efficient way to make pins was through a division of labor. In-
23   stead of ten men each separately making a pin from start to finish, each would be
24   assigned one task, for example, one man would sharpen pins all day, another
25   would polish them while a third would package them, and so on. By dividing labor
26   this way, Smith theorized that the production of pins would dramatically increase.
27   As a result, there would be more pins to sell and thus more money to be made.
28   Smith's scientific approach to rationalizing the manufacturing process for greater
29   productivity was indeed the product of Enlightenment thought.
30
31   3 ➔ A division of labor, however, was but one part of Smith's argument for creating
32   wealth. An integral part of the wealth-making process, Smith claims, is the pin
33   worker himself. He is performing his assigned task not for society's benefit nor for
34   the benefit of the company, but for his own personal gain and security. The same
35   follows with the owner of the pin factory. He too is out for personal gain, the health
36   and the wealth of the nation the least of his, and his workers', worries. Yet by pur-
37   suing individual gain, Smith argues that the worker and the factory owner are in
38   fact directly adding to the wealth of the nation by utilizing a more efficient manu-
39   facturing process, one which stimulates trade, the buying and selling of goods, lo-
40   cally, nationally, and internationally. Smith coined this process "the invisible
41   hand."
42
43   4 ➔ *The Wealth of Nations* is very much a reaction to the predominating economic
44   theory of the day, that of Mercantilism. Mercantilists posited that the wealth of a
45   nation depended on developing and maintaining national power thus it was a form
46   of economic nationalism. Spain, at the time of Columbus, is a prime example of
47   just such a nation. A nation like Spain preserved national power by accumulating
48   as much gold as possible through strong exports, the limitation of imports, and a
49   large population of poorly paid workers. ■ To develop exports, companies were
50   subsidized by the government, which also wrote laws to limit imports. ■ By limiting
51   imports, the gold used to pay for imports would stay in the country and create a
52   greater money supply and more credit. ■ Moreover, nations were geared toward ac-
53   quiring and maintaining gold at all costs, including warring with each other. ■ Ad-
54   am Smith, however, argued that trade benefitted all nations and that gold was not
55   equal to wealth. Gold, Smith said, was like any other commodity, such as wheat or
56   wool, and that it deserved no special treatment. More importantly, Smith says that
57   the wealth of a nation is not based on the hoarding of gold, but on the free flow of
58   goods manufactured in a systematic way, a way that serves the needs of the indi-
59   vidual and, ultimately, the nation as a whole. With that, Adam Smith gave birth to
60   what we now call economic theory. As Thomas Edison is to the light bulb, Adam
61   Smith is to the science of economics.

Short Reading Test Questions

<u>Directions</u>: You have 20 minutes to complete this task.

1. According to paragraph 1, when was Adam Smith born?

   a) in the late sixteenth century
   b) in the early eighteenth century
   c) in the late eighteenth century
   d) in the early seventeenth century

2. In paragraph 1, proponents is closest in meaning to...

   a) associates
   b) opponents
   c) supporters
   d) professionals

3. What is NOT true of the European Enlightenment?

   a) It was based on reason.
   b) It challenged customs and morals.
   c) It was supported by kings and queens.
   d) It valued science.

4. In paragraph 1, what does set about mean?

   a) finished
   b) set up
   c) reviewed
   d) commenced

5. In paragraph 2, to what does it refer?

   a) worker
   b) pin
   c) wire
   d) head

6. In paragraph 2, Adam Smith believes that economic wealth starts with what?

   a) Mercantilism
   b) a factory
   c) an invisible hand
   d) a division of labor

7. In paragraph 3, what does Smith mean by the "the invisible hand"?

    a) It is a rational and systematic manufacturing process creating wealth for a nation in a way that most do not notice or realize.
    b) It is a method of making pins over two hundred years ago that created wealth for Scotland.
    c) It is the government helping small businesses make money.
    d) It is an argument supporting the buying and selling of commodities, such as gold and silver.

8. In paragraph 3, why does Adam Smith mention the pin worker and the owner of the pin factory?

    a) to compare and contrast workers who benefitted the most from a new type of manufacturing process
    b) to classify the various types of workers in 1723 Scotland
    c) to define the process in which national wealth is created for both a pin worker and his employer
    d) to support his argument that a factory worker and a factory owner can both benefit financially from a systematic manufacturing process

9. Look at the four squares [■]. They indicate where the **bold** sentence below could be added to paragraph 4. Click on the square to insert the sentence into the passage.

    Witness England and Holland battling for control of present-day Manhattan in the early 1600's.

    A nation like Spain preserved national power by accumulating as much gold as possible through strong exports, the limitation of imports, and a large population of poorly paid workers. ■ To develop exports, companies were subsided by the government which also wrote laws to limit imports. ■ By limiting imports, the gold used to pay for imports would stay in the country and create a greater money supply and more credit. ■ Moreover, nations were geared toward acquiring and maintaining gold at all costs, including warring with each other. ■ Adam Smith, however, argued that free trade benefitted all nations and that gold was not equal to wealth.

10. From the passage, it can be inferred that Adam Smith probably...

    a) owned a pin factory
    b) visited a pin factory
    c) worked in a pin factory
    d) studied workers

11. Which of the following sentences best restates the essential information in the highlighted sentence in paragraph 4? Incorrect choices will change the meaning and omit important information.

    a) Adam Smith adds that the wealth of a nation depends upon serving the needs of the individual first.
    b) Smith goes on to say that free trade is the best way to create wealth.
    c) Moreover, Smith says that nations become wealthy by accumulating gold and by systematically manufacturing goods, which are then freely-traded.
    d) Smith believes that systematically manufactured goods freely-traded create more national wealth than accumulating gold.

12. Directions: The sentence in bold is the first sentence of a brief summary of the passage. Complete the summary by selecting three answer choices. Your choices will express the most important ideas in the passage. Some choices are not in the passage or do not express important ideas. **This is a 2-point question.**

The passage discusses Adam Smith's book *The Wealth of Nations.*

-
-
-

Answer Choices

1. Smith's *The Wealth of Nations* represents the start of modern economic theory.

2. Smith illustrated how a factory worker wasted time when responsible for every step in a manufacturing process.

3. Smith started to write *The Wealth of Nations* after he returned to France from a long trip to Scotland.

4. Smith argued that to create national wealth, governments should subsidize companies.

5. Smith argued that Mercantilism was not a true wealth-building system.

6. Smith's theory of "the invisible hand" was influenced by the European Enlightenment.

13. In paragraph 4, the phrase subsidized by is closest in meaning to...

    a) invested in
    b) recorded by
    c) awarded by
    d) subsumed by

14. <u>Directions</u>: Complete the following table by indicating how Adam Smith's economic theories in *The Wealth of Nations* differed from what the Mercantilists believed. **This is a 4-point question.**

Mercantilists	Adam Smith
•	•
•	•
•	•
	•

1. Nations created wealth and power by amassing gold.
2. A satisfied work force will benefit a nation's economy as a whole.
3. Imports and exports should be manufactured by the government.
4. Exports made by poorly paid workers created national wealth.
5. National wealth starts with a rational approach to manufacturing.
6. Productivity will increase if the labor force is divided systematically.
7. War with other nations is part of national and economic policy.
8. Accumulating commodities does not create national wealth.
9. Free trade is an important part of military policy.

➔ Answers page 323.
➔ Scoring multi-answer questions page 328.

Scoring the Short Reading Test

The short reading test is a total of 18 points. Add up your raw score, then convert it to a reading section score out of 30 total points using the guide below.

Sample Score	Section Score	Sample Score	Section Score
18/18 ➔	30/30	10	16
17	28	9	15
16	26	8	14
15	24	7	13
14	22	6	11
13	20	5	9
12	18	4	7
11	17	3	5

Question Types

In the reading section, there are four question types. The majority of the questions will be multiple-choice, as illustrated below.

Multiple-Choice Questions

This question type has four answer choices. Click on one of the four choices with the mouse, click *Next*, then *Okay* to confirm. This is a 1-point question.

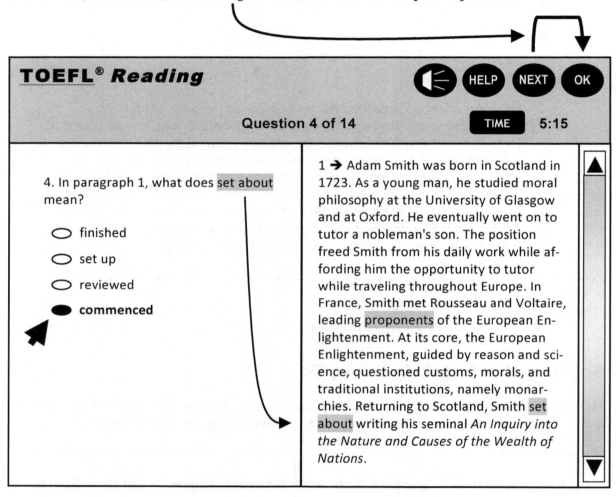

- **REMEMBER:** *This question type measures your ability to identify general and specific information in the paragraph on the right side of the screen.*

- **REMEMBER:** *You can answer the reading questions in any order.*

- **REMEMBER:** *You can change your answers but do not. Trust your intuition and move on.*

Sentence-Insertion Questions

This question has four answer choices. Each is indicated by a black square ■ in the passage on the right below. Each black square is a possible insertion point for the bold insertion sentence on the left. This is a 1-point question.

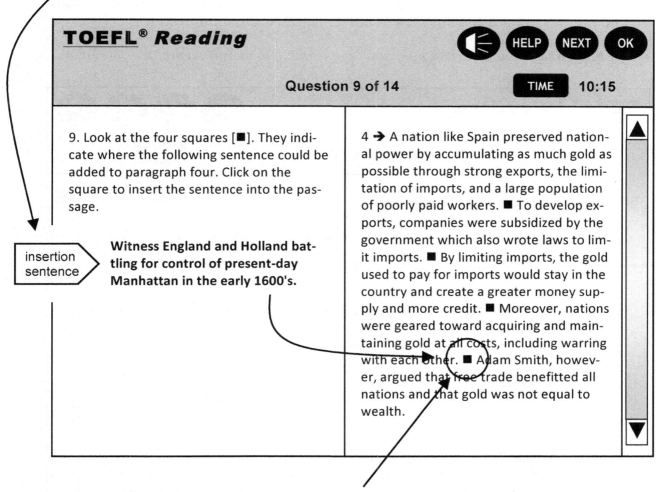

→ To answer, click on the black square ■. When you click on it, the insertion sentence will insert automatically into the paragraph, as illustrated below, line 8.

1 A nation like Spain preserved national power by accumulating as much gold as
2 possible through strong exports, the limitation of imports, and a large, popula-
3 tion of poorly paid workers. ■ To develop exports, companies were subsidized
4 by the government which also wrote laws to limit imports. ■ By limiting im-
5 ports, the gold used to pay for imports would stay in the country and create a
6 greater money supply and more credit. ■ Moreover, nations were geared toward
7 acquiring and maintaining gold at all costs, including warring with each other.
8 **Witness England and Holland battling for control of present-day Manhat-**
9 **tan in the early 1600's.** Adam Smith, however, argued that free trade benefit-
10 ted all nations and that gold was not equal to wealth.

Summary-Completion Questions

This question type starts with a topic sentence in bold. The topic sentence starts a short summary of the passage. You must complete the summary. Below the bold sentence, there will be three bullet points and six sentence choices. Choose three sentences to complete the summary. Click-drag each choice beside a bullet point. You do not have to put the answers in order. This is a 2-point question.

- **REMEMBER:** *This question measures your ability to identify general information.*

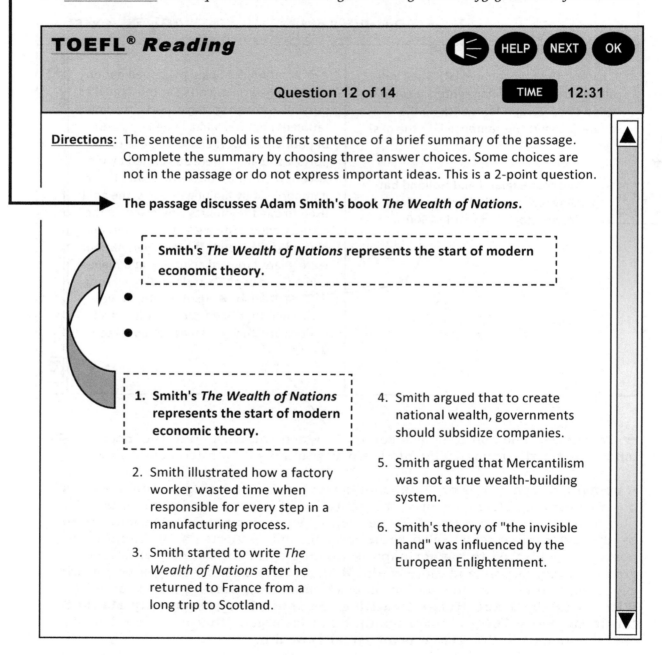

TOEFL® Reading

HELP   NEXT   OK

Question 12 of 14   TIME   12:31

Directions: The sentence in bold is the first sentence of a brief summary of the passage. Complete the summary by choosing three answer choices. Some choices are not in the passage or do not express important ideas. This is a 2-point question.

The passage discusses Adam Smith's book *The Wealth of Nations*.

- **Smith's *The Wealth of Nations* represents the start of modern economic theory.**
-
-

1. **Smith's *The Wealth of Nations* represents the start of modern economic theory.**

2. Smith illustrated how a factory worker wasted time when responsible for every step in a manufacturing process.

3. Smith started to write *The Wealth of Nations* after he returned to France from a long trip to Scotland.

4. Smith argued that to create national wealth, governments should subsidize companies.

5. Smith argued that Mercantilism was not a true wealth-building system.

6. Smith's theory of "the invisible hand" was influenced by the European Enlightenment.

Complete-a-Table Question

To complete a table, click-drag answers under the corresponding topic heading. The answers do not have to be in order. These are 3 and 4-point questions.

- **REMEMBER:** *This question measures your ability to identify specific information.*

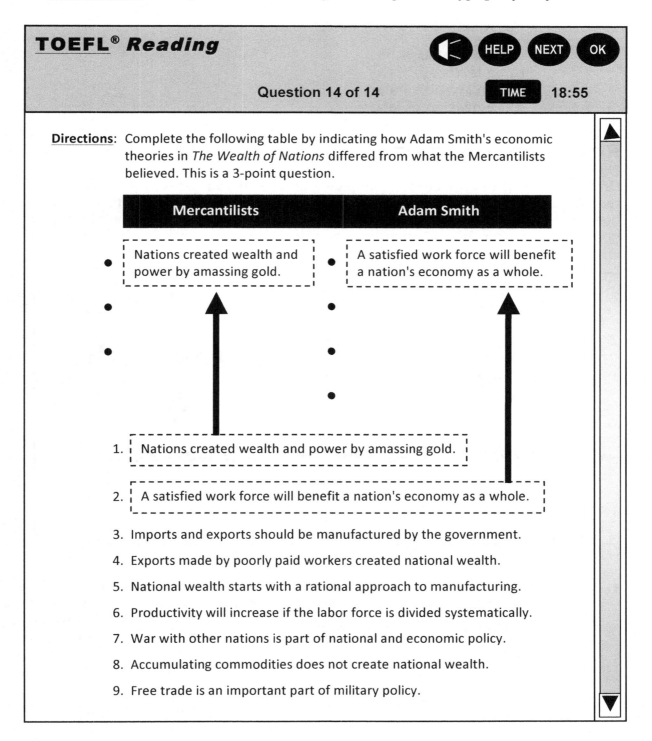

TOEFL® Reading

HELP   NEXT   OK

Question 14 of 14   TIME   18:55

Directions: Complete the following table by indicating how Adam Smith's economic theories in *The Wealth of Nations* differed from what the Mercantilists believed. This is a 3-point question.

Mercantilists	Adam Smith
Nations created wealth and power by amassing gold.	A satisfied work force will benefit a nation's economy as a whole.

1. Nations created wealth and power by amassing gold.

2. A satisfied work force will benefit a nation's economy as a whole.

3. Imports and exports should be manufactured by the government.

4. Exports made by poorly paid workers created national wealth.

5. National wealth starts with a rational approach to manufacturing.

6. Productivity will increase if the labor force is divided systematically.

7. War with other nations is part of national and economic policy.

8. Accumulating commodities does not create national wealth.

9. Free trade is an important part of military policy.

Fact Questions → *Strategies*

Each passage will have between 3-6 fact questions. These are Wh-questions (who, what, where, when, why, how). They measure your ability to identify general and specific information in the passage. Look at a sample fact question.

6. In paragraph 2, Adam Smith believes that economic wealth starts with what?

a) Mercantilism
b) a factory
c) an invisible hand
d) a division of labor

Reading Strategies

On test day, you will not see the complete passage on your screen. Instead, you will read it paragraph-by-paragraph, question-by-question. The answer to each questions will be in the paragraph on the right side of your screen, opposite the question on the left. For this question type, you do not have to scroll for the answer.

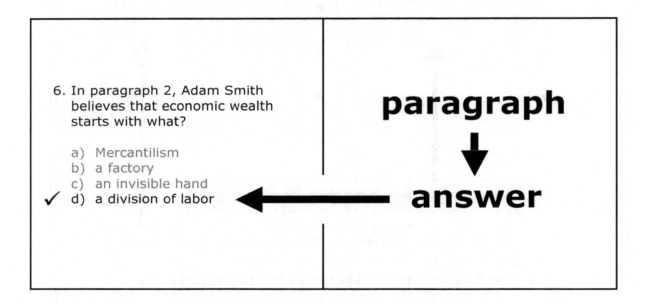

*   **WARNING:** *If you read the passage from start to finish (do a close reading), then go back and answer the questions, you will waste time. As a result, you will not be able to answer all the questions. To save time, and answer all the questions, you must scan and skim for answers using question signal words (see next page).*

Scan for Question Signal Words

When answering a fact question, first identify signal words in the question. Question signal words connect with words/synonyms in the passage, such as **economic wealth starts with** in the question below. Next, scan for the question signal words in passage. Scanning means to search quickly for targeted details, line by line. The underline answer will be located near the signal words, as illustrated below.

---

6. In paragraph 2, Adam Smith believes that **economic wealth starts with** what?

   a) Mercantilism
   b) a factory
   c) an invisible hand
   ✓ d) a division of labor

2 ➜ In *The Wealth of Nations*, Smith argues that building national **economic wealth begins with** a division of labor. Smith supports his argument by using a pin factory. In a typical pin factory of the day, each worker was responsible for making pins from start to finish. A worker would start by cutting the pin to size from a piece of wire, then straighten it, then sharpen the end, affix a head, polish it, then package it. In short, one man was responsible for each step of the pin-making process. Smith argued that such an approach was not only counterproductive but also time...

Skim for Question-Signal Words

When you skim for question signal-words, you are searching for general topic information in the paragraph. General information is found in the topic sentence (T) and the conclusion (C). Start by reading the topic sentence, then jump (skim) over the illustration (i) and read the conclusion. When you are finished, apply what you have learned to the question.

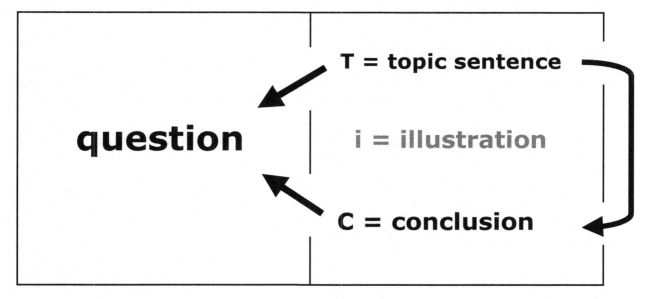

question

T = topic sentence

i = illustration

C = conclusion

Skimming and Scanning

You can combine skimming and scanning to all question types. First, skim the paragraph. Read the topic sentence, then jump to the conclusion. If the answer is not in the topic sentence or in the conclusion, scan the body of the paragraph.

- **WARNING:** *If you have "a feeling" you know the right answer, trust your feeling. Your feeling is your passive-English vocabulary talking to you. Classroom experience proves that test-takers often trust their feelings, but then change their answers only to realize that their first choice was right.*

Choice Analysis: *Process of Elimination*

When you find a possible answer, compare it to the four answer choices. Using process of elimination, eliminate choices that are: 1) off topic; 2) too general; 3) too specific; 4) not known; 5) not true; 6) not accurate.

In the following example, A is not true. Smith argues against Mercantilism. Eliminate A as a choice. C is also not true. Smith uses this metaphor (an invisible hand) to describe what happens when all steps of a rationalized manufacturing process are working as one. Also, creating wealth cannot begin with a metaphor. A metaphor is a figure of speech, not part of a manufacturing process.

6. In paragraph 2, Adam Smith believes that economic wealth starts with what?

not true	a)	Mercantilism
	b)	a factory
not true	c)	an invisible hand
	d)	a division of labor

You now have a 50-50 chance of choosing the correct answer. Both sound good. Yet one is correct and the other is the distractor.

Identifying the Distractor

Distractors look like the correct answer. They test your reading comprehension and language use proficiency. In this example, B is a topic distractor.

6. In paragraph 2, Adam Smith believes that economic wealth starts with what?

not true	a)	Mercantilism
distractor	b)	a factory
not true	c)	an invisible hand
correct	d)	a division of labor

Why is B the topic distractor? A factory is indeed an essential part of the wealth making process. However, Smith does not talk about any factory. His topic is a "pin factory"; thus, B (factory) is too general. Also, what happens inside the pin factory is the more important point. According to Smith, the labor force inside a pin factory should be divided (a division of labor), so that each man performs one job only. This, according to Smith, will result in greater productivity, which will result in a nation acquiring wealth. Therefore, D is correct.

Notes

_____

_____

_____

_____

_____

_____

_____

_____

_____

_____

_____

_____

_____

_____

_____

_____

_____

_____

_____

_____

_____

_____

_____

_____

_____

_____

Practice #1: *Fact Questions*

<u>Directions</u>: You have ten minutes to read the passage and answer the questions.

Penicillin

1. According to paragraph 1, what are capable of reproducing asexually?

a) filaments
b) hypha
c) spores
d) penicillin

2. According to paragraph 2, where did Fleming see evidence of widespread SIRS?

a) in the Royal Medical Corps
b) in St. Mary's Hospital
c) in1881 in Ayrshire, Scotland
d) in frontline soldiers

3. What did Fleming come to believe about antiseptics?

a) They were ineffective.
b) They killed deeper bacteria.
c) Lysozyme was effective.
d) They were too expensive.

4. What did Alexander Fleming find by chance in 1928?

a) Penicillium notatum
b) gram-positive bacteria
c) lysozyme
d) sepsis

1 ➔ *Penicillium chrysogenum* is a common mold, a mold being a fungus that has multi-cellular arms or filaments called hyphae. Also known as *Penicillium notatum*, *Penicillium chrysogenum* can be found living indoors on food. Its spores, units of asexual reproduction that can evolve into a new organism, are carried by the air and are a major cause of allergens in humans. In 1928, Scottish scientist Alexander Fleming discovered that *Penicillium notatum* contained a bacteria-killing antibiotic, an antibiotic Fleming named penicillin.

2 ➔ Alexander Fleming was born in 1881 in Scotland. At the age of twenty, he entered St. Mary's Hospital in London and studied medicine, then went on to become the assistant bacteriologist to Sir Almroth Wright, a pioneer in immunology and vaccine therapy. During World War One, Fleming served as a captain in the Royal Army Medical Corps and worked on the frontlines where he witnessed firsthand soldiers dying of sepsis. Sepsis, or systematic inflammatory response (SIRS), is blood poisoning due to the presence of bacteria in the blood. To fight off the bacteria, the body enters an inflammatory state accompanied by a high fever. Fleming witnessed widespread sepsis, most of which was caused by infected wounds. Antiseptics were widely available yet Fleming believed they killed only surface bacteria while failing to eradicate deeper bacteria. After the war, Fleming was determined to find a cure for sepsis. He discovered lysozyme, an enzyme found in tears. It was a natural anti-bacterial yet was ineffective against more powerful infections. In 1928, while researching the properties of staphylococci, a genus of gram-positive bacteria, he stumbled upon *Penicillium notatum*.

5. According to paragraph 3, what did the blue-green mold do?

a) It contaminated a fungus.
b) It destroyed the staphylococci.
c) It built colonies of staphylococci.
d) It turned into staphylococci cultures.

6. To what did Fleming eventually change the name mold juice?

a) staphylococci
b) penicillin
c) paratyphoid fever
d) penicillium genus

7. According to paragraph 4, by 1939 what had Fleming concluded?

a) that penicillin was a wonder drug all would benefit from
b) that he had wasted his life researching penicillin
c) that Sir William Dunn should read his 1929 research paper
d) that penicillin was not economically viable

3 ➔ By 1928, Fleming was regarded as a brilliant researcher whose laboratory was, more often than not, a mess. That same year, returning to his lab after an August holiday, Fleming discovered that his staphylococci cultures had been contaminated by a fungus. Fleming was intent on throwing the cultures out when he noticed that the staphylococci colonies had been surrounded by an invading blue-green mold. Much to Fleming's surprise, the invading mold had eradicated the staphylococci it had surrounded; whereas, those colonies of staphylococci that had not been touched by the mold were still thriving. Fleming set about isolating and growing the mold which produced a substance that killed not only staphylococci, but also a number of other disease-causing bacteria, such as pneumonia, scarlet fever, meningitis and diphtheria while having no effect on typhoid fever or paratyphoid fever. Fleming called the bacteria-killing substance "mold juice." Once he'd established that the mold was in fact part of the genus penicillium, he called it penicillin.

4 ➔ In 1929, Fleming published the results of his experiments in the British Journal of Experimental Pathology. Yet despite such initial promise, his work garnered little attention, for growing penicillium was difficult while extracting the antibiotic agent, the bacteria-killing penicillin itself, was even harder. These results, combined with tests proving that penicillin worked slowly, convinced Fleming that penicillin had no commercial appeal. By 1939, Fleming, having labored long and hard over penicillin, finally turned his attention to other matters. Penicillin, in his mind, had no future beyond his lab. Then, in that same year, the Australian scientist Howard Walter Florey, director of the Sir William Dunn School of Pathology at Oxford University, read Fleming's paper in which he described the anti-bacterial effects of penicillium. Florey immediately saw the potential of penicillium and, with the help of Ernst Chain, immediately went to work.

88
89
90
91
92
93
94
95
96
97
98
99
100
101
102
103
104
105
106
107
108

8. According to paragraph 5, what percentage of the one-hundred milligrams of penicillin that Florey and Chain made was unusable?

a) ten
b) ninety
c) one
d) one-hundred

5 ➜ With grants from the Medical Research Council in England and from the Rockefeller Foundation in the United States, Florey and Chain were able to produce one hundred milligrams of penicillin that was only ten percent pure. Then, in one of the most famous experiments in medical history, Florey injected eight mice with a lethal dose of the streptococci bacteria. He then treated four of the eight mice with the penicillin. The four non-injected mice died. Tests were then done on humans suffering from the same bacterial infections as the mice. The humans recovered at remarkable rates. However, because England was at war, there was not enough money to expand production, so Florey and Chain flew to the United States where the government became involved in large-scale production. By 1943, frontline soldiers with infections were being treated with a new wonder drug called penicillin.

pioneer: an innovator; a discoverer

staphylococci: a common type of bacteria generally harmless.

➜ Answers page 323.

Notes

_____
_____
_____
_____
_____
_____
_____
_____
_____
_____
_____
_____

Practice #2: *Fact Questions*

Directions: You have ten minutes to read the passage and answer the questions.

Biological Classification

1. According to paragraph 1, a self-sustaining biological process must have what?

a) homeostasis
b) a balance
c) chemical processes
d) a metabolism

2. According to paragraph 2, what have scientists divided into Domains?

a) Bacteria
b) Archaea
c) Life
d) complexities

3. Why are human cells eukaryotic?

a) because they contain a membrane that holds eukaryotic cells
b) because they contain genes that contain walls and membranes
c) because they are biochemically distinct from Archaea
d) because they contain a nucleus that contains genetic material

1 ➜ In biological classification, the eight major classifications are ranked hierarchically starting with Life and ending with the Common name. Life is the label given to those objects that have self-sustaining biological processes. Objects that do not signal a self-sustaining biological process are either inanimate, such as rocks, or dead. For an organism to be a self-sustaining biological process, it must have a metabolism, a metabolism being a series of integrated chemical processes that enable the organism to maintain an input-output balance called homeostasis. Homeostasis, in turn, allows a living organism to maintain its structure, to grow, and to reproduce. All living organisms on Earth, including humans, are carbon and water-based cellular structures.

2 ➜ In order to understand the vast complexities of Life, scientists have divided it into Domains. According to the three-Domain system developed by Carl Woese in 1990, Life is comprised of three Domains: Archaea, Bacteria, and Eukarya. Archaea are a large group of prokaryotes, prokaryotes being single-celled microorganisms with no nucleus. Woese discovered and named Archaea in the late 1970's. Archaea live in extreme environments, such as hot springs and deep petroleum deposits. Bacteria are also prokaryotes, yet they are genetically and biochemically distinct from Archaea. At over five nonillion (5×10^{30}), bacteria form much of the Earth's biomass. Finally, there are Eukarya. Cells within this group are called eukaryotes. These cells have a wall or membrane inside of which there is a nucleus that contains genetic material. Humans cells are eukaryotic.

43　4. According to paragraph 3, who is
44　　Carl Linnaeus?
45
46　a) the man who first identified two
47　　Kingdoms
48　b) the man who first created binomial
49　　Kingdoms
50　c) the man who first identified six
51　　Kingdoms
52　d) the first Swiss scientist
53
54
55
56　5. Into which three Phylum is the
57　　Kingdom Plantae divided?
58
59　a) Magnoliopsida, Amphia, Bryophyta
60　b) Magnoliopsida, Bryophyta,
61　　Animalia
62　c) Magnoliopsida, Chordata,
63　　Pinophyta
64　d) Magnoliopsida, Pinophyta,
65　　Bryophyta
66
67
68
69
70
71　6. What are macaques?
72
73　a) hominids
74　b) Cercopithecidae
75　c) baboons
76　d) Hominidae
77
78　7. To what does 97% refer?
79
80　a) humans
81　b) criterion
82　c) Hominidae
83　d) DNA
84
85　8. According to paragraph 5, what
86　　classification follows genus?
87
88　a) Homo sapiens
89　b) species
90　c) neanderthalis
91　d) Latin
92
93

3 ➔ Following Life and Domain is Kingdom. In 1735, Carl Linnaeus, a Swedish botanist and zoologist credited with establishing binomial nomenclature (the naming of species), believed there were two kingdoms: Vegetabilia and Animalia. Today that list has grown to six: Bacteria (prokaryotes), Protozoa (eukaryotes), Chromista (a eukaryotic supergroup), Fungi (eukaryotic organisms, such as yeast molds and mushrooms), Plantae (trees, herbs, bushes, grasses), and Animalia (multicellular eukaryotic organisms). The Kingdom Plantae is subdivided into three divisions or Phylum: Magnoliopsida, Pinophyta, Bryophyta while the Kingdom Animalia is divided into two Phylum: Chordata (vertebrates, such as humans) and Arthropoda (invertebrates, such as insects). Each Phylum is further divided into a Class. For example, Chordata is divided into two Classes: Amphibia and Mammalia. Amphibians, such as frogs and salamanders, are ectothermic or cold-blooded. However, not all Amphibia are the same; thus, they are divided into Orders based on the similarities they share. The same holds true for homeothermic Mammalians. One Order of Mammalians is Primates.

4 ➔ Primates are mammals that have large brains, walk on two or four limbs and rely on stereoscopic vision. In Order Primates, there are two distinct classifications called Families: Hominidae (hominids) and Cercopithecidae. Cercopithecidae are Old World monkeys native to Asia and Africa, monkeys such as baboons and macaques while Family Hominidae represents the great apes (gorillas, chimpanzees, orangutans) and humans. One criterion for classifying humans and apes in the same Family is that humans and apes share 97% of the same DNA.

5 ➔ Next, Family Hominidae is divided by genus. Genus is Latin meaning type. The genus Homo includes extinct early humans species. Species, the lowest order of classification, describes a group of organisms that can be classified based on similar physical characteristics and, more importantly, the ability to reproduce their kind. Early human species are Homo neanderthalis, who lived between 130,000

94
95
96
97
98
99
100
101
102　9. How many biological classifications
103　　are there?
104
105　a) 7
106　b) 6
107　c) 9
108　d) 8
109
110
111

to 30,000 years ago, and Homo habilis, who lived approximately 2.5 million years ago. These early species of the genus Homo had large brains, lived in social groups, and walked upright. The only living species of the Homo genus is the species Homo sapiens or, the Common name for which is humans.

6 ➔ Working backwards, human is the Common name for the species Homo sapiens. Homo Sapiens, in turn, belong to the Genus Homo which belongs to the Hominidae Family in the Order Primates, Primates being a part of the Class Mammalia, which is one of two sub groups in the Phylum Chordata belonging to the Kingdom Animalia, which, along with Kingdom Plantae, comprises Life as we know it.

biomass: biological material from living or non-living organisms

homeothermic: warm-blooded

➔ Answers page 323.

Vocabulary Questions → *Strategies*

Each passage will have 3-5 vocabulary questions. This question type measures your ability to understand new words, phrases and idioms by inferring their meaning from the context in which they are used. The word, phrase or idiom tested will be highlighted in the passage. Look at a sample vocabulary question.

2. In paragraph 1, proponents is closest in meaning to...

a) associates
b) opponents
c) supporters
d) professionals

Identifying the Distractor

One of the four answer choices will be a distractor. In this example, D is a homophone distractor (see page 154). Note how *proponents* and *professionals* both start with the prefix *pro*. This gives each word the same first-syllable sound. However, do not conclude that *professionals* is the correct answer simply because it sounds like *proponents*. It is not. It is a homophone distractor.

2. In paragraph 1, proponents is closest in meaning to...

a) associates
b) opponents
c) supporters
distractor d) professionals

- **WARNING:** *Do not make an answer choice based on sound. For example, night and knight sound exactly the same but have completely different meanings.*

Identifying the Distractor → *Suffixes*

A distractor can also be identified by its suffix. A suffix is a word-ending, such as *ment*. The suffix *ment* means *condition of*. For example, *excitement* means the condition of being excited. If the highlighted word has the same suffix as one of the four choices (see below), that choice is a homophone distractor.

2. What does allotment mean?

correct **a) piece**
b) ancient
distractor c) firmament
d) modern

Process of Elimination → *Antonyms*

After you identify the distractor, use the process of elimination to narrow down your choices. Start by identifying antonyms. An antonym is a word with the opposite meaning, for example B, *opponents* (see below). The prefix *op* means *opposite*. Therefore, B is not correct. The context supports this conclusion. *Rousseau and Voltaire* were not against (opponents of) the European Enlightenment. Instead, they *questioned... traditional institutions and monarchies*. If they questioned the king, they challenged his political ideas. This infers that they (Rousseau and Voltaire) opposed the king's political authority. Therefore, B is an antonym of proponents.

2. In paragraph 1, proponents is closest in meaning to...

	a) associates
antonym	b) opponents
	c) supporters
distractor	d) professionals

You now have two choices left. A is off topic. Because *Rousseau and Voltaire* were part of the European Enlightenment, they were indeed associates. However, their association is not the topic. The topic is *Rousseau and Voltaire* and *the European Enlightenment* <u>versus</u> *traditional institutions and monarchies*. If Rousseau and Voltaire were opposed to traditional institutions and monarchies, then we can infer that they were *supporters* of *the European Enlightenment*. Therefore, C is correct.

2. In paragraph 1, proponents is closest in meaning to...

off topic	a) associates
antonym	b) opponents
correct	**c) supporters**
distractor	d) professionals

Inferring Meaning → *Rhetorical Strategies*

You can infer the meaning of proponents by identifying the rhetorical strategies that create the context in which this word is used. The context for proponents is sentences 5 and 6 below.

1 2 3 4 5 6 7 8 9 10	1 → Adam Smith was born in Scotland in 1723. As a young man, he studied moral philosophy at the University of Glasgow and at Oxford. He eventually went on to tutor a nobleman's son. The position freed Smith from his daily work while affording him the opportunity to tutor while traveling throughout Europe. **5)** In France, Smith met Rousseau and Voltaire, <u>leading</u> proponents of the European Enlightenment. **6)** At its core, the European Enlightenment, guided by reason and science, questioned customs, morals, and traditional institutions, namely monarchies. Returning to Scotland, Smith set about...

Next, let's identify the rhetorical strategies that create the context. It starts with the action of <u>questioning</u> (cause) in this sentence: *the European Enlightenment, guided by reason and science, <u>questioned</u> customs, morals, and traditional institutions, namely monarchies*. Note that there is no stated effect in this sentence. Instead, the word <u>questioned</u> suggests a conflict of ideas (effect). Groups in conflict have leaders. Leaders is inferred by the participle adjective <u>leading</u>. The leaders of the European Enlightenment were *Rousseau and Voltaire*. Because *Rousseau and Voltaire* were leaders—and in conflict with monarchies (kings and queens)—we can infer that they were anti-monarchy. The opposite of anti-monarchy is pro (enlightenment). Therefore, *proponents* infers *supporters*, or C.

Look at another example. The highlighted phrase is the idiom <mark>went bust</mark>. The context is the first four sentences in paragraph five below.

1	**5 → 1)** The railroad <u>boom</u>, **however**, <mark>went bust</mark> in 1893. **2)** Like the internet bubble of 2000 and the real estate bubble of 2008, the railroad boom was a result of companies over-extending. **3)** Simply put, by 1893 there were <u>too</u> many railroads and <u>too</u> many bad loans and <u>too</u> much market speculation. **4)** This led to the <u>collapse</u> of over five hundred banks while dozens of railroads, including the Union Pacific Railroad, declared bankruptcy. Confidence in the economy was restored when gold was found in Canada's Klondike, leading to the Klondike Gold Rush of 1897.

Note in sentence one above how **however** comes between <u>boom</u> (cause) and <mark>went bust</mark> (effect). **However** signals a contrast between <u>boom</u> and <mark>went bust</mark>. From the passage, we know that boom means a time of great economic development. Therefore, we can infer that <mark>went bust</mark> is the opposite of <u>boom</u>. In other words, the end of the boom. Therefore, A is correct. A is a synonym that describes a downward direction ending unhappily. That is what happens to an economic boom: it will eventually crash (effect), as did the railroad boom.

9. What does the phrase <mark>went bust</mark> mean?

correct	**a)**	**crashed**
distractor	b)	burst
not accurate	c)	slowed
not true	d)	expanded

Sentence 3 confirms that A is the best choice. Note in sentence 3 how *too* is repeated for emphasis: *<u>too</u> many railroads; <u>too</u> many bad loans; <u>too</u> much market speculation*. This infers that the railroad boom (cause) had too many negative effects and, as a result, crashed.

Sentence 4 above confirms that A is the best choice. Note in sentence 4 the effects of the crash: *the <u>collapse</u> of over five hundred banks*; *the Union Pacific declared...bankruptcy*. Crash, in this context, is synonymous with <u>collapse</u>.

Synonyms in Context

You can also infer the meaning of a word, phrase or idiom by identifying synonyms in context. A synonym in context means that a word and its synonym will be used within the same sentence or paragraph. For example, read the highlighted sentences below starting at the end of line four. Note the highlighted word gauge. Gauge means measure. Note the prior word Measuring. Measuring is a synonym for gauge. This is an example of synonyms in context. It is also how TOEFL will teach you about the topic: by defining and clarifying words with synonym referents.

1	2 → Also, one will argue that forecasting climate change on a computer is
2	not always accurate. However, what the article fails to mention is that
3	computer modeling accurately predicts broader trends in climate change,
4	and that these trends all indicate increased warming trends. Measuring
5	the GMST is indeed a critical part in measuring climate change. However,
6	such a detailed analysis is not the only way to gauge future climate
7	change. Remember: 85% of the world's energy needs come from the
8	burning of fossil fuels...

Look at a sample question. Note the correct answer and the distractor.

3. In paragraph 2, what does gauge mean?

a) evaluate
correct   b) measure
c) weigh
distractor   d) gouge

Notes

_____

_____

_____

_____

_____

_____

_____

_____

_____

Practice #1: *Vocabulary Questions*

Directions: You have ten minutes to read the passage and answer the questions.

Flooding

1. What does take it for granted mean?

a) assume it will always change
b) assume it will always be there
c) assume it will always be granted
d) assume it will always have value

2. Myriad is closest in meaning to...

a) mystery
b) miraculous
c) many
d) wasteful

3. In a nutshell means what?

a) more importantly
b) not to mention
c) in brief
d) in a shell

4. Untold is closest in meaning to...

a) cannot be mentioned
b) cannot be counted
c) cannot be undone
d) cannot be changed

5. In paragraph 3, what does prime mean?

a) good
b) traditional
c) pristine
d) typical

1 ➔ Water. We take it for granted. Yet without it, life, as we know it, would perish. We use water in myriad ways. We use it for cooking, for cleaning, for generating electricity, and for relaxation. We use it in religious ceremonies, in agriculture, and for transportation. Suffice it to say, water's value is inestimable. And there is a lot of it. Seventy percent of the Earth is covered in water while three-quarters of the human body is water. Some theorize that human blood tastes salty because eons ago, our ancestors lived in the oceans, the salty taste of human blood evidence proving our ancestors did indeed have aquatic origins. Whatever the case maybe, water is the source of life, not only for humans but for all organisms on Earth.

2 ➔ However, much like the Roman god Janus, water has two faces. One is that of life while the other is of death. Water's dual nature as savior and destroyer is evidenced in the natural phenomenon known as flooding. In a nutshell, flooding occurs when a body of water escapes its natural boundaries and temporarily submerges the surrounding landscape. Historically, flooding has caused untold human misery and destruction. Witness the Central China floods of 1931, the greatest natural disaster ever recorded. Three rivers flooded and left over three million people dead. Yet without flooding, we might not be where we are today.

3 ➔ As a naturally occurring phenomenon, floods have been, since the dawn of time, an integral part of human evolution. A prime example is the Nile River in Egypt. For ancient Egyptians, the flooding of the Nile was an auspicious event. The Egyptians believed that the flooding was caused by the tears of the

43 6. Mundane means what?

45 a) seasonal
46 b) special
47 c) arcane
48 d) ordinary

52 7. Silt is closest in meaning to...

54 a) damage left by flooding
55 b) nutrients deposited by flood water
56 c) man-made fertilizer
57 d) crops needing water

60 8. What does the phrase holds true for
61   mean?

63 a) refers to
64 b) applies to
65 c) compares to
66 d) not true for

70 9. What does endemic mean?

72 a) renewing
73 b) beneficial
74 c) native
75 d) endangered

78 10. In paragraph 4, double-edged
79   sword is closest in meaning to...

81 a) sharp and dangerous
82 b) negative and positive
83 c) twice as dangerous
84 d) double the reward

god Isis as she cried for her dead husband, Osiris. However, a more mundane reason can be found, one that occurred then and today, two thousand miles south of Egypt in equatorial Africa. There, in the hills and mountains of present-day Rwanda, Tanzania and Ethiopia, torrential rains fell from June to September. The rain filled the lakes and rivers that fed the Nile, forcing the Nile to flood its banks as it raced north to Egypt and the Mediterranean. For the Egyptians, the annual flood symbolized rebirth. The flooding waters recharged the depleted groundwater while leaving behind a layer of silt in the fields. The silt added much needed nutrients to the heavily farmed soil. This, in turn, fertilized crops, such as flax and wheat, a valuable food source the Egyptians exported. By doing so, the early Egyptians developed wealth and became a major power in the Middle East. In short, without the annual flooding of the Nile, Egyptian civilization, as we now know it, would not exist. The same holds true for the Tigris and Euphrates Rivers flowing south through Iraq and into the Persian Gulf. Flood water caused by rain and snow melt in Syria and Turkey forced the Tigris and Euphrates to flood their banks and replenish crop fields with much needed silt. This cycle of rebirth through flooding is as old as the Earth itself, for even if man does not stand to benefit, endemic biomass does, the flooding of the Amazon is a good example of how flood water has sustained endemic biodiversity for millennia.

4 ➜ Yet flooding is indeed a double-edged sword, the aforementioned China floods of 1931 the most salient example of the destructive power of flooding water. Another, more recent example, was the 2010 Pakistan flood. Unusually heavy monsoon rains, the worst in almost a century, caused flash flooding, an unexpected and unforeseen rise in flood water, often with catastrophic effects. At one point, one-fifth of Pakistan—an area the size of England—was under water. All told, some twenty million people were affected while over two thousand died. Worse, Pakistan's infrastructure was severely disrupted with the total economic cost estimated at forty billion dollars.

93
94
95
96
97

11. Precipitous is closest in meaning to...

a) precarious
b) expected
c) slow
d) extreme

And there's a new threat on the horizon. With Arctic and Antarctica ice melting at precipitous rates, scientists predict that before the end of the century, Manhattan will be under water.

→ Answers page 324.

Notes

_____
_____
_____
_____
_____
_____
_____
_____
_____
_____
_____
_____
_____
_____
_____
_____
_____
_____
_____
_____

Practice #2: *Vocabulary Questions*

<u>Directions</u>: You have ten minutes to read the passage and answer the questions.

Wernher Von Braun

1. In paragraph 1, what does preeminent mean?

a) precious
b) richest
c) oldest
d) greatest

2. In paragraph 2, pioneer means...

a) pilot
b) leader
c) follower
d) worker

3. The idiom put his nose to the grind stone is closest in meaning to...

a) studied harder
b) studied regularly
c) studied less
d) studied with Oberth

4. What does banned mean?

a) prohibited
b) canned
c) authorized
d) supported

1 ➔ Everyone knows that America put the first man on the moon. What most don't realize, however, is that the Saturn V, the launch rocket that sent Apollo 11 astronauts Neil Armstrong, Buzz Aldrin and Michael Collins to the moon, was designed by Germans, in particular the rocket scientist and space architect Wernher Von Braun. In 1975, Von Braun was awarded America's highest science award, the National Medal of Science. Many consider Von Braun to be the preeminent rocket scientist of the twentieth century.

2 ➔ Wernher Von Braun was born into an aristocratic family on March 23, 1912 in Wirsitz, Germany, now present-day Poland. As a boy, Von Braun did not do well in school. Mathematics and physics gave him particular trouble. Then he read *Die Rakete zu den Planetenräumen* (The Rocket into Interplanetary Space) by rocket pioneer Hermann Oberth. It was a turning point. Inspired by Oberth's book, Von Braun put his nose to the grind stone and finished at the top of his class. Von Braun, envisioning that one day man would fly to the moon, went on to receive various technical degrees and became a member of the German Society for Space Travel, where he worked on liquid-fueled rocket engines with Oberth. However, the Nationalist Socialist German Workers Party, which took power in 1932, banned all work on rockets that was not government related. Braun, not wanting to give up his dream of putting a man in space, found work with the German army, designing and testing rockets. By 1934, one of his rockets had flown to a height of 3.5 kilometers. With the German army on the move, rocket development became a top priority of the German military. As a result, a large rocket facility was built at Peenemünde. There Von

5. Instrumental is closest in meaning to...

a) essential
b) industrious
c) determined
d) instructive

6. Orchestrated means what?

a) exacerbated
b) originated
c) ameliorated
d) organized

7. What does expunged mean?

a) preserved
b) reorganized
c) deleted
d) exfoliated

8. What does the cutting edge mean?

a) the most dangerous
b) the most typical
c) the sharpest
d) the most advanced

9. Containing means...?

a) limiting
b) contradicting
c) negotiating
d) imitating

Braun became the leader of "the rocket team" and was instrumental in developing the V-2, a liquid-propelled, 46-foot long ballistic missile that could hit London five-hundred miles away. The V-2, built by slave labor in underground factories, represents the birth of the rocket age, a lineage that extends through both the American and Russian post-war missile and space programs to this day.

3 ➔ In the spring of 1945, with World War Two rapidly drawing to a close, Von Braun orchestrated the surrender of himself and five hundred of his top scientists to the rapidly advancing American army. By then, the Americans were well aware of Von Braun, so much so that he had topped America's Black List, a secret list of German scientists and engineers the Americans were intent on capturing for the knowledge they possessed. Under a plan called Operation Paperclip, Von Braun and many of his colleagues secretly went to work for the American government in Fort Bliss, Texas. There, they continued to design and build rockets, their association with the Nazi party secretly expunged from their public record. Throughout the 1950's, Von Braun and his Peenemünde team represented the cutting edge of rocket technology. They built the Jupiter missile, the first missile to carry a nuclear warhead. Von Braun and his team also built the Jupiter-C, which carried the first American satellite into Earth orbit thus signaling the start of the space race. In 1955, Von Braun became a naturalized American citizen. Meanwhile, he continued to champion the idea of building rockets that would explore space. As early as 1952, his plans for space exploration included space stations and trips to Mars. He even wrote a science fiction novel exploring the possibilities. The American government, however, was more interested in containing the Russian threat than in exploring space. In 1958, the American government formed NASA (National Aeronautics and Space Program). Two years later, NASA opened the Marshall Space Flight Center and Von Braun was chosen to be the director. Von Braun agreed on one condition: that he could develop the Saturn rocket, the launch rocket that would send Apollo 11 to the moon. The Ameri-

91
92
93
94
95

96　10. In paragraph 4, what does wane
97　　　mean?
98
99　a) increase
100　b) pause
101　c) diminish
102　d) claim
103
104
105
106
107
108　11. What does affiliation with mean?
109
110　a) knowledge of
111　b) involvement with
112　c) affinity for
113　d) disinterest in
114

can government relented. And the rest is history. On July 16, 1969, Von Braun's boyhood dream of sending a man to the moon was realized when Apollo 11 commander Neil Armstrong was the first man to walk on the moon.

4 ➜ By 1970, interest in space travel began to wane. The moon had been reached and the U.S. government was cutting back on the costly Apollo program. Von Braun, however, wanted the Saturn V program to continue. His next goal was to build a rocket that would carry men to Mars. Yet it was not to be. In 1970, Von Braun was reassigned to an administrative position in Washington, DC, a position from which he soon resigned to become vice president of an aerospace company. On June 16, 1997, Wernher Von Braun died. Despite Von Braun's achievements, many continue to question his past affiliation with the Nazi party and to what extent he condoned slave labor to build Nazi Germany's rocket program. However history judges Wernher Von Braun, one thing cannot be denied: He put America on the moon.

➜ Answers page 324.

Notes

_____
_____
_____
_____
_____
_____
_____
_____
_____

Negative-Fact Questions → Strategies

Each passage will have two or fewer negative-fact questions. This question type measures your ability to identify and verify information that is not true or not stated in the passage, for example:

3. What is NOT true of the European Enlightenment?

a) It was based on reason.
b) It challenged customs and morals.
c) It was supported by kings and queens.
d) It valued science.

Question Analysis: *Signal Words*

As you analyze the question, note the signal words. In this example, they are <u>NOT true</u> and <u>European Enlightenment</u>. Next, scan the passage for the phrase **European Enlightenment** (line 6 below), the signal phrase in the question.

1	1 → Adam Smith was born in Scotland in 1723. As a young man, he studied
2	moral philosophy at the University of Glasgow and at Oxford. He eventually
3	went on to tutor a nobleman's son. The position freed Smith from his daily
4	work while affording him the opportunity to tutor while traveling throughout
5	Europe. In France, Smith met Rousseau and Voltaire, leading proponents of
6	the **European Enlightenment**. At its core, the European Enlightenment,
7	guided by reason and science, questioned customs, morals, and traditional
8	institutions, namely monarchies. Returning to Scotland, Smith set about writ-
9	ing his seminal *An Inquiry into the Nature and Causes of the Wealth of Nations*.

Choice Analysis: *Process of Elimination*

Next, in the passage above, check to see if the **European Enlightenment** was <u>based on reason</u> (choice A) or not. In the passage, it says that the European Enlightenment was <u>guided by reason</u>. Guided, in this context, means *based on*. Therefore A is true and not the answer. Repeat this check-and-verify process for the remaining three choices.

3. What is NOT true of the European Enlightenment?

a) It was <u>based on reason</u>.
b) It challenged customs and morals.
c) It was supported by kings and queens.
d) It valued science.

• **WARNING:** *Checking and verifying four answer choices is time-consuming. Watch the clock. If this question type is taking too much time, guess and move on.*

Identifying the Distractor

For this question type, there are no distractors. The answer choices are either true or false, in the passage or not, etc. In the following sample, C is correct because it is not true. It is the exception.

> 3. What is NOT true of the European Enlightenment?

true	a)	It was based on reason.
true	b)	It challenged customs and morals.
not true	**c)**	**It was supported by kings and queens.**
true	d)	It valued science.

Notes

_____

_____

_____

_____

_____

_____

_____

_____

_____

_____

_____

_____

_____

_____

_____

_____

_____

Practice #1: *Negative-Fact Questions*

<u>Directions</u>: You have ten minutes to read the passage and answer the questions.

Women of Influence

1. All of the following are true of the Bennett sisters EXCEPT?

a) There are five.
b) Their father is patient.
c) They are nobility.
d) Their mother is moody.

2. In paragraph 1, all of the following are true of Mr. Darcy EXCEPT?

a) He is kind.
b) He has a strong intellect.
c) He is Elizabeth's social equal.
d) He first met Elizabeth when visiting the Bennett's house.

1 ➔ Jane Austen's novel *Pride and Prejudice*, voted Best British novel in a 2005 BBC poll, was originally titled *First Impressions*. Austen wrote it between October 1796 and August 1797. The story centers on the Bennett family, particularly the five sisters whose mother, Mrs. Bennett—a mercurial soul always on the verge of nervous collapse—is determined to marry them off to rich husbands thus ensuring their financial futures while securing for them positions of high social status in early nineteenth century England. Mr. Bennett, a patient and level-headed man with a modest income, puts up with his wife's machinations while displaying a particular fondness for his second oldest daughter, Elizabeth. Elizabeth, with her keen intellect and independent character, watches with a critic's eye as her sisters find varying degrees of success while searching for husbands. When Mr. Darcy, a rich land owner of noble birth, visits the Bennett household, Mrs. Bennett sees another marrying opportunity for her daughters. Elizabeth, however, sees only the snobbish arrogance typical of Mr. Darcy's privileged class, one that is far and above the Bennett's station. In time, however, Elizabeth realizes that her pride has blinded her and, as a result, prejudiced her toward Mr. Darcy, a kind man whose intellect and independence mirror Elizabeth's. In short, Elizabeth and Mr. Darcy are cut from the same cloth. In this light, they are a perfect match and find happiness in wedlock.

3. In paragraph 2, what is NOT mentioned about *Pride and Prejudice*?

a) It is a comedy.
b) It is told from Elizabeth's perspective.
c) It continues to sell well.
d) It is a snapshot of English society in the early 1800's.

4. According to paragraph 3, all of the following are true of Dian Fossey EXCEPT?

a) She studied gorillas in Rwanda.
b) She was accepted into a group of gorillas.
c) She studied gorillas for thirty-five years.
d) She proved that gorillas were not Hollywood stereotypes.

5. What is NOT true of Dian Fossey?

a) National Geographic made her and Peanuts famous.
b) She was a journalist.
c) Her work ended in 1985.
d) She believed gorillas and humans shared the same traits.

6. In paragraph 4, what is NOT mentioned?

a) Where Dian Fossey studied.
b) The name of the director of the Fossey Fund.
c) The name of Fossey's publisher.
d) The impact her death had on the mountain gorillas in Parc National des Volcans.

2 ➜ *Pride and Prejudice*, a title that aptly defines the conflict Elizabeth and Mr. Darcy must face and overcome to find love, was published in 1813. The story, told from Elizabeth's point-of-view, is a window on early nineteenth century English moral values, particularly in regard to the rights of women, or the lack thereof, a condition Jane Austen observes with no small amount of satire. To date, *Pride and Prejudice* has sold over 20 million copies confirming Jane Austen as one of the most influential writers of the English language.

3 ➜ Another woman whose influence is still felt today is Dian Fossey. These days it is commonplace to see biologists on TV studying animals in the wild close up, so close it is as if the human observer were part of the animal group being studied. One of the first scientists to bridge the gap between wild animals and a human observer was Dian Fossey. Fossey did so with the mountain gorillas of Rwanda. She studied them from 1967 up to her death in 1985. Fossey's ability to study and observe wild mountain gorillas while actually being among them revolutionized not only the study of gorillas, and wildlife in general, but also changed our view of gorillas. No longer were they "King Kongs" but, as Fossey herself said, they were "dignified, highly social, gentle giants, with individual personalities, and strong family relationships." The moment Fossey was accepted into the gorilla's world occurred in 1970 when an adult male Fossey had named Peanuts, touched her hand. The moment was immortalized in a National Geographic photograph seen around the world.

4 ➜ Fossey's reputation grew with the publication of her book *Gorillas in the Mist*. By then she'd received her PhD from Cambridge and was teaching at Cornell University. Fame brought Fossey the money she needed to support her research and to establish sanctuaries for the mountain gorillas whose habitat was being destroyed by social unrest and whose numbers were being decimated by poachers. Fossey, determined to stop the unlawful killing of gorillas for meat, waged war on the poachers, so much so that many believe that it was poachers who murdered Fossey in her

88
89
90
91
92
93
94
95
96
97
98
99
100
101

cabin at Karisoke, the name of her research camp in the Parc National des Volcans in Rwanda. Despite Fossey's death, her influence lives on. Thanks to the Atlanta-based Fossey Fund, directed by Sigourney Weaver, who starred as Fossey in *Gorillas in the Mist*, the mountain gorilla population has been slowly increasing from a low of 250 in the early 1980's to an estimated 480 today. Such success is attributable to Fossey's pioneering work and to ecotourism, which brings tourists to the Parc National des Volcans so that they too might experience mountain gorillas as Dian Fossey had.

➔ Answers page 324.

Notes

_____

_____

_____

_____

_____

_____

_____

_____

_____

_____

_____

_____

_____

_____

_____

Practice #2: *Negative-Fact Questions*

<u>Directions</u>: You have ten minutes to read the passage and answer the questions.

Methods of Research

1. In paragraph 1, all of the following are true EXCEPT?

a) Quantitative research employs statistical surveys.
b) Quantitative research is scientific.
c) Qualitative research is based on personal observation.
d) Quantitative research is holistic.

2. In paragraph 2, all of the following are true EXCEPT?

a) Qualitative research targets focus groups.
b) Qualitative research is deductive.
c) Qualitative research can be biased.
d) Qualitative research tries to answer the why and how.

1 ➜ There are two methods of research: qualitative and quantitative. Qualitative research is based on events observed by the researcher while quantitative research is based on numerical data gathered by the researcher. A rainbow analogy exemplifies the two approaches. A researcher applying the qualitative approach would conclude, after personal observation, that a rainbow is an arc of colors with red on the outer edge of the arc and violet on the inner edge, with orange, yellow, blue and indigo in between. A researcher applying the quantitative approach would, in contrast, measure the varying intensities of color and the angle of refraction causing those colors, then compare those numbers to a broader statistical survey of rainbows. As you can see, quantitative research is scientific while qualitative research is holistic, a methodology based on observation and interpretation. Yet despite the differences, researchers use both with the intent of <u>compiling</u> information that is both reliable and credible.

2 ➜ To produce reliable and credible research, a researcher using the qualitative approach focuses on the why and how of decision making, specifically in regard to human behavior, such as why a child will sit in front of a computer for hours at a time or how a tribe of Amazonian Indians deals with a threat to its territory from a neighboring tribe. By observing events as they unfold—by actually being in the field—the researcher has a front row seat on trying to answer why a child is addicted to the computer or how a tribe of Amazon Indians secures its territory from incursions. The researcher does this by focusing on language, signs, and meaning. Historically, researchers in the social sciences, such as anthropologists, sociologists and psychologists, have employed the qualitative approach, one that, by its very nature, is inductive, induction being a

3. In paragraph 2, the following are mentioned EXCEPT?

a) focus group
b) anthropologist
c) neighborhood
d) computer modeling

4. In paragraph 3, the following are mentioned EXCEPT?

a) Quantitative research is non-biased.
b) Quantitative research uses mathematical models.
c) Quantitative research is used by politicians.
d) Quantitative research compiles observed data.

form of logic in which a conclusion is based on a series of observable facts. To obtain information, however, the researcher must limit the focus of his or her study. For example, if you are a researcher trying to answer the question why some children are addicted to the computer, it would not be possible for you to observe all the children in a particular city, state, or country. Instead, you would establish a context or a focus group—a group of computer-using children in a neighborhood say—a group which, by its limited size, would be accessible and easily observed. Yet by limiting the size of the study group, less data will be obtained which, in turn, might raise questions about the reliability of your research. Also, you might come under scrutiny, for readers and other researchers might ask how neutral you were when compiling data, especially if you were observing your own children using a computer.

3 ➔ In contrast, quantitative research focuses on the gathering of large amounts of empirical data, then feeding that data into mathematical models that, in turn, provide the researcher with statistics. From these statistics, a researcher can make conclusions based not on his own personal involvement with the subject but on what the numbers are telling him. This impersonal approach removes any researcher bias from the research process and, more importantly, increases the reliability of the research and any conclusions based on that research. Politicians often employ quantitative research. For example, the president wants to raise taxes but first he wants to know if the public is for or against the idea. To find out, he conducts a national opinion survey that asks the question: Are you in favor of raising taxes? The more people answer the survey, the more accurate the results. The more accurate the results, the more informed the president will be when finally deciding whether to raise taxes or not. This, then, is another difference between qualitative and quantitative research: quantitative research compiles data from much larger research groups while qualitative research is limited to what the researcher can, as an individual, practically observe.

92
93
94
95
96
97
98
99
100
101
102
103

5. Which of the following is NOT mentioned in paragraph 4?

a) When combined, quantitative and qualitative research are effective.
b) Qualitative research is a good way to prove a hypothesis based on research done quantitatively.
c) A hypothesis based on qualitative research can be confirmed using quantitative research.
d) Quantitative research can compare the results of qualitative research over a much larger surveyed area.

4 ➔ Despite their differences, the two methods of research, when used in tandem, can produce reliable and credible results. For example, a researcher has concluded through observation that Hispanics make up the majority of students in a local English-as-a-second language program. By surveying other schools in her city or state—by using quantitative research—the researcher could then compile statistical data to prove if her initial hypothesis about Hispanics and English language programs is indeed accurate.

empirical: based on observation or experience

compiling: collecting then editing data in a document

➔ Answers page 324.

Notes

_____
_____
_____
_____
_____
_____
_____
_____
_____
_____
_____
_____
_____

Inference Questions → *Strategies*

Each passage will have two or fewer inference questions. This question type measures your ability to make conclusions based on facts stated in the passage, for example:

> 10. From the passage, it can be inferred that Adam Smith probably...
>
> a) owned a pin factory
> b) visited a pin factory
> c) worked in a pin factory
> d) studied workers

Question Analysis: *Signal Words*

Look at the following question. The signal words are <u>Adam Smith probably</u>.

> 10. From the passage, it can be inferred that <u>Adam Smith probably</u>...

<u>Probably</u> means the information is not stated as fact in the passage. Therefore, you must infer it (read-between-the-lines) based on the answer choices. Do so by first scanning each answer choice for signal words. The signal words (see below) are the <u>verbs</u> and the noun *factory*. Scan the passage for the noun *factory* and the <u>verbs</u> associated with *factory*.

> a) <u>owned</u> a pin *factory*
> b) <u>visited</u> a pin *factory*
> c) <u>worked</u> in a pin *factory*
> d) <u>studied</u> workers

Choice Analysis: *Process of Elimination*

Using process of elimination, eliminate choices that are: 1) off topic; 2) too specific; 3) too general; 4) not known; 5) not true; 6) not implied; 7) not accurate. In the question below, A and C are not correct. There is not enough factual information in the passage to suggest (imply) that either of these two choices is probably true. <u>Remember</u>: Smith was writing a book, so he needed research.

> 10. From the passage, it can be inferred that Adam Smith probably...
>
> **not implied** a) owned a pin factory
> b) visited a pin factory
> **not implied** c) worked in a pin factory
> d) studied workers

You now have two choices left. One is the distractor.

Identifying the Distractor

In this example, D is the distractor. Smith did not study "workers." That description is too general. Smith, instead, studied specific workers, namely "pin workers." When did Smith study pin workers? When he visited a pin factory. Why did he visit a pin factory? To do research for his book *The Wealth of Nations*. Therefore, B is correct.

10. From the passage, it can be inferred that Adam Smith probably...

not implied   a)   owned a pin factory
correct   **b)**   **visited a pin factory**
not implied   c)   worked in a pin factory
distractor   d)   studied workers

Notes

_____

_____

_____

_____

_____

_____

_____

_____

_____

_____

_____

_____

_____

_____

_____

_____

_____

_____

_____

Practice #1: *Inference Questions*

Directions: You have ten minutes to read the passage and answer the questions.

Crypsis

1. What can be inferred about the tawny frogmouth?

a) It is a frog.
b) It is a monkey.
c) It is a bird.
d) It is a snake.

2. What can be inferred about the flounder?

a) Predators can easily see it.
b) It preys on a variety of fish.
c) Predators mistake it for sand.
d) It has the same camouflage as the tawny frogmouth.

1 ➔ Crypsis, the ability of an organism to avoid being seen by another organism, can be achieved through camouflage and mimicry. Camouflage means hiding by blending in with the environment. An organism that employs camouflage is the tawny frogmouth of Australia. When seen, the tawny frogmouth is often confused with an owl; however, the tawny frogmouth is not an owl but a nightjar. The tawny frogmouth gets its name from its large, wide beak. It is nocturnal and feeds primarily on insects. When sleeping during the day, or when threatened, the tawny frogmouth perches on a branch of a tree that is the same color as the tawny frogmouth's plumage. Camouflaged during the day this way, the tawny frogmouth is virtually invisible to the observer. Blending in with the native environment in such a manner is called cryptic coloration. This is the most common form of crypsis.

2 ➔ Another organism that benefits from cryptic coloration is the flounder. Flounders spend the majority of their time on the ocean floor; thus, evolution has provided the flounder with a speckled coloration that matches the color of the ocean floor. The flounder's ability to camouflage itself by appearing to look like the ocean floor makes it invisible to predators hoping to make a meal out of the flounder while at the same time allowing the flounder to ambush its prey, animals such as shrimp and crabs. In the aforementioned tawny frogmouth, camouflage served only one purpose: to protect. With the flounder, however, camouflage serves a dual purpose: to help it survive by avoiding being detected and possibly eaten while at the same time allowing it to ambush its prey. Tigers too rely on cryptic coloration for survival and for hunting. The tiger's vertical black and orange stripes allow it to blend in with the environment. Deer and other prey that confuse the tiger's stripes for

light and shade more often than not end up on the dinner plate.

3. In paragraph 3, it is suggested that one way a predator locates an octopus is by...

a) shape
b) sound
c) taste
d) smell

3 ➜ Disruptive camouflage is the opposite of cryptic coloration. With disruptive camouflage, an organism tries to confuse the observer by changing shape and color or, as in the octopus's case, by ejecting a cloud of black ink, which disrupts the predator's sense of smell. This allows the octopus to escape. The pufferfish, a small, slow moving fish, employs another type of disruptive camouflage. If threatened, the pufferfish balloons into a ball by filling its stomach with water. At the same time, spikes protrude from its body making the otherwise small pufferfish look like a much larger and more dangerous fish. A predator, looking for a small fish, and not wanting to risk a confrontation with a ballooned pufferfish, would move on to easier prey. However, if a predator were to attack, it would run into the pufferfish's second line of defense, the poison tetrodotoxin, a neurotoxin with no known antidote. The only vertebrate whose toxin is more lethal than the pufferfish's is the golden dart frog's.

4. What does the author suggest about the pufferfish?

a) It uses poison to kill its prey.
b) It is deadlier than the golden dart frog.
c) It is the second deadliest vertebrate in the world.
d) Its toxin has a known antidote.

5. In paragraph 4, we can infer that a sheep in wolf's clothing...

a) is a threat
b) is toxic
c) is harmless
d) is a snake

4 ➜ A second form of crypsis is mimicry. An example is the lo moth. In the center of each wing is a large black dot called an eyespot. When observed, these eyespots look like the eyes of a large predator, such as an owl. In this equation, the mimic, the lo moth, is sharing the characteristics of a different species called the model. By modeling itself after a larger animal, the lo moth sends a signal to the observer that it is a potential threat and should not be eaten. This relationship, one in which a species shares similarities with another species while pretending to be a threat, is called a Batesian mimic. Named after Henry Walter Bates, the English scientist who first observed mimicry in the wild, a Batesian mimic is a sheep in wolf's clothing. Another example is *Malpolon moilensis* or false cobra. This cobra looks and moves like its more lethal cousin, the hooded cobra, but is innocuous.

➜ Answers page 324.

Practice #2: *Inference Questions*

<u>Directions</u>: You have ten minutes to read the passage and answer the questions.

A Landmark Ruling

1 1. In paragraph 1, what can we infer
2 about the Supreme Court's
3 decision?
4
5 a) It has changed the Supreme Court.
6 b) It has limited the rights of the
7 individual in the United States.
8 c) It has dramatically changed the
9 definition of a U.S. corporation.
10 d) It has changed the constitution in
11 a way that benefits corporations.
12
13
14
15
16
17
18 2. In paragraph 2, what does the
19 author imply when he says that
20 *Hillary: The Movie* "barely appeared
21 on the radar"?
22
23 a) That *Hillary: The Movie* was widely
24 seen by many Americans then.
25 b) That *Hillary: The Movie* was seen
26 by very few Americans at the time.
27 c) That *Hillary: The Movie* was not on
28 TV during the 2008 presidential
29 primary.
30 d) That *Hillary: The Movie* was
31 banned.
32
33
34
35
36
37
38
39
40
41
42
43

1 → In January, 2010, the Supreme Court of the United States ruled on the case the US Supreme Court vs. the Federal Elections Commission. In this landmark ruling, the bitterly-divided Court ruled 5-4 that corporations enjoy the same First Amendment rights as do individuals. In other words, a corporation, no matter what the size, is considered a citizen. Microsoft, General Electric, and Exxon. In the eyes of the Supreme Court, they are all citizens—individuals—thus legally entitled to protection under the Constitution. That protection includes the right to free speech. Suffice it to say, the ruling set off a firestorm of protest. But before we get to that, let's map out how this landmark ruling came about.

2 → In 2004, Oscar-winning documentary filmmaker Michael Moore released *Fahrenheit 911*, a <u>scathing indictment</u> of how then Republican President George W. Bush failed to act during the 9/11 crisis. In Moore's film, Bush comes off looking like a man entirely unsuited to be president. In short, Moore argues that President Bush failed in a time of national crisis. The Republicans were furious. Not to be outdone, David Bossie, a veteran Republican strategist, made a film attacking Democrat Hillary Clinton, who was then starting her run for president. But the movie, titled *Hillary: The Movie*, barely appeared on the radar during the 2008 presidential primary season. Why? Because the Federal Elections Commission restricted Bossie's film from being shown. The decision to restrict the film was based on the fact that the film was made not by David Bossie himself, as an individual, but by a corporation. That corporation was Citizens United. A lower court ruled that *Hillary: The Movie* wasn't a movie at all, but instead a 90-minute attack ad telling voters not to vote for Hillary Clinton. In that light, the lower court ruled that under the current cam-

3. In paragraph 2, we can infer that David Bossie...

a) used his own money to make *Hillary: The Movie*.
b) used corporate money to make a film attacking Hillary Clinton.
c) is really a filmmaker and not a political strategist.
d) believes the Federal Elections Commission made the right decision.

4. What can we infer about the lower court's decision?

a) The Supreme Court agreed with it.
b) The Supreme Court banned it.
c) The Supreme Court voted for it.
d) The Supreme Court rejected it.

5. In paragraph 3, what does the author suggest when he says "And smoke is already on the horizon"?

a) That the Court's ruling is already having positive effects.
b) That the Court's ruling is already causing controversy.
c) That the Court's ruling was not clear.
d) That the Court's ruling is already out of date.

paign rules established by the Federal Elections Commission, Citizens United—being a legal corporate entity—was prohibited from financing political commercials. Basically, the Federal Elections Commission said corporate money has no place in American politics. What did David Bossie do? He turned around and sued the Federal Elections Commission, the argument being that Citizens United was being denied the right to free speech. In January, 2010, the Supreme Court agreed with Bossie's argument and overruled the lower court's decision. In delivering its ruling, the Supreme Court said, and I quote, "Political spending is a form of protected speech under the First Amendment, and the government may not keep corporations or unions from spending money to support or denounce individual candidates in elections." It doesn't get much clearer than that.

3 ➔ Now, you may wonder, why is this such a big deal? Why has this decision sent shock waves through the American political system? Think of it this way: the Supreme Court says that if the Ford Motor Company wants to donate a billion dollars to help elect a candidate—a candidate who will help Ford move its factories overseas—then Ford, as an individual, has every right to do so. Those opposed to the decision say that this is patently unfair. Corporate money, they argue, will go directly into political advertising which, in turn, will give an unfair advantage to a corporate-sponsored candidate. For example, imagine you are a school teacher and you decide to run for Congress and your opponent is funded by IBM or Google. In short, those who oppose corporate political funding fear that the American political system is no longer based on the one person, one vote proposition. Instead, elections will simply be bought by the candidate who has the most money, namely, corporate money. And smoke is already on the horizon. Recently it has been revealed that the American Chamber of Commerce—the largest association of businesses in America, representing every type of business from Microsoft down to your local gas station owner—has been soliciting money from foreign corpora-

94
95 6. What will the essay develop next?
96
97 a) Examples to support the Court's
98   ruling.
99 b) Examples to support the argument
       that the Court's ruling is negatively
       impacting corporations.
    c) Evidence proving that foreign money
       is already entering the American
       political system.
    d) An argument in support of ruling
       against the Chamber of Commerce.

tions with U.S. operations, money which is finding its way into the American political system regardless of what members of the Chamber of Commerce might think. Let's examine the evidence.

landmark: a turning point

scathing: bitter and severe

indictment: document served to one accused of fault or offense

→ Answers page 325.

Notes

_____

_____

_____

_____

_____

_____

_____

_____

_____

_____

_____

_____

_____

Rhetorical-Purpose Questions → *Strategies*

Each passage will have two or fewer rhetorical-purpose questions. This question type measures your ability to identify how the writer uses rhetorical strategies. The rhetorical strategies used for testing are narration, description, illustration, definition, compare-contrast, classification, process, and cause-and-effect (see page 14). Rhetorical-purpose questions can be paraphrased a variety of ways, for example:

- In paragraph 1, what was the effect of the tsunami?

- In paragraph 4, how are students classified?

- How does the author define the concept of quality control?

Look at a sample rhetorical-purpose question. The signal words are underlined.

8. In paragraph 3, why does Adam Smith mention the pin worker and the owner of the pin factory?

a) to compare and contrast workers who benefitted the most from a new type of manufacturing process

b) to classify the various types of workers in 1723 Scotland

c) to define the process in which national wealth is created for both a pin worker and his employer

d) to support his argument that a factory worker and a factory owner can both benefit financially from a systematic manufacturing process

Question Analysis: *Signal Words*

In the question above, mention means *use as an illustration*. Those illustrations are the pin worker and the owner of the pin factory.

Next, scan the answer choices for signal words. Note below how the signal words are rhetorical strategies followed by **cause**-*and-effect*.

a) to compare and contrast workers who *benefitted the most from* **a new type of manufacturing process**

b) to classify the various types of workers in 1723 Scotland

c) to define the process in which **national wealth is created** *for both a pin worker and his employer*

d) to support his argument that *a factory worker and a factory owner can both benefit financially from* **a systematic manufacturing process**

Next, scan paragraph 3 below for the signal words <u>the pin worker</u> and <u>the owner of the pin factory</u>.

1   3 ➔ A division of labor, however, was but one part of Smith's argument for creating
2   wealth. An integral part of the wealth-making process, Smith claims, is <u>the pin</u>
3   <u>worker</u> himself. He is performing his assigned task not for society's benefit nor for
4   the benefit of the company, but for his own personal gain and security. The same
5   follows with <u>the owner of the pin factory</u>. He too is out for personal gain, the health
6   and the wealth of the nation the least of his, and his workers', worries. Yet by pur-
7   suing individual gain, Smith argues that <u>the worker</u> and <u>the factory owner</u> are in
8   fact directly adding to the wealth of the nation by utilizing a more efficient manu-
9   facturing process, one which stimulates trade, the buying and selling of goods, lo-
10   cally, nationally, and internationally. Smith coined this process "the invisible
11   hand."

Choice Analysis: *Process of Elimination*

When you locate <u>the worker</u> and <u>the owner of the factory</u>, note how they are used rhetorically in the passage, then compare that usage to the four answer choices below. Eliminate choices that are not rhetorically similar and/or; 1) off topic; 2) too specific; 3) too general; 4) not known; 5) not true.

not true-too general   a) to compare and contrast workers who benefitted the most from a new type of manufacturing process

not similar-not true   b) to classify the various types of workers in 1723 Scotland

               c) to define the process in which national wealth is created for both a pin worker and his employer

               d) to support his argument that a factory worker and a factory owner can both benefit financially from a systematic manufacturing process

A is not correct because it is not true. Neither the pin worker nor the factory owner benefitted "the most." This effect suggests inequality; whereas, Smith argued that national wealth benefitted all equally. Also, in A, note the phrase "a new type of manufacturing process." Which "new type of manufacturing process"? The passage does not say; thus, this phrase is too general as well. These—combined with rhetorical strategies based on the superlative "the most"—eliminate A.

B is also incorrect because it is not rhetorically similar nor is it factually true. Adam Smith was born in 1723.

You now have two choices left. One is the distractor.

Identifying the Distractor

In this example, C is the distractor.

distractor   c) to define the process in which **national wealth is created** *for both a pin worker and his employer*

Note the inferred **cause**-and-*effect* relationship in C above. It seems correct; however, it is not. National wealth is not created for both a pin worker and his employer. It is for everyone's benefit. Also, this choice says "define the process," but what process? In the passage, Smith specifically mentions the pin-making process, but that process is not stated in C; thus, C is also too general. Therefore, by process of elimination, D is correct.

In D below, the "systematic manufacturing process" is the pin-making process, a process a factory worker (a pin worker) and a factory owner (the owner of the pin factory) "*can both benefit financially from.*" Moreover, these two illustrations (factory worker + factory owner) are evidence supporting Smith's argument paraphrased in D.

correct   d) to support his argument that *a factory worker and a factory owner can both benefit financially from* **a systematic manufacturing process**

Notes

_____

_____

_____

_____

_____

_____

_____

_____

_____

_____

_____

_____

Practice #1: *Rhetorical-Purpose Questions*

<u>Directions</u>: You have ten minutes to read the passage and answer the questions.

Cognitive Bias

1. How is the author of this passage using classification?

a) to identify and develop three common forms of cognitive bias
b) to identify and define the process of decision making
c) to illustrate how people make snap decisions
d) to contrast opposing views on the theory of cognitive bias

2. In paragraph 2, why does the author use the example of a political bandwagon?

a) to illustrate how bandwagons are used in politics, past and present
b) to compare and contrast how voters can be easily influenced
c) to classify various types of political campaign strategies
d) to illustrate the historical origin of the term bandwagon and its effect

3. What happens as a result of a cascade of information?

a) The individual concludes that he/she is right and the group is wrong.
b) The individual joins the group believing there must be truth in numbers.
c) The individual makes the correct choice based on the evidence.
d) The individual literally jumps on the bandwagon.

1 ➜ Passing judgment is human nature. Some of our judgments are accurate while others are flawed. Often a judgment is flawed because we have not taken the time to think an issue through and instead make a snap decision based on experience. A snap decision resulting in an error of judgment is called a cognitive bias. Some of the more common cognitive biases are the bandwagon effect, stereotyping, and the halo effect. Let's start with the bandwagon effect.

2 ➜ Have you ever bought something because all your friends had bought it, or tried a new restaurant simply because all your friends had? If so, then you have demonstrated the cognitive bias called the bandwagon effect. Historically, the word bandwagon describes a wagon pulled by a horse. On the wagon, a band is playing music. If you like the music, then you will follow the bandwagon, maybe even jump on. Either way, you have literally joined the group. Years ago, politicians used bandwagons to spread their messages. If many voters were following a politician's bandwagon, and you concluded that so many people must mean the politician deserves your vote, then you would have joined the bandwagon. How you came to that conclusion is known as an information cascade. An information cascade is an integral part of the bandwagon effect. It occurs when you conclude, without evidence, that if everybody is doing it, then they must be right and you must be wrong. Because you are wrong, you follow those who are right: the group or the bandwagon.

4. Why does the author mention teenagers?

a) to explain why teenagers do the things they do
b) to expand the topic of politics
c) to provide another example of a decision making process
d) to give another example of the bandwagon effect

5. What does the bandwagon effect often produce?

a) stereotypes
b) shopaholics
c) individuals
d) bargains

6. Why does the author introduce the topic of hamburgers?

a) to classify different stereotypes and how they originate
b) to contrast bargain shoppers and hamburger lovers
c) to add another step in the process of stereotyping
d) to illustrate how stereotypes are generalizations that do more harm than good

7. In paragraph 5, how does the author introduce the topic of the halo effect?

a) by using an illustration
b) by using a classification
c) by using a process
d) by using a definition

3 → The bandwagon effect is not limited to politics. It also describes why some teenagers get into trouble. Not wanting to be left out of the group, a teenager will join in even if he or she knows that what they are doing is wrong. This is one way teenagers start drinking and smoking, by jumping on the bandwagon figuratively.

4 → Another example of the bandwagon effect is Black Friday. Black Friday is a national day of sales in which millions jump on the bandwagon and flock to stores looking for pre-Christmas bargains. Do these people really need to wait in front of Wal-Mart at four a.m. in order to be first in line for the best bargains, or are they all just shopaholics? If you assume that all Black Friday shoppers are shopaholics, then you would be stereotyping. Stereotyping is another common cognitive bias. When you stereotype someone, you are concluding, without evidence, that the character traits of one individual are consistent throughout the group. For example, your friend Bill eats nothing but hamburgers. Because Bill is American, you conclude that all Americans eat hamburgers, which of course is not true, much like the fallacy that all Black Friday shoppers are shopaholics is not true. Just because you go shopping on Black Friday does not mean you are a shopaholic. True, many Black Friday shoppers are shopaholics; however, many simply want to save money or are with friends or family. Whatever the case, stereotyping can lead to offense, so be careful when making sweeping generalities based on experience rather than on sound evidence.

5 → But let's say you jump on the bandwagon anyway and join the four a.m. stampede into Wal-Mart. You want a Samsung big-screen TV so you race for the electronics department. The only problem is everybody else wanted a Samsung TV, and now they are all gone. Then a man says, "Wal-Mart TVs are just as good as Samsungs. In fact, Samsung makes Wal-Mart TVs." Is that true? You don't know. Meanwhile, the man grabs a Wal-Mart TV and everyone else jumps on the bandwagon until there is only one Wal-Mart TV left. What do

8. According to paragraph 5, what can the halo effect result in?

a) a snap decision that often results in consumer satisfaction
b) a snap decision that often ends in customer disappointment
c) a snap decision that is a bargain
d) a snap decision based on research

9. What does the Apple iPad tell us about the halo effect?

a) Apple products benefit from the halo effect.
b) Apple products are always cutting edge.
c) Apple products need no advertising.
d) Apple products are the best.

you do? You grab it. Why? Because you like Wal-Mart TVs? No. The fact is you have never heard of a Wal-Mart TV before. But you have heard of Samsung, and you know that Samsung is high quality. So what do you do? You make a snap decision based on experience: If Samsung makes Wal-Mart TVs, like the man said—and you know that Samsung is good—then Wal-Mart TVs must be good. Right? Right. Only later when you get it home do you realize that your Wal-Mart TV was made by the Cheap-O TV Company. This then is an example of the halo effect. The halo effect is a cognitive bias in which you believe that the value or quality of one thing (Samsung TV) spills over and increases the value of another thing (Wal-Mart TV).

6 → Another example is the Apple iPad. When it first came out, many questioned whether it would fly. Considering Apple's track record for delivering cutting edge products, such as the wildly successful iPod, was there any doubt? No. When the iPad arrived in stores, people lined up to buy it. Had they ever seen or used an iPad before? No. But that didn't stop sales from going through the roof. Why was the iPad such a hit? Because of the halo effect.

stampede: a mass movement based on impulse

→ Answers page 325.

Notes

_____

_____

_____

_____

_____

_____

_____

Practice #2: *Rhetorical-Purpose Questions*

Directions: You have ten minutes to read the passage and answer the questions.

The Gilded Age

1. In paragraph 1, what was the effect of the transcontinental railroad's completion in 1869?

a) It made a new class of people.
b) It put ships out of business.
c) It signaled the start of the Gilded Age.
d) It helped end the Civil War.

2. Why does the author mention Denver, Colorado?

a) to illustrate the development of a western town in the 1870's
b) to illustrate the rate at which people were moving west in 1870
c) to demonstrate how the west was linked to the east in 1869
d) to describe how the railroad was important in the Gilded Age

3. In paragraph 2, what was the direct effect of the need for steel?

a) increased spending
b) the birth of Wall Street
c) a great migration west
d) more railroads

1 ➜ The verb *to gild* means to apply a layer of gold to an object. Mark Twain used the adjectival form of this verb when he coined the phrase the Gilded Age. The Gilded Age, from 1869 to 1893, represents American economic prosperity at its height. And for good reason. The Gilded Age created many firsts, such as a new class of super-rich, men like John D. Rockefeller, J. P. Morgan, Andrew Mellon, Cornelius Vanderbilt, and Andrew Carnegie. It also witnessed the birth of the first corporations, such as General Electric and Standard Oil. Yet it was the railroad companies that were the engine that drove the Gilded Age, companies like Union Pacific and the Central Pacific Railroad. In 1869, four years after the Civil War, these two railroads linked up at Promontory Summit in Utah thereby establishing the first continental railroad in North America. Now, instead of sailing south around South America to go from New York City to San Francisco—a trip that could take three weeks, if the weather were good—the trip could now be made in six-days by train. The impact was immediate. With the east now linked with the west, thousands seeking free land and a new future headed west. When the railroad arrived in Denver in 1870, it had a population of 5,000. Ten years later it was 36,000.

2 ➜ To accommodate the movement of people and material, hundreds of new railroads were built. And they needed steel. Lots of it. Yet steel-making was, and still is, a capital-intensive business. It took money to build steel factories and to mine the ore necessary for smelting in coke ovens fueled by coal. Investment capital was needed. Banks, jumping on the bandwagon, met the demand and Wall Street, as we know it, came into its own. The boom in steel making created a demand not

4. Why does the author mention ATT, Western Union and farming?

a) because they all wanted to make a profit
b) because they all benefitted from the building of the railroad
c) because they were all American
d) because each needed steel

5. According to paragraph 3, what created the American middle-class?

a) internal promotions
b) increased productivity
c) the modern management system
d) the railroads

6. Why does the author use the example of the Singer sewing machine?

a) to demonstrate how women in the Gilded Age worked
b) to classify women's work in the late nineteenth century
c) to illustrate how the Gilded Age was a time of technological progress
d) to show how American politics and the railroads were connected

only for Wall-Street investment capital but for factory workers as well. Most of those workers were newly-arrived immigrants. The steel they made in east coast factories built rails and rail cars, all of it heading west to serve the farmers who needed to ship their beef and wheat back east by rail. In this way, the railroad spawned the farming industry and helped to expand the telegraph industry, for the fastest and easiest way to build new telegraph lines was to follow the railroads into the newly created towns dotting the west. They did, and American Telephone and Telegraph (ATT) and Western Union took their place beside Union Pacific Railroad, Carnegie Steel, Standard Oil, and Mellon Bank as being America's most profitable companies.

3 → Railroad companies are also credited with developing what today is known as the modern management system. With so much building, the railroads needed a clear chain of command to keep things running smoothly. This they did by creating clear managerial roles while establishing career goals that employees at all levels could pursue. This, combined with internal promotions, led to greater employee loyalty and productivity. Other companies soon followed suit. This gave rise to the American middle-class, especially in big east coast cities.

4 → Manufacturing too benefited from the railroad boom. One consumer item that changed millions of women's lives was the Singer sewing machine. By 1880, over three million homes had a Singer. Why was this invention so revolutionary? Prior to the Singer sewing machine, women had to stay home and make clothes for their families, a time-consuming task that left women with little or no free time for anything else. Yet the Singer sewing machine changed all that. It not only sped up the clothes-making process, but also led to the development of textile factories where clothes, such as those for railroad workers, were mass produced. The result was that clothes were cheaper and women no longer had to hand-stitch clothes for their families. With the advent of the Singer sewing machine, women now had more free time,

94
95
96
97
98
99
100
101
102
103
104
105
106
107
108
109
110

7. Why does the author compare the railroad boom to the internet and real estate bubbles of the early twenty-first century?

a) to highlight the repeating nature of economic bubbles
b) to stress that economic bubbles are bad for the economy
c) to illustrate how the railroad boom was different from later internet and real estate booms
d) to emphasize the need for more government control

time they could devote to women's rights, such as the right to vote, which they won in 1920.

5 ➜ The railroad boom, however, went bust in 1893. Like the internet bubble of 2000 and the real estate bubble of 2008, the railroad boom was a result of companies over-extending. Simply put, by 1893 there were too many railroads and too many bad loans and too much market speculation. This led to the collapse of over five hundred banks while dozens of railroads, including the Union Pacific Railroad, declared bankruptcy. Confidence in the economy was restored when gold was found in Canada's Klondike, leading to the Klondike Gold Rush of 1897.

➜ Answers page 325.

Notes

_____
_____
_____
_____
_____
_____
_____
_____
_____
_____
_____
_____
_____
_____
_____
_____

Reference Questions → *Strategies*

Each passage will have two or fewer reference questions. This grammar question measures your ability to connect words grammatically using referents (pronouns) and their antecedents (nouns). Look at a sample reference question.

5. In paragraph 2, to what does it refer?

a) worker
b) pin
c) wire
d) head

Question Analysis

Make sure you understand the question before answering. Do so by identifying the grammatical function of the highlighted referent. In this example, the referent it is a third-person pronoun (*he, she, it...*).

5. In paragraph 2, to what does it refer?

2 → In *The Wealth of Nations*, Smith argues that building national economic wealth begins with a division of labor. Smith supports his argument by using a pin factory. In a typical pin factory of the day, each worker was responsible for making pins from start to finish. A worker would start by cutting the pin to size from a piece of wire, then straighten it, then sharpen the end, affix a head, polish it, then package it. In short, one man was responsible for each step of the pin-making process...

Choice Analysis: *Process of Elimination*

Look the sample question below. B is correct.

5. In paragraph 2, to what does it refer?

a) worker
correct b) pin
c) wire
d) head

A <u>worker</u> would start by cutting the **pin** to size from a piece of <u>wire</u>, then straighten it, then sharpen the end, affix a <u>head</u>, polish it, then <u>package</u> it.

To confirm that B is correct, first identify which part of speech it is. In the sentence above, it is the object of the verb <u>package</u>. Next, using process of elimination, ask yourself: Package what? A, a <u>worker</u>? No. You cannot package a worker. Topically, that does not make sense. C, package a piece of <u>wire</u>? No. The topic is making pins not wire. D, package the <u>head</u> (of a pin)? <u>Head</u> is the object of the verb <u>affix</u>. Topically, the head of a pin becomes part of the <u>pin</u> when it is affixed (connected) to the <u>wire</u>. Because the context is the process of making a pin (head + wire = pin), the topical and grammatical answer is <u>pin</u>. This confirms that B is correct. Package what? The <u>pin</u> (the finished product).

Look at the next example.

---

1 ➜ We Americans assume that all business cultures are like ours. Nothing could be further from the truth. Many **Middle Eastern and Asian cultures** prefer to do business face-to-face. Discussing business over tea or while having dinner is an integral part of the business process in these cultures. Such traditions help develop mutual respect and trust...

If the referent is a *noun phrase*, such as these cultures above, the four answer choices will also be noun phrases. In question below, A is the correct answer.

7. In paragraph 1, what does these cultures refer to?

correct	a)	Middle Eastern and Asian cultures
not mentioned	b)	old and new cultures
not mentioned	c)	traditional and non-traditional cultures
too general	d)	foreign cultures

Confirm your choice by asking: What cultures? B, *old and new cultures*? No. They are not mentioned in this context. C, *traditional and non-traditional cultures*? No. They are not mentioned in this context either. D, *foreign cultures*? This choice is too general thus not correct. Therefore, <u>A</u> is correct.

Notes

Practice: *Reference Questions*

<u>Directions</u>: You have ten minutes to complete questions 1 to 11.

1. What does it refer to?

a) army
b) tax money
c) Roman government
d) census

2. To what does their refer?

a) manpower
b) demographers
c) heads
d) civilizations

Census taking, however, is nothing new. Many ancient civilizations regularly took a census of population, for example Rome. Because Rome had a large standing army, it needed money and men. By periodically taking a census, the Roman government knew how much tax money it could raise for the army and the available manpower it could draw from. It wasn't until the second half of the nineteenth century that the process of census taking changed. Instead of just counting heads and money, demographers started to broaden their statistic gathering to include age, occupation, marital status, and education.

3. He refers to...

a) white man
b) Rowlandson
c) God
d) Sully

4. To what does in which refer?

a) Eden
b) environment
c) message
d) Na'vi

Rowlandson's influence is still felt today. A prime example of Rowlandson's influence is the movie *Avatar*. *Avatar*, however, is very much a post-modern captivity narrative. What do I mean by that? Take a look at the story. What happens? The Na'vi—which are nothing more than Native Americans—capture Sully, a white man. Sully lives with the Na'vi yet instead of escaping with the message that faith in God will save you, he returns with the message that the white man is destroying the environment, the environment being the Na'vi and the Eden in which they live.

5. They refers to...

a) buffalo
b) cowbirds
c) family
d) nomad

6. To what does this problem refer?

a) lose their food source
b) raising a family
c) were nomadic
d) was very much an opportunist

As mentioned, the cowbird was originally a nomad, travelling with the buffalo and eating whatever the buffalo kicked up, insects, seeds, whatever. In this light, the cowbird was very much an opportunist. Yet the cowbird had a problem. Because cowbirds were nomadic, raising a family was a problem. If they stopped to raise a brood, they'd lose their food source for the buffalo were always on the move. The cowbird, ever the opportunist, resolved this problem in a unique way, one that characterizes the species to this day.

7. Of which refers to what?

a) water
b) seamount
c) variety
d) fish

Seamounts are of great interest not only to biologists but to the commercial fishing industry as well. And for good reason. The nutrient-rich water around a seamount is home to an immense variety of fish, many of which have commercial value. One such fish is the orange roughy.

---

8. To what does These organisms refer?

a) plants, algae, and photoautotrophs
b) plants, algae, and many species of bacteria
c) photosynthesis, photoautotrophs, and many species of plants
d) organisms, plants, and many species of bacteria

For plants to survive, they must convert carbon dioxide into sugar using energy from the sun. This conversion process is called photosynthesis. Organisms that depend on photosynthesis for survival are called photoautotrophs. Plants, as well as algae and many species of bacteria, fall under this classification. These organisms are unique in that they are the only ones to produce their own food by photosynthesis, a chemically complex process in which oxygen is a waste byproduct. Suffice it to say, without photo-synthesis, life on Earth would cease to exist.

---

9. Of which refers to...

a) literate, urbanized, state-level societies
b) archeologists
c) civilization
d) state-level societies

Before we proceed, we really need to define the term civilization. Within the word itself lies the root "civil" meaning to display the appropriate behavior. Yet this definition of civilization is far too broad, for what might be considered appropriate behavior in one society might be taboo in another. Simply put, archeologists apply the term civilization when describing literate, urbanized, state-level societies, the earliest of which were city-states in southwest Asia and along the Nile River.

---

10. To what does it refer?

a) hot air
b) heat
c) moisture
d) hot day

According to the National Oceanographic and Atmospheric Administration (NOAA), extreme heat is "one of the most underrated and least understood of the deadly weather phenomena." Why is this the case? First off, the danger is less obvious. Think about it. A mass of hot air settles over us and we think, okay, it's just another hot day. To cool off, our bodies perspire. This moisture evaporates. By doing so, it draws excess heat from our bodies.

11. To what does in which refer?

a) fewer
b) English canon
c) ads
d) It's

12. In which refers to?

a) day
b) by
c) goes
d) politicians

13. To what does wherein refer?

a) nature
b) language
c) process
d) usage

The comparative *fewer* is rapidly disappearing from the English canon, replaced by the ubiquitous—and grammatically incorrect—*less*. It's not uncommon to see ads in which this change is taking place, such as "Eat Mary's Ice Cream. It has less calories." Politicians also commit this grammatical faux pas. Not a day goes by in which a politician is not screaming, "Americans need to pay less taxes!" As you know, fewer takes a plural countable noun, such as, "Joe has *fewer problems* than Al," or "The effect of colony collapse disorder has resulted in *fewer honey bees*." Note that we can count calories (one calorie, two calories) and problems (one problem, two problems), and honey bees (one honey bee, two honey bees). *Less*, in contrast, takes a non countable noun, such as "English teachers make far *less money* than corporate lawyers." Can we count money (one money, two monies?) No. Sadly, the word fewer will soon be one for the history books. But that is the nature of language, a process wherein common usage often dictates grammatical form.

→ Answers page 325.

Notes

_____

_____

_____

_____

_____

_____

_____

_____

_____

Sentence-Simplification Questions → *Strategies*

Each passage will have one sentence-simplification question. This question type measures your ability to analyze how the highlighted sentence in the passage has been paraphrased. The correct answer will paraphrase the highlighted sentence. Look at a sample question.

11. Which of the following sentences best restates the essential information in the highlighted sentence in paragraph 4?

   a) Adam Smith adds that the wealth of a nation depends upon serving the needs of the individual first.

   b) Smith goes on to say that free trade is the best way to create wealth.

   c) Moreover, Smith says that nations become wealthy by accumulating gold and by systematically manufacturing goods, which are then freely traded.

   d) Smith believes that systematically manufactured goods freely traded create more national wealth than gold.

1 4 → *The Wealth of Nations* is very much a reaction to the predominating eco-
2 nomic theory of the day, that of Mercantilism. Mercantilists posited that the
3 wealth of a nation depended on developing and maintaining national power;
4 thus, it was a form of economic nationalism. Spain, at the time of Columbus, is
5 a prime example of just such a nation. A nation like Spain preserved national
6 power by accumulating as much gold as possible through strong exports, the
7 limitation of imports, and a large population of poorly paid workers. ■ To devel-
8 op exports, companies were subsidized by the government which also wrote
9 laws to limit imports. ■ By limiting imports, the gold used to pay for imports
10 would stay in the country and create a greater money supply and more credit. ■
11 Moreover, nations were geared toward acquiring and maintaining gold at all
12 costs, including warring with each other. ■ Adam Smith, however, argued that
13 trade benefitted all nations and that gold was not equal to wealth. Gold, Smith
14 said, was like any other commodity, such as wheat or wool, and that it deserved
15 no special treatment. More importantly, Smith says that the wealth of a nation
16 is not based on the hoarding of gold, but on the free flow of goods manufactured
17 in a systematic way, a way that serves the needs of the individual and, ultimate-
18 ly, the nation as a whole. With that, Adam Smith gave birth to what we now call
19 economic theory. As Thomas Edison is to the light bulb, Adam Smith is to the
20 science of economics.

Question Analysis

This task asks you to match the ideas in the highlighted sentence with one of four answer choices. The correct answer will restate the same topic, rhetorical strategies, and grammar as in the highlighted sentence.

Signal Words

Start your analysis of the highlighted sentence by identifying signal words. The signal words will help you identify which rhetorical strategies, grammar, and topics are being used to construct the highlighted sentence. In the sentence below (which is highlighted in the passage) the key signal word is **but**. **But** is a conjunction of contrast indicating that the writer is using the rhetorical strategy of compare-and-contrast.

1   More importantly, Smith says that the wealth of a nation is not based on
2   the hoarding of gold, **but** on the free flow of goods manufactured in a sys-
3   tematic way, a way that serves the needs of the individual and, ultimately,
4   the nation as a whole.

Next, identify the rhetorical strategy used in the clause before <u>but</u>. That rhetorical strategy is *effect*-and-**cause**.

More importantly, Smith says that *the wealth of a nation is not based on* **the hoarding of gold**, <u>but</u>...

Note above how the writer is paraphrasing how Smith refutes the Mercantilist argument of hoarding gold using *effect*-and-**cause**.

Next, identify the rhetorical strategy used in the clause after <u>but</u>. That rhetorical strategy is also **cause**-and-*effect*.

...<u>but</u> **on the free flow of goods manufactured in a systematic way**, *a way that serves the needs of the individual and, ultimately, the nation as a whole.*

Note above how the writer is paraphrasing Smith's counter argument against Mercantilism. Note also how **cause**-and-*effect* supports Smith's idea of systematic manufacturing and how it creates national wealth, which is his invisible-hand theory.

The signal phrase "More importantly" at the head of the sentence also indicates the writer's intent. More importantly it is an emphatic used to stress a point. That point is Smith's belief that Mercantilism is a failed system while the invisible hand is the better solution.

Mapped out below, you can see how the highlighted sentence has been constructed rhetorically, grammatically, and topically.

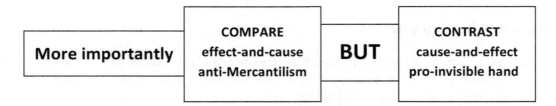

- **REMEMBER:** *The correct answer will include the same elements.*

Choice Analysis: *Process of Elimination*

After you have identified the rhetorical, grammatical, and topical elements in the highlighted sentence, compare them to those in each answer choice. By process of elimination, you will identify the answer.

➜ Choice A uses **cause**-and-*effect* and <u>illustration</u>.

    A) Adam Smith adds that *the wealth of a nation depends upon* **serving the needs of the individual first**.

➜ Choice B uses **cause**-and-*effect*.

    B) Smith goes on to say that **free trade** *is the best way to create wealth*.

➜ Choice C uses **cause**-and-*effect* and <u>illustration</u>.

    C) Moreover, Smith says that *nations become wealthy* **by accumulating <u>gold</u>** and **by systematically manufacturing goods**, **which are then freely traded.**

➜ Choice D uses <u>compare-and-contrast</u> and **cause**-and-*effect*.

    D) Smith believes that **systematically manufactured goods freely traded** *create more national wealth than gold*.

Based on rhetorical strategies alone, D is the best choice so far. To confirm that D is correct, analyze the other three choices. Look for choices that: 1) are off topic and/or are missing topics; 2) lack topic development; 3) express contrary and/or unrelated ideas; 4) contain factually wrong information; 5) are grammatically different; 6) are not rhetorically correct.

    a) Adam Smith adds that the wealth of a nation depends upon serving the needs of the individual first.

This choice is not correct because it lacks topic development. It does not include the topics of "gold" or "the free flow of goods manufactured in a systematic way," both of which are in the highlighted sentence. Also, the "wealth of a nation" does not depend on "serving the needs of the individual first." This point is factually and rhetorically wrong. Smith, instead, believes that the wealth of a nation depends on "the free flow of goods manufactured in a systematic way." The end result is that all ("the nation as a whole") benefit.

    b) Smith goes on to say that free trade is the best way to create wealth.

This choice is not correct because it lacks topic development. Yes, Smith believes that "free trade" creates wealth. But what kind of "wealth"? The highlighted sentence says "the wealth of a nation." This choice only says "wealth"; thus, it is too general. Also, this sentence uses the superlative "the best way." The highlighted sentence does not use this grammatical form.

c) Moreover, Smith says that nations become wealthy by accumulating gold and by systematically manufacturing goods, which are then freely traded.

This choice is not correct because it is factually wrong. Smith does not say that nations become wealthy by "accumulating gold." Rhetorically, this contradicts Smith's invisible hand theory. In this choice, Smith is a Mercantilist. Also, the transitions "Moreover" in the choice and "More importantly" in the highlighted sentence are not grammatically synonymous. Moreover signals the addition of added information while More importantly emphasizes a fact of greater importance. As a result, C is not correct.

d) Smith believes that systematically manufactured goods freely traded create more national wealth than gold.

Conclusion? By process of elimination, D is correct because it correctly paraphrases the highlighted sentence, rhetorically, grammatically, and topically.

Language-Use Distractors

When analyzing the answer choices, look for language-use distractors. Look at the highlighted sentence below. Note the word abolitionist, then note the **language-use distractor** in choices A, B, and C. Each distractor has the same prefix *ab* as abolitionist thus is a homophone distractor with a different meaning.

Prior to the Civil War, John Brown, a deeply religious man born in Torrington, Connecticut, was an abolitionist who fought against the south's slave-based economy.

a) John Brown, a deeply religious man born in Torrington, Connecticut, fought and **abolished** slavery in the south before the Civil War.

b) By the time the Civil War had started, John Brown, a deeply religious New England Yankee, had promised to rid the south of slavery **absolutely**.

c) Before the Civil War, John Brown, a religious man originally from Connecticut, **abhorred** the southern slave system.

d) John Brown, a New England Yankee with strong religious convictions, struggled hard to end slavery in the southern states before the Civil War.

Answer-Choice Analysis

a) John Brown, a deeply religious man born in Torrington, Connecticut, fought and abolished slavery in the south before the Civil War.

This choice is not correct. Abolitionist in the highlighted sentence is a noun while abolished in this choice is a verb. An abolitionist is a person who wants to end slavery while abolished means that John Brown, in this context, abolished (ended) slavery in the south. This fact is not stated in the highlighted sentence. This example tests language-use proficiency (OPDU**L**=C), specifically your ability to distinguish between a verb distractor (abolished) and a noun (abolitionist) with the same *ab* prefix, and how the meaning of each differs in this context.

b) By the time the Civil War had started, John Brown, a deeply religious New England Yankee, had promised to rid the south of slavery <u>absolutely</u>.

This choice is not correct. <u>Absolutely</u> is an adverb of degree meaning *completely*. The highlighted sentence does not contain an adverb that describes the degree to which John Brown will rid the south of slavery. This example tests language-use proficiency (OPDU<u>L</u>=C), specifically your ability to distinguish between an adverb distractor (absolutely) and a noun (abolitionist) with the same *ab* prefix, and how the meaning of each differs in this context.

c) Before the Civil War, John Brown, a religious man originally from Connecticut, <u>abhorred</u> the southern slave system.

This choice is not correct. The adjective <u>abhorred</u> means *to hate with extreme prejudice*. We can infer that because John Brown was an abolitionist, he <u>abhorred</u> slavery. However, because <u>abhorred</u> and <u>abolitionist</u> are not synonymous, they are topically different. That means that the highlighted sentence and this choice are also topically different. This example tests language-use proficiency (OPDU<u>L</u>=C), specifically your ability to distinguish between an adjective distractor (abhorred) and a noun (abolitionist) with the same *ab* prefix, and how the meaning of each differs in this context.

d) John Brown, a New England Yankee with strong religious convictions, struggled hard to end slavery in the southern states before the Civil War.

This choice is correct. Note that this choice contains no words with the prefix *ab*. Instead, the phrase "struggled hard to end slavery" infers <u>abolitionist</u>. What was John Brown? An <u>abolitionist</u>. What was an abolitionist? A person who "struggled hard to end slavery in the southern states before the Civil War." Therefore, this choice and the highlighted sentence are topically and grammatically united.

Practice #1: *Sentence-Simplification Questions*

<u>Directions</u>: Read each numbered sentence and the restatement below it. If the restatement is correct, put a <u>C</u> in the blank. If it is not correct, put an <u>I</u> in the blank.

1. Scientists have determined that large bodies of liquid water do not exist on Mars; thus, there is very little water vapor in the Martian atmosphere.

   Because liquid water, like lakes and oceans, is not present on Mars, the air contains few water molecules.

2. Post-impressionism is distinct from impressionism inasmuch as the post-impressionists placed more emphasis on geometric shapes and bold, arbitrary colors; whereas, the impressionists were concerned with capturing a general impression of a scene with less emphasis on line and form.

The impressionists believed that the post-impressionists, with their focus on shapes and natural colors, were less concerned with capturing the general feeling of a landscape when painting.

_____

3. Semiotics, the study of signs and symbols and signification, can be divided into the study of semantics, syntactics, and pragmatics.

The study of semiotics, signs and symbols can be subdivided into three groups: semantics, syntactics and pragmatics.

_____

4. Issue framing is a form of rhetoric in which the issue you present is delivered in such a way as to guarantee that most of your audience will agree with you.

_____ Issue framing is a form of rhetoric that can persuade an entire audience.

5. One of the earliest forms of clock was the water clock, a device that measured time by the flow of water, a method that lacks the precision of today's timepieces.

_____ Water clocks lacked precision therefore were unable to measure time.

6. Although many theories suggest that Greek fire was a form of petroleum, there is still no clear evidence proving the original chemical nature of the substance though its use as an early weapon of terror is well documented.

Greek fire is a well-documented early weapon of terror which was made from gasoline.

_____

7. In anthropology, a fossil is distinct from an artifact in that a fossil is a bone turned to stone; whereas, an artifact is a product, such as a knife or a bracelet, made by an individual living in a society.

Fossils and artifacts are different because the former is a bone that has become stone while the latter is a man-made product.

_____

8. Historically, a letter of marque granted the bearer the right to seize goods or property in the name of the government, a process which, essentially, made piracy legal.

Many years ago, if a person carried a letter of marque, it meant that he could steal things with the permission of his government.

_____

9. PEM, protein-energy malnutrition, is responsible for fifty percent of the deaths of children under five in developing nations worldwide.

PEN is responsible for fifty percent of the deaths of children worldwide in nations that are developing.

_____

10. Encomienda, a system in which the indigenous people formed the basis of Spain's colonial labor force, one that supplied the Spanish with gold and supplies, was first introduced by Columbus on the island of Hispaniola, now present-day Haiti and the Dominican Republic.

_____ On the island of Hispaniola, Christopher Columbus introduced an economic system that turned the native inhabitants into a colonial labor force.

11. While some see Gilded Age industrialists, such as John D. Rockefeller and Andrew Carnegie, as charitable individuals whose fortunes built some of Manhattan's most famous buildings, like Carnegie Hall and the Rockefeller Center, others view them as robber barons whose charitable donations were simply a way to avoid paying taxes.

_____ Some consider men like Rockefeller and Carnegie to be great philanthropists while others consider them to be nothing more than tax dodgers.

12. In 1215, the Magna Carta—a legal document that said that the king was not above the law—was signed by King John, who promptly abandoned it; it was reissued by his son, Henry the Third, albeit in a revised form, when he took the throne in 1216.

_____ King Henry of England supported then rejected the Magna Carta unlike his son, John the Third, who brought it back in 1216 even though it had been modified.

13. The herd mentality analogizes the behavior of people in large groups to the behavior of animals in herds.

_____ Behaviorally, groups of people are comparable to animals in herds.

14. Unlike most scientists who do actual experiments to prove a hypothesis, Albert Einstein instead worked out and tested his famous theory of relativity all on paper.

_____ Albert Einstein performed carefully designed experiments to prove his theories.

15. When Britains voted to exit the European Union in June of 2016, many Brits immediately regretted their actions and insisted they were instead voting to protest the inequality of globalization not Britain's place in the EU.

_____ The inequality of globalization forced Britain to leave the European Union.

16. A category five hurricane, with winds exceeding 155 mph, is the most power-ful type of hurricane, the most famous of which are Katrina in 2005 and An-drew in 1992.

_____ Hurricanes Katherine and Andrew are famous category-five hurricanes.

→ **Answers page 326.**

Practice #2: *Sentence Simplification Questions*

Directions: Read the following passages and answer the questions.

1 → The literary theory that predominated in the middle decades of the twentieth century, and is still prevalent today, is called New Criticism. Named after the 1941 book *The New Criticism* by John Crowe Ransom, New Criticism espoused an objective approach to literary analysis. Moreover, new critics argued that a literary work, be it a poem, a play, or a novel, had to be closely read in order to determine how the piece worked as a self-referential object free of external bias. By that, proponents of New Criticism meant that the aesthetic value of a work came from its inherent structure and the words therein supported by literary devices, such as analogy, metaphor, allusion, rhyme and meter, and plot. In short, the aesthetic value of a literary work rests on an objective evaluation of what lies between the covers. Prior to the New Criticism movement, literary critics judged the merits of a literary work by the author's intent, how readers reacted to the work, and by the cultural context in which the work was written. The new critics, however, argued that such an approach had little or nothing to do with the work itself as an aesthetic object. Rather, the new critics asserted that the meaning of a text could be determined only by a close reading in which the literary devices therein combined to create a theme which, in turn, helped to identify the best way to interpret the work free of external influence and bias.

1. Which of the following sentences best restates the essential information in highlighted **sentence A** in paragraph 1?

   a) New Criticism started in the 1920s and is still popular today.

   b) New Criticism was not prevalent in the twentieth century like it is today.

   c) New Criticism, dominant from 1940-1960, remains a popular form of literary criticism.

   d) Many literary theories started in the last century, particular New Criticism which is still used today.

2. Which of the following sentences best restates the essential information in highlighted **sentence B** in paragraph 1?

   a) In addition, new critics believed that a literary work had to be closely and objectively analyzed to determine if the piece were free of influence.

   b) In contrast, new critics argued that anything could be a work of art.

   c) New critics instead claimed that a literary work, such as a novel or a poem, was written with the help of external influences, such as research.

   d) New critics believe that a literary work must be a poem, a play, or a novel.

3. Which of the following sentences best restates the essential information in highlighted **sentence C** in paragraph 1?

   a) According to New Criticism, writing can be evaluated many ways.

   b) Prior to New Criticism, the best way to judge a book was by the author's intent and other cultural factors.

   c) Before New Criticism, critics judged a piece of literature by factors that had nothing to do with the work itself.

   d) New Criticism claims that critics are the best judges.

4. Which of the following sentences best restates the essential information in highlighted **sentence D** in paragraph 1?

   a) In short, the new critics argued that a literary work had to be free of external influence and bias in order to be worth reading.

   b) On the contrary, critics supported the idea that reading a book was the best way to judge its value.

   c) Instead, the new critics believed that a piece of literature could best be understood by an objective, unbiased reading of the text's literary devices.

   d) In addition, the new critics argued that a close reading of a literary work was the only way to determine if the work had a theme.

1		2 → The Socratic method, named after the Greek philosopher Socrates, is a
2	**A**	method of debate in which critical thinking is developed by asking and an-
3		swering questions in order to establish and clarify opposing viewpoints. The
4		Socratic method is an integral part of western education, particularly in law
5		school. A law professor, wanting to test his students' knowledge of a case,
6	**B**	will start by asking a student to summarize the court's ruling specific to the
7		case. The professor will then question the student to see if the student
8		agrees or disagrees with the court's ruling. Often the professor will turn dev-
9		il's advocate and challenge the student's opinion of the court's ruling. This,
10		in turn, will help the student to clarify his or her understanding of the case
11		and their position regarding it. The professor can then offer his or her opin-
12		ion, or ask another student to challenge the first student's opinion. The
13		purpose of such an exercise is not to embarrass a student by forcing him or
14	**C**	her to defend his or her ideas in public discourse, but to explore all sides of
15		an issue in order to test the logic of an argument and, more importantly,
16		how to apply the law. This approach to teaching, one in which both the
17		teacher and the students engage in ongoing debates about a particular top-
18		ic, is one of the foundations of the western educational tradition. In fact, it
19		can be argued that a successful class is one in which free and active debate
20	**D**	is encouraged by the teacher while a class in which a teacher simply lec-
21		tures with little or no discourse is of far less benefit to the student body.
22		

5. Which of the following sentences best restates the essential information in highlighted **sentence A** in paragraph 2?

   a) Socrates was a Greek philosopher famous for asking and answering important questions.

   b) Asking and answering questions to develop analytical thinking is a process of debate known as the Socratic method.

   c) The Socratic Method is a popular way to teach critical thinking.

   d) There can be no critical thinking without the Socratic method.

6. Which of the following sentences best restates the essential information in highlighted **sentence B** in paragraph 2?

   a) Measuring student knowledge of a law case begins with a summary of the court's ruling.

   b) A law professor will summarize a court's ruling before his students summarize the case.

   c) Law students must learn how to summarize to understand court rulings.

   d) Law students and professors debate rulings specific to a variety of cases.

7. Which of the following sentences best restates the essential information in highlighted **sentence C** in paragraph 2?

   a) This particular teaching method teaches students about public speaking and the law.

   b) This exercise is good practice because law students need to be able to express opinions in court.

   c) The purpose of the exercise is to help students speak more proficiently when arguing.

   d) This teaching method helps law students understand the complexities of legal issues while helping them apply the law.

8. Which of the following sentences best restates the essential information in highlighted **sentence D** in paragraph 2?

   a) By definition, a successful class is one which benefits both the students and the teacher.

   b) A class in which the teacher does all the talking is far less beneficial for the students than one in which the teacher employs the Socratic method.

   c) Students who understand the Socratic method are much smarter than those who don't.

   d) It can be argued that a successful class starts with good students.

A 3 → Marsupials are a distinct class of mammals in that they have a very short gestation period, between four to five weeks. As a result, they give birth prematurely. A joey, the name for a marsupial infant, is thus born in the fetal state. Once free of the womb, the joey crawls or wiggles helpless and blind, its long forearms designed to help it progress across its mother's fur until it finds its ways into the pouch. Because a joey cannot regulate its own body heat, it must rely on the heat inside its mother's pouch, a temperature that must remain between 30-32 Celsius in order for the joey to survive. Once inside the pouch, the joey finds a teat to which it attaches itself. Several months later, the joey will emerge from the pouch and begin the process of learning how to survive. Because female marsupials have such **B** short gestation periods, they are at less risk of environmental dangers, such as being vulnerable to predators, plus in times of drought, their chances of survival increase inasmuch as they do not need to carry a still-growing fetus to term, as do placental mammals, such as humans.

9. Which of the following sentences best restates the essential information in highlighted **sentence A** in paragraph 3?

   a) Marsupials are unique because they have a very short birthing period.

   b) Mammals have a special birthing period that lasts about a month.

   c) Marsupials are unusual mammals since they give birth every month.

   d) Mammals are distinct Marsupials who have a very short gestation period.

10. Which of the following sentences best restates the essential information in highlighted **sentence B** in paragraph 3?

   a) Owing to the fact that female marsupials have short gestation periods, they are more vulnerable to predator attack.

   b) Because of a short gestation periods, a female marsupial has a better chance of survival unlike other placental mammals.

   c) Since marsupials are vulnerable to attack and are at greater environmental risk from droughts, they must give birth quickly.

   d) Environment factors have forced marsupials to develop ways of survival that put them at less risk.

1　**A**　4 ➔ What sets the aboriginal peoples of the Pacific Northwest apart from the
2　rest of the indigenous peoples of North America is the totem pole. The making
3　of a totem pole starts with a cedar tree, the height of which can range any-
4　where from ten to two-hundred feet. The branches are removed as is the bark.
5　A carver then sculpts faces into the pole. The faces are those animals the na-
6　tive people encounter on a daily basis, animals such as ravens, killer whales,
7　eagles, bears, and salmon. Early Christian missionaries had assumed that to-
8　**B**　tem poles were shamanistic symbols and were worshipped as such; however,
9　anthropologists now know that totem poles carry no religious significance. In-
10　stead, each totem pole tells the story of the clan that erected it. Those stories
11　might be the recounting of a great battle or a great hunt. Another misconcep-
12　tion about the totem pole was that the stories were once thought to ascend in
13　a vertical order with the most important character crowning the pole. This, in
14　**C**　turn, gave rise to the popular idiom, "The low man on the totem pole," namely,
15　the person residing at the bottom of the hierarchy, such as a junior worker in
16　an office who has little or no authority compared to those above. The origin of
17　the totem pole was once a mystery too. Some have hypothesized that the scar-
18　city of old totem poles, those going back two or three centuries, suggested that
19　the tradition of carving of totem poles started when the indigenous tribes of
20　the Pacific Northwest acquired iron tools from Europeans. Anthropologists
21　now believe that ancient totem poles are rare due to the climate of the Pacific
22　Northwest. This area, stretching from Vancouver, Canada north to Alaska,
23　**D**　gets so much rain, the Pacific coast forest is considered a rainforest on par
24　with the Amazon. With so much rain and snow, and because they are made of
25　wood, most of the really old totem poles have simply rotted away.

11. Which of the following sentences best restates the essential information in
highlighted **sentence A** in paragraph 4?

a) The totem pole makes the native people of the Pacific Northwest unique.

b) Totem poles are made by many people in the Pacific Northwest.

c) The totem pole sets aboriginal people apart from indigenous people in the
Pacific Northwest.

d) Setting people apart is the purpose of the totem pole.

12. Which of the following sentences best restates the essential information in
highlighted **sentence B** in paragraph 4?

a) Early Christians believed in shamanistic rituals and totem poles.

b) Early Christian assumptions about the religious significance of totem poles
have been proven wrong by anthropologists.

c) Early Christians first identified the importance of totem poles yet only
anthropologists understand their symbolic significance.

d) Early Christian missionaries and anthropologists agree on the symbolic
significance of totem poles.

13. Which of the following sentences best restates the essential information in highlighted **sentence C** in paragraph 4?

    a) The idiom "the low man on the totem pole" is an English idiom that defines a person of low social standing.

    b) A person with no authority will often be found carved at the bottom of a totem pole.

    c) The expression "the low man on the pole" was started by the native tribes of the Northwest as a means of describing a position of great authority.

    d) A person with no authority will often think of totem poles when he or she hears an idiom.

14. Which of the following sentences best restates the essential information in highlighted **sentence D** in paragraph 4?

    a) The Pacific coast rainforest gets as much rain as the Amazon.

    b) The Pacific coast is as big as the Amazon rainforest.

    c) The Pacific coast rainforest, extending from Canada to Alaska, gets almost as much rainfall as does the Amazon.

    d) The Amazon and the Pacific coast rainforest are the same size and get as much rain.

1
2
3
4

5 ➜ Nobody would disagree that violent video games are designed with killing in mind, just like no one would disagree that problem-solution scenarios in which an anti-hero blasts his way to freedom reinforce detrimental behavior in adolescents. But wait. Where are the parents in all this?

15. Which of the following sentences best restates the essential information in the highlighted sentence in paragraph 5?

    a) Everybody would agree that video games have a negative influence on kids.

    b) Nobody would disagree that video games are about death and destruction and that children love to watch the behavior of heroes.

    c) Adolescents prefer to watch violent video games, a fact nobody would disagree with.

    d) Some would disagree that violent video games are designed with killing in mind and that heroes are a bad influence on adolescent viewers.

A

B

6 → In AD 476, the Western Roman Empire, its territories controlled by corrupt and ineffective governors, fell to an invading army of Goths. This event was a turning point in world history, for it marks the end of classical antiquity and the beginning of the Early Middle Ages in Europe. The Early Middle Ages (circa 500 to 1000 AD) was a time of social and economic chaos. With the collapse of the Western Roman Empire, long distance trade was abandoned, for the trade routes built by Rome and secured by its once-powerful army were now under the control of varying Germanic tribes constantly at war with each other. The precipitous decline in trade directly affected manufacturing. Pottery, for example, was an industry that vanished almost overnight, as did the trade in luxury goods, such as silk and spices from the Far East and salt from Africa. With them went the merchant class, men whose money was the tax base upon which Rome had survived. The Early Middle Ages was in such turmoil that it is often referred to as the Dark Ages. The Roman Empire, which had been a stabilizing economic and cultural force for over five hundred years, had given way to a Europe in which anarchy reigned supreme. Out of the chaos rose various Germanic tribes, one of which was the Franks, the ruler of which was Charles Martel, or Charles "The Hammer." Martel is credited with devising what today is known as the feudal system. In order to wage war and protect his ever-expanding empire, Martel needed to maintain a large standing army. That army was made up of heavily armored horseman called vassals. The vassals, who would later on be known as knights, swore allegiance to Martel. In return, Martel granted them large tracts of land called fiefs. The vassals then leased their land to peasant farmers. The peasants, little more than slaves, were heavily taxed for their work, the money going to Martel for the purpose of expanding the Frankish empire which, by the 800's, included most of western Europe and was under the control of Martel's grandson, Charlemagne. Charlemagne had by then established a central court in Aachen in present-day Germany. For protecting the Pope Leo III, he was crowned the Holy Roman Emperor, for Charlemagne's empire did indeed mirror that of ancient Rome's. With Charlemagne creating a stable social order, there was a renewed interest in writing, art, architecture, and the study of scripture. This period is known as the Carolingian Renaissance, a period many historians believe was the precursor to the European Renaissance, circa 1300-1600. When Charlemagne died in 814, he was succeeded by his son, Louis the Pius. Upon his death, his three sons divided the empire into three kingdoms, territories which would eventually evolve into present-day France, Germany and Italy.

C

D

E

F

G

H

16. Which of the following sentences best restates the essential information in highlighted **sentence A** in paragraph 6?

   a) In AD 476, the Rome was invaded by an army of Goths, which supported Rome's corrupt and ineffective governors.

   b) The territories of the Western Empire had been, by AD 476, invaded and destroyed by an invading army of Goths, who replaced corrupt and ineffective governors.

c) In AD 467, the Western Roman Empire fell because it had no defense.

d) The Western Roman Empire was conquered by an army of invaders in AD 476.

17. Which of the following sentences best restates the essential information in highlighted **sentence B** in paragraph 6?

a) The Early Middle ages was stable both politically and economically.

b) The Early Middle Ages was in social and economic chaos.

c) The Middle Ages lasted about five hundred years.

d) Social and economic problems were common in the Middle Ages.

18. Which of the following sentences best restates the essential information in highlighted **sentence C** in paragraph 6?

a) Trading in luxury goods, such as pottery, suddenly disappeared.

b) Many industries vanished, such as silk making, pottery and salt.

c) Luxury goods gained a new popularity in Africa and the Middle East.

d) Pottery was no longer made while luxury goods were no longer imported.

19. Which of the following sentences best restates the essential information in highlighted **sentence D** in paragraph 6?

a) The stability of Rome gave way to an unstable Europe.

b) Rome reigned supreme when Europe was full of anarchy.

c) European anarchy gave way to Rome's stabilizing influence.

d) For five hundred years, Rome and Europe were in chaos.

20. Which of the following sentences best restates the essential information in highlighted **sentence E** in paragraph 6?

a) A permanent army was essential to sustain Martel's empire.

b) Martel didn't need to wage war to expand his army and his empire.

c) Martel expanded his army as he expanded his empire.

d) Martel needed to build and protect his empire.

21. Which of the following sentences best restates the essential information in highlighted **sentence F** in paragraph 6?

    a) The taxes Martel forced from peasants helped him conquer western Europe, an empire eventually ruled by his son, Charlemagne.

    b) By 800, most of the peasants of western Europe were under the control of Charlemagne and Martel.

    c) For the purpose of expanding his empire, Martel forced peasants to pay taxes, money that eventually went to Martel's son, Charlemagne.

    d) Martel taxed peasants in order to expand the Frankish Empire which, by 800, was ruled by Charlemagne, Martel's grandson.

22. Which of the following sentences best restates the essential information in highlighted **sentence G** in paragraph 6?

    a) Charlemagne was interested in writing, art, architecture and scripture.

    b) A renewed interest in art and religion created stability under Charlemagne.

    c) A stable social order depends on an interest in the arts and scripture.

    d) Social stability created a revival in the arts and religion.

23. Which of the following sentences best restates the essential information in highlighted **sentence H** in paragraph 6?

    a) France, Germany and Italy were once ruled by Charlemagne's son.

    b) After his death, Charlemagne's sons invaded France, Germany, and Italy.

    c) Charlemagne's three sons inherited his empire.

    d) Charlemagne divided his kingdom between his three sons.

➔ Answers page 326.

Sentence-Insertion Questions → *Strategies*

Each passage will have one sentence-insertion question. For this question, you will insert a sentence into a paragraph. By doing so, you are developing the paragraph grammatically, topically, and rhetorically. When the sentence is inserted in the right place, the paragraph will demonstrate Coherence (OPDUL=C).

Look at the following question.

9. Look at the four squares [■]. They indicate where the following sentence could be added to paragraph 4. Click on the square to insert the sentence into the passage.

insertion sentence > **Witness England and Holland battling for control of present-day Manhattan in the early 1600's.**

1 A nation like Spain preserved national power by accumulating as much gold
2 as possible through strong exports, the limitation of imports, and a large
3 population of poorly paid workers. ■ To develop exports, companies were
4 subsidized by the government, which also wrote laws to limit imports. ■ By
5 limiting imports, the gold used to pay for imports would stay in the country
6 and create a greater money supply and more credit. ■ Moreover, nations
7 were geared toward acquiring and maintaining gold at all costs, including
8 warring with each other. ■ Adam Smith, however, argued that free trade
9 benefitted all nations and that gold was not equal to wealth.

To choose an answer, click on <u>one</u> black square. For this example, square four is the correct insertion point, so you would click on it.

- **REMEMBER:** *On test day, when you click on a black square, the insertion sentence will insert, like the sample below.*

1 A nation like Spain preserved national power by accumulating as much gold
2 as possible through strong exports, the limitation of imports, and a large,
3 population of poorly paid workers. ■ To develop exports, companies were
4 subsidized by the government, which also wrote laws to limit imports. ■ By
5 limiting imports, the gold used to pay for imports would stay in the country
6 and create a greater money supply and more credit. ■ Moreover, nations
7 were geared toward acquiring and maintaining gold at all costs, including
8 warring with each other. ■ **Witness England and Holland battling for**
9 **control of present-day Manhattan in the early 1600's.** Adam Smith,
10 however, argued that free trade benefitted all nations and that gold was not
11 equal to wealth.

- **REMEMBER:** *You can change your answer, but don't. Trust your intuition.*

Insertion-Sentence Analysis

For this task, you must figure out where the insertion sentence (the piece) fits into the paragraph (the puzzle). Start by dividing the insertion sentence into three sections: head / middle / end.

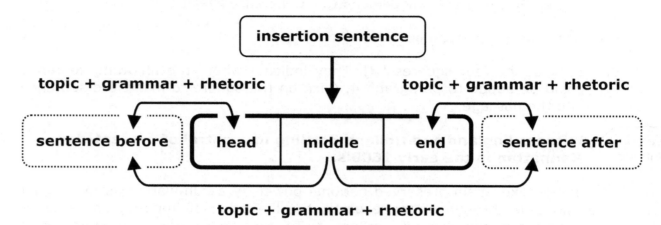

Each section of the insertion sentence will connect to the sentence before it and after it topically, grammatically, and rhetorically. This task measures your ability to identify these integrated connections.

Analyzing the Insertion Sentence

When analyzing the insertion sentence, start at the head. The head will often contain a transitional signal word, such as <u>Witness</u> in the sample insertion sentence.

<u>Witness</u> / *England and Holland* battling for control of present-day Manhattan / in the early 1600's.

<u>Witness</u>, in this context, is a verb. It is also a synonym for the transitional phrase *for example*. <u>Witness</u>, therefore, grammatically signals the rhetorical purpose of the insertion sentence: to provide illustrations that will develop the topic *in the sentence before*. Those examples are **England and Holland**. They are the noun objects of the verb <u>Witness</u>. Also, **England and Holland** refer back to the plural noun **nations** and to the phrase **each other** in the sentence before.

Moreover, **nations** were geared toward acquiring and maintaining gold at all costs, including warring with **each other**. Witness **England and Holland** battling for control of present-day Manhattan in the early 1600's. Adam Smith...

Therefore, insertion point four is correct grammatically, topically and rhetorically. As a result, the paragraph demonstrates OPDUL=<u>C</u>.

Choice Analysis: *Process of Elimination*

To confirm your choice, use process of elimination.

The first insertion point (A) is not correct (see below. Note: For demonstration purposes, the black squares have been replaced by corresponding letters).

If you insert the insertion sentence at (A) below, the paragraph will lack coherence. Why? Because the insertion sentence is developing the topics of *England and Holland*. However, *England and Holland* are not mentioned in sentence one. The topics of sentence 1 are <u>Spain</u>, <u>exports</u> and <u>imports</u>. Note in sentence 2 how the infinitive phrase <u>To develop</u> continues the topics of <u>exports</u> and <u>imports</u>. Therefore, sentence 1 and 2 cannot be separated because they are topically, grammatically, and rhetorically connected, with sentence 2 giving an example of how exports were developed: they *were subsidized by the government*.

1	1) A nation like <u>Spain</u> preserved national power by accumulating as much
2	gold as possible through strong <u>exports</u>, the limitation of <u>imports</u>, and a large
3	population of poorly paid workers. **(A)** 2) To develop <u>exports</u>, companies
4	*were subsidized by the government,* which also wrote laws to limit <u>imports</u>.

The second insertion point (B) below is also not correct. In sentence 2, the topics of **exports** and **imports** are continued. Note at the head of sentence 3 the transitional phrase *By limiting imports*. This phrase refers to the topics of <u>exports</u> and <u>imports</u> in sentence 1 and 2. It also signals a continuation of these topics in sentence 3. In sentence 2, note the **cause**-*and*-*effect* relationship: **To develop exports, companies were subsidized by the government which also wrote laws** *to limit imports*. The cause-and-effect result of import-limiting laws is described in sentence 3: **By limiting imports, the gold used to pay for imports** *would stay in the country and create a greater money supply and more credit*. Therefore, sentences 1, 2 and 3 cannot be separated because they are topically, grammatically, and rhetorically connected.

1	1) A nation like Spain preserved national power by accumulating as much
2	gold as possible through strong **exports**, the limitation of **imports**, and a
3	large population of poorly paid workers. (A) 2) <u>To develop **exports**</u>, <u>compa-</u>
4	<u>nies were subsidized by the government, which also wrote laws to limit **im-**</u>
5	<u>**ports**</u>. **(B)** 3) <u>By limiting **imports**</u>, the gold used to pay for **imports** would
6	stay in the country and create a greater money supply and more credit.

The third insertion point (C) (see next page) is also not correct. The topic of <u>gold</u> in sentence 3 is continued in sentence 4. Sentence 4 uses the rhetorical strategies of description and illustration to describe how the <u>gold</u> in sentence 3 was acquired: through <u>warring</u>. At the head of sentence 4, note the transitional signal word <u>Moreover</u>. <u>Moreover</u> is a synonym for *In addition*. In this context, sentence 4 is adding more information to develop the topic of <u>gold</u> in sentence 3. Therefore, grammatically, topically, and rhetorically sentence 3 and 4 cannot be separated.

1) A nation like Spain preserved national power by accumulating as much gold as possible through strong exports, the limitation of imports, and a large population of poorly paid workers. (A) 2) To develop exports, companies were subsidized by the government, which also wrote laws to limit imports. (B) 3) By limiting imports, the **gold** used to pay for imports would stay in the country and create a greater money supply and more credit. **(C)** 4) Moreover, nations were geared toward acquiring and maintaining <u>gold</u> at all costs, including <u>warring</u> with each other. (D) **Witness *England and Holland* battling for control of present-day Manhattan <u>in the early 1600's</u>.** Adam Smith, <u>however</u>, argued that free trade benefitted all nations and that gold was not equal to wealth.

By process of elimination, the fourth insertion point (D) is correct.

Signal Words

When analyzing the insertion sentence, look for signal words at the head of the insertion sentence. They provide a good indication of where the insertion sentence can be inserted into the paragraph grammatically. The following are transitional signal words often found at the head of the insertion sentence.

Addition	Sequence	Restatement	Consequence
Also,	After...	In other words,	As a result,
Additionally,	As soon as...	To clarify,	Accordingly,
Moreover,	At first,	In essence,	For this reason,
Furthermore,	At last...	Essentially,	For those reasons,
Further,	Finally,	To paraphrase,	Consequently,
For example,	Before long,	In brief,	Subsequently,
For instance,	In the first place,	In a nutshell,	Therefore,
To illustrate,	Meanwhile,	In other words,	Thereupon,
Besides that,	Next,	Basically,	Thus,
Likewise,	Soon after,	Simply put,	Hence,

Emphasis	Contrast	Similarity	Conclusion
Truly,	Yet,	Likewise,	In conclusion,
Indeed,	But,	Together with...	To conclude,
In fact,	However,	Coupled with...	In sum,
Again,	In contrast,	In the same way...	To sum up,
Of course,	Conversely,	In the same manner,	In the end,
Suffice it to say,	On the contrary,	In a like manner,	All in all,
In the same fashion,	On the one hand,	In the same fashion,	Finally,
Equally important...	Despite...	Similarly...	Lastly,
To repeat,	Even so,	Correspondingly,	In closing,
With this in mind,	Nevertheless,	Much like...	Naturally,

Signal Words: *Pronouns*

If the head of the insertion sentence has none of the signal words on the previous page, look for pronouns. In the insertion sentence below, It is a pronoun signal word at the head of the insertion sentence. Note how It is followed by *is a process*.

> It *is a process* that begins with a set of initial conditions, called input, then provides an output, a result, based on a fixed set of rules or instructions.

The clause It *is a process* refers to a specific topic in the sentence before. But which topic and which sentence? Look at the paragraph below. Insertion point (A) looks correct. The word process in sentence 1 is topically connected to process in the insertion sentence. However, do not be distracted by one word. If you insert the insertion sentence at (A), the paragraph will lack coherence. Why? Because rhetorically, sentence 1 is a general definition that is defined and developed in sentence 2. In other words, sentence 1 is a general statement and sentence 2 is a specific statement supporting sentence 1. This topic progression is indicated by the transitional signal phrase More specifically at the head of sentence 2. Therefore, sentence 1 and 2 cannot be separated because they are connected grammatically, topically, and rhetorically.

1 1) An algorithm is a process that performs a series of operations aimed at
2 solving a problem. **(A)** 2) More specifically, an algorithm has a starting point
3 followed by a sequence of well-defined instructions terminating at an end
4 point. **(B)** 3) Algorithms lie at the heart of computer software. **(C)** 4) Soft-
5 ware, as you know, is basically a sequence of instructions aimed at carrying
6 out a task. 5) That task is called a computation. **(D)** 6) A more common
7 form of algorithm is a recipe for, oh, I don't know—let's say brownies. 7) The
8 recipe tells you where to start, the steps to follow, and what the outcome will
9 be. 8) An algorithm, however, cannot stop you from eating them all.

- **REMEMBER:** *The rhetorical relationship between the insertion sentence and the sentence before often moves from general (sentence before) to specific (insertion sentence). Look for this relationship when identifying rhetorical and grammatical connections.*

> **sentence before = general** ➡ **insertion sentence = specific**

The correct insertion point is (D). It, in the insertion sentence, refers to the noun computation. What is a computation? Answer: It *is a process*. Rhetorically, the insertion sentence defines computation (*It is a process...*), then describes that process (*...that begins with a set of initial conditions, called input, then provides an output, a result, based on a fixed set of rules or instructions*).

5) That task is called a computation. **(D)** It *is a process* that begins with a set of initial conditions called input, then provides an output, a result, based on a fixed set of rules or instructions. 7) A more common...

Insertion Sentences: *No Signal Words*

The insertion sentence may have no transitional signal words at the head, in the middle, or at the end. If the insertion sentence has no transitional signal words, identify the rhetorical strategy(ies). In the insertion sentence below, the rhetorical strategy is cause-and-effect and definition.

> *Animal behavior can be classified* **according to the time of day an animal is active**.

Next, determine if the insertion sentence is a general statement or a specific statement. The example above is a general statement. That suggests that this insertion sentence is either a topic sentence or a concluding sentence. The insertion point for the insertion sentence is (A).

1	**Animal behavior can be classified according to the time of day an an-**
2	**imal is active.** Animals, such as horses, elephants, and most birds, are said
3	to be <u>diurnal</u> because they are active during the day and rest at night. ■
4	Those animals active at dawn and dusk are said to be <u>crepuscular</u>. ■ Beetles,
5	skunks, and rabbits fall into this category. ■ The third group are those ani-
6	mals that sleep during the day and are active at night. They are called <u>noc-</u>
7	<u>turnal</u>. A good example is the bat...

To confirm that (A) is the correct insertion point, analyze the sentences that follow it. Topically, grammatically, and rhetorically, the sentences that follow are examples that support the topic (animal behavior) in the insertion sentence. The three supporting examples (<u>diurnal</u>, <u>crepuscular</u>, <u>nocturnal</u>) describe each behavioral type. The result is a classification and a definition of animal behavior. Combined, the first four sentences topically, grammatically, and rhetorically support the general statement that is the insertion sentence thus will come after it. Therefore, (A) is the correct insertion point.

1	**(A)** 1) Animals, such as horses, elephants, and most birds, are said to be <u>di-</u>
2	<u>urnal</u> because they are active during the day and rest at night. **(B)** 2) Those
3	animals active at dawn and dusk are said to be <u>crepuscular</u>. **(C)** 3) Beetles,
4	skunks, and rabbits fall into this category. **(D)** 4) The third group are those
5	animals that sleep during the day and are active at night. 5) They are called
6	<u>nocturnal</u>. 6) A good example is the bat. Bats have highly-developed eye-
7	sight, hearing and smell. 7) This helps them avoid predators and locate food.
8	8) Being nocturnal also helps them avoid high temperatures during the day,
9	especially in deserts where temperatures can reach well over one-hundred
10	degrees Fahrenheit. 9) There are two types of bat: micro-bats, or true bats,
11	and mega-bats, also called fruit bats. 10) Let's start with mega-bats.

If the insertion sentence is a general statement, but not the topic sentence, it might be a concluding sentence, such as the next example. Note that the insertion sentence below has no transitional signal words at the head, in the middle, or at the end.

> Darwin's theory revolutionized scientific thought, for according to Darwin, natural selection proved that divine creation played no part in the creation and evolution of organisms.

The insertion point for this insertion sentence is (D) or the fourth square.

1
2
3
4
5
6
7
8

■ 1) Charles Darwin is famous for his groundbreaking book *On the Origin of Species* published in 1851. ■ 2) In it, *Darwin theorized that all organisms evolved through natural selection*. ■ 3) Natural selection, as defined by Darwin, is the process in which an organism inherits traits that make it more likely to survive and successfully reproduce, and thus become more common. 4) ■ **Darwin's theory revolutionized scientific thought,** for according to Darwin, natural selection proved that divine creation played no part in the creation and evolution of organisms.

In the insertion sentence, the phrase **Darwin's theory revolutionized scientific thought** sounds like a topic sentence. However, in sentence 2, note how the prepositional phrase In it (line 2) refers back to *On the Origin of Species* in sentence 1. Note also in sentence 2 how the book's theory is summarized (...*Darwin theorized that all organisms evolved through natural selection*). The noun phrase natural selection at the end of sentence 2 is then developed in sentence 3. Therefore, sentences 1, 2, and 3 are grammatically, topically, and rhetorically connected. By process of elimination, the correct insertion point is D or insertion point 4.

Notes

_____

_____

_____

_____

_____

_____

_____

_____

_____

_____

Practice: *Sentence-Insertion Questions*

<u>Directions</u>: You have 20 minutes to complete the following.

---

1. Click on the square [■] to insert the bold sentence into the passage.

The most common of these are aspirin and ibuprofen while capsaicin, the main capsaicinoid in chili peppers, is applied topically.

1 Costal cartilage is the cartilage that connects the ribs to the sternum. The con-
2 dition in which the costal cartilage between the ribs becomes inflamed is known
3 as costochondritis. Strenuous exercise can bring it on and the pain can be quite
4 intense. ■ However, even in the most extreme cases, costochondritis is consid-
5 ered benign. ■ Treatment usually consists of rest and analgesics. ■ If the pain
6 is too great, then steroid injections, even surgery, are options. ■ Symptoms of
7 costochondritis are quite similar to those indicative of heart attack. Therefore,
8 medical attention should be sought if the pain persists.

2. Click on the square [■] to insert the bold sentence into the passage.

One of the most influential post-war art movements was that of pop art.

1 ■ Flowering in mid-1950's Britain and late 1950's America, pop art was a reac-
2 tion to the elitism of abstract expressionism. ■ Instead of employing paint on
3 canvas, artists, such as Andy Warhol, instead found inspiration in popular im-
4 ages found in advertising, comic books, and commercial products; hence, the
5 name pop art. ■ In this way, pop art was a direct reflection of post-war America,
6 one in which the mass production of consumer products and television adver-
7 tising were dominant culture forces. ■

3. Click on the square [■] to insert the bold sentence into the passage.

The Iranian calendar today is based on Khayyám's measurements.

1   Omar Khayyám, born in Persia in 1048 AD, was a polymath, a man whose ge-
2   nius ranged from astronomy to philosophy to poetry. Recognized as one of the
3   greatest medieval mathematicians, Khayyám authored the *Treatise on Demon-*
4   *stration of Problems of Algebra.* ■ In it, Khayyám provides a geometric method
5   for solving cubic equations. ■ Khayyám's contributions to algebra eventually
6   found their way to Europe, as did the work of many other influential Persian
7   mathematicians. ■ In astronomy, Khayyám measured a solar year and con-
8   cluded that it was 365.2421 days. ■ Yet despite his scientific achievements,
9   Omar Khayyám is most famous for his poetry, in particular his book of poems
10 *The Rubáiyát of Omar Khayyám. The Rubáiyát* consists of about one thousand
11 quatrains, a quatrain being a poem consisting of four lines or rubaais.

4. Click on the square [■] to insert the bold sentence into the passage.

Another striking feature of the electric eel is that, unlike other fish, it breathes air directly, surfacing every ten minutes or so to gulp down air, air which accounts for eighty percent of its oxygen requirement.

1 The electric eel is an apex predator found in the Amazon and Orinoco Rivers of
2 South America. Like its name says, it is indeed electric, dangerously so. The
3 charge it produces can reach up to one amp at 800 volts, enough to incapaci-
4 tate half a dozen people. Such a lethal evolutionary attribute is produced in
5 body-length organs filled with cells called electroplaques. When the eel is rest-
6 ing, proteins force positively charged ions out of these cell. The electroplaque
7 cells are then negatively charged. ■ When the eel needs to create an electric
8 shock, it opens the cell walls and lets the positive ions rush back in thus creat-
9 ing a charge. ■ The electric eel, which is not a true eel but a knifefish—a spe-
10 cies of fish with long thin bodies and no fins—employs the charge when hunt-
11 ing, for protection, and to attract a mate. ■ Why an electric eel doesn't shock it-
12 self remains a mystery. ■

5. Click on the square [■] to insert the bold sentence into the passage.

Nowadays commercial producers rely on centrifugation to facilitate the separation process.

1 The process of making olive oil has changed little since olives were first used as
2 a food source over six thousand years ago in the eastern Mediterranean. The
3 process starts with picking the fruit, either by hand or by machine. To preserve
4 freshness, the fruit is taken immediately to the processing facility. There, the
5 fruit is cleaned with water while any remaining leaves and debris are removed.
6 Next, the fruit is put into a mill which crushes the fruit into a paste. This is a
7 critical step for it tears the flesh cells thus releasing the oil from the vacuoles.
8 Malaxing, or mixing the paste, is next. This can last for up to forty-five minutes.
9 This is another critical step, for it allows droplets of oil to form into larger ones.
10 Heating can expedite the process; however, heating can reduce the quality of
11 the oil. ■ Finally, the paste is pressed, a process in which the oil itself is sepa-
12 rated from the pulp. ■ Traditionally, the paste was ground between two mill
13 stones, a process that is commonly called the "first pressing" or "cold pressing."
14 ■ These terms, however, are somewhat obsolete. ■

6. Click on the square [■] to insert the bold sentence into the passage.

This process, one that gives the comet an atmosphere, is called sublimation.

1 A comet—a loose mixture of dust, ice, and rock particles—is distinct from a me-
2 teorite in that a comet is a small solar system body; whereas, a meteorite is a
3 piece of space debris that survives an impact with Earth. While falling to Earth,
4 a meteorite will begin to heat up as it meets resistance from the atmosphere.
5 That resistance is in the form of friction. The heat is so intense the meteorite
6 turns into a fireball. When appearing in the night sky, meteors trail a long glow-
7 ing trail; thus, they are called falling stars or shooting stars. A comet also has a

8 tail. Like a meteorite, a comet's tail is also due to heating. ■ When a comet
9 passes close to the Sun, the area enveloping the comet, the coma, heats up. ■
10 Within the coma, solids turn to gas. ■ As the comet orbits the Sun, the subli-
11 mated particles trail behind the comet for a great distance. ■ Such a sight has,
12 over the years, instilled fear, so much so that comets are traditionally seen as
13 bad omens; whereas, the tradition is to make a wish when seeing a shooting
14 star.

7. Click on the square [■] to insert the bold sentence into the passage.

This system of representation, based on a census of population, is the foundation of the American electoral system.

1 In the United States, a census is taken every ten years. ■ This information is
2 essential for a variety of reasons, in particular the establishment of political dis-
3 tricts. ■ By determining the size of a population in a given state, the federal
4 government can then apportion the state into Congressional districts based not
5 on geography but on population. ■ This ensures equal representation in Con-
6 gress wherein populous states, such as California, are awarded more Congres-
7 sional representatives while states with fewer people, such as Montana, are
8 awarded fewer Congressional representatives. ■

8. Click on the square [■] to insert the bold sentence into the passage.

At fourteen, guided by "a rebellious temperament," he dropped out of school and went to work for the railroad.

1 Samuel Dashiell Hammett was born in 1894 on a farm in Maryland. ■ In 1915,
2 at the age of twenty-one, he joined the Pinkerton Detective Agency. ■ As a Pink-
3 erton operative, or "Op," Hammett saw everything from "petty theft to murder."
4 ■ In 1918, Hammett left Pinkerton's, joined the army and contracted influenza.
5 ■ Soon after he developed tuberculosis. He left the army and went back to
6 Pinkerton's, but poor health forced him to resign. In 1922, weakened by disease
7 and in need of work, Hammett, encouraged by a friend, turned to writing.

9. Click on the square [■] to insert the bold sentence into the passage.

The result, the Situationists believed, was that the individual was no longer a participant in life but a slave controlled by false images created by capitalist interests.

1 ■ As a political movement, the Situationist International combined Marxist ide-
2 ology and Surrealism to wage war against consumerism. ■ The Situationists,
3 founded in 1957, argued that mainstream capitalism, through the mass media,
4 was destroying the experience of daily life through false images, the worst of-
5 fender being consumer advertising. ■ The group's main proponent was Guy
6 Debord. ■ Debord argued that authentic social life had been replaced with false
7 representations. Debord wanted to wake up the spectator drugged by advertis-
8 ing. The Situationists did so by creating "situations," mass events in which peo-
9 ple turned their backs on the mass media and came together as one.

10. Click on the square [■] to insert the bold sentence into the passage.

Historians believe that as many as 20,000 Roman soldiers died.

1 Next we'll explore the Battle of Teutoburg Forest. This engagement occurred in
2 9 CE. ■ By that date, Rome had successfully conquered western Europe and
3 was turning east with the aim of conquering what is today's Germany east of
4 the Rhine River. ■ Determined to subdue the Germanic tribes once and for
5 all, three Legions under Varus marched east of the Rhine and right into a
6 trap. ■ The Germanic tribes, led by Arminius, an ex-Roman cavalry officer,
7 annihilated the Roman army to a man. ■ Historians also believe that this—
8 the complete destruction of an elite Roman army—marked the start of the de-
9 cline of the Roman Empire. Finally, we'll travel to Waterloo, a small town in
10 Belgium. There, on June 18, 1815, Napoleon Bonaparte, back from exile—and
11 determined to rule as Emperor once again—was defeated by a combined Brit-
12 ish and Prussian force.

11. Click on the square [■] to insert the bold sentence into the passage.

It is then that the runner moves in for the kill.

1 The sand people of the Kalahari Desert are the only tribe left on Earth who
2 use what many scientists consider to be the oldest method of hunting known
3 to man: the persistence hunt. On foot, under a hot African sun and armed on-
4 ly with spears, the hunters locate a herd of kudu, kudu being a species of
5 large antelope. The hunters then move the herd using only hand signals to
6 communicate. By continually moving the herd, the hunters tire their prey. ■
7 Hours later, the hunters will isolate one animal, usually a male whose heavy
8 horns have caused him to tire faster than the females. ■ At this point, with a
9 kudu separated from the herd, one hunter, the fastest of the group, continues
10 the hunt alone. ■ This hunter, called "the runner," chases the lone kudu for
11 hours until, exhausted from the heat, it stops to rest. ■

12. Click on the square [■] to insert the bold sentence into the passage.

The opposite half was occupied by livestock, typically a cow for milk, chickens for meat and eggs, and a horse that pulled the plow.

During the Middle Ages, peasant families lived in rural houses close to the fields in which they worked, land which was controlled by a lord in a castle. A typical peasant house, usually built by the family themselves, was a primitive shelter that provided little more than a place to eat and sleep. ■ Construction materials included earth and wood for the walls and thatching for the roof. The most common rural structure was the longhouse or house-barn. ■ Rectangular in shape, this dwelling had doors on opposite ends and on the sides thus ensuring cross ventilation. ■ Inside, the floor plan was divided in half with one end forming the hearth, the place where the family prepared and ate their meals and slept. ■

➜ Answers page 327.

296 - TOEFL STRATEGIES by Bruce Stirling

Prose-Summary Questions → *Strategies*

Each passage will have one prose-summary question. This question type comes at the end of the passage. This question type measures your ability to understand the passage as a whole and complete a summary of it. The correct answers will summarize the passage's main ideas. The six answer choices will be a mix of general ideas, details, off-topic ideas, and information that is not true or too general.

- **REMEMBER:** *To complete this task, you must choose three correct general ideas.*

Look at the following question. The directions will be followed by a topic sentence in bold. The topic sentence is the start of the summary.

12. Directions: The sentence in bold is the first sentence of a brief summary of the passage. Complete the summary by selecting three answer choices. Your choices will express the most important ideas in the passage. Some choices are not in the passage or do not express important ideas. This is a 2-point question.

   The passage discusses Adam Smith's book *The Wealth of Nations.*

   - •
   - •
   - •

- **REMEMBER:** *You do not need to put your choices in order.*

Answer Choices

1. Smith's *The Wealth of Nations* represents the start of modern economic theory.

2. Smith illustrated how a factory worker wasted time when responsible for every step in a manufacturing process.

3. Smith started to write *The Wealth of Nations* after he returned to France from a long trip to Scotland.

4. Smith argued that to create national wealth, governments should subsidize companies.

5. Smith argued that Mercantilism was not a true wealth-building system.

6. Smith's theory of "the invisible hand" was influenced by the European Enlightenment.

Question Analysis

Before you choose answers, make sure you understand the question and the directions. The directions are paraphrased below.

Directions: The sentence in bold is the topic sentence of a summary of the passage. Complete the summary by selecting three answers. The correct answers will be general statements expressing the main ideas in the passage. Wrong answers will be off topic, not true, too specific, or too general.

Analyzing the Topic Sentence

In the sample topic sentence below, note that it is a general statement describing the topic to be summarized.

The passage discusses Adam Smith's book *The Wealth of Nations*.

- **REMEMBER:** *Read the topic sentence carefully. Make sure you understand the topic. Many test-takers answer incorrectly because they did not take the time to analyze the topic sentence. In the example above, all correct answers will be topically connected to the book Smith wrote, The Wealth of Nations, in a general way.*

Answer-Choice Analysis

After you identify the topic in the topic sentence, analyze the six answer choices. To make a selection, click-drag the answer beside a bullet point (see page 218). When analyzing each choice, ask: A) Is this choice a general or specific idea? In the choices below, choices 1, 5 and 6 are general statements. Choice 2 is too general while choice 3 is not true. B) Is this choice off-topic and/or not true? Choice 4 is not true. It contradicts the passage. Choices 1, 5 and 6 are therefore correct.

Answer Choices

general >
1. Smith's *The Wealth of Nations* represents the start of modern   economic theory.

not true <
4. Smith argued that to create national wealth, governments should subsidize companies.

too general >
2. Smith illustrated how a factory worker wasted time when responsible for every step in a manufacturing process.

general <
5. Smith argued that Mercantilism   was not a true wealth-building   system.

not true >
3. Smith started to write *The Wealth of Nations* after he returned to France from a long trip to Scotland.

general <
6. Smith's theory of "the invisible   hand" was influenced by the   European Enlightenment.

- **REMEMBER:** *Some choices will be very close. You must decide which choices are best compared to the others by process of elimination.*

Time-Saving Strategy

If you are running out of time, use the following strategies to increase your chances of answering correctly.

1. Do not go back and skim and scan for information. If you do, you will run out of time. By this point, you should be familiar with the topic of the passage and the supporting details.

2. Focus on the answer choices. Look for details in each. If a choice contains details, such as dates, names, or a step in a process, or suggests a process, do not choose it. It might be true, but it is too specific. This will leave choices that are off topic, not true, or too general. Eliminate choices you feel are wrong. By doing so, you will narrow your choices down to general statements. Select them.

3. Eliminate choices that are not topically related to each other or to the topic sentence. Note below how choices 1, 5, and 6 are correct because they are general statements, they are topically related to the topic sentence, and they are true.

Answer Choices

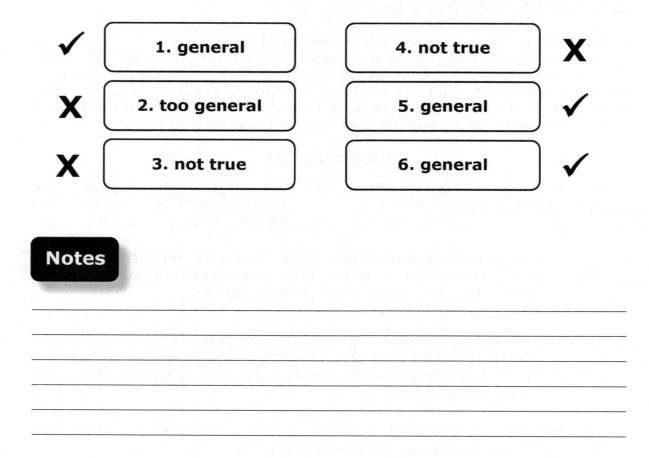

✓ 1. general   4. not true ✗

✗ 2. too general   5. general ✓

✗ 3. not true   6. general ✓

Notes

_____

_____

_____

_____

_____

_____

Practice #1: *Prose-Summary Questions*

<u>Directions</u>: You have five minutes to read <u>each</u> passage and answer the question.

Jonathan James

1   1 ➜ In the world of computer hackers, one name stands out: Jonathan James. Be-
2   tween August and October of 1999, James, aged 16, hacked into the computers of
3   BellSouth. Next, he hacked the Miami-Dade school system. Soon after, he hit the
4   computers of the Defense Reduction Agency, a division of the United States De-
5   partment of Defense. James installed a sniffer, a piece of hidden software that in-
6   tercepted thousands of passwords giving him almost complete access to Depart-
7   ment of Defense computers, including the computers of NASA. From the NASA
8   computers, James downloaded the software that controlled the temperature and
9   the humidity on the Space Station. On January 26, 2000, James was arrested and
10   incarcerated, making him the first juvenile to be jailed for computer hacking. Why
11   did he do it? As James himself said, "I was just looking around, playing around.
12   What was fun for me was a challenge to see what I could pull off." James commit-
13   ted suicide in May, 2008 after federal authorities accused him of being part of a
14   conspiracy that had committed the largest computer identify theft in American his-
15   tory, the hacking into the computers of retailers TJ Maxx, Marshalls, Boston Mar-
16   ket, Barnes and Noble, and many others.

1.   <u>Directions</u>: The sentence in bold is the first sentence of a brief summary of the passage. Complete the summary by selecting three answer choices. Your choices will express the most important ideas in the passage. Some choices are not in the passage or do not express important ideas.

The passage discusses the hacking life of Jonathan James.

-
-
-

Answer Choices

1. At 16, he hacked into the computers of Bell South.

2. He illegally gained access to Defense Department computers.

3. He was sorry for what he did.

4. He was arrested and jailed in 2001.

5. He worked for the FBI as a government hacker.

6. He was part of the largest computer theft in history.

➜ **2 points for all 3 correct. One wrong = 0.**

➜ Answers page 327.

F. Scott Fitzgerald

1 **1 →** One of the more tragic figures in American literary history is F. Scott Fitzger-
2 ald. Fitzgerald died in Hollywood on December 21, 1940, at the age of 44. He'd
3 been trying to revive his career by writing screenplays which he despised. Yet, al-
4 ways desperate for money, Fitzgerald had no choice but to serve Hollywood. No
5 longer was he the golden boy whose short stories of rebellious young men and
6 women defined the Jazz Age, a name Fitzgerald himself had coined to describe the
7 1920's. In 1920, at age 25, Fitzgerald rocketed to the top of the literary world with
8 his first novel, *This Side of Paradise*. Soon after, the Saturday Evening Post was
9 paying him $4,000.00 for his short stories, an incredible sum even by today's
10 standards. In 1925, Fitzgerald published *The Great Gatsby*. Fitzgerald went on to
11 write *Tender is the Night* in 1934, but it failed to sell. With the Depression eclipsing
12 the Jazz Age, with his short stories no longer in demand, and burdened by a men-
13 tally unstable wife, Fitzgerald hit rock bottom. In 1937, he settled in Los Angeles
14 where he landed a six-month writing contract with MGM yet he continued to drink
15 heavily while producing nothing of substance. Fitzgerald died believing he was a
16 failure while *The Great Gatsby* lives on, a novel many critics consider the greatest
17 American novel ever written.

2. <u>Directions</u>: The sentence in bold is the first sentence of a brief summary of the passage. Complete the summary by selecting three answer choices. Your choices will express the most important ideas in the passage. Some choices are not in the passage or do not express important ideas.

The passage discusses the work of F. Scott Fitzgerald.

- •

- •

- •

Answer Choices

1. He wrote many great stage plays for Hollywood.

2. He died at the age of 44 in Hollywood believing he was a failure.

3. *The Great Gatsby* is considered the greatest American novel.

4. *This Side of Paradise* made him famous at an early age.

5. He is credited with creating the name The Jazz Age.

6. *Tender is the Night* was not popular.

→ 2 points for all 3 correct. One wrong = 0.

→ Answers page 327.

Practice #2: *Prose-Summary Questions*

Directions: You have ten minutes to read <u>each</u> passage and answer the question.

Passage One: The Tulip Bubble

1 → The seventeenth century is known as the Dutch Golden Age. During this period, the Dutch empire, centered in the port city of Amsterdam, stretched from Manhattan Island in North America to the spice islands in Southeast Asia. The engine
that drove the Dutch empire was the Dutch East India Company, a company considered to be the world's first multi-national corporation. Funded by shareholders
and the Bank of Amsterdam, the Dutch East India Company was, by 1640, the
dominant force in the world economy. Ships arriving in Amsterdam were filled with
exotic cargo, such as nutmeg, cinnamon, and pepper from the islands of Indonesia.
They also carried silk, tea, and porcelain from China and beaver fur from Manhattan. Dutch merchants became fabulously wealthy. They had their portraits painted
by Rembrandt and Vermeer, and sought ways to reinvest their money. One investment opportunity was in tulips.

2 → The tulip is a flowering plant that grows from a bulb similar in appearance to
an onion. In North America, tulips are one of the first flowering plants to emerge in
early spring. In North America, the tulip is synonymous with Dutch culture, as are
windmills and wooden shoes. However, the tulip is not native to the Netherlands.
The tulip arrived in Holland from the Ottoman Empire sometime in the mid sixteenth century, the Ottoman empire encompassing present-day Turkey, Syria, and
Iraq. Tulip cultivation took off in 1593 when famed Flemish botanist Carolus Clusius started to grow tulips for research. Clusius was interested in "tulip breaking,"
a natural phenomenon that resulted in multi-colored tulips. His neighbors, so the
story goes, were so captivated by Clusius's tulips they stole some bulbs which they
sold. And with that, tulipmania was on. Almost overnight, the tulip became a status symbol, a much coveted luxury item sought by rich and poor alike.

3 → Dutch tulips were classified according to color. Solid red, yellow, and white
were called Couleren while multi-colored, striped tulips were called rosen (red or
pink vertical stripes on a white background), violetten, (purple or lilac stripes on a
white background), and bizarden (red or purple stripes on a yellow background).
Today, botanists know that tulip striping, the thing that made them so valuable in
the early seventeenth century, is caused by a virus known as the tulip breaking
virus. At the time, however, this fact was not known. What is known is that world's
first economic bubble was created by the Dutch buying and selling of tulip bulbs.

4 → Much like stocks on Wall Street today, tulips were traded with buyers hoping
to turn around and sell their bulbs at much higher prices, prices that had nothing
to do with reality. For example, for one tulip bulb, a man traded twelve acres of
land while another bought forty bulbs for 100,000 florins. At the time, a skilled la-
borer earned less than one-hundred-and-fifty florins a year. Perhaps the most out-
rageous trade was the man who traded for one bulb "a silver drinking cup, a suit of
clothes, a complete bed, 1,000 pounds of cheese, two tons of butter, four tons of

43 beer, two barrels of wine, twelve fat sheep, eight fat swine, four fat oxen, four lasts
44 of rye, [and] four lasts of wheat." When the mania reached its peak in the winter of
45 1636, buyers were no longer willing to plant their bulbs come spring. They deemed
46 it too risky. Instead, the trend was to have parties in which people viewed unplant-
47 ed tulip bulbs arranged on tables.
48
49 5 ➔ In the winter of 1636, every Dutchman it seemed was trying to cash in on the
50 tulip craze. The government could do nothing to stop it. Money kept pouring into
51 the tulip market and prices kept going up with no one actually taking possession of
52 the bulbs they had purchased. Moreover, the Dutch, like Americans and the 1929
53 stock market, were convinced that the good times were here to stay. By the winter
54 of 1637, however, Dutch tulip traders could no longer find buyers willing to pay
55 such exorbitant prices for their bulbs. Panic erupted when one buyer failed to show
56 up to claim his purchase. Within days, prices plummeted. The tulip bubble had
57 finally burst.

1.   Directions: The sentence in bold is the first sentence of a brief summary of
     the passage. Complete the summary by selecting three answer choices.
     Your choices will express the most important ideas in the passage. Some
     choices are not in the passage or do not express important ideas.

     The passage discusses the Dutch tulip bubble.

     -

     -

     -

Answer Choices

1. In the sixteenth century, tulips
   were classified by color: red,
   white, and yellow.

2. The Dutch mania for tulips
   started when bulbs from a
   botanist's garden were stolen,
   then sold as status symbols.

3. During the Dutch Golden Age,
   many exotic products were imported into Amsterdam, including spices and flowers.

4. The price for one tulip bulb was
   often more than a common
   man made in one year.

5. Speculators drove the price of
   tulip bulbs so high, the market
   finally collapsed due to a lack
   of buyers.

6. The Dutch East India company
   was a major grower of tulip
   bulbs.

➔ **2 points for all 3 correct. One wrong = 0.**

➔ Answers page 327.

Passage Two: *The Women of Liberia Mass Action for Peace*

1 1 ➜ Of all the peace movements in recent years, one in particular stands out: *The*
2 *Women of Liberia Mass Action for Peace.* In 2003, the movement, through non-
3 violent protest, ended the second Liberian civil war and ousted president Charles
4 Taylor. Taylor, a warlord who had overthrown his predecessor, was accused of a
5 plethora of crimes including crimes against humanity for the brutal repression of
6 his fellow Liberians. Rebel groups, supported by neighboring Guinea and Côte d'Iv-
7 oire, attempted to overthrow Taylor. In early 2003, the rebels controlled most of the
8 countryside and were laying siege to the capital of Monrovia. Taylor fought back
9 with paramilitary units he called Small Boy Units. These units marked a new type
10 of warfare. Instead of regular soldiers, Small Boy Units consisted of war-orphaned
11 boys as young as eight. To entice boys to join his army, Taylor promised gifts and
12 assault weapons. Taylor ordered his Small Boy Units to terrorize the civilian popu-
13 lation using any means possible, including rape and torture. Small Boy Units were
14 particularly savage. Because of their lack of maturity, the boys believed that they
15 were invincible thus feared nothing as they terrorized the populace and battled the
16 invading rebels. Peace conferences were held, but the fighting continued with civil-
17 ians caught in the middle. By 2003, Liberia had been in a state of constant civil
18 war for thirteen years. Finally, one woman said enough. That woman was Leymah
19 Gbowee.
20
21 2 ➜ At the age of seventeen, Leymah Gbowee moved from central Liberia where she
22 was born to the capital Monrovia. Trained as a trauma counselor, she helped child
23 soldiers who had fought in Taylor's Small Boy Units. By doing so, Gbowee wit-
24 nessed firsthand the physical and psychological damage Taylor had visited upon
25 the people of Liberia. Determined to stop the war, Gbowee brought Christian and
26 Muslim mothers together and formed *The Women of Liberia Mass Action for Peace.*
27 United, the mothers of Liberia believed that "Regardless of whom you pray to, dur-
28 ing war our experience as a community and as mothers [is] the same."
29
30 3 ➜ Dressed in white, the Christian and Muslim mothers staged daily, non-violent
31 protests in the fish market of the capital. With their numbers growing, the WLMAP
32 forced Taylor to attend peace talks in neighboring Ghana. The talks were held in
33 the presidential palace with Gbowee and a delegation from the WLMAP there to
34 monitor the talks. The talks, however, broke down when the warring parties re-
35 fused to negotiate. With the delegates threatening to leave, Gbowee and her delega-
36 tion took action. They blocked the doors and windows of the presidential palace
37 and would not let the delegates leave without a resolution. In the end, Taylor re-
38 signed as president of Liberia and found refuge in Nigeria. With Taylor's exit, Libe-
39 ria's second civil war came to an end. Elections were held and Ellen Johnson Sir-
40 leaf was elected president thus making her the first female head of an African
41 state. These changes would not have been possible if it were not for Leymah
42 Gbowee and her determination to bring peace to Liberia.
43
44 4 ➜ The achievements of Leymah Gbowee and the WLMAP are documented in the
45 movie *Pray the Devil Back to Hell* by Gini Reticker and Abigail E. Disney. To date,
46 the film has won many awards while Leymah Gbowee herself has received many
47 prestigious honors, including the John F. Kennedy Profile in Courage Award and
48 the Nobel Peace Prize. Leymah Gbowee continues to fight for peace and women's

49 rights as the executive director of the Women Peace and Security Network, Africa
50 (WIPSEN), an organization devoted to building relationships to support and pro-
51 mote women and youth throughout West Africa.

1. Directions: The sentence in bold is the first sentence of a brief summary of
    the passage. Complete the summary by selecting three answer choices.
    Your choices will express the most important ideas in the passage. Some
    choices are not in the passage or do not express important ideas.

    The passage discusses the achievements Leymah Gbowee.

    -
    -
    -

Answer Choices

1. Leymah Gbowee protested
   against Liberia's second civil
   war by successfully organizing
   peaceful demonstrations in
   which Christian and Muslim
   mothers united.

2. Leymah Gbowee helped child
   soldiers become responsible
   members of society once again.

3. She was trained a trauma
   counselor.

4. As a result of Leymah
   Gbowee's peace efforts, Liberia
   elected Africa's first male
   president.

5. Leymah Gbowee has received
   many awards, including the
   Nobel Peace Prize.

6. Leymah Gbowee's actions at
   the Ghana peace conference
   helped end Liberia's second
   civil war.

→ **2 points for all 3 correct. One wrong = 0.**

→ Answers page 327.

Passage Three: *Knock-offs*

1 → Today, we're going to look at another factor that can severely impact a company's bottomline. That issue is knock-offs. Essentially, a knock-off is a copy of an original, trademarked product or design illegally manufactured for sale and distribution. More importantly, in the U.S., a trademarked product is a government registered mark, a mark that gives a brand its unique identity. Copy that trademark—knock off some Nike Air-Maxs with the Nike symbol on them—and you're breaking the law.

2 → A good place to find knock-offs is on Fifth Avenue. Why Fifth Avenue? Tourists. Many of them would love to buy something on Fifth Avenue but, let's face it, Fifth Avenue is not exactly Wal-Mart. Your average tourist is not about to shell out five-hundred bucks for a Dolce-and-Gabanna belt when just down the street, there's a tout selling a knock-off from a suitcase. The tourist, wanting a Dolce-and-Gabanna belt, sees the knock-off, and hey, the tourist isn't stupid. Who cares if it's fake? That belt looks real enough, especially the logo, you know, the brand mark. How much is the knock-off? Twenty bucks, if that? And the original? Five hundred? A thousand? And accessories are just the tip of the iceberg. Knock-offs are having the greatest impact on pharmaceuticals. In fact, today's Wall Street Journal has a front page story on it. According to the article, the U.S. population age 65 and older stands at 40 million or 2.9 percent of the current population. That's about one in every eight Americans. By 2030, that number will double to 80 million.

3 → Why are these numbers significant? Because people over 65 need medication for everything from arthritis to cholesterol to cancer. A woman in the article is taking twenty different pills every day. So let's say you are that woman. You have a fixed monthly income of one-thousand dollars. Out of that thousand, you must pay for rent, bills and food. You're also taking a variety of medications, some of which cost a hundred bucks a pill. When you add it up, you can't afford such expensive medication. So what do you do? You look for cheaper alternatives and end up buying a knock-off. And what, you might ask, is the big deal, especially if those bogus pills are saving you—and thousands like you—money? The problem is there's no government oversight or quality control on the manufacturing side. As a result, a knock-off manufacturer can simply fill capsules with sugar, put a name like Pfizer on it, and customers think they're getting the real deal when in fact they're not.

4 → So let's bring it full circle, shall we? How does all this impact the bottomline? First off, companies can lose the incentive to innovate. If I'm a drug company, let's say, and my products are continually being ripped off, what is the point in developing new products if I know that I will lose money in the long run? Also, the more my products are knocked off, the more consumers will begin to suspect my products. In other words, one bad apple can hurt the whole bunch. This, in turn, will result in a significant loss of brand equity. Also, if I manufacture drugs, I can lose significant market share to knock-offs that are chemically the same as the drugs I'm producing. The consumer is not stupid. Word gets around. They know what works and what doesn't. If a knock-off sells for fifty bucks, and the original sells for two hundred—and it works, stops the pain—it's pretty obvious which one you're going to buy.

49 5 ➔ Are companies fighting back? Indeed, they are. A famous case is Tiffany ver-
50 sus eBay. Tiffany claimed that eBay was infringing upon Tiffany's trademark, the
51 Tiffany name itself, by publishing advertising on eBay, advertising in which people
52 were selling counterfeit Tiffany products via eBay. According to Tiffany, more than
53 thirty percent of the so-called Tiffany jewelry on eBay is fake. The court, however,
54 ruled against Tiffany saying that Tiffany, quote, "has the sole burden to police the
55 improper use of its trademark." In other words, if someone is counterfeiting your
56 products, it is your job to stop them.

1. Directions: The sentence in bold is the first sentence of a brief summary of the passage. Complete the summary by selecting three answer choices. Your choices will express the most important ideas in the passage. Some choices are not in the passage or do not express important ideas.

The passage discusses the effect knock-offs have on a company.

-
-
-

Answer Choices

1. The incentive to innovate can be impacted severely.

2. Belts and other accessories are some of the most common knock-offs on eBay.

3. Market share can be greatly reduced.

4. A company's brands can lose their value.

5. Americans over 65 will be forced to spend more money on health care.

6. Pharmaceutical companies, such as Tiffany and Pfizer, are directly affected by counterfeit products.

➔ **2 points for all 3 correct. One wrong = 0.**

➔ Answers page 327.

Complete-a-Table Questions → *Strategies*

Each passage will have one complete-a-table question. This question type comes at the end of the passage. This question measures your ability to identify details in the passage and connect them topically to main topic headings in a table, for example, vegetables and fruit below. To answer, click-drag your choices under the applicable topic heading.

- **REMEMBER**: *You do not need to put your choices in order.*

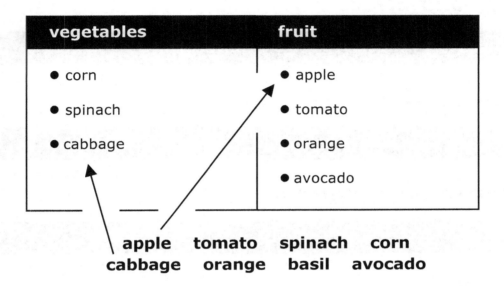

vegetables	fruit
• corn	• apple
• spinach	• tomato
• cabbage	• orange
	• avocado

apple   tomato   spinach   corn
cabbage   orange   basil   avocado

Question Analysis

Start your question analysis by identifying the rhetorical strategy in the task description (see below). This sample is asking you to **compare-and-contrast** the details of <u>Adam Smith's economic theories</u> (arguments) to the details of the *Mercantilist* argument.

14. <u>Directions</u>: Complete the following table by indicating how <u>Adam Smith's economic theories</u> in *The Wealth of Nations* **differed from** *what the Mercantilists believed*. This is a 4-point question.

    Note: If you get all seven answers correct, you will score 4 points.

    Determine your score for this question using the following chart.

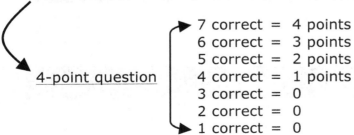

    4-point question
    7 correct = 4 points
    6 correct = 3 points
    5 correct = 2 points
    4 correct = 1 points
    3 correct = 0
    2 correct = 0
    1 correct = 0

The rhetorical strategy in the topic heading could be any of the following rhetorical strategies. Note below how the process of comparing-and-contrasting is inferred in each heading.

Illustration

Examples of A	Examples of B

Cause-and-Effect

Causes	Effects

Pros and Cons

Pros	Cons

Compare-and-Contrast

Topic A	Topic B	Topic C

Definition

Definition of A	Definition of B

Process

Process A	Process B

Description

Description of A	Description of B	Description of C

Classification

Luxury cars	Mid-sized cars	Compacts

Choice Analysis

Start your answer choice selection by identifying the signal words in each choice. For example, in choice one below, the signal words are **amassing gold**. Next, scan the passage for **amassing gold** and confirm whether sentence one is correct. Repeat this process for all choices.

- **REMEMBER:** *Two choices will be incorrect. They will be off topic, not true, too general, not known, and/or not stated in the passage. Choice 3 below is not stated in the passage. Choice 9 is also not stated in the passage. Both choices are too general as well.*

  1. Nations created wealth and power by **amassing gold**.

  2. A **satisfied work force** will benefit a nation's economy as a whole.

  3. **Imports and exports** should be manufactured by a government.

  4. Exports made by **poorly paid workers** created national wealth.

  5. National wealth starts with a **rational approach** to manufacturing.

  6. Productivity will increase if the **labor force is divided** systematically.

  7. **War with other nations** is part of national and economic policy.

  8. **Accumulating commodities** does not create national wealth.

  9. **Trading** is part of **military policy**.

- **WARNING:** *Watch the clock. Analyzing the choices and scanning for answers will take time. If you are running out of time, guess and move on. Never leave an answer blank.*

Notes

_____

_____

_____

_____

_____

_____

Practice #1: *Complete-a-Table Questions*

<u>Directions</u>: You have ten minutes to read the following two passages and answer the questions.

Refining

1   1 ➜ A barrel of crude oil is the oil industry's standard unit of measurement. One
2   barrel contains 42 gallons or 159 liters. Within that barrel of crude is a complex
3   mixture of molecules called hydrocarbons. Hydrocarbons are what's left of plants
4   and animals that lived billions of years ago. This organic matter, deep within the
5   Earth, is heated by the Earth which, over time, turns it into crude oil hence the
6   term fossil fuel. To make consumer petroleum products from a barrel of crude oil,
7   products such as gasoline and diesel fuel, the hydrocarbons must be separated.
8   That separation process is done at a refinery through a process called fractional
9   distillation. Fractional distillation starts by boiling raw, unprocessed crude oil. The
10 hydrocarbons in the oil all have different boiling points. This means they can be
11 separated through distillation, a process in which the raw crude oil is changed into
12 its gaseous form through boiling. When a particular hydrocarbon reaches its boil-
13 ing point, it changes from a solid to a vapor. This vapor is then drained off into a
14 separate holding tank where it is cooled and condensed into liquid form. The light-
15 est products, those which have the lowest boiling point, such as gasoline, exit from
16 the top of the boiler while the heaviest products—those with the highest boiling
17 points, such as lubricating oil—exit from the bottom.

1.   <u>Directions</u>: Complete the table by indicating how hydrocarbons differ from
     fractional distillation. This is a 4-point question.

Hydrocarbons	Fractional Distillation
•	•
•	•
•	•
•	

1. occurs at a refinery
2. change to vapor when boiled
3. the process of boiling crude oil
4. boiling changes it to a solid from a vapor
5. separated by distilling

6. mixture of molecules called gasoline
7. turns solid crude oil into vapor
8. plant and animal-based
9. found in crude oil

➜ Answers page 327.   ➜ Scoring multi-answer questions page 328.

Slang and Jargon

1 → There seems to be some confusion as to the difference between slang and jargon. Remember that jargon is a type of slang. The difference is that I can learn jargon—for example computer jargon—and I can become a systems engineer or an app designer. Moreover—and this is key—jargon is inclusive. That means I can learn computer jargon, invented words like virus and mouse, and computer professionals will accept me. In other words, learn the code, join the group; thus, jargon is inclusive. Slang, in its purest sense, however, is an excluding code. I can learn, for example, all the rap slang I want, such as "Yo, s'up homey? Dawg, bust a move!" or "Crib cost beaucoup Benjamins," but will Fifty Cent or Lil Wayne or Snoop Dog accept me into their group, their gang? After all, I know the language, the code, right? Not likely. In this light, slang is like a wall, a wall of invented words designed for two purposes: to exclude me from the group and to keep outsiders—other gangs and the police—from figuring out what we, our gang, are saying. Of course, rap slang is only one kind of slang. Teenagers use slang all the time, skateboarders in particular.

2. Directions: Complete the table by indicating how slang and jargon differ. This is a 4-point question.

Slang	Jargon
•	•
•	•
•	•
•	

1. type of slang
2. skateboarders
3. Fifteen Cent
4. like a wall
5. inclusive code

6. started in the USA
7. rap
8. virus, mouse
9. excluding code

→ Answers page 327.
→ Scoring multi-answer questions page 328.

Practice #2: *Complete-a-Table Questions*

<u>Directions</u>: You have 20 minutes to read <u>all</u> three passages and answer the questions.

Passage One: *Impressionists and Pre-Raphaelites*

1   **1 ➜** The nineteenth century witnessed many art movements. However, one in par-
2   ticular tends to overshadow all the rest. That art movement is Impressionism, a
3   school of painting that originated in France in the late 1860's.
4
5   **2 ➜** The Impressionists were a radical group of painters who broke all the rules of
6   academic painting. In Europe at the time, academic painters were traditionalists
7   who gave the public what they wanted: great canvases that depicted heroic figures
8   and ancient scenes painted with brushwork so fine some paintings looked more
9   like photographs. The Impressionists, however, refuted such a conservative ap-
10   proach to painting. Instead of painting indoors, as did the academics, the Impres-
11   sionists took their easels outside and painted "en plein air," in the open air. Instead
12   of painting classical scenes which glorified a heroic past, the Impressionists paint-
13   ed scenes of everyday life, such as sailboats on a river and bustling city streets. In-
14   stead of spending hours on one painting, the Impressionists strove to capture the
15   moment with broken brush strokes using mixed and unmixed paint as a means of
16   recreating the physical properties of light. Critics were outraged. This new style of
17   painting was not painting in the formal, classical sense but were sketches and im-
18   pressions. Hence the term impressionists.
19
20   **3 ➜** Initially, the Impressionists and their revolutionary approach to painting was
21   rejected by the French art world, a closed and cliquish world that was dictated by
22   the tastes of the Académie des Beaux-Arts. The academy gave its stamp of approval
23   to those artists it favored while rejecting those it deemed too radical. Those radicals
24   were the Impressionists, men like Edouard Manet and his painting *Dejeuner sur*
25   *l'herbe* (Luncheon on the Grass), a painting many critics believe represents the
26   start of modernist painting yet at the time outraged the conventional art world.
27   Undaunted, Manet and the Impressionists charted their own course and soon the
28   art world realized that the work of Manet, Renoir, Monet and Degas, among others,
29   was indeed making an impact, one that persists to this day. In fact, impressionist
30   paintings are so ubiquitous, it would be easy to assume that it was the only art
31   movement of any significance during the nineteenth century. Nothing could be fur-
32   ther from the truth. Twenty miles across the English Channel, some twenty years
33   before the Impressionists shook the French art world, the school of painting known
34   as the Pre-Raphaelite Brotherhood was shaking the foundations of the British art
35   world.
36
37   **4 ➜** The Pre-Raphaelite Brotherhood was formed in 1848 by John Everett Millais,
38   Dante Gabriel Rossetti, and William Holman Hunt. Like all great art movements, it
39   rejected the old in favor of the new. In this light, the Pre-Raphaelite Brotherhood
40   was similar to the Impressionists some twenty years later. However, where the Im-
41   pressionists captured impressions outside in natural light, the Pre-Raphaelite
42   Brotherhood drew inspiration from romantic poetry and medieval themes, and con-

43 veyed them on large canvases painted in studios. The subjects were bathed in a
44 realistic light and were rendered with great attention to detail. This radical new ap-
45 proach to painting, one in which romanticism and naturalism merged, rejected the
46 predominating Mannerist school in which the human form was exaggerated in set-
47 tings that were both unreal and filled with hard, unnatural light.
48
49 5 ➔ Like the Impressionists, the Pre-Raphaelite Brotherhood outraged the art es-
50 tablishment with their radical new approach to painting. One painting in particu-
51 lar, *Christ in the House of His Parents* by John Millais, caused a firestorm of criti-
52 cism. Critics, including Charles Dickens, claimed the painting was blasphemous.
53 Worse, Dickens said Mary, the mother of Christ, was ugly when in fact Millais had
54 based her on his sister-in-law, Mary Hodgkinson. The Pre-Raphaelite Brother-
55 hood's love of medieval themes and details also drew sharp rebukes. Yet, like the
56 Impressionists, the Pre-Raphaelite Brotherhood refused to be swayed by popular
57 opinion. Today, paintings, such as Millais's *Ophelia*, Rossetti's *Beata Beatrix*, and
58 Hunt's *Scapegoat* are acknowledged masterpieces. Moreover, the influence of the
59 Pre-Raphaelite Brotherhood can be seen in the protean work of William Morris, a
60 prolific artist and textile designer who founded the decorative art firm William,
61 Marshall and Faulkner, a commercial art house that, in 1860, signaled the begin-
62 ning of the decorative arts, a movement that spawned the Arts and Crafts move-
63 ment and Art Nouveau, of which Louis Comfort Tiffany was a central figure.

1. <u>Directions</u>: Complete the table by indicating how the Impressionists' theory of art differed from the Pre-Raphaelite Brotherhood's theory of art. This is a 4-point question.

Impressionists	Pre-Raphaelite Brotherhood
•	•
•	•
•	•
•	

1. Painting outdoors was preferred to painting in a studio.
2. They found inspiration in romantic poetry and medieval themes.
3. They were influenced by Mannerism.
4. They captured the feeling of a scene rather than every detail.
5. They rejected the academic school of painting with its heroic themes.
6. They utilized big canvases.
7. They captured the physical properties of light in paint.
8. Naturalism was important even though they worked inside.
9. It was founded in 1838.

➔ Answers: page 328.   ➔ Scoring multi-answer questions page 328

Passage Two: *Housing in the Middle Ages*

1 → During the Middle Ages, peasant families lived in rural houses close to the fields in which they worked, land which was controlled by a lord in a castle. A typical peasant house, usually built by the family themselves, was a primitive shelter that provided little more than a place to eat and sleep. Construction materials included earth and wood for the walls and thatching for the roof. The most common rural structure was the longhouse or house-barn. Rectangular in shape, this dwelling had doors on opposite ends and on the sides thus ensuring cross ventilation. Inside, the floor plan was divided in half with one end forming the hearth, the place where the family prepared and ate their meals and slept. The opposite half was occupied by livestock, typically a cow for milk, chickens for meat and eggs, and a horse that pulled the plow. In winter, the heat rising off the animals kept the structure warm. Because there was no chimney, the interior was often smoky. The exit for the smoke was through holes at either end of the roof. Fire was a constant threat as was the risk of contracting diseases from living in such close proximity to animals.

2 → Those with more money and social status, namely land-owning families, lived in houses separate from the livestock. The house consisted of two floors. The first floor was the hall, the place where the family ate and entertained around a central fireplace. For the landowner, the hall was of central importance for it was there that the landowner fed his family and his servants, the meals themselves a measure of the landowner's wealth and hospitality. Above the hall was a private family room called the solar. It consisted of beds and a fireplace for heating and was reached by a private staircase. On the ground floor off the hall were the buttery and the pantry. The pantry, a name still in use today, was a storage room for dry foodstuffs, such as flour and spices, while the buttery was cold storage for perishables, such as butter, cheese, and eggs.

3 → Houses built in cities and towns, unlike rural houses, were built in rows and often shared the same walls. As a result, they occupied less horizontal space while raising vertically several floors. On the ground floor facing the street there was often a shop behind which were the living quarters. The kitchen too was located on the ground floor with a small light court separating it from the house. This transitional space prevented odors and fire from spreading from the kitchen to the rest of the house. Because houses were built so close, and made of wood and thatch, they were highly combustible. During the Middle Ages, cities were often engulfed in flames, the source of which was often traceable to a kitchen fire. The city of London experienced two such conflagrations, the Great Fire of 1135 and the Great Fire of 1212.

4 → At the top of the social ladder were the nobility. They resided in fortified residences called castles. Early castles were built of wood and earth, and evolved into massive stone edifices, many of which were surrounded by a water barrier called a moat. Castles were built in places of strategic importance, such as on a trade route or at the mouth of a harbor. Militarily, they provided protection from invaders and offered a base from which raids could be launched. Inside their high stone walls were stables, granaries, and workshops, all of which served the noble, his family, and his staff. The land surrounding the castle was farmed by peasants who, in times of trouble, sought the protection of the lord. In return, the peasants served

50 as soldiers under the lord and paid for the use of his land through taxes and by
51 sharing part of the harvest; thus, the castle also served as a center of administra-
52 tion.

2. <u>Directions</u>: Complete the table by matching the construction type to the house type. This is a 4-point question.

Peasant House	Land-Owner House
●	●
●	●
●	●
●	

1. shaped like a rectangle

2. had a storage room for dairy products

3. had a private second floor accessible by stairs

4. had granaries and workshops

5. humans and animals shared the one main room

6. four doors on the ground floor

7. had a great hall for eating and entertaining

8. no chimney

9. surrounded by a moat

➔ Answers: page 328.
➔ Scoring multi-answer questions page 328.

Passage Three: *The Panama Canal*

1 → The Panama Canal is one of the great engineering feats of the modern era. Stretching forty miles across the Isthmus of Panama, the canal connects the Atlantic Ocean to the east with the Pacific Ocean to the west. Before the canal opened in 1914, a ship sailing from New York to San Francisco south around South America had to travel fourteen-thousand miles. The Panama Canal cut that distance in half.

2 → Connecting the Atlantic and the Pacific had been envisioned as early as 1513. In September of that year, Spanish explorer and conquistador Vasco Núñez de Balboa was the first European to lay eyes on the Pacific Ocean after having crossed the Isthmus of Panama, home to one of the most inhospitable jungles on Earth. However, it wasn't until 1888 that the French, led by Ferdinand de Lesseps, began construction on the canal. By then, de Lesseps was famous the world over for building the Suez Canal, a waterway that connects the Mediterranean Ocean and the Red Sea. In 1856, de Lesseps, a diplomat by trade, was awarded the concession to build the Suez Canal from Said Pasha, the viceroy of Egypt. With that concession, de Lesseps started the Suez Canal Company. The indefatigable de Lesseps gathered a team of international engineers and employed thousands of workers. After ten years of digging, much of it done by forced labor, the Suez Canal opened on November 17, 1869 to much fanfare. With the completion of the Suez Canal, and the completion of the American transcontinental railroad six months earlier, the world could now be traversed without stopping. As for de Lesseps, the man who dug a canal through the desert, his popularity soared. In May 1879, when the Geographical Society in Paris voted to build a canal across the Isthmus of Panama, de Lesseps was chosen to lead the project.

3 → From the outset, construction of the Panama Canal was plagued with problems. Malaria and yellow fever decimated the workers while landslides from torrential rains buried dredges and filled in land that had been excavated. To raise money for the failing project, de Lesseps encouraged the average Frenchman to do his patriotic duty and buy shares in the Panama Canal Company. Banking on his reputation as the man who had built the Suez Canal, de Lesseps raised the necessary capital. Yet scandal soon broke out. De Lesseps and a number of others had bribed journalists and politicians to lie about the failing canal. The value of the company's stock plummeted. Millions of people lost everything overnight. The Panama Canal Scandal, as it was called, marked the end of French construction on the canal, and the end for de Lesseps as a free-wheeling entrepreneur and canal builder. All told, with the canal unfinished, some 20,000 canal workers, the majority of whom had been recruited from islands in the Caribbean, had succumbed to disease and work-related accidents.

4 → In 1904, the United States government under President Theodore Roosevelt, bought the Panama Canal Company from the French. At the time, Panama was Colombian territory. The Americans offered to buy Panama from Colombia but the government of Colombia steadfastly refused. Soon after, Panamanian separatists revolted against Colombia. With the support of the American military, the Panamanians won their independence and the nation of Panama was formed. In return, Panama granted America the right to build a canal and administer it indefinitely. In August, 1914 the canal was finished two years ahead of schedule. Yet the world

49 paid scant attention for all heads were turned toward Europe where World War
50 One had started that very same month and year.
51
52 5 ➔ Despite the political controversy surrounding the Panama Canal even to this
53 day, its construction is notable for many milestones. One was the eradication of
54 yellow fever, a disease that had decimated the French workforce. Scientists identi-
55 fied the mosquito as the carrier of the disease; thus, living and working quarters
56 were regularly fumigated. The result was a dramatic reduction in yellow fever and
57 malaria deaths. Another milestone lies in the construction of the canal itself. It is
58 the world's first all-electric installation. The raising and the lowering of the locks,
59 and the trains that move ships into position, are all powered by electric motors de-
60 signed and built by General Electric, a company started by Thomas Edison.

3. Directions: Complete the table by contrasting de Lesseps' building of the
    Suez Canal and the Panama Canal. This is a 4-point question.

Suez Canal	Panama Canal
●	●
●	●
●	●
●	

1. finished in 1914

2. took ten years to build

3. was unfinished

4. was started before Panama was independent

5. used forced labor

6. 20,000 workers died building it

7. connected the Mediterranean Ocean and the Red Sea

8. made de Lesseps famous

9. was designed by Thomas Edison

➔ Answers: page 328.

➔ Scoring multi-answer questions page 328.

Answer Key

Pg.	Task	?#	Answers	Distractor
	Office-Hours	1	D	B
136	Off-Hrs Questions	2	B	A
		3	B, C	A
		4	C	A
		5	C	B
140	Content Questions	1	B	C
		2	D	A
		3	C	A
		4	D	B
143	Purpose Questions	1	C	A
		2	C	D
		3	D	C
		4	B	D
145	Single-Answer	1	C	D
	Detail Questions	2	B	A
		3	A	B
		4	D	B
		5	C	B
		6	B	D
148	Multi-Answer	1	A, D, E	B
	Detail Questions	2	C, D	A
		3	A, D, E	C
		4	B, C	D
156	Question-First	1	D	B
	Function Questions	2	C	D
		3	B	D
		4	B	D
157	Segment-First	1	B	A
	Function Questions	2	B	C
		3	D	A
		4	A	C

Pg.	Task	?#	Answers	Distractor
160	Direct-Attitude	1	C	B
	Questions	2	A	D
		3	C	D
		4	D	B
163	Inferred-Attitude	1	B	C
	Questions	2	D	C
		3	D	A
		4	C	B
165	Inferred-Action	1	A	C
	Questions	2	B	A
		3	B	C
		4	D	A
	Service-Encounter	1	B	A
167	Serv-Enc... Questions	2	C	D
		3	A, C, D	B
		4	D	B
		5	B	A
168	Content Questions	1	A	B
		2	A	C
		3	C	A
		4	C	D
169	Purpose Questions	1	D	B
		2	B	C
		3	D	A
		4	D	A
170	Single-Answer	1	B	A
	Detail Questions	2	C	A
		3	A	C
		4	C	B
		5	D	A
		6	C	A
171	Multi-Answer	1	B, C	D
	Detail Questions	2	A, D	B
		3	C, D	A
		4	A, C	D

Pg.	Task	?#	Answers	Distractor
172	Question-First	1	D	C
	Function Questions	2	D	A
		3	D	A
		4	B	C
173	Segment-First	1	B	A
	Function Questions	2	B	C
		3	A	B
		4	B	A
174	Direct-Attitude	1	C	A
	Questions	2	A	D
		3	D	C
		4	C	D
175	Inferred-Attitude	1	D	B
	Questions	2	C	A
		3	C	D
		4	C	B
176	Inferred-Action	1	B	C
	Questions	2	A	C
		3	C	B
		4	D	A
	Lecture → Professor	1	D	A
180	Lecture Questions	2	B	A
		3	A, C, E	B
		4	A	B
		5	1.C 2.A 3.D 4.B	
		6	Y, N, Y, N, Y	
182	Content Questions	1	C	D
		2	B	D
		3	A	D
		4	C	D
183	Purpose Questions	1	D	A
		2	C	A
		3	C	A
		4	C	B

Pg.	Task	?#	Answers	Distractor
184	Single-Answer	1	A	C
	Detail Questions	2	D	A
		3	C	B
		4	C	D
		5	D	A
		6	B	D
185	Multi-Answer	1	A, C, E	B
	Detail Questions	2	B, C, D	E
		3	B, C, D	A
		4	B, D	C
186	Question-First	1	D	B
	Function Question	2	B	D
		3	C	B
		4	A	B
		5	D	A
		6	B	D
		7	D	B
		8	A	C
188	Segment-First	1	C	A
	Function Question	2	D	C
		3	C	B
		4	A	C
189	Direct-Attitude	1	B	C
	Questions	2	C	D
		3	D	C
		4	B	D
190	Inferred-Attitude	1	D	B
	Questions	2	A	C
		3	A	D
		4	D	B
191	Inferred-Action	1	C	B
	Questions	2	C	B
		3	C	B
		4	C	B

Pg.	Task	?#	Answers	Distractor
192	Ordering Questions	1	1.A 2.D 3.B 4.C	
		2	1.C 2.D 3.B 4.A	
		3	1.D 2.B 3.C 4.A	
		4	1.C 2.A 3.B 4.D	
194	Yes-No Questions	1	N, Y, N, Y, N	
		2	Y, Y, N, N, Y	
		3	Y, Y, Y, N, Y	
		4	Y, Y, N, N, N	
198	Connecting Questions	1	C. Teutoburg Forest = Varus	
			B. Marathon = Darius	
			A. Waterloo = Napoleon	
		2	B. willow bark = aches-pains	
			C. milk thistle = liver health	
			A. aloe vera = burns-wounds	
		3	A. cytoplasmic... = contains genome	
			C. exterior = flagella for motion	
			B. envelope = protective filter	
		4	B. fry = six months old	
			A. alevin = lives off yolk sack	
			C. smolt = mature in Pacific	
	Professor-Students	1	C	A
204	Discussion Questions	2	B	A
		3	B	A
		4	A, C, E	D
		5	1.C 2.D 3.B 4.A	
		6	N, N, Y, Y, Y	
206	Practice #1: Discussion	1	D	A
		2	B	A
		3	A	B
		4	1.D 2.C 3.A 4.B	
		5	V, TH, V, TH, V	
		6	A	C

Pg.	Task	?#	Answers	Distractor
208	Practice #2: Discussion	1	D	C
		2	B	A
		3	C	A
		4	C	D
		5	C, O, C, O, C	
		6	C	A
210	**READING SECTION**			
212	Adam Smith and The	1	B	D
	Wealth of Nations	2	C	D
		3	C	
		4	D	B
		5	B	C
		6	D	B
		7	A	B
		8	D	C
		9	square 4	
		10	B	D
		11	D	C
		12	1, 5, 6	
		13	A	D
		14	Mercantilists = 1, 4, 7	
			Adam Smith = 2, 5, 6, 8	
224	Practice #1	1	C	D
	Fact Questions	2	D	A
	Penicillin	3	A	B
		4	A	B
		5	B	D
		6	B	D
		7	D	B
		8	B	A
227	Practice #2	1	D	A
	Fact Questions	2	C	D
	Biological Classification	3	D	B
		4	A	B
		5	D	B
		6	B	C
		7	D	B
		8	B	A

Pg.	Task	?#	Answers	Distractor
	Biological Classification	9	D	A
234	Practice #1	1	B	C
	Vocabulary Questions	2	C	A
	Flooding	3	C	D
		4	B	C
		5	A	C
		6	D	C
		7	B	A
		8	B	D
		9	C	D
		10	B	D
		11	D	A
237	Practice #2	1	D	A
	Vocabulary Questions	2	B	A
	Wernher Von Braun	3	A	B
		4	A	B
		5	A	D
		6	D	C
		7	C	D
		8	D	C
		9	A	B
		10	C	B
		11	B	C
242	Practice #1	1	C	
	Negative Fact	2	C	
	Questions	3	A	
	Women of Influence	4	C	
		5	B	
		6	C	
245	Practice #2	1	D	
	Negative Fact	2	B	
	Questions	3	D	
	Methods of Research	4	D	
		5	B	
250	Practice #1	1	C	A
	Inference Questions	2	C	B
	Crypsis	3	D	A

Pg.	Task	?#	Answers	Distractor
	Crypsis	4	C	A
		5	C	A
252	Practice #2	1	C	D
	Inference Questions	2	B	C
	A Landmark Ruling	3	B	A
		4	D	B
		5	B	C
		6	C	D
258	Practice #1	1	A	B
	Rhetorical Purpose	2	D	A
	Cognitive Bias	3	B	C
		4	D	A
		5	A	B
		6	D	A
		7	A	C
		8	B	C
		9	A	D
261	Practice #2	1	C	A
	Rhetorical Purpose	2	B	A
	The Gilded Age	3	B	D
		4	B	A
		5	D	C
		6	C	A
		7	A	B
266	Practice	1	C	B
	Reference Questions	2	B	C
		3	D	C
		4	A	B
		5	B	C
		6	A	B
		7	D	B
		8	B	C
		9	A	D
		10	C	A
		11	C	D
		12	A	D
		13	C	B

Pg.	Task	?#	Answers	Distractor
273	Practice #1	1	C	
	Sentence Simplification	2	I	
		3	I	
		4	I	
		5	I	
		6	I	
		7	C	
		8	C	
		9	I	
		10	C	
		11	C	
		12	I	
		13	C	
		14	I	
		15	I	
		16	1	
276	Practice #2	1	C	A
	Sentence Simplification	2	A	C
		3	C	B
		4	C	D
		5	B	C
		6	A	C
		7	D	C
		8	B	A
		9	A	B
		10	B	C
		11	A	C
		12	B	C
		13	A	C
		14	A	D
		15	A	D
		16	D	C
		17	B	D
		18	D	A
		19	A	B
		20	A	C
		21	D	C
		22	D	A
		23	C	A

Pg.	Task	?#	Answers	Distractor
292	Practice	1	3	
	Sentence-Insertion	2	1	
	Questions	3	4	
		4	4	
		5	4	
		6	3	
		7	4	
		8	1	
		9	3	
		10	4	
		11	4	
		12	4	
299	Practice #1: Prose-	1	1, 2, 6	3 not true
	Summary Questions			4 not true
	Jonathan James...			5 unknown
300	*F. Scott Fitzgerald...*	2	3, 4, 6	1 not true
				2 off topic
				5 off topic
302	Practice #2: Passage	1	2, 4, 5	1 off topic
	One Prose-Summary:			3 off topic
	The Tulip Bubble			6 unknown
304	Passage Two:	1	1, 5, 6	2 unknown
	Women of Liberia...			3 off topic
				4 not true
306	Passage Three:	1	1, 3, 4	2 unknown
	Knock-Offs			5 off topic
				6 not true
310	Practice #1: *Complete-*	1	Hydrocarbons 2, 5, 8, 9	4 reversed
	a-Table Questions		Fractional Dis... 3, 7, 1	6 not true
	Refining...			
311	*Slang and Jargon*	2	Slang 2, 4, 7, 9	3 spelling
			Jargon 1, 5, 8	6 not true

Pg.	Task	?#	Answers	Distractor
313	Practice: Passage One	1	Impressionists 1, 4, 5, 7	3 not true
	Complete-a-Table		Pre-Raphaelites 2, 6, 8	9 not true
	Impressionists...			
315	Passage Two:	2	Peasant House 1, 5, 6, 8	4 = castle
	Housing...		Land-Owner House 2, 3, 7	9 = castle
317	Passage Three	3	Suez Canal 2, 5, 7, 8	1 not true
	Panama Canal		Panama Canal 3, 4, 6	9 not true

Scoring Multi-Answer Questions

Using the following guide when scoring multi-answer questions (✓ means correct).

1-point question = 2 ✓ = 1 point
1 ✓ = 0

2-point question = 3 ✓ = 2 points
2 ✓ = 0
1 ✓ = 0

2-point question = 4 ✓ = 2 points
3 ✓ = 1 point
2 ✓ = 0
1 ✓ = 0

3-point question = 5 ✓ = 3 points
4 ✓ = 2 points
3 ✓ = 1 point
2 ✓ = 0
1 ✓ = 0

4-point question = 7 ✓ = 4 points
6 ✓ = 3 points
5 ✓ = 2 points
4 ✓ = 1 points
3 ✓ = 0
2 ✓ = 0
1 ✓ = 0

Independent Writing → *Proficiency Checklist*

Rate your independent-writing responses using OPDUL=C, then score them using the rating guide on the next page.

O = Does it (essay) demonstrate proficient Organization?

- deduction   Yes ___ No ___
- induction   Yes ___ No ___

P = Does it demonstrate a proficient Progression of ideas?

- general-specific   Yes ___ No ___
- specific-general   Yes ___ No ___

D = Does it demonstrate proficient Development?

- introduction   Yes ___ No ___
- body   Yes ___ No ___
- conclusion   Yes ___ No ___

U = Does it demonstrate proficient Unity?

- topical   Yes ___ No ___
- grammatical   Yes ___ No ___

L = Does it demonstrate proficient Language-Use?

- word choice   Yes ___ No ___
- idioms   Yes ___ No ___
- sentence variety   Yes ___ No ___

C = Does it demonstrate Coherence?

- Yes ___ No ___

Comments: _____

_____

_____

_____

_____

Independent Writing → *Rating Guide*

→ <u>Rating</u>: 4.0 - 5.0 ---

A response in this range is <u>C</u>oherent because it demonstrates proficiency in **all** of the following areas.

<u>O</u> Demonstrates a clear and consistent method of organization.

<u>P</u> Demonstrates a clear and consistent progression of ideas.

<u>D</u> Demonstrates clear and consistent development of the intro, body, and conclusion; the supporting illustrations are well developed; *however, some areas might lack development and/or an idea might not be completely explained.*

<u>U</u> Demonstrates topical and grammatical unity; *however, some topical and/or grammatical connections might not be clear or accurate. These errors are minor and do not affect coherence.*

<u>L</u> Demonstrates consistent language use; *however, some word choice and/or idiom usage might not be clear or accurate, and/or there might be syntax errors. These errors are minor and do not affect coherence.*

→ <u>Rating</u>: 2.5 - 3.5 ---

A response in this range demonstrates a lack of proficiency in **one or more** areas.

<u>O</u> Demonstrates organization; *however, it might not always be clear or consistent.*

<u>P</u> Demonstrates a progression of ideas; *however, it might not always be clear or consistent.*

<u>D</u> Demonstrates development; *however, the introduction, body, and/or conclusion might lack development, and/or might not provide enough supporting examples or be sufficiently explained.*

<u>U</u> Demonstrates topical and grammatical unity; *however, there might be topical digressions and/or connections that are not always clear or accurate.*

<u>L</u> Demonstrates basic but accurate language use with limited sentence variety; *however, inaccurate word choice and/or idiom usage, and/or syntax errors might make the meaning of some sentences unclear.*

→ <u>Rating</u>: 1.0 - 2.0 ---

A response in this range demonstrates a serious lack of proficiency in **one or more** areas of OPDUL.

Integrated Writing → *Proficiency Checklist*

Rate your integrated-writing responses using OPDUL=C, then score them using the rating guide on the next page.

O = Does it (summary) demonstrate proficient Organization?

- block-style   Yes ___ No ___
- point-by-point   Yes ___ No ___

P = Does it demonstrate a proficient Progression of ideas?

- general-specific   Yes ___ No ___
- specific-general   Yes ___ No ___

D = Does it demonstrate proficient Development-Summarization?

- introductions   Yes ___ No ___
- bodies   Yes ___ No ___
- conclusions   Yes ___ No ___

U = Does it demonstrate proficient Unity-Synthesis?

- topical   Yes ___ No ___
- grammatical   Yes ___ No ___

L = Does it demonstrate proficient Language-Use-Paraphrasing?

- word choice   Yes ___ No ___
- idioms   Yes ___ No ___
- sentence variety   Yes ___ No ___

C = Does it demonstrate Coherence?

- Yes ___ No ___

Comments: _____

_____

_____

_____

_____

Integrated Writing → *Rating Guide*

→ Rating: 4.0 - 5.0 ---

A response in this range is <u>C</u>oherent because it demonstrates proficiency in **all** of the following areas.

<u>O</u> Demonstrates a clear and consistent method of organization that accurately shows how the main lecture points argue against the main reading points.

<u>P</u> Demonstrates a clear and consistent progression of ideas.

<u>D</u> Demonstrates development-summarization of the intro, body, and conclusion of both the lecture and reading; the main points are clear and well developed; *however, some points might lack development and/or a lecture point might not be completely explained.*

<u>U</u> Demonstrates unity-synthesis; *however, some topical and/or grammatical connections between the lecture and the reading might not be clear or accurate. These errors are minor and do not affect coherence.*

<u>L</u> Demonstrates consistent and accurate language-use paraphrasing; *however, some word choice and/or idiom usage might not be accurate or clear, and/or there might be syntax errors. These errors are minor and do not affect coherence.*

→ Rating: 2.5 - 3.5 ---

A response in this range demonstrates a lack of proficiency in **one or more** areas.

<u>O</u> Demonstrates organization; *however, the connection between the main lecture points and the main reading points is not always clear or consistent.*

<u>P</u> Demonstrates a progression of ideas; *however, it might not always be clear or consistent.*

<u>D</u> Demonstrates development-summarization; *however, the main points in the intro, body, and/or conclusion of the lecture and/or the reading might lack development, and/or a main point in the lecture might be missing.*

<u>U</u> Demonstrates topical and grammatical unity; *however, the connection between the main lecture and reading points is not always clear or accurate.*

<u>L</u> Demonstrates basic language-use paraphrasing with limited sentence variety; *frequent and inaccurate word choice and/or idiom usage, and/or errors in syntax make the meaning of some sentences and connections unclear.*

→ Rating: 1.0 - 2.0 ---

A response in this range demonstrates a serious lack of proficiency in **one or more** areas of OPDUL.

Independent Speaking → *Proficiency Checklist*

Rate your independent-speaking responses using OPDUL=C, then score them using the rating guide on the next page.

O = Does it (response) demonstrate proficient Organization?

- deduction   Yes ___ No ___
- induction   Yes ___ No ___

P = Does it demonstrate a proficient Progression of ideas?

- general-specific   Yes ___ No ___
- specific-general   Yes ___ No ___

D = Does it demonstrate proficient Development?

- introduction   Yes ___ No ___
- body   Yes ___ No ___
- conclusion   Yes ___ No ___

U = Does it demonstrate proficient Unity?

- topical   Yes ___ No ___
- grammatical   Yes ___ No ___

L = Does it demonstrate proficient Language-Use?

- word choice   Yes ___ No ___
- idioms   Yes ___ No ___
- sentence variety   Yes ___ No ___
- ease-of-understanding   Yes ___ No ___

C = Does it demonstrate Coherence?

- Yes ___ No ___

Comments: _____

_____

_____

_____

_____

Independent Speaking → *Rating Guide*

→ Rating: 3.5 - 4.0 --

A response in this range is Coherent because it demonstrates proficiency in **all** of the following areas.

O Demonstrates a clear and consistent method of organization.

P Demonstrates a clear and consistent progression of ideas.

D Demonstrates development of the intro, body, and conclusion; the illustrations are clear and well developed; minor omissions do not affect coherence.

U Demonstrates topical and grammatical unity; the relationship between ideas is clear and accurate both topically and grammatically.

L Demonstrates clear and accurate language use; minor errors in word choice and/or idiom usage, and/or syntax do not affect coherence. The delivery demonstrates proficient fluency, pronunciation and automaticity; minor difficulties do not affect coherence, or require listener effort to understand.

→ Rating: 2.5 - 3.0 --

A response in this range demonstrates proficiency in at least **two** areas.

O Demonstrates organization.

P Demonstrates a progression of ideas.

D Demonstrates limited development; *the intro, body, and/or conclusion might lack development, particularly the example in the body.*

U Demonstrates topical and grammatical unity; *however, the connection between ideas might not always be clear or accurate.*

L Demonstrates a limited range of word choice and/or idiom usage, and/or sentence variety; inaccurate word choice and/or idiom usage, and/or syntax errors might make the meaning of some words/sentences unclear. Difficulties in one or more areas of fluency, pronunciation, and automaticity require listener effort to understand.

→ Rating: 1.5 – 2.0 --

A response in this range demonstrates a serious lack of proficiency in **two** areas of OPDUL.

→ Rating: 0.0 - 1.0 --

A response in this range demonstrates a serious lack of proficiency in **all** areas of OPDUL.

Integrated Speaking → *Proficiency Checklist*

Rate your integrated-speaking responses using OPDUL=C, then score them using the rating guide on the next page.

O = Does it (response) demonstrate proficient Organization?

- deduction   Yes __ No __
- induction   Yes __ No __

P = Does it demonstrate a proficient Progression of ideas?

- general-specific   Yes __ No __
- specific-general   Yes __ No __

D = Does it demonstrate proficient Development-Summarization?

- introductions   Yes __ No __
- bodies   Yes __ No __
- conclusions   Yes __ No __

U = Does it demonstrate proficient Unity-Synthesis?

- topical   Yes __ No __
- grammatical   Yes __ No __

L = Does it demonstrate proficient Language-Use-Paraphrasing?

- word choice   Yes __ No __
- idioms   Yes __ No __
- sentence variety   Yes __ No __
- ease-of-understanding Yes __ No __

C = Does it demonstrate Coherence?

- Yes __ No __

Comments: _____

_____

_____

_____

_____

Integrated Speaking → *Rating Guide*

Rate your integrated speaking responses using OPDUL=C, then score them using the rating guide on the next page.

→ Rating: 3.5 - 4.0 --

A response in this range is <u>C</u>oherent because it demonstrates proficiency in **all** of the following areas.

O Demonstrates a clear and consistent method of organization.

P Demonstrates a clear and consistent progression of ideas.

D Demonstrates development-summarization of the intro, body, and conclusion; the main idea and supporting illustrations are well developed; minor omissions do not affect coherence.

U Demonstrates unity-synthesis; the relationship between ideas is clear and accurate both topically and grammatically.

L Demonstrates clear and accurate language-use paraphrasing; minor errors in word choice and/or idiom usage, and/or syntax do not affect coherence. The delivery demonstrates consistent and accurate fluency, pronunciation and automaticity; minor difficulties do not affect coherence.

→ Rating: 2.5 - 3.0 --

A response in this range demonstrates proficiency in at least **two** areas.

O Demonstrates organization.

P Demonstrates a progression of ideas; however, it might not always be accurate or clear.

D Demonstrates development-summarization; *however, the intro, body and/or conclusion might be incomplete due to a lack of details and/or a point not being sufficiently explained.*

U Demonstrates unity-synthesis; *however, the connection between ideas might not always be clear/accurate and/or consistent due to a lack of topical and/or grammatical unity.*

L Demonstrates limited language-use paraphrasing; word choice and/or idiom usage, and/or syntax might be inaccurate/incomplete making the meaning of words/sentences unclear. Minor difficulties in fluency and/or pronunciation and/or automaticity require listener effort to understand.

→ Rating: 1.5 – 2.0 --

Demonstrates a serious lack of proficiency in **two** areas of OPDUL.

→ Rating: 0.0 - 1.0 --

Demonstrates a serious lack of proficiency in **all** areas of OPDUL.

Audio Scripts

Integrated Writing Task – Pg. 41

Sample Lecture: Big Oil - Track #1 – Page 41

Prof: 1 ➔ On the contrary, oil companies do more harm than good.

2 ➔ For starters, big oil eliminates jobs to increase profits. Last year, oil companies reduced their work force by 25% while profits were up 50% percent. This trend does not appear to be changing.

3 ➔ Also, oil companies avoid paying taxes by moving overseas. One company, Hamilton, moved to Dubai to reduce its U.S. corporate tax rate. How does this help our roads and bridges?

4 ➔ Worse, petroleum products are the number one cause of global warming. Every day, cars pour billions of tons of CO2 into the atmosphere. CO2 has been directly linked to the greenhouse effect.

5 ➔ The evidence is clear. Oil companies do more harm than good.

Sample Lecture: Internet Music - Track #2 - Page 46

Prof: 1 ➔ It happens every second of every day all over the world. One click and that new song—the one you didn't pay for—is on your iPod. You may think it's legal. After all, downloading music is fast and easy, right? Think again. It goes without saying that downloading music off the web without paying for it is a crime.

2 ➔ I know. I know. Some will argue that "It's my democratic right to download music without paying for it." Nonsense. The internet might have started out with the intention of being a democracy but believe me, those days are long gone. The internet these days is about two things: information and money. Big money. One of the biggest money makers on the web is music, and music is protected by law. If you download U2's latest album, let's say, and you don't pay for it, then you are breaking the copyright law that says U2 owns that music. It is their property and you just stole it. If you want to listen to U2, you've got to buy it, no ifs, ands or buts.

3 ➔ Also, the artist has a legal right to get paid for his or her work no matter how or where it is downloaded. How would you like it if somebody were stealing your music? This is exactly what Napster was doing. Napster was the first peer-to-peer music sharing site. Musicians, however, took Napster to court for not paying royalties, money owed each time a song was downloaded via Napster. Napster argued that it was just helping friends share music. The courts disagreed. Napster paid a big fine and is now a pay site.

4 ➔ Moreover, illegally downloading music off the web is not a privacy issue. If you break the law by illegally downloading music, you are a criminal. I'm sorry, but you can't have it both ways. You can't break the law and hide behind the privacy issue. The law is clear. Criminals have no right to privacy. Period.

5 ➔ It bears repeating that downloading music without paying for it is a crime no matter what anyone says about "the freedom of cyberspace." Just because downloading music is fast and easy doesn't mean you have the right to steal it.

Task #1 – Teleconferencing: Track #3 - Page 58

Narrator: Listen to a lecture in a business class.

Prof: 1 ➔ We Americans assume that all business cultures are like ours. Nothing could be further from the truth. Many Middle Eastern and Asian cultures prefer to do business face-to-face. Discussing business over tea or while having dinner is an integral part of the business process in these cultures. Such traditions help develop mutual respect and trust not only between business partners but between international employees working for the same company. Unfortunately, in the rush for convenience and cost saving, Americans fail to appreciate that not all business cultures view teleconferencing as the ultimate business solution.

2 ➔ The article goes on to say that blue-chip companies saved an average of $40 million last year by cutting travel costs. What the article doesn't tell you is that for every dollar saved by cutting travel costs, these same companies paid two dollars to upgrade their intranet systems. Teleconferencing might be fast and easy, but it's certainly not cheap, especially when companies need to continually upgrade their computer systems if they want to stay competitive.

3 ➔ Some would argue that teleconferencing is the perfect tool for problem solving, especially when operating under a deadline. Yet how do you know if the information you are receiving is timely and accurate? A good example is the American who called up a colleague in Japan. Because the Japanese colleague was new and did not want to lose face, and because the American was his boss, he told the American exactly what he wanted to hear. The American believed he had the solution to his problem only to realize later that the information was not accurate.

Task #2 - Track #4 - Global Warming – Page 59

Narrator: Directions. Now listen to a lecture on the same topic.

Prof: 1 ➔ It's amazing how some scientists bend the facts to serve their own agendas. That said, let me shed some light on the carbon sink issue. The CO_2 released from carbon sinks has a different isotopic ratio than the CO_2 produced by our burning of fossils fuels. In other words, carbon-sink CO_2 and fossil-fuel CO_2 have different fingerprints. This fact, ignored by the article, proves that the rise of CO_2 in the atmosphere during the 20th century is indeed man-made, and that global warming will only increase.

2 ➔ Also, one will argue that forecasting climate change on a computer is not always accurate. However, what the article fails to mention is that computer modeling accurately predicts broader trends in climate change, and that these trends all indicate increased warming trends. Measuring the GMST is indeed a critical part of measuring climate change. However, such a detailed analysis is not the only way to gauge future climate change. Remember: 85% of the world's energy needs come from the burning of fossil fuels. Where does all that CO_2 go? Into the atmosphere as greenhouse gases. You don't need a computer model to conclude that all that CO_2 poses a serious problem.

3 ➔ Global warming is a natural phenomenon we are just beginning to understand? What is this guy smoking? Researchers at Texas A&M have proven that increased water vapor serves to amplify the warming process. In other words, water vapor is like gasoline poured onto an already raging fire. That fire is those greenhouse gases already present in the atmosphere. How do we stop that fire? By substantially reducing our dependence on fossil fuels.

Narrator: Now get ready to write your response. Summarize the points made in the lecture and show how they cast doubt on the points made in the reading. You have 20 minutes to complete this task.

Task #3 - Track #5 - America and Oil - Page 60

Narrator: Directions. Now listen to a lecture on the same topic.

Prof: 1 ➔ The oil debate refuses to die, and for good reason: we are addicted to oil. Like a junkie, we just can't live without it. However, like a drug addict, if we don't stop, our addiction will eventually kill us despite what the so-called oil experts think.

2 ➔ Yes, it's true that millions work in the U.S. petroleum industry. It is also true that U.S. oil companies are moving overseas in record numbers. Why? Because big oil is about one thing: making money for their shareholders. They do so by reducing their tax burden as much as possible. This is achieved by moving to countries with low corporate tax rates. These same countries have few regulations regarding environmental safety; thus, oil companies can avoid investing in environmental protection technologies required in the U.S.

3 ➔ As for convenience? Let's face it. Convenience kills. Go to the remotest islands in the Pacific Ocean, and what do you find? Plastic water bottles and disposable razors piled up on the shores. Even more depressing is the fact in the North Pacific there is a floating garbage dump the size of Texas. This garbage dump is comprised mainly of plastic bottles. My esteemed colleague is all for convenience, just as long as he doesn't have to look at its effects. In other words, out of sight, out of mind.

4 ➔ The fact that we are being held hostage by oil-rich countries who hate us is our own fault. Since World War II, the U.S. has supported dozens of dictators in order secure a steady source of cheap oil at any price. As for offshore oil freeing us from foreign oil, nothing could be further from the truth. Statistics indicate that our offshore reserves represent only eight-percent of our total oil needs. Who are the hostages in this debate? The American people being fed the lie that our future energy needs lie just offshore.

5 ➔ Statistics are very persuasive. Here are a few of my own. That 8,000 barrels mentioned in the article? Most of it comes from countries like Nigeria. Since 1958, over 13 million barrels of oil have spilled in the Niger Delta, Nigeria's main oil producing area. That's one *Exxon Valdez* supertanker every year. Worse, little, if any, of that oil has been cleaned up. If that isn't an argument for freeing our addiction to oil, I don't know what is.

Narrator: Now get ready to write your response. Summarize the points made in the lecture and show how they cast doubt on the points made in the reading. You have 20 minutes to complete this task.

Task #4 - Track #6 - Computer Games - Page 61

Narrator: Directions. Now listen to a lecture on the same topic.

Prof: 1 ➔ When parents or educators want to blame something for all the ills of our youth, they immediately point the figure at video games and brand them as being anti-social destroyers of youth and all that we hold sacred and dear. Well, excuse me if I disagree.

2 ➔ Nobody would disagree that violent video games are designed with killing in mind, just like no would disagree that problem-solution scenarios in which an anti-hero blasts his way to freedom reinforces detrimental behavior in adolescents. But wait just a minute here. Where are the parents in this equation? If such games are so perilous to the youth of our nation, then turn the darn things off and tell the kids to go bounce a ball. Blaming a video game for poisoning a kid's behavior is like saying guns kill people. Wrong. Guns don't kill

people. People kill people. Likewise, video games don't make bad kids. Parents make bad kids. Period.

3 ➔ Let's move on to the idea that video games create a "false sense of reality." Look around you. What do you see? Surprise. Surprise. The world is built on false realities. Movies, internet social networks, music videos, even rock concerts. I mean, come on, who hasn't walked away from a rock concert thinking, "Man, I wanna be a rock star!" I sure did. I still do! Talk about delusions. So let's put the hyperbole aside and call a spade a spade, shall we? False realities have always been here, and they always will.

4 ➔ Finally, the woman issue. Seriously, if you're looking for feminine role models in a violent video game—any video game—then you're the one who needs to take a good hard look in the mirror. Video games are not repositories of virtue nor are they purveyors of moral rectitude. Far from it. They are what they are: entertainment vehicles, pure, plain and simple. To think otherwise is to miss the point completely, that point being that, like it or not, violent video games are symbols of free speech. That's right. Democracy in action. If you don't like what you're hearing, turn them off. The choice is yours.

Narrator: Now get ready to write your response. Summarize the points made in the lecture and show how they cast doubt on the points made in the reading. You have 20 minutes to complete this task.

Task #5 - Track #7 - Standardized Testing – Page 62

Narrator: Directions. Now listen to a lecture on the same topic.

Prof: 1 ➔ Proponents of standardized testing are quick to wave the flag of comparative statistics as being the best way to measure academic performance. Yet, what supporters of standardized testing fail to realize is that, in their rush for statistics, they have boiled education down to a game, a game in which there are winners and losers. I'm sorry, but education is not about dividing students into winners and losers. It's about uniting with a focus on equality, the very thing standardized testing destroys by pointing the finger at those schools with lower-than-average scores.

2 ➔ The article goes on to describe how teachers benefit from standardized testing. By using statistics, teachers know which subjects to focus on to increase scores, the example being math. Okay, so math is a problem. But why does it suddenly become a teaching priority? Why should English or history suffer? The reason is clear: this is not about providing students with a balanced education. It's about satisfying administrators and their constant demand for higher scores, for higher scores suggest that all is well when, more often than not, statistics lie, for if too much emphasis is placed on one subject, other subjects will suffer in turn. And who is to blame for that? Teachers trying to please administrators while ignoring the needs of their students.

3 ➔ My biggest complaint with standardized testing is that someone is always to blame. If it's not the student's fault for getting a low score, then it must be the teacher's. If only it were so simple. What if, on test day, a student were tired, or sick, or had family problems, or wasn't getting enough to eat? Are teachers to blame for all these variables? If you believe in low-scoring test results, then you have to say yes: bad teaching is to blame for poor student scores. Unfortunately, many excellent teachers have been fired because standardized testing has provided such leaps of logic.

4 ➔ Let's be honest. Standardized testing is a numbers game played by administrators and teachers with the students left out in the cold. The sooner we get rid of standardized testing the better.

Narrator: Now get ready to write your response. Summarize the points made in the lecture and show how they cast doubt on the points made in the reading. You have 20 minutes to complete this task.

Task #6 - Track #8 - Organic Food - Page 63

Narrator: Directions. Now listen to a lecture on the same topic.

Prof: 1 ➔ A major trend in the food industry is the increasing popularity of organic food. Yes, organic is more expensive. There's no denying that, just as there's no denying the health risks associated with eating non organic strawberries. Most are unaware that non-organic strawberries are one of the most chemically-contaminated fruits you can buy. Why? Because farmers apply two chemicals to every crop: a pesticide to protect the fruit from insects and a fungicide to protect the roots from fungus. Both the pesticide and the fungicide contain chemicals that have been linked to breast cancer in woman and to a 50% reduction in sperm count in men. By eating organic strawberries, you can substantially reduce your exposure to these risks.

2 ➔ The author goes on to say that organic food is hard to find. This is simply not true. All you have to do is go to your local grocery store and you will find organic food. Many of the bigger stores, for example, even have organic sections. Not only that but Wal-Mart now offers a wide variety of organic produce. In fact, I buy a lot of organic products at Wal-Mart, such as milk and cottage cheese and, yes, even organic rice.

3 ➔ As for non-organic versus organic milk, of course, there's no difference in taste. Why should there be? The whole point of organic milk is not to change the taste but to eliminate pesticides and other man-made chemicals from the milk production process. A big part of that process is the genetically engineered growth hormone rBGH. Farmers give their cows rBGH which, in turn, makes the cows produce far more milk than is naturally possible. Worse, rBGH stays in the milk and enters your body when you drink it. Moreover, research has linked rBGH to colon, breast and prostate cancer.

4 ➔ In the end, buying organic is an investment in your health. Personally, I don't mind paying a little extra. At least I know what I'm eating.

Narrator: Now get ready to write your response. Summarize the points made in the lecture and show how they cast doubt on the points made in the reading. You have 20 minutes to complete this task.

Task #7 - Track #9 – Cell Phones - Page 64

Narrator: Directions. Now listen to a lecture on the same topic.

Prof: 1 ➔ According to the article you read for homework, cell phones are a silent killer threatening us all. If you believe that, then you also believe in the tooth fairy. Let me set the record straight.

2 ➔ Cell phones do not cause cancer. Period. Why not? Because cell-phone radiation is non-ionizing. What does that mean? It means that cell-phone radiation has too few electrons thus cannot cause cancer unlike ionizing radiation produced by X-rays. Moreover, cell-phone RF-levels are tested and retested by the manufacturers to ensure that radiation levels meet the strict standards set by the Federal Communications Commissions. That said, put to rest any notion that you might be harming yourself whenever you make a call.

3 ➔ And, yes, cell phones can be a distraction, but they are not the only distraction on the roads today. Drive along any interstate and you'll be distracted by any number of things, from billboards to speeding transport trucks

to construction crews, not to mention little Jilly and Billy screaming for attention in the back seat. Suffice it to say, the world is full of distractions. 4 ➔ As for colony-collapse disorder, cell-phone usage is only one of many factors that must be taken into account. Other factors include the bacterial infection called foulbrood and the varroa mite, an infectious insect that preys on bee larvae. Climate change too is suspected. Global warming has brought new and invasive species. One such species, the Asian hornet, has spread across Europe and into Britain. The Asian hornet raids hives for bee larvae and the bees are powerless to stop this invader. To say that the cell phone threatens honey bees with extinction is like saying hamburgers are responsible for childhood obesity without considering chocolate and high-fructose breakfast cereals.

Narrator: Now get ready to write your response. Summarize the points made in the lecture and show how they cast doubt on the points made in the reading. You have 20 minutes to complete this task.

Speaking Section – Pg. 66

Task #3 - Integrated Speaking – Pg. 82

Sample Dialogue - Organic-Food Policy - Track #10 – Page 84

Narrator: Now listen as two students discuss the announcement.

Man: Hi, Wendy.

Woman: Hey, Tom. Have you heard about the new organic food policy?

Man: Yeah. What a great idea. It's about time the school did something to improve the food around here.

Woman: If you ask me, I think the new policy is all wrong.

Man: Why?

Woman: Because organic food is way more expensive. In some cases, at least fifty percent more. Add that to labor costs, you know, money to pay the cafeteria staff, and I'm going to be paying a lot more for my coffee and the milk I put in it. I hate to think what a salad will cost. Organic may be cheaper in the future, but right now it's for people with money not poor students like me.

Man: But think of all the health benefits. You'll be eating food that doesn't have any chemicals or antibiotics in it. Not only that but all that good organic food will be lower in fat and calories. I mean, that's got to be good, right?

Woman: Don't be fooled. A hamburger is a hamburger whether the meat is organic or not. Both will have the same amount of fat and calories. The only difference is the organic hamburger has no pesticides or antibiotics in it.

Man: Well, I still think it's a good idea. By offering organic food, we'll be eating a lot better. Even the snacks in the vending machines will be organic. It's definitely the wave of the future. Best of all, we'll be helping local farmers.

Woman: What I don't like is the university telling us what we can and can't eat. Not everybody wants to eat organic, you know. If I want to eat non organic, that's my choice. Sorry, but the school should not be in the health care business.

Task #1 - Track #11 – New Bookstore Policy - Page 93

Narrator: Directions. Now listen as two students discuss the announcement.

Woman: Hey, Steve. Have you heard about the campus bookstore going digital? What a great idea. Digital texts are definitely the wave of the future. Now, instead of lining up to buy texts, we can just download them at home.

Man: I don't know. Whenever I read a computer screen for a long time, I get wicked headaches. I prefer paper, really. With a regular book, I can study for hours and not feel like my brain is melting. Believe me, I'm not looking forward to studying organic chemistry off a computer screen.

Woman: You should upgrade. Get a computer with a better screen, like my iPad. It's amazing. The screen resolution is so good, I no longer buy regular books. Upgrade, definitely. Your brain will thank you for it.

Man: I'm sorry but upgrading my computer is a luxury I can't afford, what with my car and rent. But with this new policy, I'll have to buy one. Obviously, the school thinks students are made of money.

Woman: Think of it this way: going digital is good for the environment. Think of all the trees you'll be saving. Mother Nature will thank you for it.

Man: What I don't like is there's longer a buy-back. It was great, the book store buying back all our old texts at the end of the semester. But now, with this new policy, I'm out a couple hundred bucks easy. With that money, I could've bought a new computer.

Woman: Try selling your old texts on eBay.

Man: You just read my mind.

Narrator: Now get ready to answer the prompt. The man gives his opinion about the new policy. State his position and explain the reasons he gives for holding that opinion. You have 30 seconds to develop your response and 60 seconds to speak.

Task #2 - Track #12 – New Dress-Code Policy – Page 93

Narrator: Directions. Now listen as two students discuss the announcement.

Woman: A dress code? Give me a break.

Man: That's the new policy. Starting next semester.

Woman: Where does the school get off telling us what we can or can't wear? Hel-lo. This is the United States. Last I heard it was a democracy. What I wear is none of the school's business. I'm paying them to educate me not to deny me the right to wear shorts.

Man: I can understand the policy. Some students really push the envelope when it comes to fashion. I mean, c'mon. School is not the place to be flashing skin or walking around dressed like a rock star. It's distracting. Seriously. This is a university not a club.

Woman: Where does it stop? That's what I want to know. First clothes, then what? Are they going to tell us what to read? What to eat? What to think? Give them an inch and they'll take a mile, believe me.

Man: When I went to high school, we all wore the same uniform and nobody complained. Uniforms created greater equality. Also, I didn't have to worry about what I was going to wear every day.

Woman: Sorry, but that analogy doesn't cut it. High school uniforms are simply a way to control adolescents with way too much energy. This is a university. We're supposed to be responsible adults, remember? By taking away our right to dress as we please, the school no longer trusts us. They're treating us like kids, and I don't like it.

Narrator: Now get ready to answer the prompt. The woman expresses her opinion about the announcement. State her opinion and explain the reasons she gives for holding that opinion. You have 30 seconds to develop your response and 60 seconds to speak.

Task #3 - Track #13 – New School Mascot - Page 94

Narrator: Directions. Now listen as two students discuss the announcement.

Woman: So, Phil, what's your pick for the new school mascot?
Man: What are the choices again?
Woman: A bear and a chicken. I'm voting for the chicken.
Man: You want the symbol of our school to be a chicken? You can't be serious.
Woman: I am. Think about it. What other school has a chicken mascot?
Man: Alice....
Woman: Every other school has an eagle, a bear...
Man: I like bears.
Woman Or some kind of dog. Bor-ing. But a chicken? That would make our school unique.
Man: It'll make everybody laugh at us. The Greenwich College Chickens? No way. No way.
Woman: But that's the point. Why does a mascot have to be serious? Why can't a mascot be fun, like a chicken, or a goat, or a giraffe even? Education is way too serious.
Man: Alice...
Woman: What?
Man: Earth to Alice.
Woman: What!
Man: We eat chickens.
Woman: Go on.
Man: Read the announcement. A chicken does not "symbolize the strength and traditions of our three-hundred-year-old institution." A bear, however, represents strength and determination, the school motto, remember? Seriously. Vote for the bear. It's going to win hands down.
Woman: Yeah, well, don't count your chickens before they're hatched.

Narrator: Now get ready to answer the prompt. The woman expresses her opinion about the announcement. State her opinion and explain the reasons she gives for holding that opinion. You have 30 seconds to develop your response and 60 seconds to speak.

Task #4 - Track #14 - No-Pets Policy - Page 95

Narrator: Directions. Now listen as two students discuss the announcement.

Man: It's about time the school did something. My dormitory is like a zoo.
Woman: I take it you don't like animals.
Man: No. Actually, I love animals. It's my allergies that don't like animals. Cats are the worst. There're six on my floor alone. Six! I can hardly sleep I sneeze so much. It's so bad, I'm falling behind.
Woman: Yeah. I can see where you're coming from. Still, before this new policy, there was no law against having a pet in a dorm, so you can't really blame someone for having a pet.
Man: If you'd heard the noise at night, you'd be singing another tune. The dogs in the next dorm just bark and bark. One starts and they all start. It's driving me crazy. What I wouldn't give for a good night's sleep.

Woman: The school really should have a dorm that allows pets. I know a school in Vermont that does that. Supposedly having a pet at school increases your grade-point average.

Man: I fail to see how a snake can improve my grade-point average.

Woman: A snake? Who's got a snake?

Man: My roommate. You ever tried studying for a physics exam with a six-foot snake crawling across your desk? Fun. And my physics professor wonders why I got a B- on the last test.

Woman: A snake is definitely pushing it. But to tell you the truth, I'm not sure if this new policy will really change things. People love their pets. And if they want one, they'll have one, policy or not.

Narrator: Now get ready to answer the prompt. The man gives his opinion about the new policy. State his position and explain the reasons he gives for holding that opinion. You have 30 seconds to develop your response and 60 seconds to speak.

Task #5 - Track #15 – No-Laptops Policy - Page 95

Narrator: Directions. Now listen as two students discuss the announcement.

Woman: You've got to be kidding. No laptops in class? Where did you hear this?

Man: I read it on the school web site. Starting Monday, you can't use a laptop in class. If you do, you'll be asked to leave or turn it off . Actually, I think it's a good idea. In my psychology class, everybody's taking notes on their laptops. That's forty people all typing away. You can't believe the noise.

Woman: But my laptop is my life. I always take notes with it. And now they expect me to use a pen? Forget it. Writing by hand is too slow. Not only that but I'll have to rewrite my notes when I get home. Talk about a waste of time. This new policy is definitely going to make a lot of people angry.

Man: I don't think so. The school is just trying to improve classroom conditions. Imagine trying to teach when everybody is looking at their computers and not at you. Laptops are definitely coming between the teacher and the students.

Woman: What angers me is the school said I had to buy a laptop. It was a requirement. So I bought one even though I couldn't afford it. And now the school is telling me not to use the laptop they told me I had to buy? Ridiculous. If I can't use my laptop in class, then the school should refund the cost of buying it. It's only fair.

Narrator: Now get ready to answer the prompt. The woman expresses her opinion about the new policy. State her opinion and explain the reasons she gives for maintaining that position. You have 30 seconds to develop your response and 60 seconds to speak.

Task #6 - Track #16 – New-School President - Page 96

Narrator: Directions. Now listen as two students discuss the announcement.

Man: Did you say William Alfred Liddell?

Woman: That's right. Haven't you heard? He's our new president. His business record is impressive. Why the face?

Man: Because Wild Bill Liddell is famous for tearing schools apart.

Woman: Just what Old Lovell needs. The buildings are ancient, enrollment is at an all-time low, and our teams are a joke. It's about time we had a money-man running the show. Let's face it, education is all about money. And if Wild Bill means business, if he can shake this place up, he's got my vote.

Man: The last school Liddell ran, Saint Lionel's prep, he ran into the ground.

Woman:	What do you mean?
Man:	Saint Lionel's brought Wild Bill in to turn things around. He fired half the teaching staff and closed half the buildings. Not only that but he sold off a big chunk of school property, this beautiful old forest, to a golf course developer to raise money. In less than a year Saint Lionel's closed. Wild Bill was obviously more interested in the bottomline than in education.
Woman:	So what do suggest? That Old Lovell stay the course? If we do, we hit the iceberg. If this school needs a boss like William Liddell, I say go for it. It's about time this place had a wake-up call.
Man:	Here's another reason why I'm leaving. Tuition just went up.
Woman:	What?
Man:	This place is too rich for me.
Woman:	Wait. Wait. Why did tuition go up?
Man:	Ask Wild Bill.

Narrator:	Now get ready to answer the prompt. The woman expresses her opinion about the announcement. State her opinion and explain the reasons she gives for holding that opinion. You have 30 seconds to develop your response and 60 seconds to speak.

Task #4 - Integrated Speaking – Pg. 97

Sample Lecture - Animal Behavior - Track #17 – Page 100

Narrator:	Directions. Now listen to a lecture on animal behavior.

Prof:	1 ➔ Good afternoon. In this lecture, we'll focus on a common nocturnal animal: the bat. There are two types of bat: micro-bats, or true bats, and mega-bats, also called fruit bats.
	2 ➔ Let's start with mega-bats. Size-wise, mega-bats are from two to sixteen inches in length. Mega-bats have extremely sensitive sight and smell. This helps them locate the flowers and fruit upon which they feed. It is while eating that mega-bats play an important role in the distribution of plants. Like bees, mega-bats serve as pollinators. When they lick nectar or eat flowers, their bodies become covered in pollen which they, in turn, carry to other trees and plants, thereby acting as pollinators. In fact, many of the fruits and vegetables on our tables, such as bananas and peaches, would not be there if mega-bats did not pollinate plants and trees.
	3 ➔ Next are micro-bats. As the name implies, micro-bats are quite small, about the size of a mouse. To find food, micro-bats use echolocation, high-frequency sounds they bounce off insects. The most common micro-bat is the vesper or evening bat. Like mega-bats, micro-bats play an important role in the environment. The average vesper bat, for example, can eat one-thousand mosquitoes in one night. By doing so, they control the mosquito population.

Task #1 - Track #18 - Bestsellers - Page 106

Narrator:	Directions. Now listen to a lecture on the same topic.

Prof:	1 ➔ In early America, circa 1650, the center of publishing was in the Massachusetts Bay Colony. Leaders of the colony printed religious pamphlets as a means of keeping up settler morale, for the early settlers were on the edge of a savage new frontier. One such settler was Mary Rowlandson.
	2 ➔ In 1657, Rowlandson was captured by Indians. After eleven weeks, a ransom was paid and Rowlandson was freed. She went on to write about her experience in a book titled *The Sovereignty and Goodness of God: Being a Narrative of the Cap-*

tivity and Restoration of Mrs. Mary Rowlandson. In her book, Rowlandson describes the ordeal of being captured by Indians. By doing so, Rowlandson created the genre of writing known as the captivity narrative. Simply put, the captivity narrative describes how a god-fearing person is captured by godless devils called Indians. In the end, the god-fearing person, backed by an undying faith in God, is freed thus proving that good always conquers evil. Rowlandson's book was so popular it went through four editions and became America's first bestseller.

Narrator: Now get ready to answer the prompt. How do the reading and the lecture add to our understanding of the term bestseller in a contemporary and in an historical sense? You have 30 seconds to develop your response and 60 seconds speak.

Task #2 - Track #19 - The Green Revolution - Page 106

Narrator: Directions. Now listen to a lecture on the same topic.

Prof: 1 ➜ The benefits of the Green Revolution cannot be denied. Yet, as with all revolutions, it takes time to measure the full impact of change, both in the short and the long term.

2 ➜ During the Green Revolution, only a select few crops were grown. Those crops, such as wheat, were grown on a massive scale. As a result, soil quality decreased dramatically as the wheat drained nutrients from the soil. Instead of letting the land regenerate by letting it go fallow, or rest, for a year—as was the traditional practice—farmers instead added synthetic fertilizers to boast crop yields. The result was the complete exhaustion of soil quality, so much so that today many large expanses of land are simply dead.

3 ➜ At the same time that a wheat crop was being fed a diet of synthetic fertilizer, it was also being protected against insects with pesticides, such as DDT. DDT, along with many other synthetic pesticides, has since proven to be carcinogenic. DDT was so dangerous, in fact, it was banned because it was wiping out the American bald eagle. And where did all that fertilizer and pesticide end up? In the water system. This caused an explosion of water plants, such as algae, that thrives on nitrogen-rich fertilizers. This, in turn, reduced the oxygen level to the point where today, many once-healthy bodies of water are now dead zones.

Narrator: Now get ready to answer the prompt. What is the Green Revolution and what are its short and long term effects? You have 30 seconds to develop your response and 60 seconds to speak.

Task #3 - Track #20 - Seamounts - Page 107

Narrator: Directions. Now listen to a lecture on the same topic.

Prof: 1 ➜ Seamounts are of great interest not only to biologists but to the commercial fishing industry as well. And for good reason. The nutrient-rich water around a seamount is home to an immense variety of fish, many of which have commercial value. One such fish is the orange roughy.

2 ➜ In the mid 1970's, orange roughy was found in great numbers around seamounts near New Zealand. The greatest concentrations were found one kilometer down, a depth once thought impossible to fish. But this did not stop the fishing industry. No longer did depth protect the fish. Helped by new GPS technology, bottom trawling was born. Bottom trawling involves dragging a net across the ocean floor. This is a very destructive form of fishing for not only does the net catch orange roughy, but it also destroys the ocean floor and catches

other species that are not commercially valuable. This method of fishing was so effective, and the demand for orange roughy so great, that they were practically wiped out.

3 ➔ Another fish directly impacted by bottom trawling is the armorhead. In the 1960's, huge numbers of armorheads were discovered around seamounts northwest of Hawaii. In no time at all, Russian and Japanese fishing fleets virtually wiped out the armorhead. Like orange roughy, armorhead stocks have yet to recover.

Narrator: Now get ready to answer the prompt. Seamounts are under threat. Why? Using information from the reading and the lecture, illustrate the threat and the reason for it. You have 30 seconds to develop your response and 60 seconds to speak.

Task #4 - Track #21 - Brown-Headed Cowbird - Page 107

Narrator: Directions. Now listen to a lecture on the same topic.

Prof: 1 ➔ In this lecture, we'll take a closer look at the breeding habits of the brown-headed cowbird.

2 ➔ The cowbird is what's called a brood parasite. Let me explain. As mentioned, the cowbird was originally a nomad, travelling with the buffalo and eating whatever the buffalo kicked up, insects, seeds, whatever. In this light, the cowbird was very much an opportunist. Yet the cowbird had a problem. Because they were nomadic, raising a family was a problem. If they stopped to raise a brood, they'd lose their food source, for the buffalo were always on the move. The cowbird, ever the opportunist, resolved this problem in a unique way, one that characterizes the species to this day.

3 ➔ When it comes time to lay her eggs, the female cowbird, instead of building a nest, deposits her eggs in the nest of another, much smaller host bird. The cowbird eggs then hatch. Because the cowbird chicks are much bigger than the host chicks, the host brood dies while the mother bird—unable to tell the difference between her own brood and the cowbird brood—is forced to feed the baby cowbirds till they fly off. This parasitic process—one in which one animal takes advantage of another—makes the brown-headed cowbird a true brood parasite.

Narrator: Now get ready to answer the prompt. The brown-headed cowbird is a brood parasite. How do the reading and lecture define and develop this classification? You have 30 seconds to develop your response and 60 seconds to speak.

Task #5 - Track #22 – Census of Population - Page 108

Narrator: Directions. Now listen to a lecture on the same topic.

Prof: 1 ➔ In the United States, a census is taken every ten years. This information is essential for a variety of reasons, in particular the establishment of political districts. By determining the size of a population in a given state, the federal government can then apportion the state into Congressional districts based not on geography but on population. This ensures equal representation in Congress wherein populous states, such as California, are awarded more Congressional representatives while states with fewer people, such as Montana, are awarded fewer Congressional representatives. This system of representation, based on a census of population, is the foundation of the American electoral system.

2➔ Census taking, however, is nothing new. Many ancient civilizations regularly took a census of population, for example Rome. Because Rome had a large standing army, it needed money and men. By periodically taking a census, the Roman government knew how much tax money it could raise for the army and the available manpower it could draw from.

Narrator: Now get ready to answer the prompt. Summarize the points made in the lecture and show how they add to and support the information in the reading. You have 30 seconds to develop your response and 60 seconds to speak.

Task #5 - Integrated Speaking – Pg. 109

Sample Dialogue - Harvard Law - Track #23 - Page 110

Narrator: Listen to a sample dialogue.

Man: Hi, Betty. What's wrong?
Woman: Well, there's good news and bad.
Man: Okay, so what's the good news?
Woman: I got accepted into Harvard law.
Man: Congratulations! That's fantastic.
Woman: Thanks. Now for the bad news. Harvard is not cheap. I nearly died when I saw the tuition.
Man: Yeah, but it's Harvard. Ivy League.
Woman: I know. I want to go, but I can't afford it. I already have four years' worth of undergrad loans at this school. If I do three years of Harvard law, I'll be even more in debt. I'm not sure what to do.
Man: What about applying for a scholarship? How are your grades?
Woman: I'm at the top of my class.
Man: There you go. You'd have a really good chance of getting a scholarship. Some scholarships pay all your tuition. If you don't get a full scholarship, you should at least get something for books. I got a scholarship here, and boy did I save a bundle.
Woman: Applying for a scholarship is definitely an option. I'll have to check it out.
Man: You could also take time off and work for a year or two, you know, postpone admittance. That way you could save money for tuition. You might not be able to pay off the full cost, but you could at least pay off some of it. That way you'd owe less in the long run.
Woman: Yeah. Obviously, I have a decision to make.

Task #1 - Track 24 - Pet Policy - Page 118

Narrator: Directions. Listen to a conversation between two students.

Man: Hey, Mary. You look upset. What's wrong?
Woman: Hi, Steve. Oh, it's nothing, really.
Man: C'mon...
Woman: Well, there's this new school policy.
Man: The one about pets?
Woman: Yeah. I don't know what to do. It's breaking my heart. I can't give Pete up. I just can't. It'd be like giving away my, you know, child.
Man: You're going to have to do something. The school is really cracking down on pets. Have you considered putting Pete up for adoption? You could get him a good home and you'd feel better knowing he was okay. You could probably arrange to see him on weekends.

Woman: I thought about that. But I've had Pete for so long. Oh, who thought up this stupid policy? Do you know how many pets there are? Practically everyone's got one. Julie. Sylvia. Jason. He just got a new puppy.
Man: Doesn't matter. Rules are rules.
Woman: I hate rules.
Man: Why don't you donate Pete to a zoo?
Woman: A zoo? I never thought of that.
Man: You should give it a try. Pete would have a nice, safe home with all the mice he could eat. And he wouldn't get lonely. People would be stopping by to see him all the time. Talk about living.
Woman: Do you know anyone who would take Pete? Your parents maybe?
Man: My parents? Are you kidding. My mother hates snakes.

Narrator: Now get ready to answer the prompt. The students discuss two solutions to the woman's problem. Identify the problem and the solutions, then state which solution you think is best and why. You have 20 seconds to develop your response and 60 seconds to speak.

Task #2 - Track 25 - Euthanasia Debate – Page 118

Narrator: Directions. Listen to a conversation between two students.

Man: Hey, Sue. You got a minute?
Woman: Sure, Brian. What's up?
Man: I'm taking Political Science. Part of my course requirement is to debate some hot-button issue, you know, like amnesty for illegals or gay marriage.
Woman: So what's the problem? Why so wound up?
Man: The topic is euthanasia. I'm supposed to argue against it, but I'm pro euthanasia. I believe people have the right to die whenever and however they please. Call it freedom of choice. Call it whatever. No way am I arguing against a person's right to choose.
Woman: Know what I think? I think you're blowing this thing way out of proportion. I also think Professor Smith gave you the con side as a way of teaching you.
Man: Teaching me? Teaching me what?
Woman: Think about it. By arguing the opposite of what you believe, maybe Professor Smith wants you to see both sides of the argument. Maybe this is really an exercise in understanding. In that case, I think you should do it. I mean, life is not always about getting your own way, you know.
Man: True.
Woman: Another option is to tell Professor Smith you refuse to debate on moral grounds. You'd be true to your beliefs, and I'm sure he'd understand. But he might also fail you, so you're definitely taking a risk if you back out. Look. There's Professor Smith now. So, what're you going to do?
Man: I don't know. I'm still debating.

Narrator: Now get ready to answer the prompt. The students discuss two solutions to the man's problem. Identify the problem and the solutions, then state which solution you think is best and why. You have 20 seconds to develop your response and 60 seconds to speak.

Task #3 - Track #26 - Job Offer - Page 118

Narrator: Directions. Listen to a conversation between two students.

Man: Hey, Sylvia. Did you get the job?
Woman: I did.
Man: Congratulations. You don't look so thrilled.

Woman:	I am. Very. But I've got a choice to make. I applied for a part-time position, right?
Man:	Right.
Woman:	So I go for the interview and, before you know it, they're offering me a full-time position with benefits.
Man:	Whoa. So what're you going to do?
Woman:	That's the $64,000.00 question.
Man:	Why don't you tell them you'll work part-time, then do full-time when you graduate? That way you could finish your education and have a job when you graduate. They might even pay for the rest of your education that way.
Woman:	Oh, I don't know. Asking them to pay for my education when they've already offered so much seems a bit, you know, greedy.
Man:	Okay. So quit school. Serious. You've got a once-in-a-lifetime job offer. With the economy the way it is, you'd be crazy not to take it. Best of all, the pressure of finding a job would be gone, just like that.
Woman:	But what about my master's degree?
Man:	Work for a few years, then finish it part-time in the evening. People do it all the time, work and go to school at the same time. By working, you could pay for your master's if your company won't pay. What was that job again?
Woman:	Entertainment director on a cruise ship. It goes all over the world. Miami. Rio. Greece.
Man:	Sweet.
Narrator:	Now get ready to answer the prompt. The students discuss two solutions to the woman's problem. Identify the problem and the solutions, then state which solution you think is best and why. You have 20 seconds to develop your response and 60 seconds to speak.

Task #4 - Track #27 - Roommate Problems - Page 119

Narrator:	Directions. Listen to a conversation between two students.
Woman:	Hey, Jack. How's your new roommate?
Man:	Don't ask. The guy is a disaster.
Woman:	Worse than Frank?
Man:	You have no idea. And exams are coming up.
Woman:	So what're you going to do?
Man:	Short of dropping out? I have no idea.
Woman:	Move out. Serious. That would be the simplest solution. Just tell the guy, "Sorry, dude, I can't live this way." Why waste energy on something you don't need? Go for it. Be free. Just leave. Focus on what matters: exams.
Man:	But I like my dorm. The top floor has the best view of the lake and the breeze in summer is great. Also, I don't know where I'd go. Apartments in town aren't exactly cheap, you know.
Woman:	Okay, then go to the housing office. Write out a complaint detailing why you want a new roommate and then let them take care of it. That's their job. Remember: You're paying a lot for this education. You have the right to be satisfied.
Man:	But then it would get around that I complain about people. I'm not sure if that's the way I want to go. Maybe as a last resort.
Narrator:	Now get ready to answer the prompt. The students discuss two solutions to the man's problem. Identify the problem and the solutions, then state which solution you think is best and why. You have 20 seconds to develop your response and 60 seconds to speak

Task #5 - Track #28 - Professor Plagiarizes - Page 119

Narrator: Directions. Listen to a conversation between two students.

Man: Are you sure?
Woman: Yes. My professor plagiarized my essay, not just a few words, but an entire page verbatim in his last research paper.
Man: This happened once before. A student accused her professor of plagiarism.
Woman: And?
Man: The professor was fired.
Woman: Great. Maybe I should just forget the whole thing. Maybe I should be flattered that a professor borrowed my work, and just shut up about it.
Man: Marilynn, the man did not borrow your work. He stole it. If you'd done this, stolen his work, you would've been kicked out of school in two seconds. No. There's no way you can back down. You've got to confront the man. You need to take your essay and his paper to his office, and tell him in no uncertain terms that what he did was wrong.
Woman: But he's one of the most popular professors.
Man: He's a thief.
Woman: He gave me an A+ —for the essay he plagiarized!
Man: Look, if you don't want to confront him, then you've got to go to the Dean. This is a serious breach of academic ethics. The sooner you confront the man, the better. Who knows how many other student essays he's plagiarized?
Woman: But if I go to the Dean, it'll be all over the school in no time.
Man: Yeah, well, I know what I'd do.

Narrator: Now get ready to answer the prompt. The students discuss two solutions to the woman's problem. Identify the problem and the solutions, then state which solution you think is best and why. You have 20 seconds to develop your response and 60 seconds to speak.

Task #6 - Integrated Speaking – Pg. 120

Sample Lecture: Animal Behavior - Track #29 - Page 121

Narrator: Listen to a lecture in a zoology class.

Prof: 1 ➜ Animal behavior can be classified according to the time of day an animal is active. Animals, such as horses, elephants, and most birds, are said to be diurnal because they are active during the day and rest at night. Those animals active at dawn and dusk are said to be crepuscular. Beetles, skunks, and rabbits fall into this category. The third group are those animals that sleep during the day and are active at night. They are called nocturnal. A good example is the bat. Bats have highly-developed eyesight, hearing and smell. This helps them avoid predators and locate food. Being nocturnal also helps them avoid high temperatures during the day, especially in deserts where temperatures can reach well over one-hundred degrees Fahrenheit. There are two types of bat: micro bats, or true bats, and mega-bats, also called fruit bats. Let's start with mega-bats.
2 ➜ Size wise, mega-bats range from two to sixteen inches in length. Mega-bats have extremely sensitive sight and smell. This helps them locate the flowers and fruit upon which they feed. It is while eating that mega-bats play an important role in the distribution of plants. Like bees, mega-bats serve as pollinators. When they lick nectar or eat flowers, their bodies become covered in pollen which they, in turn, carry to other trees and plants, thereby acting as pollinators.

In fact, many of the fruits and vegetables on our tables, such as bananas and peaches, would not be there if mega-bats did not pollinate plants and trees. 3 ➜ Next are micro-bats. As the name implies, micro-bats are quite small, about the size of a mouse. To find food, micro-bats use echolocation, high-frequency sounds they bounce off insects. The most common micro-bat is the vesper or evening bat. Like mega-bats, micro-bats play an important role in the environment. The average vesper bat, for example, can eat one-thousand mosquitoes in one night. By doing so, they control the mosquito population.

Task #1 - Track #30 - Charles Darwin - Page 128

Narrator: Directions. Listen to a lecture in a biology class.

Prof: 1 ➜ In Darwin's lifetime, *On the Origin of Species* sold well; however, it did not sell as well as another popular Darwin book. That book, published in 1881, is titled *The Formation of Vegetable Mould Through the Action of Worms, With Observations on Their Habits*. With the publication of this book, Darwin revolutionized soil and agricultural science. Let's take a look at how he did it. 2 ➜ While most people saw earthworms as an ugly, useless nuisance, Darwin realized their value through a series of experiments. However, his research was overtaken by the writing of *On the Origin of Species*. Later in life, Darwin returned to his study of earthworms and proved that earthworms were not useless pests but, in fact, played a crucial role in maintaining healthy soil. Darwin observed that earthworms were busy at work turning over the soil by eating it and excreting it. The turning of soil allowed water to penetrate more deeply and allowed more oxygen to enter the ground while the fertilizing added nutrients. 3 ➜ Darwin proved the earthworm's value by doing a simple experiment. In a field near his house, Darwin scattered small pieces of coal. In time, the earthworms had moved so much soil that the pieces of coal had settled deep in the soil, proving that the worms were indeed at work turning the soil. With this discovery, Darwin proved that the common earthworm was not a pest but an essential part of the agricultural process.

Narrator: Now get ready to answer the prompt. According to the lecture, how did Charles Darwin revolutionize agricultural science? You have 20 seconds to develop your response and 60 seconds to speak.

Task #2 - Track #31 – Estrogen and HRT - Page 128

Narrator: Directions. Listen to a lecture in a women's studies class.

Prof: 1 ➜ In women, estrogen regulates the development of female sexual characteristics and reproduction. As a woman reaches middle-age, around age 45, the estrogen level decreases. Indications of decreased estrogen are hot flashes, mood swings, and weak or broken bones due to a loss of bone mass. 2 ➜ It wasn't until the early 1960's that author Robert Wilson in his book *Feminine Forever* recommended that women could stop the aging process by taking estrogen pills. Suddenly, women started taking estrogen and were feeling much better for it. However, in the early 1970's, a rise in uterine cancer was connected to an increase in estrogen usage, so women stopped taking estrogen almost overnight. In the late 1970's, doctors did an about-face and said that it was okay to take estrogen combined with another hormone, progestin. By the 1990's, doctors were so enthusiastic about the estrogen-progestin combination that they were telling women that hormone replacement therapy (HRT for short) was the solution to stopping heart attacks. In short, HRT was a life-saver. By 2000, almost six-million women in the United States were taking some form of HRT. That, then, is a brief history of estrogen use in America. But is the news all good? No.

3 ➔ A lot of research has been done on estrogen, the most striking of which was a report by the Women's Health Initiative. Of the 16,000 women they were studying, HRT had increased the risk of heart attack by 29%, breast cancer by 24%, blood clots by 100%, and stroke by 41%. The evidence was clear: hormone-replacement therapy was life-threatening.

Narrator: Now get ready to answer the prompt. The lecture talks about hormone replacement therapy (HRT). Summarize the recent history of HRT usage in the United States and its impact on women's health. You have 20 seconds to develop your response and 60 seconds to speak.

Task #3 - Track #32 - White-Collar Crime - Page 129

Narrator: Directions. Listen to a lecture in a sociology class.

Prof: 1 ➔ Most have never heard of Professor Edwin Sutherland, yet we've all heard the phrase white collar crime. Sutherland came to define white-collar crime as a "crime committed by a person of respectability and high social status in the course of his occupation," a perfect example of which is Bernard L. Madoff.
2 ➔ On December 11, 2008, the business world was rocked by news no one could believe. Even now, people are still shaking their heads. On that December day, Bernard L. Madoff was arrested for securities fraud. Madoff freely confessed that his private investment fund was in fact a Ponzi scheme, a criminal enterprise in which Madoff took money from one party and, instead of investing it as promised, gave it to another party while taking a cut in the process.
3 ➔ How did Madoff get away with it and for so long? The answer is simple. Madoff was one of the most respected men on Wall Street. He'd served as chairman of the Board of Directors of the National Association of Securities Dealers and was one of the first to champion electronic trading. He was active in high society as well, serving on the boards of prestigious universities and charities. In short, Bernie Madoff commanded so much business and social respect that no one ever suspected that he was running a criminal enterprise. And why would people suspect him? After all, his private investment fund was making people rich, even in bad times. Yet when the stock market crashed in the fall of 2008, Madoff's house of cards crashed with it. With stock prices falling, Madoff investors suddenly wanted their money back. The only problem was Madoff could not return their investments. The money had simply vanished.

Narrator: Now get ready to answer the prompt. How does the lecture define and develop the concept of white-collar crime? You have 20 seconds to develop your response and 60 seconds to speak.

Task #4 - Track #33 - Space Junk - Page 129

Narrator: Directions. Listen to a lecture in an astronomy class.

Prof: 1 ➔ The space race ended when America landed men on the moon on July 16, 1969. Today, the exploration of space continues with the Space Shuttle making regular trips to the International Space Station where scientists are developing new technologies that might one day take us to Mars.
2 ➔ Now, let's change gears and talk about the side of the space race you rarely hear about. In man's race to conquer space, we've created a huge problem with

no apparent solution. That problem is space junk. At last count, there were over ten thousand man-made objects in low-Earth orbit. What worries scientists most is the larger pieces of space junk, such as satellites. When big pieces of space junk collide, they literally explode. This, in turn, creates thousands of smaller pieces of junk, all of which are orbiting the Earth at more than 17,000-miles-per hour. Combined, these smaller pieces of space junk create a corrosive effect when they hit other objects, much like sandblasting a building. This rain of space junk can seriously damage not only operating satellites, but it's also a threat to all space flights, manned or otherwise.

3 ➔ The ever-increasing problem of space junk has become known as the Kessler Syndrome. Donald Kessler, a NASA scientist, describes a scenario in which there is so much space junk colliding and dividing that one day it will be too dangerous for man to travel into space. In other words, the garbage orbiting the Earth will destroy anyone and anything that tries to enter it.

Narrator: Now get ready to answer the prompt. According to the lecture, what are the origins of space junk and why is it a problem? You have 20 seconds to develop your response and 60 seconds to speak.

Task #5 - Track #34 - Sharks - Page 129

Narrator: Directions. Listen to a lecture in a marine biology class.

Prof: 1 ➔ All sharks are carnivorous. Some sharks, like the tiger shark, will eat just about anything. However, most sharks are more selective, such as the whale shark, which feeds only on plankton, microscopic organisms on the bottom of the ocean food chain. The most feared shark is the great white. However, despite Hollywood's best efforts, experts do not consider the great white to be the most dangerous. That label goes to the bull shark.

2 ➔ The bull shark, also known as the whaler shark, gets its name from its stocky body, flat nose, and aggressive behavior. Bull sharks can reach a length of six-and-a-half feet and are commonly found patrolling shorelines near populated areas. They will eat anything that comes their way, including garbage and other sharks. What makes the bull shark so aggressive is that their bodies contain more testosterone than any other animal. This makes them arguably the most aggressive predator on the planet. But it doesn't stop there. Bull sharks thrive in any kind of water, including fresh water. Scientists have found bull sharks thousands of miles up the Amazon and as far up the Mississippi River as Illinois. In Nicaragua, bull sharks have even been seen jumping rapids like salmon to get upstream. In Australia, a bull shark travelled eighty miles up an inland waterway system and killed a swimmer.

Narrator: Now get ready to answer the prompt. What does the lecture teach us about sharks? You have 20 seconds to develop your response and 60 seconds to speak.

Task #6 - Track #35 – Aristotle's Three Appeals - Page 130

Narrator: Directions. Listen to a lecture in a composition class.

Prof: 1 ➔ According to Aristotle, there are three modes of appeal: logos, pathos, and ethos. Let's start with logos. Logos, or logic, appeals to reason. One way to appeal to reason is by using deduction. Deduction—and we'll come back to this later on—is a form of reasoning in which you make a conclusion based on a series of related facts or premises. When deducing, you start with a major premise, such as...Oh, I don't know *All English teachers are poor*. This general statement is followed by a specific statement or minor premise, such as *Bob is an English teacher*. From these two premises, a conclusion logically follows: *Bob is poor*. Induction is another form of logic that appeals to reason. When inducing, you combine a series of related facts, such as *Joan loves apples*; *Joan loves blueberries*; *Joan loves mangos*. From these facts, we can make a conclusion: *Joan loves fruit*.

2 ➔ Pathos, in contrast, is an appeal to the emotions. By appealing to the emotions, the arguer can evoke sympathy from an audience. Sympathy, in turn, makes an argument more persuasive.

3 ➔ Next we have ethos. Ethos is an appeal to character. For example, from whom would you buy a laptop computer, a man in a business suit or a man in a T-shirt? Ethically, some might eschew the man in a T-shirt, a T-shirt being the antithesis of business attire therefore unethical, not trustworthy.

4 ➔ Those, then, are Aristotle's three appeals. It's important to remember that a successful argument—a persuasive argument—combines all three appeals.

Narrator: Now get ready to respond. According to the lecture, what are Aristotle's three appeals? Use examples to support your summary. You have 20 seconds to develop your response and 60 seconds to speak.

Listening Section - 131

Office-Hours Conversations – Pg. 132

Track #36 - Sample: Office-Hours Conversation - Page 135

Narrator: Sample. Office-hours conversation. Directions. Listen to a sample conversation, then answer the questions on the next page. Do not look at the questions. On test day, you will not see the questions as you listen. Remember to answer all the questions. You will not lose points for a wrong answer. Now listen as a student talks to a professor.

Student: Professor Morgan? Hi. Do you have a minute?

Prof: Sure, Sue. Come in. What's up?

Student: I have a question about my essay you just gave back. Where should I start? I worked really hard on it and...Well, I thought I'd get a better grade. But...Yeah. Talk about a shock. Anyway, can you tell me why I got such a low grade?

Prof: Sure. Do you have the essay with you?

Student: Yes. Right here. It's on the question of legalizing marijuana. You asked us to pick a side and argue in favor of it. I took the pro side.

Prof: Yes. Now I remember. Let me take a look at it. Right. Right.

Student: Is it too short? Is that why I didn't get an A?

Prof: No. Length is really not an issue. Let me rephrase that. There's no connection between length and quality. Some might disagree, but frankly, some of the best essays I've graded have been short, not one-page short, mind you, but, you know, a couple of really focused pages that address the subject with no extra verbiage. Some of the worst essays I've seen have been...Well, let's just leave it at that, shall we?

Student: Well, if length isn't a problem, then what is?

Prof: Well, it all starts with your opinion. Show me which sentence is your opinion?

Student: It's this one right...here.

Prof: Sorry, but that's not an opinion. You're simply telling me what you'll write about. Remember, your opinion must be arguable. Since you're arguing the pro side of the marijuana issue, you really need to state what you believe in no uncertain terms. By doing do so, your audience will know from the start where you stand.

Student: That's exactly what I was having trouble with. My opinion.

Prof: Try this. Simply say, *Personally, I believe that...*, and then add what you believe. For example, *I believe that Americans should have the right to choose* or *I believe that marijuana should be legalized for medical purposes.* Got it?

Student: Yeah. Okay. I see.

Prof: Also, your opinion must be supportable. When I say supportable, I mean each sentence—sorry, I meant each body paragraph—must have one specific topic, then you must develop that topic in detail. Look at body paragraph one. You start off by saying *legalizing marijuana would be good for the economy* in the first sentence, then you suddenly switch to *it has many medical benefits* in the next sentence. This signals a clear lack of development of both topics.

Student: But that's what I believe.

Prof: Yes. But now we're talking the mechanics of developing and supporting your opinion. Do so by giving each supporting topic its own body paragraph. In this case, *legalizing marijuana would be good for the economy* is the topic of your first body paragraph, and the medical benefits is the topic of your second body paragraph.

Student: You mean, do what I did in paragraph three?

Prof: Exactly. In body paragraph three, you focus on how legalizing marijuana will decrease the crime rate. However, you still need to develop this topic in detail. Give an example. One with statistics. You know what I mean. Do the same for body paragraphs one and two. Remember: The more you develop your supporting examples, the more persuasive your argument will be. Right now, you're just scratching the surface. To be honest, this reads more like a first draft.

Student: I see what you mean. Can I rewrite it for a higher grade?

Prof: Sure. Can you have it on my desk by nine tomorrow morning?

Student: By nine? I'll try.

Narrator: Now get ready to answer the questions. Answer each question based on what is stated or implied in the conversation.

1. What are the student and the professor mainly discussing?
2. Why does the student visit the professor?
3. In which areas does the student's essay need revising? Select two. This is a 1-point question.
4. What does the professor think about short essays?

🎧 5. Listen again to part of the conversation, then answer the question.

Prof: Remember: The more you develop your supporting examples, the more persuasive your argument will be. Right now, you're just scratching the surface. To be honest, this reads more like a first draft.

Narrator: What does the professor imply when she says this?

Prof: Right now, you're just scratching the surface.

Track #37 – Practice: Content Questions - Page 140

Narrator: Practice. Content questions. Directions. Listen to each prompt, then answer the question.

Narrator: **1. Listen as a student talks to a professor.**

Student: Professor Peters?
Prof: Hi, Phyllis. Thanks for dropping by. Were you able to transfer?
Student: Not yet. The registrar said I had to wait a week.
Prof: That class is always full. Professor Cameron is really popular. You sure you don't want to take my class?
Student: No offense, professor, but chemistry is not what I'm aiming for.
Prof: What happened to pre-med?
Student: It's history. Back to square one, I guess.
Prof: Don't worry. Finding your major is all part of the process. Let me know if you need any more help.
Student: Thanks, professor.

Narrator: Now get ready to answer the question. What is topic of discussion?

Narrator: **2. Listen as a student talks to a professor.**

Prof: Hi, Gina.
Student: You wanted to see me, professor Austin?
Prof: I do. You've been missing in action, lately. So far you've missed six classes.
Student: Really? Are you sure?
Prof: That's what my records show. Your homework is all up to date and you completed your presentation. It's just your attendance.
Student: How many classes can I miss?
Prof: The limit is five. How's your attendance in other classes?
Student: About the same. This new job I have really eats up a lot of my time.
Prof: Just to let you know, if you miss anymore classes, I will have no choice but to lower you a grade overall.
Student: Can you show me the last day I was absent?
Prof: Sure. It's on my spreadsheet here. You missed, let's see...You missed last Friday. That makes six absences.
Student: But I was here last Friday.
Prof: Are you sure?
Student: Yes. You asked me to summarize the different types of earthquakes and...
Prof: Ah, you said you were in an earthquake last year in San Francisco. Right. Now I remember. How did that work out, anyway? You didn't really say.
Student: I was terrified. The windows fell out of the hotel I was in and the building shook for about three seconds, but nobody was hurt. The weird thing was it's like I had absolutely no control. I just had to ride it out.
Prof: I was in Thailand back when that big earthquake hit in 2004. I thought the world was coming to an end. It hit 9.1 on the Richter scale.
Student: Whoa.
Prof: You know what? I'm confusing you with the other Gina. Gina...?
Student: Jones.
Prof: Right.
Student: It happens a lot, actually.
Prof: I can imagine. So you've only missed five classes. My apologies.

Narrator: Now get ready to answer the question. What are the speakers mainly talking about?

Narrator: **3. Listen as a student talks to a professor.**

Student: You know, professor, it's not as easy as I thought.
Prof: Like most things it takes practice.
Student: The worst part is I'm so nervous. What should I do?
Prof: Before you give your presentation tomorrow, do some breathing exercises, you know, breathe in, breathe out. That's what I always do. It works for me.
Student: I hope I don't blow it.
Prof: Don't worry. You'll be fine.

Narrator: Now get ready to answer the question. What is the student's problem?

Narrator: **4. Listen as a student talks to a professor.**

Student: Professor Morrison?
Prof: Hi, Bill. Come in. We need to talk. Were you answering questions with your iPhone last class?
Student: Ah...Yeah. I was. Why?
Prof: And the class text is on your iPhone, I take it?
Student: Oh, yeah. That's right.
Prof: All one thousand pages?
Student: Ah, yeah. The quality's amazing. Want to see?
Prof: Ah, no. I didn't know that the assigned text was downloadable. Where did you get it from, if you don't mind my asking?
Student: I downloaded it from this site in, you know...Europe. Why?
Prof: I assume it's legal, this site in Europe?
Student: Actually, over there they have different laws about downloading material. They're not as uptight about it as we are.
Prof: That's not the point. The point is you are supposed to buy a hard copy of the course text.
Student: What if I don't have the money?
Prof: Then try the library. They always have copies on reserve.
Student: What if all the copies have been checked out?
Prof: Have you checked?
Student: I have. Every day. All out.
Prof: Look, I'm not trying to play cop, okay? It's just that when you enroll in a course, you have to buy a hard copy of the text. Those are the rules. The nature of the game. What about a used one?
Student: Used or new it's all the same. When added up, my average text book cost is over $700.00. That might not be a lot of money to you, but it is to me. I have two part-time jobs and I still can't make ends meet. I mean, can you blame me for trying to save some money?
Prof: Okay, so where does that leave us?

Narrator: Now get ready to answer the question. What is the focus of the conversation?

Track #38 – Practice: Purpose Questions - Page 143

Narrator: Practice. Purpose questions. Directions. Listen to each prompt, then answer the question.

Narrator: 1. Listen as a student talks to a professor.

Prof: Hi, Raquel. I got your email. Tell me again why you need my signature?
Student: The lab tech won't let me work at night without it.
Prof: That's strange. I've never had to approve anything before.
Student: It's for security. That's what the lab tech said. She's so persnickety.
Prof: Just my signature? Anything else?
Student: Nope. If you could sign this permission form, that would be great.
Prof: Sure. No problem.

Narrator: Now get ready to answer the question. Why does the student visit the professor?

Narrator: 2. Listen as a student talks to a professor.

Prof: Hi, Lilian. What's up?
Student: I was wondering, professor, if my friend could sit in on one of your lectures. She's thinking of taking your course, but would like to know a little bit more about it first. You know, kind of like test the waters first.
Prof: Generally, it's not the school's policy to allow non-registered students to attend lectures.
Student: I understand.
Prof: Here's what I suggest. Tell your friend to email me and I can talk to her privately. That's probably the best option.
Student: Actually, I have two friends who want to talk to you.

Narrator: Now get ready to answer the question. What is the student's purpose for talking to her professor?

Narrator: 3. Listen as a student talks to a professor.

Student: Could you explain that again, professor?
Prof: Sure. As I said in class, one essential difference between Canada and the United States is the individual's view of government. Americans have a long distrust of government going back to the Revolution. As a result, they hate paying taxes and generally view the government as a threat to individual rights.
Student: And Canadians?
Prof: Canadians are more willing to trust their government. The relationship is more a social compact with universal health care playing a big part. Rarely, if ever, will you hear a Canadian complaining about health care or claiming that his or her *rights* are being denied.
Student: In class, you said something about Canadians having an inferiority complex. What's that all about?
Prof: Right. Many Canadians are stuck on the idea that if you're really want to make it big, you have to go south to Harvard and Hollywood, the reason being that making it in America is the true measure of success. I'm sure this attitude is changing, what with globalization, but think about it: What was the last Canadian movie you saw?
Student: Ah...

Prof:	Exactly. But you know all the Canadian actors, right? Jim Carey, the guy who plays Austin Powers, Kim Catrall in *Sex and the City*, Keifer Sutherland in *24*, Michael J. Fox, you know, *Back to the Future*, and James Cameron, director of *Avatar*.
Student:	Really? James Cameron is Canadian?
Prof:	Born and raised. And that's just film. Now, as all that talent flows south, American culture floods north, so much so that American culture threatens to eliminate any sense of Canadian identity. To combat this, the Canadian government must, you know, step up to the plate and financially support indigenous industries, like publishing and film, with tax money. In short, Canadian tax money is a way of preserving the Canadian identity against American cultural hegemony. Once again, the social compact is in play here. Most Canadians think that's a good thing. Here in America, that would never happen. Washington investing in Hollywood? Forget it.
Student:	So what would happen if the Canadian government withdrew its tax support of indigenous industries like film and publishing?
Prof:	What would happen? You do the math.
Narrator:	Now get ready to answer the question. What does the student need clarified?

Narrator: 4. Listen as a student talks to a professor.

Prof:	Hey, Jane.
Student:	You wanted to see me, professor?
Prof:	Right. Come in. Close the door.
Student:	Is this about what I said in class? I apologize if I came off sounding too strong. But I really believe what I said about a woman's right to choose.
Prof:	No need to apologize. Your argument was bang on. It blew me away. In fact, I think you should put it in writing.
Student:	You mean, an essay?
Prof:	Exactly. It stands a good chance of being published.
Student:	Really? No way.
Prof:	Sure.
Student:	That's great. Really. But I have no clue how to go about it.
Prof:	You mean getting it out there?
Student:	Yeah. I mean, where do I start?
Prof:	Start by putting it down on paper, of course. I'll help you with the editing and formatting.
Students:	Thanks.
Prof:	At the same time google academic journals, you know, Yale, Princeton, Harvard.
Student:	Harvard? Really?
Prof:	Why not? Start at the top. That's what I always say.
Student:	Why academic journals?
Prof:	Often they're theme-related. The trick is to find a journal related to what you're writing about. Women's issues are very topical, so you stand a good chance of getting published.
Student:	What about getting an agent?
Prof:	You can try. But the thing about agents is that they're in the business of making money. That means they want a commercial product. Your essay, while good, is not what I would call commercial.
Student:	Right. I understand. No money. Just bragging rights.

Narrator: Now get ready to answer the question. Why did the professor ask to see the student?

Track #39 – Practice: Single-Answer Detail Questions - Pg. 145

Narrator: Practice. Single-answer detail questions. Directions. Listen as a student talks to a professor, then answer the questions.

Student: Professor Dirk? Is this a good time?
Prof: Cindy. It's always a good time. Come in. Come in.
Student: I've been reviewing my notes and what you said last time we met.
Prof: Good. Good. And? What's wrong? Cold feet?
Student: Frozen, actually. I know that it's all part of the scientific process, but I'm not sure if I can go through with it, you know, vivisection. I know all the arguments—that it's for science, and it's how progress is made, and to fight disease we have no other choice—but I just can't do it. I can't hurt a living animal.
Prof: Keep in mind, Cindy, that we breed these mice especially for this purpose. They are not pets; they have no names, have very little human contact. They are simply objects of investigation, an essential link—a critical link—in medical research. Did you know that in the twentieth century almost every medical achievement was based on animal testing? Even today, right now, schools and labs all over the country are doing the same thing: using animals to advance the cause of mankind.
Student: Right. Is it possible to do it digitally?
Prof: Vivisection? I'm afraid not. True, we have some pretty amazing software, but a computer can't extract DNA. And that's what this assignment is all about: cells extracted to process DNA. One day I'm sure it'll all be done virtually, but that is then and this is now. Like it or not, vivisection is the only way to get the target DNA—and to complete the assignment.
Student: Would it be all right if I just watched?
Prof: I'm afraid not. This is a hands-on assignment. It constitutes 40% of your final grade. I really need to see the extraction process from start to finish. That said, class starts in ten minutes. So, what've you decided?
Student   I've decided that I'm not cut out for this.
Prof: But you want to be a vet, yes?
Student: I did. I'm great at chemistry and biology. I am. I even thought I could work with animals in a lab, but obviously I can't. The thing is I never would have known that if I hadn't taken this course. The thought of experimenting on a living animal no matter what the reason is...Well, I think you know where I stand.
Prof: Then you're dropping the course. Is that what I'm hearing?
Student: I am. That's why I came by. I wanted to thank you for all your help, and for listening to me, strange as it must seem.
Prof: It's not strange at all. Life is full of crossroads. What about your other courses?
Student: I'll finish them and take a break for a while. Maybe work for a year of two. I need to rethink just what it is I want to do. Being a vet obviously isn't in the cards.

Narrator: Now get ready to answer the questions.

1. What can't the student do?
2. What are the "objects of investigation?"
3. What can't be done virtually?
4. What percentage of the final grade is the assignment?
5. What is the student dropping out of?
6. The professor says, "Life is full of..."

Track #40 - Practice: Multi-Answer Detail Questions - Page 148

Narrator: Practice. Multi-answer detail questions. Directions. Listen to each prompt, then answer the question.

Narrator: 1. Listen as a student talks to a professor. This is a two-point question.

Student: So, ah, professor, let me get this straight. To complete this assignment, I need to give a ten-minute presentation and hand in a written summary of my presentation. Correct?

Prof: No. A summary is not necessary. Just a bibliography.

Student: Properly annotated, right?

Prof: No. Just give me the author, publisher, and date of publication.

Student: What about when the author was born?

Prof: Not necessary.

Student: Okay. Ah, one more thing. What about the interviews I did?

Prof: Really? You did interviews? Great. Who did you talk to?

Student: I talked to Professor William Foster.

Prof: Bill Foster? The Bill Foster? From Oxford?

Student: Yes. I ran into him by chance at a bookstore downtown. I just walked up to him and said, "Are you Professor Foster, the one who wrote *Metaphysical Moments in the New Millennium*? And he said yes. I asked him if I could talk to him about it and he said sure. We actually talked for about two hours in a Starbucks. It was amazing. He is so smart. And funny. He had me in stitches. I thought he was so serious. I mean, you look at his photos and you'd think he was this grumpy old curmudgeon, what with that beard and all the crazy hair. Boy, was I wrong. Talk about judging a book by its cover.

Prof: You're very lucky. Normally William Wellington Foster doesn't give interviews or travel. I can't remember the last time he left the UK. Did you get his autograph?

Student: I did.

Prof: He didn't mind?

Student: Not at all. I also interviewed Karen Scott, you know, the famous feminist writer who wrote *Listening to the Apple of Your Eye*. I'm not sure if I'll use her, but it was pretty interesting. She disagrees with pretty much everything Foster says, so it was a great counterpoint.

Prof: You've been working hard. Excellent.

Student: So what should I do?

Prof: Hand in a list of all those you interviewed.

Student: Okay. When's it all due?

Prof: A week from Monday.

Narrator: Now get ready to answer the question. What must the student do to complete the assignment? Select three.

Narrator: 2. Listen as a student talks to a professor. This is a one-point question.

Prof: Hi, Liz. I got your email. You said you needed some help?

Student: Yes. I'm applying for a summer internship at Amnesty International.

Prof: Great. The experience will keep you in good stead.

Student: I need a letter recommendation. I was wondering if you could...

Prof: Sure. How many do you need?

Student: Two, actually. With your signature on each.

Prof: Consider it done. Anything else?

Student: Yes. They might call and interview you. Would you mind?

Prof: Not at all. Ah, any idea when they might call?

Student:	No. But I can find out.
Prof:	Great. That'd be a big help. So, are you going to work stateside or abroad?
Student:	I'm not sure. There's an opening in their Rome office. I speak Italian, so I'd definitely go if they'd ask me. But it's not paid, so that's a problem.
Prof:	You know, I have a friend working for Amnesty International, an old classmate from NYU. She's pretty high-ranking. I could talk to her, see if she could hire you on. The pay wouldn't be much, mind you, but at least you'd get your foot in the door.
Student:	Thanks, professor. That's very generous. Really. But let me sleep on it. Okay?
Narrator:	Now get ready to answer the question. What does the student need from her professor? Select two.

Narrator: 3. Listen as a student talks to a professor. This is a two-point question.

Student:	Professor Salander?
Prof:	Oh, hi, Liz. Did you get my message?
Student:	I did. Thanks. By the way, thanks to you I got the job.
Prof:	Job?
Student:	Helping Professor Larson.
Prof:	Right. Congrats. Isn't Professor Larson a kick?
Student:	Totally. He's got me doing tons of research. And get this. He wants me to go to the Amazon over Christmas and help him tag jaguars!
Prof:	Fantastic. Just remember to take a lot of bug spray and malaria pills.
Student:	Really?
Prof:	Forewarned is forearmed, right?
Student:	Right. I'm taking my laptop too, but I'm not sure how I'll get power. I mean, it's the Amazon, right? Not a lot of outlets in a jungle.
Prof:	Try solar.
Student:	Really? You mean like a solar-powered laptop?
Prof:	No. A charger. I took one to the Peru on my last dig. I set it out on a rock every morning. It's basically a small sheet of photovoltaic cells. They capture sunlight and turn it into electricity. It sure is handy. Believe me.
Student:	That's exactly what I need.
Prof:	As a matter of fact, it's right here in my drawer. A few hours in the sun and this thing will charge anything. You want to borrow it?
Student:	Really?
Prof:	It's not doing anything sitting here in the drawer.
Narrator:	Now get ready to answer the question. What will the student take to the Amazon? Select three.

Narrator: 4. Listen as a student talks to a professor. This is a one-point question.

Prof:	There are two graduate English degrees, Norma. An MA, a master of arts, and a doctorate, a PhD.
Student:	What's the difference between an MA and an MFA?
Prof:	The focus of an MA is research. For example, you choose an area you want to study, like—oh, I don't know, let's say early Greek tragedies—and you study it with the aim of one day teaching it.
Student:	And an MFA?
Prof:	The focus of an MFA is on writing. It's geared more toward those who want to write fiction or non-fiction. In that sense, it's more an art course, like, you know, music or graphic design.
Student:	So which do you recommend?

Narrator: Now get ready to answer the question. Which two graduate English degrees does the professor describe? Select two.

Track #41 - Practice: Question-First Function Questions - Pg. 156

Narrator: Practice. Question-first function questions. Directions. Answer each question based on what is stated or implied.

Narrator: 1. Why does the professor say this?

Prof: Toni, you know that each homework assignment is due at the end of the every week. I would love to bend the rules for you, but that would not be fair to other students. That said, you have till Friday to put things right.

Narrator: 2. Why does the professor say this?

Prof: As I mentioned in class, Carlos—last class—because Rome had a large standing army—this huge, massive army—it constantly needed money and men. By periodically taking a census of population—you know, counting heads basically—the Roman government knew how much tax money it could raise for the army and the available manpower it could draw from.

Narrator: 3. Why does the professor say this?

Prof: Look, Bill, I can't meet today. I have a faculty meeting in five minutes. Take a rain check? How about we aim for...ah, noon tomorrow?

Narrator: 4. Why does the student say this?

Student: I did the research as you suggested and discovered something amazing. I mean, I don't know how to put this. It's...Well, you'll see. It'll totally blow you away. You got a minute, professor?

Track #42 - Practice: Segment-First Function Questions - Pg. 157

Narrator: Practice. Segment-first function questions. Directions. Answer each question based on what is stated or implied.

Narrator: 1. Listen to part of a conversation, then answer the question.

Prof: No. Length is really not an issue. Let me rephrase that. There is no connection between length and quality. Some might disagree, but frankly, some of the best essays I've graded have been short.

Narrator: Why does the professor say this?

Prof: Let me rephrase that.

Narrator: **2. Listen to part of a conversation, then answer the question.** 🎧

Prof: The thing to remember about internet piracy is this: It's a plague, a plague costing consumers and businesses billions, a plague that is only getting worse.

Narrator: Why does the professor say this?

Prof: It's a plague, a plague costing consumers and businesses billions, a plague that is only getting worse.

Narrator: **3. Listen to part of a conversation, then answer the question.** 🎧

Woman: So for a teaching job, a PhD will definitely improve my chances of getting hired?
Prof: There's no guarantee, but yes. You have an MBA, right?
Woman: Yes. In finance.
Prof: Well, there's always Wall Street. You don't need a PhD to trade stocks and bonds. Surprisingly, though, a lot of business research is done by those with PhD's in quantitative finance. They use computer modeling. It's all the rage. You could write your ticket with a background like that.

Narrator: What does the professor mean when he says this?

Prof: It's all the rage.

Narrator: **4. Listen to part of a conversation, then answer the question.** 🎧

Student: Professor Page, what exactly is rock and roll? I missed it in class.
Prof: Good question, Jimmy. Rock and roll is basically blues with an attitude. Let me try that again. Rock and roll is a salad, a big musical salad with the heart of a rebel. Ah, now I'm mixing metaphors.

Narrator: What does the professor mean when she says this?

Prof: Ah, now I'm mixing metaphors.

Track #43 - Practice: Direct-Attitude Questions - Page 160

Narrator: Practice. Direct-attitude questions. Directions. Listen to each prompt, then answer the questions.

Narrator: **1. Listen as a student talks to a professor.**

Student: Professor Pickett, do you have a minute?
Prof: Hi, Justine. Sure. What's up?
Student: I just wanted to get your opinion on something.
Prof: Shoot.
Student: Do you think I stand a chance in the debate tomorrow?
Prof: Not only do I think you've got a chance—you and the rest of the debating team—but I think we are going to clean Harvard's clock.

Narrator: What does the professor believe?

Narrator: **2. Listen as a student talks to a professor.**

Prof: Hey, Tina. Thanks for dropping by. So what did you think of your presentation? I didn't get the chance to ask you in class.

Student: Personally? To be honest? I think I nailed it.

Narrator: What does the student believe?

Narrator: **3. Listen as a student talks to a professor.**

Student: Rewrite, professor? You mean, my essay? Again?

Prof: Yes. I'm giving you the chance to improve your grade.

Student: But I like what I wrote. It's how I feel, what I believe. Besides, grades really don't mean that much to me.

Narrator: What is the student's opinion of grades?

Narrator: **4. Listen as a student talks to a professor.**

Student: What did you think of my thesis, Professor?

Prof: Let's see. You say, and I quote, "Videos games are a popular form of entertainment." That's not a thesis, Charleen. It's a fact and thus not arguable.

Student: But it's true.

Prof: Right. True because it's a fact.

Student: Oh. Right. I get it.

Narrator: What is the professor's opinion of the student's thesis?

Track #44 - Practice: Inferred-Attitude Questions - Page 163

Narrator: Practice. Inferred-attitude questions. Directions. Listen to each prompt, then answer the question.

Narrator: **1. Listen as a student talks to a professor.**

Student: Professor Bergman? Hi. Got a minute?

Prof: Sure Peggy. What's up?

Student: It's about the debate tomorrow.

Prof: You're arguing for more government, correct?

Student: Less.

Prof: Right. So, all prepared?

Student: I think so. Anyway, the reason I stopped you is because, well, tomorrow's supposed to be a really nice day, and I thought it'd be kind of cool to do the debate outside on the quad. It'd be a nice change of pace, don't you think? You know, on the grass under a tree. We could get some food too. Maybe some pizza or something.

Prof: Or something.

Student: Well, what do think?

Prof: I don't.

Narrator: What can we infer about having the debate outside?

Narrator: **2. Listen as a student talks to a professor.**

Prof: "Computer games are the best thing since sliced bread." Really, Lilian? That's your thesis?
Student: Ah, yeah. Why? It's an opinion, right?
Prof: It is.
Student: So what's the matter?
Prof: Don't get me wrong. I'm all for analogies as a way to start an essay. But this one? It seems, how should I put it—like a fish out of water. Do you catch my drift?
Student: Right. Lose the cliché.

Narrator: What can we infer from the conversation?

Narrator: **3. Listen as a student talks to a professor.**

Prof: Hi, Peter. Thanks for dropping by.
Student: Sure. What's wrong? I know. It's my cell phone, right?
Prof: It is rather annoying. Right in the middle of class. Can't you turn it off?
Student: I can. But I'm expecting an important call. It's about a job. I interviewed and everything. If I turn my phone off, I might miss it.
Prof: What about vibrating mode?
Student: Yeah. I can do that. But I might miss the call, and I really need this job. Serious. The job market has really gone south. I've been looking for ages. What's this?
Prof: It's the school policy regarding cell phone use in classrooms.
Student: I got one, thanks. You handed them out on the first day of class.
Prof: Maybe you should review it. Point number one in particular. Read it carefully so we can avoid having this conversation again.

Narrator: What is the professor suggesting?

Narrator: **4. Listen as a student talks to another student.**

Woman: But that's the point. Why does a mascot have to be serious? Why can't a mascot be fun, like a chicken or a goat, or a giraffe even? Education is way too serious.
Man: Alice...
Woman: What?
Man: Earth to Alice.
Woman: What!

Narrator: How does the man feel about having a chicken for a mascot?

Track #45 - Practice: Inferred-Action Questions - Page 165

Narrator: Practice. Inferred-action questions. Directions. Listen to each prompt, then answer the question.

Narrator: **1. Listen as a student talks to a professor.**

Prof: "Proponents of standardized testing are quick to wave the flag of comparative statistics as being the best way to measure academic performance." I like that. I do. Very good. Drives the point home. "Yet what supporters of standardized testing fail to realize is that, in their rush for statistics, they have boiled education down to a game, a game in which there are winners and losers. I'm sorry, but education is not about winners and losers." And that is your point, Josh. And it's a good one. Excellent essay. Bravo. Well done.

Student: Really, professor? You're joking, right?

Prof: No. That's why I wanted to see you. This is an excellent piece of writing. Well researched, well developed. You've hit the nail right on the head. Not only that but you've worked hard. You should be proud.

Student: Thanks.

Narrator: What will the professor probably do?

Narrator: 2. Listen as a student talks to a professor.

Student: Professor Keaton, that was a great point you made in a class, you know, the one about how video games teach a false sense of reality. I was at the mall yesterday and there was this new military recruiting center. I couldn't believe it. It was like walking into a video game store.

Prof: I've heard about these new high-tech recruiting centers.

Student: You should see the stuff they've got. You can climb into an Apache or an F-16, and suddenly you're flying over a desert, or an ocean—like it's the real thing. Not only that, but you get shot at. It's like you're in a...in a...

Prof: A war?

Student: Yeah. I mean, it was real—but it wasn't—just like what you were talking about in class, you know, creating a false sense of reality using virtual images.

Prof: Right. So, Henry, did you sign up?

Narrator: We can infer from the conversation that the professor has not...

Narrator: 3. Listen as a student talks to a professor.

Prof: Really, Claudia? But, in the end, don't we have to sacrifice some freedom to be safe?

Student: It depends, professor, on how you define safe?

Prof: Okay, fair enough. So how do you define it?

Student: Simple. What I do in the privacy of my home is nobody's business but my own. Period. I don't need the government telling me what I can or can't do with my computer or anything else. The United States is a democracy not a dictatorship.

Narrator: From the conversation, we can infer that the student will probably continue to...

Narrator: 4. Listen as a student talks to a professor.

Student: As you can see, I'm still not sure what direction I should take after graduating. You'd think with a PhD I could write my ticket.

Prof: There's always Wall Street, you know. You don't need a PhD to trade stocks and bonds. Surprisingly, though, a lot of business research is done by those with PhD's, particularly in quantitative finance. They use computer modeling. It's all the rage. The money's not too bad either.

Student: I like the idea of Wall Street. I do. And thanks for the advice, professor, but I think I need to broaden my horizons.

Narrator: What will the student probably do?

Track #46 - Sample: Service-Encounter Conversation - Pg. 166

Narrator: Sample. Service-Encounter Conversation. Directions. Listen to a sample conversation, then answer the questions on the next page. Do not look at the questions. On test day, you will not see the questions as you listen. Remember to answer all the questions. You will not lose points for a wrong answer. Now listen as a student talks to a member of the school's IT support staff.

Student: Hi. Is this IT support?

Support: Yes, it is. How can I help you? Let me guess. Your computer got hit by the email virus going round and you want to know how to restore your corrupted files, right?

Student: Actually, my computer didn't get hit.

Support: Oh, one of the lucky ones. So, what's up?

Student: I just bought an iPod Touch.

Support: Sweet. How much?

Student: A lot. Look, the reason I'm calling is because I can't connect my iPod to the internet.

Support: You mean the school's wireless network?

Student: Right.

Support: What exactly is the problem?

Student: When I open my email, a dialogue box asks me to log on to the school's wireless network. I log on with my school ID and my password, just like with my laptop, then another dialogue box pops up and says, "No wireless network." How can there be no wireless network when everybody around me is connected? I'm like totally confused. This never happens with my laptop. What am I doing wrong? It's something really simple, right?

Support: Probably security. What kind of encryption are you using?

Student: Excuse me?

Support: Encryption. The school's wireless network is encrypted.

Student: I'm sorry. I don't follow.

Support: Encryption basically means the wireless signal floating around the school here— well, not so much floating but, you know, covering—has been scrambled into a secret code that can only be opened by the right security setting on the device you're using. The old kind of wireless encryption is called WEP. That's short for wired-equivalent privacy. The school stopped using it two years ago because it had serious security issues. We now use WPA. That's short for wi-fi protected access. Your iPod is probably set for WEP.

Student: Ahhh...Right. Can you just tell me how to set it up? I'm kind of in a hurry here.

Support: Sure. Boot up your iPod. Go to your home screen. Open settings, then go to network. See it?

Student: Network. Network. Right.

Support: Open network, then open Wi-Fi.

Student: Okay. It's open.

Support: At the top of the screen, you should see security. Open it.

Student: Open security. Got it.

Support: You should see a menu that gives you a choice of encryption settings starting with WEP. See it?

Student: Got it. There's WEP followed by WPA and WPA2. Those are wireless security settings?

Support: Bingo. The school uses WPA, so select it and you should be good to go.

Student: Oh, my God. You're a genius!

Support: Sweet. Anything else I can help you with?

Student: Nope. That's it.

Support: Hey, would you mind filling out a survey? It's about how well I solved your problem. It would only take a sec.

Student: Sure. No, problem.

Narrator: Now get ready to answer the questions. Answer each question based on what is stated or implied in the conversation.

1. What are the student and the IT staffer mainly discussing?
2. What is the student's problem?
3. What are the wireless security settings? Select three.

 4. Why does the student say this?

Student: Oh, my God. You're a genius!

 5. Listen again to part of the conversation, then answer the question.

Support: What exactly is the problem?

Student: When I open my email, a dialogue box asks me to log on to the school's wireless network. I log on with my school ID and my password, just like with my laptop, then another dialogue box pops up and says, "No wireless network." How can there be no wireless network when everybody around me is connected? I'm like totally confused. This never happens with my laptop. What am I doing wrong? It's something really simple, right?

Support: Probably security. What kind of encryption are you using?

Student: Excuse me?

Support: Encryption. The school's wireless network is encrypted.

Student: I'm sorry. I don't follow.

Narrator: What does the student mean by this?

Student: I'm sorry. I don't follow.

Track #47 - Practice: Content Questions - Page 168

Narrator: Practice. Content questions. Directions. Listen to each prompt, then answer the question.

Narrator: 1. Listen as a student talks to a security guard.

Student: Really? I got a ticket for parking in the wrong spot? But I thought student parking was red.

Security: Staff is red. Students yellow. Visitors blue.

Student: You know, somebody should repaint the lines. They're really hard to see.

Security: Here. Give me your ticket. We'll let it slide this time.

Student: Thanks.

Security: And remember.

Student: Yes?

Security: The garage closes at eleven.

Narrator: What is main topic of discussion?

Narrator: **2. Listen as a student talks to an admin.**

Student: Hi. Can you tell me if my student ID ready?

Admin: Sure. Name?

Student: Jane Smitts. I had my picture taken yesterday.

Admin: Let me check. Smart. Smith. Smitts. Here you go. That'll be ten dollars.

Student: Ten dollars? I have to shell out ten bucks for an ID? Excuse me? Since when do I have to pay for my student ID?

Admin: Since the new policy. Cash or charge?

Student: Wa...Wait. I don't get it. New policy? What new policy? I thought getting a student ID was part of my tuition.

Admin: It was. But because of government cutbacks, the school now has to charge extra for IDs. It was announced in a school-wide memo.

Student: Memo? What memo?

Admin: An email memo. It was sent out to all students and faculty two months ago. Cash or charge?

Student: I didn't get a memo.

Admin: It's posted right here.

Student: What if I don't want to pay?

Admin: All students are required to carry a digital photo ID. If security stops you, or you need access a lab or to use the library, you'll need to identify yourself.

Student: What if I just hold up my tuition receipt? That would prove I'm a student here, right?

Admin: It would. But the new policy says you must carry a digital photo ID.

Student: Okay. So if you were me, what would you do?

Admin: I'm really not the person to ask.

Student: Who is?

Admin: The registrar. Cynthia Nichols. Second floor. Room 310. Next.

Narrator: What is the focus of the conversation?

Narrator: **3. Listen as a student talks to a security guard.**

Security: Are you the student who called security?

Student: Yes. The bio lab is supposed to be open but the door's locked. Can you unlock it for me? I really have to complete an assignment by tomorrow morning. If I don't, my head's going to be on the chopping block.

Security: No problem. And you are?

Student: Kenichi. Kenichi Mori. Just call me George.

Security: Right. There you go, George. The door's open.

Student: Thanks. What happens if I have to step out for a minute?

Security: The door will lock. Are you alone?

Student: Yes.

Security: Then give security a ring. I'll scoot on by and open it for you. Also, I'll need to see some ID.

Student: Sure. There you go.

Security: Thanks.

Narrator: What is subject of discussion?

Narrator: **4. Listen as a student talks to a librarian.**

Admin: What's the title of that book again?

Student:	*PowerPoint for Dummies.*
Admin:	*PowerPoint for Dummies*? I'm afraid not. The school library doesn't carry those titles.
Student:	Really? Why not?
Admin:	I can't say for sure. Probably because they send the wrong message.
Student:	Really? But I use them all the time. They're fast and easy. And cheap.
Admin:	Hey, if it works? Anything else?
Student:	Ah, yeah. I'm also looking for another book. Just let check my notes. It's for my philosophy class.
Admin:	With Professor Reamer?
Student:	Yeah.
Admin:	I had her. Isn't she great?
Student:	Yeah—and tough. She's got us burning the midnight oil.
Admin:	She does make you hit the books. So you're probably looking for Kant, right?
Student:	No. Not Kant.
Admin:	Kierkegaard?
Student:	No. Oh, what is it? It's right on the tip of my tongue.
Admin:	Schopenhauer?
Student:	We've done all those guys. Here it is. *The Birth of Tragedy.*
Admin:	Nietzsche. Right. *The Birth of Tragedy.* Let me see if it's available. Napster. Negotiating. Neologisms. Nietzsche. You're in luck. It's on the shelf. Number N789.PH34. Here I'll right down.
Student:	Thanks. Which floor?
Admin:	Fourth.
Narrator:	What is the subject of discussion?

Track #48 - Practice: Purpose Questions - Page 169

Narrator:	Practice. Purpose questions. Directions. Listen to each prompt, then answer the question.

Narrator: 1. Listen as a student talks to an admin.

Admin:	So which scholarship did you have in mind?
Student:	One with full tuition. You know, for the whole year.
Admin:	There's a lot of competition for those. Suffice it to say, they go fast.
Student:	So I'm too late?
Admin:	For this year? Yes. Would like to apply for next year?
Student:	Actually, I need the money now. Are there any scholarships I can apply for?
Admin:	Let me take a look. What's your major?
Student:	Philology.
Admin:	Philology. A philosopher, huh?
Student:	Yeah. Sorta.
Admin:	Okay. Philology. There's no scholarship specific to that discipline.
Student:	What is there?
Admin:	There's the Scott-Shackleton Scholarship for Polar Research. It's five-thousand dollars.
Student:	I don't think so. Anything else?
Admin	There's the Pierce-Val Scholarship for Economics. It's one thousand, and...Let's see. What else? How about this? The Parker-Bowles Research Scholarship for the Enrichment of the Humanities.
Student:	Humanities? That's a pretty broad area.

Admin: It's a ten-thousand dollar research grant. Are you researching anything related to the humanities?
Student: No. I'm still in first year. Looks like I'm out of luck then.
Admin: Can I suggest something?
Student: Sure.
Admin: Philology is definitely a humanity.
Student: I know. But, like I said, I'm not researching anything.
Admin: There's no harm in applying. Hey, you never know?

Narrator: Why does the student visit financial aid?

Narrator: 2. Listen as a student talks to maintenance.

Staffer: Hello? Campus Maintenance.
Student: Hi. I'm a student over in Noble Hall. Dorm Eight.
Staffer: Let me guess. The toilet, right?
Student: Ah, no. Not this time. The raccoon. He's back.
Staffer: In the garbage?
Student: Actually, he's parked under my bed. Can you come over and, you know, talk to him?
Staffer: Don't try and touch him.
Student: I wasn't planning to. Actually, I was planning to study calculus. I have an exam tomorrow, but my guest is a bit of a...What should I say? Distraction?
Staffer: Understood. I'm on my way.

Narrator: Why does the student call maintenance?

Narrator: 3. Listen as a student talks to a security guard.

Student: Hi. I'd like to report a stolen laptop.
Security: Are you sure it was stolen?
Student: Definitely.
Security: Ah, where and when?
Student: I forgot it in the library this morning. When I went back to look, it was gone. Man, my life was on that thing.
Security: What kind of laptop is it?
Student: A MacBook Air. I just bought it.
Security: Drag.
Student: Tell me about it. Has it turned up? Probably not, huh?
Security: As a matter of fact...
Student: Oh, man. Awright! Thank you so much!
Security: Don't thank me. Thank the library. One of the staff saw it and dropped it off about an hour ago.

Narrator: Why does the student visit security?

Narrator: 4. Listen as a student talks to an admin.

Student: Hi. I'd like to buy some tickets, please.
Admin: Sure. Which sport? Football? Soccer? Lacrosse? Field hockey?
Student"   Lacrosse, please. Can I get twenty?
Admin: Twenty?

Student:	Yeah. My boyfriend's team is playing and he asked me to get tickets for his family.
Admin:	Big family.
Student:	Tell me about it.
Admin:	You know, if you purchase twenty-five tickets, I can give you a twenty-percent discount, with a student ID, of course.
Student:	I only need twenty. Besides, what would I do with the other five?
Admin:	Keep them for the next game.
Student:	So they're transferable? The tickets?
Admin:	That's right. Only for faculty and students though.
Student:	For lacrosse or any sport?
Admin:	Any sport.
Student:	Basketball too?
Admin:	That's right. Basketball tickets sold out ages ago.
Student:	What if I don't use them? The other five. Can I get a refund?
Admin:	No. You have to use them. So, what's it going to be?
Student:	Oh, man. Decisions. Decisions.
Admin:	You know, since our ladies basketball team became number one in the country, people have been scrambling to buy tickets. You can't believe the demand. In fact, I just heard a pair sold on eBay for five-hundred bucks for tomorrow night's game—and we're not even playing a ranked team. You buy twenty-five tickets with a twenty-percent student discount and you'll be sitting in the catbird seat, believe me.
Student:	All right. I'm sold. Give me twenty-five with the discount.
Narrator:	Why does the student talk to the admin?

Track #49 - Practice: Single-Answer Detail Questions - Pg. 170

| Narrator: | Practice. Single-answer detail questions. Directions. Listen as a student talks to a campus employee, then answer the questions. |

Student:	Hello?
Admin:	Yes? Oh, come in. Can I help you?
Student:	Are you Bill Jenkins? The gallery manager?
Admin:	I am.
Student:	Professor Gainsborough said I should talk to you about having a show here in the gallery.
Admin: very	Oh, right. You must Sylvia. So nice to meet you. Professor Gainsborough speaks very highly of you.
Student:	Really?
Admin:	He does. So tell me. What did you have in mind?
Student:	I'd like to exhibit my graduate portfolio.
Admin:	Great. What medium?
Student:	I'm not sure how to classify it. Lately, I've been combining photographs and old computer parts.
Admin:	Oh, really?
Student:	I found them, actually. The computer parts. In a dumpster. In fact, I find all my material. I can't remember the last time I bought something.
Admin:	Found art. I see. Sounds intriguing. Do you have anything I can look at?
Student:	Yes. I brought some examples. It's not exactly mainstream. Most of the time I'm pushing the envelope.
Admin:	Oh, I like this. Does it have a title?
Student:	No. I just number them.
Admin:	Why's that?

Student:	Well, I can never think of a good title. They all sound, you know, lame. So how is the schedule? You must be really booked.
Admin:	Let me check. Ah, next month...Let's see, Gloria Samuels will show for the first two weeks. She works in oil. Landscapes. Very traditional. Ah, after Gloria, for the last two weeks of the month, it's David Hopkins.
Student:	Really? David Hopkins the sculptor?
Admin:	The one and only. Straight from a show in London. Have you heard?
Student:	No. What?
Admin:	The Queen bought one of his pieces. Ah, will you price your work?
Student:	You mean sell it?
Admin:	That's right. How about next Monday? Emily Lopez was slated to show, but she had to cancel. She called just before you walked in. Mind you, it would only be for a week. That's the best I can do, I'm afraid. It's short notice, I know but...
Student:	No. No. Next Monday would be great. What should I do?
Admin:	Well, today's Thursday. I suggest we meet here tomorrow morning. Let's say, ah, nine? Bring whatever work you want to show and we'll go from there. The current show, Joseph Sands—have you seen it?
Student:	Yes. I'm not a big fan of expressionism. Not that it's bad. It's just not my cup of tea.
Admin:	To each his own. Anyway, Joseph will be out of here Saturday night. That gives us all day Sunday to get your show up and running.
Student:	What about pricing? I'd really like to try and sell a few pieces.
Admin:	Pricing is up to you. That said, I wouldn't go crazy. For example, this piece here...
Student:	Number nine?
Admin:	Easily five hundred.
Student:	Five hundred?
Admin:	Maybe more. You know, I think I'll call Karen Goldblatt. She's the editor of Art House Magazine. She really should see these. She'll know how to price them.
Narrator:	Now get ready to answer the questions.

1. To whom does the student speak?
2. What can't the student remember?
3. What is the student pushing with her art?
4. How long will the student's exhibition last?
5. How many days does the student have to prepare her exhibition?
6. Who is Karen Goldblatt?

Track #50 - Practice: Multi-Answer Detail Questions - Page 171

Narrator:	Practice. Multi-answer detail questions. Directions. Listen to each prompt, then answer the question.

Narrator: 1. Listen as a student talks to an admin. This is a 1-point question.

Admin:	High grades are essential. That's a given for a scholarship. And letters.
Student:	You mean letters of recommendation?
Admin:	Yes.
Student:	What about volunteering?
Admin:	Not essential, but it doesn't hurt to put it down. Here's the application form.
Narrator:	What information is required for the scholarship application? Select two.

Narrator: **2. Listen as a student talks to a librarian. This is a 1-point question.**

Student: Hi, I'd like to put three books on reserve.
Admin: Okay. Which ones?
Student: I'd like to reserve *Howard's Human Prehistory*, *Mitchell's Methods of Archeology*, and *Swift-Lee's*—sorry, *Swift-Scott's Guide to Ancient Tools*.
Admin: That's it?
Student: Yes. Thanks. When will they be available?
Admin: Let me check. *Prehistory and Tools* should be available next week. *Methods of Archeology*? Could be a while. It's very popular.
Student: Then scratch it.

Narrator: Which books does the student put on reserve? Select two.

Narrator: **3. Listen as a student talks to an admin. This is a 1-point question.**

Student: Right. So how much are the tickets?
Admin: For twenty-five?
Student: Yes.
Admin: That will be...Just a second. Five-hundred dollars.
Student: Whoa. Is that the student rate with the discount?
Admin: Yes. How would you like to pay?
Student: Just a sec. How about Visa? Half cash, half Visa?
Admin: Whatever works.
Student: Sorry. It'll have to be MasterCard. My Visa's maxxed out.

Narrator: How will the student pay for the tickets? Select two.

Narrator: **4. Listen as a student talks to a campus employee. This is a 1-point question.**

Student: Excuse me? Excuse me?
Worker: Yo.
Student: I got the wrong order. I wanted a turkey wrap with avocado, and sprouts.
Worker: Avocado and sprouts? Not chicken with onions, cheese and jalapenos?
Student: No.
Worker: Sure?
Student: Positive.
Worker: Who ordered the chicken wrap with onions, cheese, and jalapenos?
Student: Not me. Can I get a Coke too?
Worker: Pepsi okay?
Student: Whatever.

Narrator: What did the student order? Select two.

Track #51 - Practice: Question-First Function Questions - Pg. 172

Narrator: Practice. Question-first function questions. Directions. Answer each question based on what is stated or implied.

Narrator: **1. Why does the student say this?** 🎧

Student: My Visa's maxxed out.

Narrator: 2. Why does the admin say this?

Staffer: High grades are essential. That's a given for a scholarship.

Narrator: 3. Why does the student say this?

Student: It's just not my cup of tea.

Narrator: 4. Why does the student say this?

Student: I have to shell out ten bucks for an ID?

Track #52 – Practice: Segment-First Function Questions - Pg. 173

Narrator: Practice. Segment-first function questions. Directions. Listen to each prompt, then answer the question.

Narrator: 1. Listen to part of a conversation, then answer the question.

Admin: Let me check. *Prehistory and Tools* should be available next week. *Methods of Archeology*? Could be a while. It's very popular.

Student: Then scratch it.

Narrator: Why does the student say this?

Student: Then scratch it.

Narrator: 2. Listen to part of a conversation, then answer the question.

Student: Really? I got a ticket for parking in the wrong spot? But I thought student parking was red.
Security: Staff is red. Students yellow. Visitors blue.
Student: You know, somebody should repaint the lines. They're really hard to see.
Security: Here. Give me your ticket. We'll let it slide this time.

Narrator: What does security mean by this?

Security: We'll let it slide this time.

Narrator: 3. Listen to part of a conversation, then answer the question.

Student: Hi. I like to buy some tickets, please.
Admin: Sure. Which sport? Football? Soccer? Lacrosse? Field hockey?
Student: Lacrosse, please. Can I get twenty?
Admin: Twenty?
Student: Yeah. My boyfriend's team is playing and he asked me to get tickets for his family.
Admin: Big family.
Student: Tell me about it.

Narrator: What does the student mean by this?

Student: Tell me about it.

Narrator: 4. Listen to part of a conversation, then answer the question.

Worker: Who ordered the chicken wrap with onions, cheese and jalapenos?
Student: Not me. Can I get a Coke too?
Worker: Pepsi okay?
Student: Whatever.

Narrator: What does the student mean by this?

Student: Whatever.

Track #53 - Practice: Direct-Attitude Questions - Page 174

Narrator: Practice. Direct-attitude questions. Directions. Listen to each prompt, then answer the question.

Narrator: 1. Listen then answer the question.

Admin: Congratulations. You got a scholarship.
Student: I did? Great. It's really a load off my mind.

Narrator: How does the student feel about getting a scholarship?

Narrator: 2. Listen then answer the question.

Admin: Do you often read *Dummies* books?
Student: Sure. All the time. They cover practically every subject. Web design. Photoshop. How to play the piano. Pets. You name it. I buy them because you get more bang for your buck.

Narrator: What is the student's opinion of *Dummies* books?

Narrator: 3. Listen then answer the question.

Admin: Found art. I see. Sounds intriguing. Do you have anything I can look at?
Student: Yes. I brought some examples. It's not exactly mainstream. Most of the time I'm pushing the envelope.
Admin: Oh, I like this. Does it have a title?
Student: No. I just number them.
Admin: Why's that?
Student: Well, I can never think of a good title. They all sound, you know, lame. So how is the schedule?

Narrator: How does the student feel about putting titles on her work?

Narrator: 4. Listen then answer the question.

Student: Oh, man. Decisions. Decisions.

Admin: You know, since our ladies basketball team became number one in the country, people have been scrambling to buy tickets. You can't believe the demand. In fact, I just heard a pair sold on eBay for five-hundred bucks for tomorrow night's game—and we're not even playing a ranked team. You buy twenty-five tickets with a twenty-percent student discount and you'll be sitting in the catbird seat, believe me.

Narrator: What does the admin think about buying so many tickets?

Track #54 - Practice: Inferred-Attitude Questions - Page 175

Narrator: Practice. Inferred-attitude questions. Directions. Listen to each prompt, then answer the question.

Narrator: 1. Listen then answer the question.

Student: Ten dollars? I have to shell out ten bucks for an ID?

Narrator: How does the student feel about the new policy?

Narrator: 2. Listen then answer the question.

Student: Hi, I'd like to return this book for resale.
Admin: Sorry, we're not reselling used texts anymore.
Student: Really? Since when?
Admin: Since last month when the bookstore started selling ebooks.
Student: So what should I do?
Admin: Try selling them on eBay.
Student: eBay? Yeah, right. Me and a million other guys.

Narrator: What does the student think about selling his used texts on eBay?

Narrator: 3. Listen then answer the question.

Student: Hi, I'd like to apply for grad school.
Admin: Great. Which program are you interested in?
Student: One that'll help me make the most money in the shortest time possible.
Admin: O-kay.

Narrator: How does the admin react to the student's request?

Narrator: 4. Listen then answer the question.

Security: Hey, you can't park there. Hey!
Student: Ah, sorry. I'm a new student here.
Security: Student parking's on the third floor. You need to get a tag.
Student: How do I do that?
Security   Police office. Fourth floor. FitzGerald Building. Here. Use this temporary tag till you get a new one.

Student: Dude. All right. You are the man.

Narrator: How does the student feel about the staffer's help?

Track #55 - Practice: Inferred-Action Questions - Page 176

Narrator: Practice. Inferred-action questions. Directions. Listen to each prompt, then answer the question.

Narrator: 1. Listen then answer the question.

Student: Hi. I've come to pick up my scholarship money.
Admin: For that, you'll need to go to financial aid. They'll take care of you.

Narrator: Where will the student probably go?

Narrator: 2. Listen then answer the question.

Staffer: Campus Security. Briana speaking.
Student: Hi. I lost my cell phone this morning. Has anyone turned one in?
Staffer: A few.
Student: Any iPhones? One with a pink silicon sleeve with little red hearts on it?
Staffer: Red hearts? Just a sec...You're in luck.

Narrator: What will the student probably do?

Narrator: 3. Listen then answer the question.

Student: Hi, my name is Lisa Jones. I have a couple of books on reserve. Have they come in yet?
Admin: Let me check. Yes, they have.
Student: Great.
Admin: I see you have an outstanding late fee on *Fundamentals of Physics*. A dollar to be exact. You'll need to pay that first before you sign out any more books.

Narrator: What will the student probably do?

Narrator: 4. Listen then answer the question.

Admin: Hi, can I help you?
Student: I'd like to sign up for the total workout fitness class starting next week.
Admin: Great. Fill out this form.
Student: How much is it?
Admin: Twenty dollars. You'll need a medical release form too.

Narrator: What will the student probably do?

Professor-Only – Pg. 177

Narrator: Sample. Professor-only lecture. Directions. Listen to a sample lecture, then answer the questions on the next page. Do not look at the questions. On test day, you will not see the questions as you listen. Remember to answer all the questions. You will not lose points for a wrong answer. Now listen to part of a lecture in a composition class.

Prof: 1 ➔ According to Aristotle, an argument can be made more persuasive by using three appeals: logos, pathos, and ethos.

2 ➔ Let's start with logos. Logos, or logic, appeals to reason. One way to appeal to reason is by using deduction. Deduction—and we'll come back to this later on—is a form of reasoning in which you make a conclusion based on a series of related facts or premises. Let's work through an example. First, you start with a major premise, such as...Oh, I don't know—*All English teachers are poor.* This general statement is followed by a specific statement or minor premise, in this case *Bob is an English teacher.* From these two premises, a conclusion logically follows: *Bob is poor.* Put it all together and it reads like this: *All English teachers are poor. Bob is an English teacher. Bob is poor.* As you can see, deduction can be pretty persuasive. Its closed or formal structure leaves no doubt as to Bob's financial situation relative to his profession.

3 ➔ Induction is another form of logic that appeals to reason. When inducing, you combine a series of related facts, such as *Joan loves apples; Joan loves blueberries; Joan loves mangos.* From these facts, we can make a conclusion, in this case *Joan loves fruit.* Does she love all fruit? We don't know. She might abhor apricots. As you can see, induction is not as closed or conclusive as deduction. Still, add numbers to an inductive mix and the logic behind an argument whether to invest in a company can be quite appealing. For example, *ABC Company made a $20 billion profit last year; ABC made a $40 billion profit this year; ABC will make a $60 billion profit next year.* Conclusion? You do the math.

4 ➔ Pathos, in contrast, is an appeal to the emotions. By appealing to the emotions, the arguer can evoke sympathy from an audience. Sympathy, in turn, makes an argument more persuasive. Movies regularly employ pathos. Did you cry when E.T. finally went home? Were you terrified when Titanic sank or when Jaws rose out of the water, teeth flashing? If so, then the director persuaded you that two-dimensional images on a movie screen are so real, so life-like, you reacted to them emotionally. Pathos can also support logos. For example, photographs often support news stories. What better way to evoke audience anger at an oil company than to place a photo of an oil-covered pelican next to an article about an oil spill.

5 ➔ Next we have ethos. Ethos is an appeal to character. For example, from whom would you buy a computer, a man in a business suit or a man in a T-shirt? Ethically, some might eschew the man in the T-shirt, a T-shirt being the antithesis of business attire therefore unethical, not trustworthy. However, such ethical conclusions have been turned on their heads, especially in America. Case in point: Whenever Apple introduces a new product, CEO Steve Jobs introduces the product wearing jeans and a T-Shirt. Does Jobs' choice of clothes diminish the quality of the product? No. If anything, Jobs' casual look enhances Apple's cool factor. As you can see, what was once ethically unacceptable—wearing jeans to work—is now perfectly acceptable.

6 ➔ Those, then, are Aristotle's three appeals. It's important to remember that a successful argument—a persuasive argument—combines all three appeals. Look at President Obama. As an argument for president, his life story was quite compelling. Why? Because it was defined by the three appeals. As a youth, he was a community organizer (ethos and pathos). He then studied law at Harvard (logos and ethos). After he graduated, he taught constitutional law at the University of Chicago (logos

and ethos). He then became a U.S. senator (logos, pathos and ethos). Combined, these three appeals made Barack Obama a persuasive argument to be president of the United States.

7 ➔ That said, keep in mind, however, that even when supported by all three appeals, there is no guarantee that a politician seeking office—or any other argument—will persuade an audience, for if any of the three appeals come under the fire, the audience will fail to be persuaded.

Narrator: Now get ready to answer the questions. Answer each based on what is stated or implied in the lecture.

    1. What is the topic of the lecture?
    2. What is the purpose of the lecture?
    3. According to Aristotle, which appeals make a lecture more persuasive? Select three. This is a 2-point question.

    4. Why does the professor say this?

Prof: That said, keep in mind, however, that even when supported by all three appeals, there is no guarantee that a politician seeking office—or any other argument—will persuade an audience, for if any of the three appeals come under the fire, the audience will fail to be persuaded.

    5. The professor describes President Obama's personal history. Put President Obama's personal history in the proper order. This is a 2-point question.

    6. In the lecture, the professor describes Aristotle's three appeals and their functions in an argument. Indicate whether each of the following is a function of Aristotle's three appeals. This is a 3-point question.

Track #57 - Practice: Content Questions - Page 182

Narrator: Practice. Content questions. Directions. Listen to each prompt, then answer the question.

Narrator: 1. Listen to a professor, then answer the question.

Prof: For plants to survive, they must convert carbon dioxide into sugar using energy from the sun. This conversion process is called photosynthesis. Organisms that depend on photosynthesis for survival are called photoautotrophs. Plants, as well as algae and many species of bacteria, fall under this classification. These organisms are unique in that they are the only ones to produce their own food by photosynthesis, a chemically-complex process in which oxygen is a waste by-product. Suffice it to say, without photosynthesis, life on Earth would cease to exist.

Narrator: What is the main topic of the lecture?

Narrator: 2. Listen to a professor, then answer the question.

Prof: An algorithm is a process that performs a series of operations aimed at solving a problem. More specifically, an algorithm has a starting point followed by a sequence of well-defined instructions terminating at an end point. Algorithms lie at the heart of computer software. Software, as you know, is basically a sequence of instructions aimed at carrying out a task. That task is called a computation.

It is a process that begins with a set of initial conditions, called input, then provides an output, a result, based on a fixed set of rules or instructions. A more common form of algorithm is a recipe for, oh, I don't know—let's say brownies. The recipe tells you where to start, the steps to follow, and what the outcome will be. An algorithm, however, cannot stop you from eating them all.

Narrator: What is the focus of the lecture?

Narrator: **3. Listen to a professor, then answer the question.**

Prof: Archeologists agree that a major turning point in world history was the appearance of literate civilizations in southwest Asia and along the Nile River. This period dates from about the fourth millennium BCE to around 1,200 BCE. Yet before we proceed, we really need to define the term civilization. Within the word itself lies the root "civil" meaning to display the appropriate behavior. Yet this definition of civilization is far too broad, for what might be considered appropriate behavior in one society might be taboo in another. Simply put, archeologists apply the term civilization when describing literate, urbanized, state-level societies, the earliest of which were city-states in southwest Asia and along the Nile River. The wealth of these city-states was derived from many sources, a major one of which was agriculture. To record the buying and selling of a grain like wheat, a system of record keeping was developed, one in which marks and symbols were carved into tablets or pressed into clay. Primitive, indeed, but arguably the world's first spreadsheets. To understand them, one had to read thus with writing came reading. Soon taxes were being recorded and laws written. This, in turn, created a system of government officials to collect the tax and a military to enforce the laws. This was indeed a turning point. Suddenly, everyone knew their position in society based on what was written; thus, it can be said that the earliest civilizations were built on the written word, as is ours today.

Narrator: What is the main topic of the lecture?

Narrator: **4. Listen to a professor, then answer the question.**

Prof: Ancient Egyptians used a formal writing system called hieroglyphs. Hieroglyphs combine logographic as well as alphabetic elements. For years, scholars were unable to decipher the meaning of hieroglyphs. The Rosetta Stone changed all that. In 1799, a French soldier, part of Napoleon's expedition to Egypt, discovered it in a temple. On it was a decree by King Ptolemy V in engraved text. The decree is in three languages: Egyptian hieroglyphs, Egyptian demotic script, and ancient Greek. Scholars who knew ancient Greek suddenly had a means by which they could finally translate hieroglyphs. In 1801, the British defeated the French in Egypt and the Rosetta Stone fell into British hands, where it has remained ever since. This, then, has led to the debate about who actually owns the Rosetta Stone, a debate that persists to this day.

Narrator: What is the focus of the lecture?

Track #58 - Practice: Purpose Questions - Page 183

Narrator: Practice. Purpose questions. Directions. Listen to each prompt, then answer the question.

Narrator: 1. Listen to a professor, then answer the question.

Prof: Okay. A quick review. The goal of thinking. What is it? To make sense of the world. How do we do that? By acquiring knowledge. Okay, so how do we acquire knowledge? Good question. With the brain, obviously. But seriously. We acquire knowledge with tools—thinking tools. Last time we identified four of those tools: memory, association, reason, and pattern discernment and recognition. To that list add experience, invention, experimentation, and intuition. Right. So before we begin, jump in with any questions you might have.

Narrator: Why does the professor introduce four more thinking tools?

Narrator: 2. Listen to a professor, then answer the question.

Prof: It goes without saying that Frank Sinatra was in a league of his own. Who can deny his artistry and influence? Yet besides his dazzling blue eyes and self-effacing smile, what made teenage girls—bobby-soxers as they were called back in the 1940's—crazy about Frank Sinatra? One thing was his breathing technique. While singing, instead of taking a breath in the middle of a long phrase like singers of the day always did, Sinatra would sing through to the end without taking a breath. The bobby-soxers loved it. They felt as if Sinatra really knew the words and was talking directly to them. In other words, Sinatra's breathing technique was pure passion. That is one reason why a young Francis Albert Sinatra set the world on fire back in the 1940's. Another reason was his work ethic.

Narrator: Why does the professor describe Frank Sinatra's breathing style?

Narrator: 3. Listen to a professor, then answer the question.

Prof: So far, we've been talking about preindustrial societies, societies which were essentially agrarian-based with political and economic power concentrated in the hands of a king or despot. An industrial society, quite the contrary, is one in which power and economic influence are dispersed throughout society and, more importantly—and this is the point that needs stressing—industrial societies are based on fossil fuels; whereas, preindustrial societies are not.

Narrator: Why does the professor stress fossil fuels?

Narrator: 4. Listen to a professor, then answer the question.

Prof: This may come as a surprise, but hurricanes and tornadoes do not account for the most weather-related deaths in the United States. Heat and drought do. According to NOAA—the National Oceanographic and Atmospheric Administration—extreme heat is "one of the most underrated and least understood of the deadly weather phenomena." Why is this the case? First off, the danger is less obvious. Think about it. A mass of hot air settles over us and we think, okay, it's just another hot day. To cool off, our bodies perspire. The moisture evaporates. By doing so, it draws excess heat from our bodies. If we don't drink enough water, we perspire less and the excess heat stays in the body. As a result, our core body temperature rises dramatically and we risk death from heatstroke. This is what happened in Europe in 2003 when over 26,000 people died in the hottest summer on record.

Narrator: Why does the professor mention Europe in 2003?

Track #59 - Practice: Single-Answer Detail Questions - Pg. 184

Narrator: Practice. Single-answer detail questions. Directions. Listen to a lecture about education, then answer the questions.

Prof: 1 ➔ In America, public education had its genesis in the New England colonies of Massachusetts, Connecticut and New Hampshire. At the time, circa 1600, these colonies were settled by two main religious groups: the Puritans and the Congregationalists; both were Protestant, both were fiercely independent, both rejected the centralized power of Catholicism, and both shared the belief that educating children was critical to the survival of their beliefs; thus, the earliest form of public education in America was funded by the Protestant church with the tenets of Protestantism the core curriculum.

2 ➔ The first publicly supported high school in America, the Boston Latin School, was founded in 1635. Now, I need to be clear here. Publicly supported doesn't mean what it means today: a public-school system funded by tax dollars. Quite the contrary, back in 1635, public education meant that church money paid for books and teachers' salaries while students had to pay tuition. These so-called public schools, of which the Boston Latin School was the first, educated an elite, all-male student body in Latin and Greek, the humanities, and philosophy with an emphasis on religious studies, for it was assumed that the students would become teachers or ministers espousing the Protestant faith.

3 ➔ At the same time, immigrants were arriving in the New England colonies. These immigrants, many of whom were Catholic, soon came into conflict with the Puritans and the Congregationalists over the issue of public education. The Catholics viewed the English-dominated public education system as simply a way in which the English Protestants could impose their religious views. As a result, the Catholics rejected the Protestant-based, public-school system and created a system of private Catholic schools, a system which survives to this day.

4 ➔ As you can see, the educational system in colonial America was very much a religious conflict. Keep in mind, however, that these schools, for Catholics and Protestants alike, were for the sons of the rich and politically powerful. For those boys on the lower end of the social scale, charity or "common schools" were set up. While public money paid for books and teachers, students still had to pay tuition, money most simply did not have. Instead, most school-age boys became apprentices learning a trade. As for girls, they were educated at home by mothers and grandmothers. Girls learned how to cook and sew with the aim of being a good housewife; thus, the literacy rate among women was very low.

5 ➔ By the early nineteenth century, the common or public school system was in dire straits. The schools were poorly equipped, one-room buildings with poorly paid, poorly trained teachers. Students, if they attended classes, attended in winter and only for a few weeks. The rest of the time they worked in agriculture or in the growing number of factories, for the industrial revolution was picking up steam, particularly in big east coast cities like Boston, New York and Philadelphia.

6 ➔ In 1837, with the public-school system hitting rock bottom, Horace Mann, a social reformer and a powerful Massachusetts politician, decided enough was enough. Mann—a leader in the temperance movement and a builder of insane asylums—was appointed secretary of Massachusetts' newly created Board of Education, the first of its kind in America. Mann, believing that all children

should learn in common schools, set about reforming the public school system. He established institutes to train teachers. He increased teacher salaries, increased the school year to six months, and raised money for books and school construction. Mann pursued these reforms because he believed that public education would result in greater economic prosperity for the individual, the state and the country while teaching respect for private property. This, Mann argued, would decrease the crime rate, for the industrial revolution had created a rising class of urban poor. By providing public money for public schools, Mann viewed education as a means of controlling the crime rate; thus, "moral training", as Mann called it, was part of the curriculum along with standardized lessons and classroom drills. This, Mann also argued, would create greater equality for the masses and greater economic prosperity for all.

Narrator: Now get ready to answer the questions.

1. The first public schools in America were...
2. In which year was the Boston Latin School founded?
3. According to the lecture, the literacy rate for women in colonial America was...
4. What was the condition of the public school system in 1837?
5. How did Horace Mann change the school year?
6. According to the lecture, what did Horace Mann believe?

Track #60 - Practice: Multi-Answer Detail Questions - Page 185

Narrator: Practice. Multi-answer detail questions. Directions. Listen to each prompt, then answer the question.

Narrator: 1. Listen then answer the question. This is a 2-point question.

Prof: The Roman Army was a highly-disciplined and highly-feared military force that, by 300 BCE, had made the Republic of Rome an unrivalled empire controlling eastern Europe and much of the Mediterranean. The basic unit of the Roman Army was the legion. A legion was comprised of approximately 4,200 legionnaires. These men, both professional and conscript, were each equipped with three weapons: a pugio, a long dagger or knife, a gladius, a short thrusting sword (from which the word "gladiator" is derived), and a pilum, a two-meter javelin. With a shield for protection, and dressed in body armor, the legionnaire was a killing machine. Imagine the terror the tribes of Europe felt when the Roman army came marching over the hill.

Narrator: What three weapons did a Roman legionnaire carry? Select three.

Narrator: 2. Listen then answer the question. This is a 2-point question.

Prof: A business plan has three essential parts starting with a formal statement that outlines a set of specific goals. Those goals will be either for profit or not-for profit. A for-profit business plan will describe goals aimed at the creation of wealth; whereas, a not-for profit business plan will focus on a mission statement in order to receive tax-exempt status from the government. Next, the business plan will describe the reason why the stated goals are attainable. Depending on the plan, those reasons will be supported by a market analysis and a competitor analysis, and whatever research is necessary to attain the stated goal. Finally, a business plan will state how the business will go about achieving those goals. In other words, a plan of action. Let's begin by defining the first part of a business plan: defining the goals.

Narrator: What are the essential parts of a business plan? Select three.

Narrator: 3. Listen then answer the question. This is a 2-point question.

Prof: A critical part of a marine biologist's research is to compile data by observing events and by collecting samples. However, because the oceans are so vast, and because most of what is going on is happening below the waves, marine biologists must devise ways to observe and collect samples. Some use nets and dredges for gathering samples while others use computers for compiling data. Still others perform experiments in labs designed to recreate specific ocean environments. However, the best way, and frankly the only way, to observe and collect data is to get your feet wet. In other words, you've got to enter the ocean itself and see things with the naked eye. One way is to dive in scuba gear or in specially equipped research submersibles. The other is to employ specially designed video equipment with bait to attract the animal in question. No matter what the method of research, the goal of the marine biologist—it goes without saying—is to collect data in a manner that leaves the marine environment undisturbed.

Narrator: According to the professor, the best ways to study marine life are... Select three.

Narrator: 4. Listen then answer the question. This is a 1-point question.

Prof: If you walk around New York City today, with its skyscrapers and densely packed districts, it's hard to imagine that during the American Revolutionary War, two battles took place there in the fall of 1776. The first was the Battle of Long Island, also known as the Battle of Brooklyn or the Battle of Brooklyn Heights. This battle was the first major battle of the American Revolutionary War, coming soon after the United States declared Independence from Britain. At the Battle of Brooklyn Heights, a superior British force attacked and forced the Continental Army, led by George Washington, to retreat to present-day Harlem on Manhattan Island. There, the Americans and the British fought again with the British withdrawing to regroup. Historians call this engagement the Battle of Harlem Heights. Washington, fearing a British trap at Harlem, retreated north to present-day White Plains.

Narrator: What were the first major battles of the American Revolutionary War? Select two.

Track #61 - Practice: Question-First Function Questions - Pg. 186

Narrator: Practice. Question-first function questions. Directions. Answer each question based on what is stated or implied.

Narrator: **1. Why does the professor say this?**

Prof: It goes without saying that Frank Sinatra was in a league of his own.

Narrator: 2. Why does the professor say this?

Prof: No matter what the method of research, the goal of the marine biologist—it goes without saying—is to collect data in a manner that leaves the marine environment undisturbed.

Narrator: **3. Why does the professor say this?**

Prof: Yet this definition of civilization is far too broad, for what might be considered appropriate behavior in one society might be taboo in another.

Narrator: **4. Why does the professor say this?**

Prof: If you walk around New York City today, with its skyscrapers and densely packed districts, it's hard to imagine that during the American Revolutionary War, two battles took place there in the fall of 1776.

Narrator: **5. Why does the professor say this?**

Prof: This may come as a surprise, but hurricanes and tornadoes do not account for the most weather-related deaths in the United States.

Narrator: **6. Why does the professor say this?**

Prof: Census taking, however, is nothing new. Many ancient civilizations regularly took a census of population, for example Rome. Because Rome had a large standing army, it needed money and men. By periodically taking a census, the Roman government knew how much tax money it could raise for the army and the available manpower it could draw from.

Narrator: **7. Why does the professor say this?**

Prof: Global warming has brought new and invasive species. One such species, the Asian hornet, has spread across Europe and into Britain. The Asian hornet raids hives for bee larvae and the bees are powerless to stop this invader.

Narrator: **8. Why does the professor say this?**

Prof: On December 11, 2008, the business world was rocked by news no one could believe. Even now, people are still shaking their heads.

Track #62 - Practice: Segment-First Function Questions - Pg. 188

Narrator: Practice. Segment-first function questions. Directions. Answer each question based on what is stated or implied.

Narrator: **1. Listen to part of a lecture, then answer the question.**

Prof: In 1801, the British defeated the French in Egypt and the Rosetta Stone fell into British hands, where it has remained ever since. This, then, has led to the debate about who actually owns the Rosetta Stone, a debate that persists to this day.

Narrator: Why does the professor say this?

Prof: This, then, has led to the debate about who actually owns the Rosetta Stone, a debate that persists to this day.

Narrator: 2. Listen to part of a lecture, then answer the question.

Prof: Last time we identified four of those tools: memory, association, reason, and pattern discernment and recognition. To that list add experience, invention, experimentation, and intuition. Right. So before we begin, jump in with any questions you might have.

Narrator: Why does the professor say this?

Prof: Right. So before we begin, jump in with any questions you might have.

Narrator: 3. Listen to part of a lecture, then answer the question.

Prof: It goes without saying that Frank Sinatra was in a league of his own. Who can deny his artistry and influence? Yet besides his dazzling blue eyes and self-effacing smile, what made teenage girls—bobby-soxers as they were called back in the 1940's—crazy about Frank Sinatra?

Narrator: Why does the professor say this?

Prof: Yet besides his dazzling blue eyes and self-effacing smile, what made teenage girls—bobby-soxers as they were called back in the 1940's—crazy about Frank Sinatra?

Narrator: 4. Listen to part of a lecture, then answer the question.

Prof: A more common form of algorithm is a recipe for, oh, I don't know—let's say brownies. The recipe tells you where to start, the steps to follow, and what the outcome will be. An algorithm, however, cannot stop you from eating them all.

Narrator: Why does the professor say this?

Prof: Oh, I don't know—let's say brownies.

Track #63 - Practice: Direct-Attitude Questions - Pg. 189

Narrator: Practice. Direct-attitude questions. Directions. Listen to each prompt, then answer the question.

Narrator: 1. Listen then answer the question.

Prof: Many buy into the argument that corporate rehiring is an indication that the economy is finally turning around. However, corporate hiring figures are only one way of gauging economic health. In my estimation, a better indicator of a market turnaround is home sales. Why home sales? Because the American economy is based on the construction of houses. Think about it. Manufacturing is linked to the home. You buy a home, you need a car—and a washing machine, and a lawnmower, and a computer, and a flat-screen TV. And on and on. Once homes start selling, only then will I believe that the economy has turned the corner.

Narrator: The professor thinks corporate rehiring is...

Narrator: **2. Listen then answer the question.**

Prof: Offshore drilling? To meet our energy needs and free us from foreign oil? Sorry, but the jury is still out on that one.

Narrator: What is the professor's position on drilling for oil offshore?

Narrator: **3. Listen then answer the question.**

Prof: Thomas Edison falls into two camps. You either love him for his achievements or hate him for his complete lack of scruples. All that aside, no one can argue with the fact that he coined some pretty memorable lines, such as this one: "Genius is one-percent inspiration and ninety-nine percent perspiration."

Narrator: What is the professor's view of Thomas Edison?

Narrator: **4. Listen then answer the question.**

Prof: To risk beating a dead horse, I will say it again. Despite what the lobbyists say, genetically-modified food is not fit for human consumption. Period.

Narrator: The professor thinks that genetically modified food is...

Track #64 - Practice: Inferred-Attitude Questions - Page 190

Narrator: Practice. Inferred-attitude questions. Directions. Listen to each prompt, then answer the question.

Narrator: **1. Listen then answer the question.**

Prof: Put a killer whale and a great white shark together, and which one will come out the winner? That answer was made clear off the Farallon Islands in October, 1997. The Farallons are home to thousands of elephant seals, a rich food source for great whites. On that October day, a great white was hunting when it was attacked and eaten by a killer whale. This incident, captured on video, turned conventional wisdom on its head: the great white does not rule the waves after all. Even more shocking was the fact that on that very same day, the one hundred-or-so great whites that had been hunting off the Farallons at the time of the killer whale attack suddenly disappeared. Vanished like scared rats. Even now I'm shaking my head.

Narrator: How does the professor feel about what happened off the Farallon Islands?

Narrator: **2. Listen then answer the question.**

Prof: As a computer company, Apple, with its cutting-edge products, is the envy of its rivals, a position once held by Microsoft, a company founded by Bill Gates, a Harvard drop-out and the focus of today's lecture.

Narrator: What is the professor's view of Microsoft?

Narrator: **3. Listen then answer the question.**

Prof: Perhaps the greatest mystery concerning Cro-Magnon man is why did he paint on the walls of caves? Not just sketches but enormous murals of wild horses and deer, painted with such masterly detail they practically come alive even after 20,000 years. Were these paintings part of a shamanistic ritual? Was Cro-Magnon man simply bored and looking for distraction, or do we see in all the bison and aurox, man's first attempt at asking the question we still ask to this day: Who am I? Of course, seeing the paintings in person is best; however, their power is not diminished even in these slides.

Narrator: What is the professor's opinion of Cro-Magnon cave art?

Narrator: **4. Listen then answer the question.**

Prof: I know. I know. Some say President John F. Kennedy was assassinated by Cuban Nationalists for failing to invade communist Cuba while others claim Kennedy was assassinated by the military-industrial complex seeking to profit from the Viet Nam conflict, a conflict Kennedy was, at the time of his death, determined to end. I also know that if I had a dime for every time I heard those two theories, I'd be rich by now.

Narrator: The professor believes that...

Track #65 - Practice: Inferred-Action Questions - Page 191

Narrator: Practice. Inferred-action questions. Directions. Listen to each prompt, then answer the question.

Narrator: **1. Listen then answer the question.**

Prof: 1 ➜ There seems to be some confusion as to the difference between slang and jargon. Remember that jargon is a type slang. The difference is that I can learn jargon—for example computer jargon—and I can become a systems engineer or an app designer. Moreover—and this is key—jargon is inclusive. That means I can learn computer jargon, invented words like virus and mouse, and computer professionals will accept me. In other words, learn the code, join the group; thus, jargon is inclusive
2 ➜ Slang, in its purest sense, however, is an excluding code. I can learn, for example, all the rap slang I want, such as "Yo, s'up homey? Dawg, bust a move!" or "Crib cost beaucoup Benjamins," but will Fifty Cent or Lil Wayne or Snoop Dog accept me into their group, their gang? After all, I know the language, the code, right? Not likely. In this light, slang is like a wall, a wall of invented words designed for two purposes: to exclude me from the group and to keep outsiders—other gangs and the police—from figuring out what we, our gang, are saying. Of course, rap slang is only one kind of slang. Teenagers use slang all the time, skateboarders in particular. Any skateboarders out there? Ah, yes. Quite a few.

Narrator: What will the professor probably do next?

Narrator: 2. Listen then answer the question.

Prof: While singing, instead of taking a breath in the middle of a long phrase like singers of the day always did, Sinatra would sing through to the end without taking a breath. The bobby-soxers loved it. They felt as if Sinatra really knew the words and was talking directly to them. In other words, Sinatra's breathing technique was pure passion. That is one reason why a young Francis Albert Sinatra set the world on fire back in the 1940's. Another reason was his work ethic.

Narrator: What will the professor talk about next?

Narrator: 3. Listen then answer the question.

Prof: That brings us to the end of the lecture. Just to recap, napping for twenty-minutes each day restores energy, increases productivity, and boosts memory. In Greece, researchers found that men who napped three times a week had a thirty-seven percent lower risk of heart-related deaths. The benefits of napping speak for themselves. Personally, I do it all the time. That said, you know where I'll be. If you have a question, email me.

Narrator: What will the professor probably do next?

Narrator: 4. Listen then answer the question.

Prof: The process of making a hand axe, you might think, is no big deal. After all, what's so hard about knocking the sides off a round rock to make a razor-sharp cutting edge, right? I mean, if some Cro-Magnon guy could do it way back when, I can do it too. Easier said than done. Watch.

Narrator: What will the professor demonstrate?

Track #66 - Practice: Ordering Questions - Page 192

Narrator: Practice. Ordering questions. Directions. Listen to each prompt, then answer the question.

Narrator: 1. Listen then answer the question.

Prof: In the fall, when a sockeye salmon is approximately five-years old, it leaves the Pacific Ocean, where it has grown to maturity, and returns to the home river where it was born. Once in the home river—how sockeye return to the river of their birth remains a mystery—the sockeye navigates upstream and spawns in shallow water, then dies. In a few months, between January and April, the eggs turn into alevin, a tiny fish with the yolk sack still attached. The alevin live off the yolk and grow into fry. After a period of growth, they will head downstream in late spring, making the transition from the fresh water of the home river to the salt water of the ocean as smolt. Once in the ocean, the smolt will grow into adults, then return to the home river in five years to begin the cycle all over again.

Narrator: The professor talks about the sockeye salmon. Put the life cycle of the sockeye in the correct order. This is a 2-point question.

Narrator: **2. Listen then answer the question.**

Prof: In the world of computer hackers, one name stands out: Jonathan James, a.k.a. cOmrade. Between August and October of 1999, James, aged 16, hacked into the computers of BellSouth. Next, he hacked the Miami-Dade school system. Soon after, he hit the computers of the Defense Reduction Agency, a division of the United States Department of Defense. James installed a sniffer, a piece of hidden software that intercepted thousands of passwords, giving him almost complete access to Department of Defense computers, including the computers of NASA. From the NASA computers, James downloaded the software that controlled the temperature and the humidity on the Space Station. On January 26, 2000, James was arrested and incarcerated, making him the first juvenile to be jailed for computer hacking. Why did he do it? As James himself said, "I was just looking around, playing around. What was fun for me was a challenge to see what I could pull off." James committed suicide in May, 2008 after federal authorities accused him of being part of a conspiracy that had committed the largest computer identify theft in American history, the hacking into of the computers of retailers TJ Maxx, Marshalls, Boston Market, Barnes and Noble, and many others.

Narrator: The professor talks about Jonathan James. Put James' computer hacking career in the proper order. This is a 2-point question.

Narrator: **3. Listen then answer the question.**

Prof: One of the more tragic figures in American literary history is F. Scott Fitzgerald. Fitzgerald died in Hollywood on December 21, 1940, at the age of 44. He'd been trying to revive his career by writing screenplays which he despised. Yet, always desperate for money, Fitzgerald had no choice but to serve Hollywood. No longer was he the golden boy whose short stories of rebellious young men and women defined the Jazz Age, a name Fitzgerald himself had coined to describe the 1920's. In 1920, at age 25, Fitzgerald rocketed to the top of the literary world with his first novel, *This Side of Paradise*. Soon after, the Saturday Evening Post was paying him $4,000.00 for his short stories, an incredible sum even by today's standards. In 1925, Fitzgerald published *The Great Gatsby*. Fitzgerald went on to write *Tender is the Night* in 1934, but it failed to sell. With the Depression eclipsing the Jazz Age, with his short stories no longer in demand, and burdened by a mentally-unstable wife, Fitzgerald hit rock bottom. In 1937, he settled in Los Angeles where he landed a six-month writing contract with MGM yet he continued to drink heavily while producing nothing of substance. Fitzgerald died believing he was a failure while *The Great Gatsby* lives on, a novel many critics consider the greatest American novel ever written.

Narrator: The professor describes the life of F. Scott Fitzgerald. Put Fitzgerald's writing career in the proper order. This is a 2-point question.

Narrator: **4. Listen then answer the question.**

Prof: The sand people of the Kalahari Desert are the only tribe left on Earth who use what many scientists consider to be the oldest method of hunting known to man: the persistence hunt. On foot, under a scorching African sun and armed only with spears, the hunters locate a herd of kudu, kudu being a species of large antelope. The hunters then move the herd using only hand signals to communicate. By continually moving the herd, the hunters tire their prey.

Hours later, the hunters will isolate one animal, usually a male whose heavy horns have caused him to tire faster than the females. At this point, with the sun pounding down, and a kudu separated from the herd, one hunter, the fastest of the group, continues the hunt alone. This hunter, called "the runner," chases the lone kudu for hours until, exhausted from the heat, it stops to rest. It is then that the runner moves in for the kill.

Narrator: The professor talks about the persistence hunt. Put the steps of the persistence hunt in order. This is a 2-point question.

Track #67 - Practice: Yes-No Questions - Page 194

Narrator: Practice. Yes-no Questions. Directions. Listen to each prompt, then answer the question.

Narrator: **1. Listen then answer the question.**

Prof: Despite its ominous sounding name, Black Friday is not the day the world ends. Instead, it is the traditional beginning of the Christmas-shopping season in the United States. An east-coast term dating back to 1966, Black Friday is now a nationwide event. It is not an official holiday, per se; however, because it falls on the Friday between Thanksgiving Day and the weekend after Thanksgiving, many workers take Friday off. For retailers, Black Friday is a bellwether. If consumer spending is up on Black Friday, it generally means that consumer spending over the Christmas period will also be up. This will be good news for retailers and manufacturers alike. Following hot on the heels of Black Friday is Cyber Monday, the official start of the online Christmas-shopping season. Smart consumers have learned to wait for Cyber Monday to buy big-ticket items like TVs and computers, for Cyber Monday bargains are generally better than anything offered by traditional Black Friday brick-and-mortar retailers.

Narrator: The professor describes Black Friday. Indicate whether each of the following is true of Black Friday in the United States. This is a 3-point question.

Narrator: **2. Listen then answer the question.**

Prof: 1 ➔ Microcredit is a system of finance wherein banks lend very small amounts of money to the extremely poor, people who would have no access to credit otherwise. The idea originated with Muhammad Yunus, a Bangladeshi economist. The result was the Grameen Bank of Bangladesh. The bank extends microloans, or grameencredit, to the impoverished without collateral. The poor, in turn, use these loans to generate income through self-employment. A key point to remember is that the loans are for groups only, the average size of which is five. The members can choose who will participate in the group but they cannot be related. This form of group financing is called solidarity lending. This approach spreads the cost of repaying the loan across a group of borrowers. It also discourages free riders while encouraging group decision making and financial responsibility. As a result, the group builds up wealth and exits poverty. It is a radical approach to financing that has proven successful in Bangladesh and in India. In fact, microcredit is now so popular that many banks worldwide offer microloans. For his work, Muhammad Yunus and Grameen Bank were jointly awarded the Nobel Peace Prize for economics in 2006. 2 ➔ Recently, however, microcredit has come under a cloud due to unscrupulous lending practices whereby banks—without questioning the borrower's ability to repay—lend borrowers huge, high-interest rate loans they cannot possibly repay. As a result, an alarming number of borrowers have simply walked away from their loans. The same thing happened in America in 2007 when mortgage lenders extended huge, high-interest loans to borrowers who could not possibly repay them. The result was the near collapse of the global economy.

Narrator: The professor talks about microcredit. Indicate whether each of the following is true of microcredit. This is a 3-point question.

Narrator: 3. Listen then answer the question.

Prof: As a political movement, the Situationist International combined Marxist ideology and Surrealism to wage war against consumerism. The Situationists, founded in 1957, argued that mainstream capitalism, through the mass media, was destroying the experience of daily life through false images, the worst offender being consumer advertising. The result, the Situationists believed, was that the individual was no longer a participant in life but a slave controlled by false images created by capitalist interests. The group's main proponent was Guy Debord. Debord argued that authentic social life had been replaced with false representations. Debord wanted to wake up the spectator drugged by advertising. The Situationists did so by creating "situations," mass events in which people turned their backs on the mass media and came together as one. Only through situations, Debord argued, could individuals free themselves from capitalism and, thereby, reclaim the freedom of experiencing life in its original sense, namely as an individual free of the capitalist influence. The largest and most famous situation was the General Strike in France in 1968. Today, the Situationist International, having long since dissolved, has found new voice in various anarchist movements.

Narrator: The professor talks about the Situationist International. Indicate whether each of the following is true of the Situationist International. This is a 3-point question.

Narrator: 4. Listen then answer the question.

Prof: 1 ➔ Hybrid cars are all the rage these days. Yet are they all that fuel-efficient? Will they actually save you money in the long run? And are they really environmentally friendly? Let's take a closer look under the hood.
2 ➔ A hybrid car is basically two engines: one gas, one electric. A hybrid is engineered this way to be fuel efficient, averaging 50 miles to the gallon. However, those two engines, plus the huge battery in the back, mean that the cost of buying a hybrid is substantially higher than a good old gas car. A regular gas car will cost on average $4,000.00 less than a hybrid. If the hybrid costs $18,000.00, let's say, then the owner—to justify the hybrid as a fuel-saver—must somehow make up the $4,000.00 difference in fuel costs. What's happening in the news, even as we speak? That's right. The price of gas is once again going up. If gas prices go up, it's going to be virtually impossible for the hybrid owner to make up the $4,000.00 cost difference. So why buy a hybrid? That's the $64,000.00 question.
3 ➔ And, of course, there's always the hybrid's dirty little secret: the nickel it takes to make a hybrid's battery. Where does that nickel—all one-hundred-and-seventeen pounds of it—come from? Canada. How is it extracted? By digging massive holes in the Earth. Not very environmentally-friendly, I'm afraid.

Narrator: The professor talks about hybrid cars. According to the professor, which of the following are true of hybrid cars? This is a 3-point question.

Track #68 - Practice: Connecting Questions - Page 198

Narrator: Practice. Connecting questions. Listen to each prompt, then answer the question.

Narrator: 1. Listen then answer the question.

Prof: 1 ➔ Today, we'll begin our look at three major battles that changed the course of history. After a brief intro of each, we'll analyze each in depth and identify how that military event determined the social landscape as we now know it. The battles we'll focus on are Marathon, Teutoburg Forest, and Waterloo.
2 ➔ First Marathon. The Battle of Marathon took place in 490 BCE. Persian King Darius, attempting to conquer Greece, landed on Greek soil near the town of Marathon with a massive army. The much smaller Greek army, using hoplites or citizen soldiers, pushed the invader back into the sea. This victory preserved Greece and gave us classical Greece as we know it.
3 ➔ Next, we'll explore the Battle of Teutoburg Forest. This engagement occurred in 9 CE. By that date, Rome had successfully conquered western Europe and was turning east with the aim of conquering what is today's Germany east of the Rhine River. Determined to subdue the Germanic tribes once and for all, three Legions under Varus marched east of the Rhine and right into a trap. The Germanic tribes, led by Arminius, an ex-Roman cavalry officer, annihilated the Roman army to a man. Historians believe that as many as 20,000 Roman soldiers died. Historians also believe that this—the complete destruction of an elite Roman army—marked the start of the decline of the Roman Empire
4 ➔ Finally, we'll travel to Waterloo, a small town in Belgium. There, on June 18, 1815, Napoleon Bonaparte, back from exile—and determined to rule as Emperor once again—was defeated by a combined British and Prussian force. It was a close battle. As the British commander, the Duke of Wellington, said, it was "A near miss thing."

Narrator: The professor describes three military battles that changed history. Match each battle with each defeated military leader. This is a 2-point question.

Narrator: 2. Listen then answer the question.

Prof: 1 ➔ Herbalism is a traditional plant-based medicine. It is also known as botanical medicine, herbology, and phytotherapy. Herbalism has a long history stretching back to the dawn of time. Today, over 122 compounds used in modern medicine have been derived from plant sources. Some of the more common herbal medicines in use today are milk thistle, a thistle extract used for centuries to maintain liver health, aloe vera, a traditional remedy for burns and wounds, and willow bark, a tree bark extract the Greeks used for aches and pains, the main ingredient of which has been synthesized into today's aspirin.
2 ➔ Despite herbalism's long tradition, doubt remains as to the efficacy of plant-based medicines. Moreover, the dangers are all too real. For example, comfrey can cause liver damage and ginseng can cause insomnia and schizophrenia. Moreover, unscrupulous manufacturers can vary the quality and quantity of the herb in question which, in turn, poses another danger. What should you do? Consult your physician and proceed with caution.

Narrator: The professor identifies three herbs used for plant-based medicine. Match each herb with its corresponding application. This is a 2-point question.

Narrator: 3. Listen then answer the question.

Prof: There are two types of cells: eukaryotic and prokaryotic. Prokaryote cells are simpler and smaller. They have three architectural regions: the exterior, consisting of projecting flagella and pili used for motion; the cell envelope, a plasma membrane giving the cell rigidity and serving as a protective filter, and the cytoplasmic region, a region that contains the genome condensed in a nucleoid. Eukaryotic cells are much larger than prokaryotic cells yet retain a similar structure. The major difference between the two cell types is that the interior of a eukaryotic cell is divided into membrane-bound compartments in which specific metabolic processes occur.

Narrator: The professor describes the parts of a prokaryote cell. Connect each part of a prokaryote cell with its corresponding function. This is a 2-point question.

Narrator: 4. Listen then answer the question.

Prof: In the fall, when a sockeye salmon is approximately five-years old, it leaves the Pacific Ocean, where it has grown to maturity, and returns to the home river where it was born. Once in the home river—how sockeye return to the river of their birth remains a mystery—the sockeye navigates upstream and spawns in shallow water, then dies. In a few months, between January and April, the eggs turn into alevin, a tiny fish with the yolk sack still attached. The alevin live off the yolk and grow into fry. After a period of growth, they will head downstream in late spring, making the transition from the fresh water of the home river to the salt water of the ocean as smolt. Once in the ocean, the smolt will grow into adults, then return to the home river in five years to begin the cycle all over again.

Narrator: The professor illustrates the life cycle of the sockeye salmon. Match each stage of the sockeye salmon's life cycle with a corresponding description of that stage. This is a 2-point question.

Professor-Students – Pg. 200

Track #69 - Sample Discussion - Page 203

Narrator: Sample discussion. Professor-Students. Directions. Listen to a sample discussion, then answer the questions on the next page. Do not look at the questions. On test day, you will not see the questions as you listen. Remember to answer all the questions. You will not be penalized for a wrong answer. Now listen to part of a discussion in an environmental class.

Prof: Today, we're going to discuss a man-made problem that's impacting oceans worldwide, a problem with no solution in sight. That problem is right in front you. When you're finished with them, hopefully—as concerned and responsible citizens—you'll recycle so they won't end up on a Pacific island or a Cape Cod beach. Of course, you all know what I'm talking about: the ubiquitous polyethylene terephthalate. That said, let me begin by giving you a few eye-popping stats. Every year, Americans buy over 50 billion—yes, billion—bottles of water. That equates to 1,500 bottles consumed every second—every second. That number beggars the imagination. Of that number, eight out of ten end up in a landfill with the remaining twenty-percent recycled. And those numbers are only in America. What about the rest of the world? What about countries that can't afford to build expensive recycling plants? And what about all those bottles that are not recycled or dumped in landfills, in America and worldwide? Where does all that polyethylene terephthalate end up? Carol?

Carol: In the oceans.

Prof: Exactly. Can you elaborate on the homework?

Carol: Sure. According to the reading, there's this huge floating patch of garbage in the North Pacific. It's made up mostly of plastic bottles, but you can also find fish nets and micro pellets used for abrasive cleaning, plus all the stuff tossed off freighters and cruise ships. All this garbage is being swept along on what's called the North Pacific gyre.

Prof: Sorry, what exactly is that? A gyre?

Carol: It's the prevailing ocean current. In the North Pacific, the gyre moves west along the equator, then up past Japan to Alaska, then down the west coast of North America to the equator again. It's kind of like water spinning in a toilet bowl.

Prof: Good. So what's the connection between the North Pacific gyre and pelagic plastic?

Ann: Sorry, professor, what does pelagic mean again?

Prof: It means living or occurring at sea. The albatross, for example, is a pelagic bird. Carol?

Carol: Right, so where was I? Okay, so the stuff, I mean, you know, all that pelagic plastic, is swept along clockwise by the gyre. Eventually all that plastic junk finds its way into the center of the gyre and becomes stationary, you know, just sits there in an area called the Horse Latitudes, this area of calm in the center of the gyre. Years ago sailors would get trapped there due to a lack of wind and current. Today, it's basically one big, continuously-fed garbage dump in which pelagic plastic is the prevailing contaminant.

Prof: And it isn't going anywhere. In fact, it's spreading due to the decomposing nature of the contaminants themselves. Ann, can you jump in here and talk about the photodegradation process?

Ann: So when all this floating plastic is exposed to the sun, it begins to photodegrade until it reaches the molecular level. For example, take this book. Let's say it's floating in the center of the gyre, okay? The first thing to go are the covers, then the pages decompose freeing all the words. Next, the words break apart into letters. Finally, the ink in the letters photodecomposes into molecules. All that ends up in the gyre forming this thick, soupy liquid full of floating plastic particles that look like confetti.

Prof: A sea of confetti. That's a good way to put it. Beautiful, I'm sure, what with all that colored plastic floating around, but deadly. Very. All that particulate matter? It doesn't sink. Instead, it stays in the upper water column where it poses a significant threat to endemic wildlife. Pelagic birds, for example, consume the particulate matter mistaking it for food. They, in turn, feed it to their young who die of starvation or are poisoned by the toxic nature of polyethylene terephthalate. Other contaminants identified in the patch are PCB, DDT and PAH. When ingested, some of these toxins imitate estradiol which, as you know, is a naturally occurring estrogenic hormone secreted mainly by the ovaries. You can imagine the effect these toxins have on the reproduction systems of endemic species, such as whales. Fish too ingest the decomposed plastic and become contaminated.

Carol: Professor, is it possible to clean it up?

Prof: So far? No. The particulate matter is so small, you need extremely fine nets—micronets basically—to scoop it up. But even if we had such nets, remember, the

North Pacific is vast. It would take an armada constantly going back and forth to even put a dent in all that plastic while at the same time, new plastic—tons of it—is entering the gyre every day. How many bottles of water do Americans drink every year?

Carol: Fifty billion.

Prof: Precisely. And that statistic is already out of date.

Ann: That's a lot of garbage.

Prof: It is. And the thing is, we don't even know how big the patch is. Satellites can't pick up the particulate matter because it's too small. Not only that but when you're parked in the middle of it on a boat or a ship, you can't see it. The particulate matter is that small. So, how big is the great North Pacific garbage patch? Well, some say it's the size of Texas. Others claim it's twice the size of the U.S. Big no matter how you cut it. Okay, so that's the North Pacific. Worldwide how many gyres are there?

Carol: Five.

Prof: So if the center of the North Pacific gyre is one huge, floating garbage dump, what does that tell us about the other four gyres?

Narrator: Now get ready to answer the questions. Answer each question based on what is stated or implied in the discussion.

1. What is the discussion mainly about?
2. What is the purpose of the discussion?

3. Why does the professor say this?

Prof: That number beggars the imagination.

Narrator: 4. Which pelagic species does the professor mention? Select three. This is a 2-point question.

Narrator: 5. The professor describes how plastic becomes part of the eco-system. Put those steps in order. This is a 2-point question.

Narrator: 6. In the lecture, the professor describes the Horse Latitudes. Indicate whether each of the following is a characteristic of the Horse Latitudes. This is a 3-point question.

Track #70 - Practice: Discussion #1 - Page 206

Narrator: Practice. Discussion one. Directions. Listen to a sample discussion, then answer the questions on the next page. Do not look at the questions. On test day, you will not see the questions as you listen. Remember to answer all the questions. You will not be penalized for a wrong answer. Now listen to part of a discussion in a computer class.

Prof: Welcome everybody. Hope you had a good weekend. Today, we're going to start with Ann. Ann was assigned the task of researching malware. Ann? What did you come up with?

Ann: A lot, actually. I'm sure you all know what malware means, but just in case, malware is short for malicious software. It's software designed with the purpose of entering your computer without your permission. It's like somebody suddenly enters your house or apartment and starts checking the place out. By the way, if you have any questions, just stop me. Okay? Great. So where was I? Ah, right. Malware. Malware comes in all shapes and sizes. There are viruses, Trojan horses, spyware, adware, scareware. Most of it is spread by the internet. Here's a great fact I found. According to Symantec, there's more malware being released every year than legitimate software.

Prof:	Ann, where did it all start?
Ann:	You mean, what was the first piece of malware?
Prof:	Yes. Were you able to find out?
Ann:	I was. It was a virus, actually. Starting around 1949, computer scientists began writing about computer viruses and how they could reproduce like human viruses. The first computer virus, you know, the first real piece of code, didn't appear until 1972. That was the Creeper Virus.
Betty:	1972? Was the internet even around then?
Ann:	No, it wasn't. Not as we know it. Back then, they had something called ARPANET. That's short for Advanced Research Projects Agency Network. It all started during the Cold War in the 1950's. The U.S. military needed a way to make sure that its military computers stayed connected if attacked, so the government got all these guys from Harvard and MIT to design an interconnected information system. They did and called it ARPANET. ARPANET is basically the start of the internet as we know it. Anyway, a guy named Bob Thomas was working on ARPANET when he created the Creeper virus. He did it as an experiment to see if it would work, and it did. He sent it to computers on ARPANET and it started reproducing. However, it never left ARPANET and was harmless. Like I said, it was just an experiment. The first computer virus to appear outside a lab was the Elk Clone. It was created by Richard Skrenta in 1981. The Elk Clone attacked Apple computers.
Prof:	Ann, how did it get on Apple computers in the first place?
Ann:	By floppy disk. Back then, people shared them and that's how the Elk Clone spread. When it infected a computer, it would display a poem. Pretty tame, really. In1986, the first PC virus, the Brain, was created by the Farooq Alvi Brothers. And get this. They created it as a way of preventing the medical software they'd developed from being pirated. If you copied their software off the internet, or wherever, you'd get a warning saying something like, "Warning! You've just been infected. Call us for the vaccination."
Prof:	So what's the difference between a virus and a Trojan horse?
Ann:	A computer virus can reproduce just like, say, the flu virus. You know the flu virus is invading your body when you feel really sick. That's because the virus is overwhelming your body's defense system. It's the same with computer viruses. They reproduce and overwhelm the host computer. That's what happened to me once. I got a virus that made all the words on my screen melt.
Betty	How did you get it?
Ann:	Probably on a flash drive. That's how a lot of viruses travel, by portable media.
Betty:	So what did you do?
Ann:	I had to reformat my hard drive and reload all my programs.
Betty:	Drag.
Ann:	Tell me about it. A Trojan horse, on the other hand, is a piece of malware designed not just to mess up your computer but to control it without your knowing it. Trojan horses often show up as legitimate links in emails. This tricks the user into opening the link just like the Trojan horse the Greeks used to trick the Trojans into opening Troy. And we all know what happened to the Trojans, don't we?
Prof:	And once in a host computer, then what?
Ann:	It can do any number of things, like start sending spam to everyone on your email list or downloading bank files and passwords.
Betty:	So let me see if I've got this straight. A Trojan horse seeks to control or steal from a host computer, whereas a virus simply disrupts or crashes a computer. Correct?
Ann:	You got it.

Narrator: Now get ready to answer the questions. Answer each question based on what is stated or implied in the discussion.

    1. What is the discussion mainly about?
    2. What is the purpose of the discussion?

    3. Why does the student say this?

Student: And we all know what happened to the Trojans, don't we?

    4. The student describes the history of computer viruses. Put that history in order. This is a 2-point question.
    5. In the discussion, the student describes Trojan horses and computer viruses. Identify the characteristics of each. This is a 3-point question.

    6. Listen to part of the discussion, then answer the question.

Betty: So what did you do?
Ann: I had to reformat my hard drive and reload all my programs.
Betty: Drag.

Narrator: Why does the student say this?

Betty: Drag.

Track #71 - Practice: Discussion #2 - Page 208

Narrator: Practice. Discussion two. Directions. Listen to a sample discussion, then answer the questions on the next page. Do not look at the questions. On test day, you will not see the questions as you listen. Remember to answer all the questions. You will not be penalized for a wrong answer. Now listen to part of a discussion in a biology class.

Prof: Homeostasis. We talked about it last class. Before we push on, however, let's revisit what we know. Who wants to start us off? Linda?
Linda: In a nutshell, homeostasis is a process—a system-regulating process—that helps an organism maintain a stable internal environment or balance. That system can be either open or closed.
Prof: Good. Very succinct. Can you give us an example of a closed system?
Linda: A closed system? Ah, let's see. A computer network. And the Earth.
Prof: And what exactly is a system? Harold?
Harold: A system—all systems actually—is a series of interdependent parts forming an integrated whole with a common purpose.
Prof: So how is the Earth a closed system? How does that work? Linda?
Linda: Because, like you said, a system is closed if it has a definable border. For Earth, that definable border is the atmosphere dividing us from whatever's out there.
Prof: And what can pass through our atmosphere, the Earth's border, so to speak?
Linda: Only the sun's energy, you know, heat, which the Earth absorbs. As the Earth cools, it gives off heat. By doing so, the temperature of the Earth is maintained. It's just like the human body. To maintain a balance, we sweat to keep cool and shiver to keep warm. Also, with the Earth, mass cannot pass through the Earth's atmospheric border.
Prof: What do you mean by mass?

Linda: I mean, large objects. Solids. You also mentioned last class that a closed system is an isolated system, which is exactly what the Earth is. We're just floating around in space like a self-contained bubble protected by a border—the atmosphere—through which heat energy enters and leaves. This creates a balance which is what homeostasis is all about.

Prof: And within that balance, life, as we know it, exists. Excellent. As Linda said, homeostasis is all about a system maintaining a balance. The word homeostasis itself actually means *staying the same* or *in one place*, just like the Earth circling the sun, year in, year out, absorbing heat, losing heat. That, then, is what homeostasis is all about: balance. And there are—as I said last lecture—two ways a system can maintain homeostasis, by being either closed or open. Okay, so we've identified a closed system. What about an open one? Harold? You want to take the wheel?

Harold: Sure. An open system is one in which mass and energy can both cross a border. In doing so, they cross from one environment into the next, and back again. In other words, an open system, to be homeostatic, must be permeable. Countries, for example, are open systems. Well, most, anyway. Take us, for example, you know, the U.S. People and products—mass and energy—flow back and forth across our borders every day. The result is a stable, system-regulating process or society. Economists call this a steady-state economy.

Prof: Great. Can you give us a biological example?

Harold: The human body. To survive, to maintain homeostasis, we must constantly take in energy in the form of mass, you know, food. And when we're finished processing that food, that mass, we get rid of it to maintain the balance.

Prof: And the human body is also a closed system, right?

Harold Parts of it, yes.

Prof: For example?

Harold: The circulatory system. Blood is pumped from the heart through a series of veins and arteries, and back again. Objects with mass, like food, cannot permeate this system; however, energy, such as oxygen and carbon dioxide, come and go, as well nutrient-based energy that comes from digested food.

Linda: Professor, can we circle back to the Earth for a sec?

Prof: Sure.

Linda: What about meteors? Aren't they a kind of mass penetrating the Earth's atmospheric border? And wouldn't that then make the Earth an open system?

Prof: Good point. But no. Meteors burn up in the Earth's atmosphere long before they reach the Earth's surface. Of course, there is always the possibility that an asteroid will hit the Earth, such as the one that wiped out the dinosaurs 65 million years. It was so big, it failed to burn up. But those are few and far between. Also, it's important to remember that a system demonstrates homeostasis only when there is a balance. The asteroid that wiped out the dinosaurs is an excellent of how a mass penetrated the Earth's atmospheric border and destroyed that balance.

Narrator: Now get ready to answer the questions. Answer each question based on what is stated or implied in the discussion.

1. What is the topic of the discussion?
2. What is the purpose of the discussion?
3. According to the discussion, all systems have what?

4. Why does the professor say this?

Prof: Good. Very succinct.

5. In the discussion, the following topics are mentioned. Identify which are open systems and which are closed systems. This is a 3-point question.

6. Listen to part of the discussion, then answer the question.

Student: An open system is one in which mass and energy can both cross a border. In doing so, they cross from one environment into the next, and back again. In other words, an open system, to be homeostatic, must be permeable.

Narrator: Why does the student say this?

Student: In other words, an open system, to be homeostatic, must be permeable.

Notes

_____
_____
_____
_____
_____
_____
_____
_____
_____
_____
_____
_____
_____
_____
_____
_____
_____
_____
_____
_____

Typing Test

Typing proficiently is an essential TOEFL writing strategy. The faster and more accurately you type in English, the more you will develop the topic you are writing about. Poor typing will result in a lack of <u>Development</u>, more <u>Language-Use</u> errors, and a lower writing score.

How proficient is your English typing? Take the test and find out.

- **REMEMBER:** *You will use a standard keyboard on test day. A standard keyboard is not touch sensitive like a laptop keyboard.*

Directions: You have one minute to type the 60-word passage below. If you make one mistake, you can type 59 words-per-minute (60 words – 1 mistake = 59 words per minute), two mistakes, 58 wpm, etc.

Note: A letter(s) not capitalized is a mistake; a comma in the wrong place is a mistake; a missing comma/period is a mistake.

Topical unity means you focus on one topic from start to finish. If you suddenly introduce a new and unrelated topic, you are changing topics. For example, you are writing about pizza when you suddenly change to TOEFL. This obvious change in topic direction is called a topic digression. This will result in a lack of topical unity and coherence.

- **WARNING:** *If you type fewer than 30 words-per-minute, you need typing practice. If you need typing practice, see <u>500 Words, Phrases and Idioms for the TOEFL iBT plus Typing Strategies</u> by Bruce Stirling.*

Also by Bruce Stirling

Speaking and Writing Strategies for the TOEFL® iBT
Nova Press, Los Angeles USA

Practice Tests for the TOEFL® iBT
Nova Press, Los Angeles USA

500 Words, Phrases and Idioms for the TOEFL® iBT
***plus* Typing Strategies**
Nova Press, Los Angeles USA

Speaking and Writing Strategies for the TOEFL® iBT
Chinese translation
Foreign Language Teaching and Research Press
Beijing, China

TOEFL Strategies: *Quick Reference Guide*
Amazon.com

Business English: *Speaking and Writing Strategies*
Amazon.com

Business Idioms in America
Nova Press, Los Angeles USA

* * *

Visit Bruce Stirling at www.LinkedIn.com

Audio Files

You may download the audio files from the following webpage:

testprepcenter.com/download

Notes

CPSIA information can be obtained
at www.ICGtesting.com
Printed in the USA
LVOW04*1137281117
557775LV00005B/13/P

9 781944 595265